EDUCATIONAL FREEDOM
IN EASTERN EUROPE

EDUCATIONAL FREEDOM
IN EASTERN EUROPE

Charles L. Glenn

CATO
INSTITUTE
Washington D.C.

An earlier version of this book was prepared for the Office of Educational
Research and Improvement, Programs for the Improvement of Practice,
U.S. Department of Education under purchase order number 43-3J47-0-
00875. It does not necessarily represent positions or policies of the U.S.
Department of Education, and no official endorsement should be inferred.

Library of Congress Cataloging-in-Publication Data

Glenn, Charles Leslie, 1938–
    Educational Freedom in Eastern Europe / by Charles L. Glenn.
      p.   cm.
    Originally published: Washington, D.C. : Programs for the
  Improvement of Practice, Office of Educational Research and
  Improvement, U.S. Dept. of Education, 1994. With added chapter.
    Includes bibliographical references and index.
    ISBN 1-882577-20-5 (cloth).—ISBN 1-882577-21-3 (paper)
    1. Education—Europe, Eastern.   2. Academic freedom—Europe,
Eastern.   I. Title
[LA622.G54   1994]
370'.947—dc20   95-34490
                                                                      CIP

Cover Design by Randy White.

Printed in the United States of America.

CATO INSTITUTE
1000 Massachusetts Ave., N.W.
Washington, D.C. 20001

"How good it would be to break the monopoly
of the Communists in Education."

—Wojciech Starzyński, 1987

Contents

Foreword

School choice is the hottest idea in educational reform. In fact, it's somewhat disconcerting to realize that, even though the United States prides itself on individualism and free markets, parents in many other countries have more freedom of choice in education than Americans do. As Charles Glenn demonstrated in *Choice of Schools in Six Nations*, parents in countries such as Australia, Germany, France, Belgium, and the Netherlands can choose private, even religious, schools rather than public schools without incurring any financial penalty. Most recently Sweden, long the model social-democratic state, has instituted an education voucher program. Parents in those countries thus have a choice not only in the quality of the school their children will attend but in the kinds of moral and religious values that will be taught, a choice American parents can exercise only by paying a significant price for private rather than public education.

Now, in *Educational Freedom in Eastern Europe*, Charles Glenn points out that parents in the ex-Communist countries are being granted more educational freedom than American parents. Not only can they freely choose nongovernment schools; they can also work with others to create new independent schools. Glenn estimates that over 1,000 such schools now receive public funding in Poland, Russia, Hungary, and other post-Communist nations.

After visiting the United States to study education reform here, Katarzyna Skórzyńska, a young Solidarity activist who headed Poland's Office of Innovation and Independent Schools, noted some disappointing similarities with Poland. "You have the same people who oppose choice as in my country. The trade unions and the education bureaucrats. The difference is that in my country their failures have completely discredited those groups."

To be sure, progress in developing civil society and educational freedom is uneven. In the concluding chapter of this book, written two years after the survey chapters for reasons discussed below,

Glenn's optimism has been tempered by experience. "In each of the countries of Eastern Europe," he writes, "though to a widely varying extent, the all-encompassing bureaucracy of the communist era remains largely in place, as do the habits and attitudes that sustain its power." It is not an easy task to undo decades of totalitarian domination of a country's schools. Still, *Educational Freedom in Eastern Europe* gives us hope that one of the many happy results of the fall of the Soviet empire will be increased freedom for families, students, and schools.

Educational Freedom in Eastern Europe was first published by the U.S. Department of Education. Many readers may wonder why the Cato Institute would publish a government report, interesting though it might be. In the answer to that question lies a tale.

Charles Glenn, for 21 years the Massachusetts state official responsible for urban education and civil rights, was first appointed by Gov. Michael Dukakis as chief of the Office of Educational Equity in the state Department of Education. The author of the Boston busing plan, he was described by J. Anthony Lukas in *Common Ground* as "a veteran of the civil rights movement" with "a passionate zeal on racial issues." Discouraged by the results of the busing plan, he looked for alternative ways to bring about school integration and experimented with the use of magnet schools. He discovered that giving families more choice in education led not only to integration but to improved educational outcomes. That led to his further involvement with educational freedom issues in the United States and Europe. He also became a highly respected scholar, the author of *The Myth of the Common School* and dozens of articles.

Late in the Reagan administration, he was commissioned by the Department of Education (ED) to prepare a report on how other nations handle parental choice of schools. That study was published, in an edition of 6,000 copies, as *Choice of Schools in Six Nations* in 1989. Around that time, Glenn met the Solidarity-appointed officials of the new Polish government, who were encouraging the establishment of hundreds of alternative schools. Officials in the ED asked him to undertake a second study, on the emerging educational freedom in Eastern Europe. The project grew as the Eastern European dominoes fell, and ED officials gave him an initial and then a second contract.

Glenn completed the study with the help of dozens of collaborators in the various countries, some of them paid out of his contract funds and others volunteering their help. He collected more than a hundred relevant texts and put a number of graduate students to work translating from the various languages. The study was completed in 1991 and received favorable reviews from the experts consulted by ED.

Then the project seemed to become bogged down in bureaucratic obstacles and delays. Mid-level officials in the department sat on the text for months without explanation, to the great frustration of the program officer assigned to the project. It was apparently only after a reporter began inquiring about the delays that it was moved slowly forward to publication. It seems likely that some ED bureaucrats, not overly enthusiastic about educational freedom, were trying to run out the clock in anticipation of a Clinton victory. Finally, in December 1992, the text was cleared and sent to the printers.

Then, within a week after the inauguration, in late January 1993, the publication was canceled. Glenn was paid in full but was told that the book would be published only in electronic form. So far as can be determined, that did not take place. Perhaps the government, admirably looking for places to save money, concluded that neither education nor Eastern Europe was a subject of widespread interest.

About a year later, Glenn was told that the book *would* be published, but in a print run of only 200 and for obviously limited distribution. Presumably, officials realized the potential for embarrassment over a study paid for but never published. The study was released in March 1994.

The distinguished education historian Diane Ravitch saw much of this bureaucratic sabotage from the inside—well, almost from the inside—as the third-ranking official in the ED for the last two years of the Bush administration. Her observations are worth quoting at length:

> What happened to Charles Glenn's study is itself an instructive lesson in the power of the bureaucracy to control policy from below. In the summer of 1991, I was sworn in as Assistant Secretary of Education, in charge of the Office of Educational Research and Improvement (OERI). Soon after assuming office, I asked for a list of the publications that were "in the pipeline." Glenn's study was on the list, and I was told that it was not yet finished. Months later, I was told that reviewers were reading it. Since trade publishing houses usually take nine months to publish a book, and academic presses take even longer, I was not alarmed by

the slow progress of the Glenn book. Then sometime in the summer or fall of 1992, I received a call from a reporter who told me that he had heard that the Glenn book had been "deep-sixed" or buried. This was news to me, and I demanded a fast response on its whereabouts. I was told that nothing unusual had happened, that Glenn's book was not a high priority, and that I had to understand that the government moves slowly. In fact, as now seems clear, those who controlled the release of the book held it back just long enough to make sure that it would never be published. They gambled that the Democrats would win, and their gamble succeeded.

I would be more apt to attribute the misfortune of Glenn's study to bad luck or bureaucratic bungling except that it was not a unique occurrence. When I took office, I told the top staff that I was very interested in assembling the research on the academic results of single-sex schools. The research director commissioned an independent review of the research literature and planned a conference of scholars and practitioners. By February 1992, we had in hand a research paper that showed that girls benefited significantly from single-sex education but that single-sex schools had virtually disappeared from the public sector over the past thirty years and were fast diminishing in the private sector. What was once a common form of schooling in the United States—and is still common in many other countries—was on its way to extinction, in part because of the erroneous perception that single-sex schooling is illegal or somehow socially unwise. At the conference, we also gathered some interesting papers from participants. Before the summer, everything was in hand for a first-rate, provocative publication on an important issue. I regularly asked for updates on the progress of the report. Like Glenn's study, there was always some small hangup, one more obstacle in the way. When at last it was finished, it needed to be reviewed and approved by every other office in the Department of Education, and any one of them could raise a question that would send it back for another round of reviews.

Despite my intense interest in this publication, it never appeared. Its quiet suppression was even more peculiar in view of the fact that Congress was considering major legislation on "gender equity" at the behest of the American Association of University Women. The AAUW, I learned in debates with its leaders, was not interested in single-sex schooling but in pushing through legislation that would authorize the expenditure of hundreds of millions of dollars for gender equity training. Calling attention to the efficacy of single-sex schools was, in their view, a diversion from their political agenda, which was to make gender equity a major federal priority.

I do not blame the Clinton administration for abandoning a project that promotes policies inimical to its own. That's politics. No one would have expected the Reagan or Bush administration to publish a book commissioned by the Carter administration that attacked school choice. Since my successor as Assistant Secretary came from the staff of the National Education Association, she was certainly not going to support publication of Glenn's book, nor would Secretary of Education Richard Riley, who repeatedly expressed the Clinton administration's adamant opposition to school choice that included nonstate schools.

The determination to bury Charles Glenn's book was made by mid-level civil servants, which ought not be surprising. Career bureaucrats are not likely to admire a study that questions the power of career bureaucrats and that endorses public funding for parents who choose nongovernmental schools.

During my stint in the federal government, I relied on the loyalty of career officials; I had no choice, because in my agency of nearly 500 people, I was able to hire fewer than 10 people. Yet ultimately, it is clear that those who work in the federal government are inherently more sympathetic to those who seek to enlarge government power (a view that confirms their value and authority) and inherently antagonistic to those who seek to lessen or diffuse it, for obvious reasons. It is in the very nature of bureaucracy to seek to perpetuate itself. Elected officials and those they appoint to administer the federal government are seen by career civil servants as "Christmas help," in charge for a season and then out. And they are right. Administrations come and go, but the bureaucracy is forever.

By their acts you shall know them: The bureaucracy did not like this book or its message.

And that is where the Cato Institute comes in. We believe that educational freedom is a crucially important issue for free societies, both here and in the budding civil societies of Eastern Europe. We decided not to let the Clinton administration stifle the distribution of this valuable study, so we determined to publish it ourselves and distribute it widely, through bookstores and other means. We asked Charles Glenn to write a concluding chapter, bringing the story up to date and drawing lessons for the United States. He did that, though obviously he was not able to undertake another investigation as thorough as his research on the first two years of reform.

When we look at his draft of a concluding chapter that he submitted to the ED in March 1992, we can perhaps understand why the project almost ground to a halt and why the ED version did not include a conclusion. Glenn wrote, for instance,

> The experience of Soviet education since 1917, and of education in Eastern Europe from the post-war years to 1989, illustrates the danger of seeking to use schooling as an instrument of State power, in an effort to remold humanity and to eliminate loyalties and beliefs competing with those considered useful by the State.
>
> Unfortunately, this ambition is not unknown in the United States and other Western democracies, where interest groups within the educational establishment and special interest groups have sought to manipulate the content of public schooling to advance their agendas. The strength of the conviction that schooling *should* be used in this manner, even within a free society, provides much of the moral fervor expressed in opposition to parental choice of nongovernment schooling.

He went on to point out "the enduring power of bureaucracy" and collectivism to frustrate the exercise of educational freedom. And he concluded,

> The dead hand of bureaucracy can be almost as constraining under a democratic system as under a decayed totalitarian system. What is so devastating about educational bureaucracy is that it always acts in the name of the highest motivations: justice, accountability, social harmony, the interests of children, a well-informed citizenry and work-force. . . . Western educational policy should learn from this painful process that half-way reforms will not bring about fundamental change of the sort that is needed.

Perhaps it is not surprising that such sentiments were not welcome at the U.S. Department of Education, nor among Clinton officials determined to use the ED to improve thousands of American schools through centralized leadership from Washington.

Now Charles Glenn's important study is available to all Americans. And now it is time for American parents to have as much freedom to choose the schools their children will attend as parents in Sweden, Poland, and Russia.

DAVID BOAZ

Acknowledgments

The information from each of the nations discussed in this study was collected by the author primarily during the first half of 1991, and the first draft was prepared by January 1992. Developments since 1991 are therefore in general not reflected in the narrative. The primary exception is developments in Russia, where the author served as member of an advisory commission in September 1992.

This study could not have been prepared without the assistance of several graduate students who prepared summaries and translations of materials in languages which the author is unable to read. The intelligence and discernment with which they undertook this difficult task is gratefully acknowledged.

Bissera Antikarova (Bulgarian and Russian)
Ivana Mazalkova (Czech and Slovak)
Malgorzata Radziszewska-Hedderick (Polish)

The individuals listed below either provided source materials and other information, commented upon drafts of the study, made other valuable suggestions, or helped in all three ways. They are of course not responsible for the judgments expressed in the study.

Bulgaria

Hristo Hristov and Valentina Krusteva, Ministry of Public Education, Sofia

Czech Republic

Oldrich Botlik, Prague

Zdenek Janacek, Zlin

Hana Nováková, Vyzumny ustav pedagogicky, Prague

Jan Prucha, Director of Educational Research, Charles University, Prague

Jana Strakova, První Obnovené Reálné Gymnázium, Prague

Eliška Walterová, Deputy Director of Educational Research, Charles University

Estonia

Rein Taagepera, University of California, Irvine [United States]

Hungary

Judit Borbáthné Bánhegyi, Lutheran Gimnazium, Budapest

Péter Lukács, Hungarian Institute for Educational Research

Péter Soltész, Ministry of Culture and Education

Wim E. Westerman, Christian Pedagogical Study Center, Hoevelaken [The Netherlands]

Germany

Oskar Anweiler, Institut für Pädagogik, Ruhr-Universität Bochum

Hans-Georg Hofmann, University of California, Los Angeles

Siegfried Jenkner, Fachbereich Erziehungswissenschaften, Hannover

Guenther Lange, (formerly) Ministerium für Bildung und Wissenschaft

Heinz Rose, Sektion Berufspädagogik, University of Technology, Dresden 8023

   [Professors Anweiler and Jenkner provided a wealth of information on Eastern Europe as well as on Germany]

Lithuania

Aurimas Juozaitis, Deputy Minister, Vilnius

Stanislavas Taišerskis, Prienai 3rd Middle School

Poland

Katarzyna Bogucka-Krenz, Gdansk

Stanislaw Czachorowski, Teachers Training College, Olsztyn

Kazimierz Kossak-Glowczewski, University of Gdańsk

Bogdan Krawczyk, former editor, *Edukacja i Dialog*, Warsaw

Zbyszko Melosik, Institute of Education, Poznań

Aleksander Nalaskowski, Copernicus University, Toruń

Zbigniew Sawiński, Institute of Sociology, University of Warsaw

Michał J. Sawecki, Independent Educational Center, Szczecin

Katarzyna Skórzyńska and Jerzy Pomianowski, formerly of the Ministerstwo Edukacji Narodowej, Warsaw

Wojciech Starzyński, Civic Educational Association, Warsaw

Miroslaw Szymansky, Director, IBE Institute for Educational Research, Warsaw

Romania

Sorin Antohi, Paris

Cezar Birzea, Elena Malec and Monica Cuciureanu, Institute for Educational Sciences, Bucharest

Russia

Derenic N. Abramyan, Chief Specialist of the Constitutional Commission, Moscow

Ger P. van den Berg, Documentation Office for East European Law, Leiden University [The Netherlands]

Zoya Pavlovna Doschinskaya, Legal Department, Russian Federation Ministry of Education, Moscow

N. J. Dunstan, Center for Russian and East European Studies, University of Birmingham [United Kingdom]

Nikolai A. Khromenkov, Rector, Moscow Pedagogical University

Mikhail L. Levitski, Moscow Pedagogical Institute

Katlijn Malfliet, Institute for Central and East European Studies, Leuven [Belgium]

Jerry Mintz, Alternative Education Resource Organization [United States]

Elena Sergeevna Seninskaya, Office of Nonstate Educational Institutions, Department for Innovation and Nonstate Programs, Russian Federation Ministry of Education, Moscow

Jane Simonyan, "Kosmos" School, Moscow

Larisa Ivanovna Sokolova, Kindergarten 1076, Moscow

Jeanne Sutherland, London

Anatoly M. Tsirulnikov, Center of Pedagogical Innovations, Ministry of Education, Moscow

Slovakia

Stefan Švec, Katedra Pedagogiky, Univerzita Komenskeho, Bratislava

I am also grateful for comments and suggestions from the following American colleagues:

John Bernbaum, Vice President, Christian College Coalition

Stephen Kerr, College of Education, University of Washington

Miriam Mareček, Boston University School of Education

Howard Mehlinger, Institute for the Study of Soviet Education, Indiana University

Gerald Read, Center for the Study of Socialist Education, Kent State University

Felissa Tibbitts, Harvard Graduate School of Education

Janet Vaillant, Soviet and East European Language and Area Center, Harvard

This report was prepared under a contract with the Research Applications Division, Office of Educational Research and Improvement/Programs for the Improvement of Practice, as a sequel to my earlier study for OERI, *Choice of Schools in Six Nations*, which reported on Western Europe and Canada. I am grateful for the consistent support and advocacy of Dr. Robert Hickson over the past two years, and for his diligence in finding materials with a broad perspective on events in the post-Communist world.

1. Communism, Schools, and Civil Society

A fundamental goal of all Communist regimes, beginning with the one established in Russia in 1917, has been to create a new type of humanity that would be incapable of less than full devotion to the Party and its leadership.

The new humanity, Communist theoreticians promised, would bear no traces of value systems—peasant or bourgeois—that were condemned by the forward movement of history. There would no longer be a place for selfish individualism, nor would religious belief or ethnicity compete with identities defined by the state. "Socialism will be possible," as Krupskaya wrote, "only when the psychology of people is radically changed."[1]

The goal of changing human nature defines totalitarian rule, which is not satisfied with external obedience, with passive acquiescence in absolute rule, but seeks to gain willing inner adherence as well.

This goal does not necessarily imply the use of schooling to create the new humanity. After all, one of the most frequently quoted aphorisms of Marx was that

> the mode of production in material life determines the general character of the social, political and spiritual processes in life. It is not the consciousness of men that determines their existence, but, on the contrary, their social existence determines their consciousness.[2]

Consistent with this belief, making schooling an instrument to reshape the people was not a priority in the first years of Communist rule in Russia. "On the whole, the Bolsheviks did not consider culture and education nearly as important as politics or economics, particularly in the early years after the October Revolution when the party was primarily concerned with consolidating power."[3]

Over time, however, the Communist regime came to recognize that the Russian and other peoples of their empire continued to be rooted in ancestral beliefs and attitudes and "that economic and political changes, no matter how fundamental, alone could not radically alter human behavior to create the new Soviet citizen."[4]

The effort to impose a worldview that was intolerant of any rivals began toward the end of the 1920s and took on major proportions with increasing urbanization and universal education. As Russian émigré Alexander Zinoviev put it, "As the cultural level of a society rises, as living conditions improve, as people become more educated, as an opposition develops and other phenomena that directly or indirectly threaten [Communist] society's monolithic ideology, there is need for more effort and more ideology." By the last years of the Communist regime,

> everyone is subjected to the influence of ideology from birth to death, systematically and with a strikingly pedantic consistency. The number of people employed professionally in the ideological field is enormous. The number of people who in one way or another are forced to carry out bits of ideological work is innumerable.[5]

Although the task of inculcating—and continually updating—a worldview and an understanding of the demands of the Communist Party line was shared by many institutions in each of the nations covered by this study, formal schooling was naturally central. Schools were expected to give consistent attention to shaping the values and attitudes of their pupils: to teach Marxism-Leninism and to combat any sign of rival beliefs.

The recent collapse of Communist hegemony in nation after nation of Eastern Europe, and ultimately in the Soviet Union, startled most informed observers. Some had described these systems as fundamentally successful in meeting the challenges they faced, as stable working societies "in which the leadership and various sections of society were almost harmoniously involved in macrosocial processes such as modernization and urbanization."[6] Others, while more critical of the economic and social accomplishments of Communism, had argued that the process of remaking human nature had been generally successful and precluded effective resistance to Communist rule.

Zbigniew Rau has pointed out in an important essay that Communists and some of their critics shared the belief that "there is no such thing as individual human nature, since all human activity is socially

2

learned and determined by the kind of society that people live in."
In Bukharin's image, a human being was nothing more than "a
sausage skin stuffed by environmental influences."[7] From that perspective, it seemed obvious that a concerted effort to employ formal
schooling and a wide range of other socializing experiences to change
human nature would lead inevitably to the desired result. As Zinoviev put it, *Homo sovieticus* "totally supports his leadership because
he possesses the standardized consciousness formed by the ideology."[8] Or, again,

> under Communism man lives from the cradle to the grave
> in a powerful "magnet field" of ideological influence. He is
> a particle in it receiving a particular "charge," position and
> orientation. Once created, this field renews and strengthens
> itself and becomes continually more professional and
> effective. . . . Ideology doesn't only organize people's con-
> sciousness, it creates the social intellect of society as a whole
> and an intellectual stereotype for individual members of
> society.[9]

Rau finds a more nuanced version of the same assumption in the
Polish émigré writer Czeslaw Milosz's 1953 book *The Captive Mind*,
in which the author predicted that even those intellectuals who
practiced an inner resistance to the control of the Communist regime
would come eventually to accept its inevitability. "Forty or fifty
years of this education . . . must create a new and irretrievable species
of mankind. The 'new man' is not merely a postulate. He is beginning
to become a reality."

But was this process of acceptance inevitable? Were the efforts of
Communist societies to shape a new human nature successful?
Recent events seem to have disproved Zinoviev's claim that "this
society is not only stable; it is in the highest degree stable," just as
they have dramatically falsified his claim that "the Communist
regime deals successfully with national problems, as Soviet experience has shown. . . . Any expectation that conflicts between nationalities will cause the ruin of the Soviet Empire derives from a total
misconception of the real situation in the country."[10]

Václav Havel argued in his influential essay "The Power of the
Powerless" (1978) that, although ideology was "one of the pillars
of the system's external stability," it was "built on a very unstable
foundation. It is built on lies. It works only as long as people are

3

willing to live within the lie." There comes a point, however, when a growing number of individuals become determined to "live within the truth." They go beyond protecting a private sphere of consciousness from manipulation by the Communist system, and begin to act in ways that show a "newfound sense of higher responsibility."

> The point where living within the truth ceases to be a mere negation of living with a lie and becomes articulate in a particular way, is the point at which something is born that might be called the "independent spiritual, social and political life of society." . . . [This] includes everything from self-education and thinking about the world, through free creative activity and its communication to others, to the most varied free, civic activities, including instances of independent social self-organization.[11]

But are such efforts, under a totalitarian system, only futile gestures by a minority of intellectuals and other dissidents who have no real power to transform the social order? The question remains relevant even after the political collapse of communism, since the vacuum that it has left seems likely to be filled by new forms of authoritarianism unless men and women at all levels begin acting in a fashion for which the socialization process under Communist regimes may have unfitted them. Neither a free market, nor a democratic political system, nor a healthy society can function without the active involvement of individuals who are both autonomous and responsible, capable of acting freely and voluntarily cooperating with others through a host of formal and informal associations.

Political reform alone will not be enough. As Jacques Maritain observed, "Family, economic, cultural, educational, religious life matter as much as does political life to the very existence and prosperity of the body politic."[12] Some observers fear that the effort of Communist regimes to eliminate the "civil society," all forms of social organization not directly subordinated to the state and Party, may have done profound damage to the ability of these societies to respond to the demands of freedom. These critics "are preoccupied with that hypertrophy of central authority which became so very characteristic of Communist society, and with the achievement of the erosion or total destruction of rival centres of countervailing power."[13]

4

Civil society, a central concern of this study of education in the former Soviet bloc, has been defined in various ways. Michael Walzer writes that the "words 'civil society' name the space of uncoerced human association and also the set of relational networks—formed for the sake of family, faith, interest, and ideology—that fill this space."[14] Zbigniew Rau defines it as a

> historically evolved form of society that presupposes the existence of a space in which individuals and their associations compete with each other in the pursuit of their values. This space lies between those relationships which result from family commitments and those which involve the individual's obligations toward the state. Civil society is therefore a space free from both family influence and state power.[15]

A primary strategy of Communist regimes was to eliminate or subordinate all expressions of the civil society to their direct control: "The state dissolved the institutions of civil society and replaced the normative order of that society with one of its own making. . . . Political parties, business associations, trade unions, learned societies, religious organizations, and publishing houses were abolished or put under the control of the state."[16]

Ironically, however, the tremendous stress of Communist regimes upon mobilizing the entire population to support the goals of economic and social transformation had an unanticipated consequence of reviving what the regimes had earlier destroyed. "The continuous processes of social mobilization, the expansion of education, and the growth of numerous professional groups and organizations created in Soviet Russia a much greater range of nuclei, the kernels of civil society."[17]

The conviction has grown that economic and political reforms in the nations of the former Soviet bloc will not be successful without a revival of this civil society. Efforts from the center during Gorbachev's campaign of perestroika to insist upon new forms of behavior—harder work, less abuse of alcohol, more economic initiative—within a system that was fundamentally unchanged proved largely incapable of reaching the desired results, confirming Martin Malia's insistence upon "the intrinsic irreformability of communism."[18] Or, as Victor Zaslavsky put it,

> Perestroika was essentially a political revolution that destroyed the old political order but neither shattered the

5

institutional structure of the economy nor changed the state-dependent mentality of the population.[19]

Are processes at work within the formerly Communist societies that will lead to new and more positive forms of social organization? Malia takes the pessimistic view that the "creation of a mature, diversified civil society in the East still lies many years in the future"; the economies will not revive as hoped, despite political changes, because the necessary changes "require initiative on the part of society, and the rudimentary civil society that emerged from the collapse of communism is too weak for such a response."[20]

Václav Havel gave a different response in his 1978 essay: "The attempt at political reform [in the Prague Spring of 1968] was not the cause of society's reawakening, but rather the final outcome of that reawakening." Disagreeing with the Marxist-Leninist assumption that human nature would change in response to changes in the economic and political order, Havel insisted that political and economic reform could only occur through "profound existential and moral changes in society."[21] Through initiatives independent of state and Party control, those determined to reject the lies imposed upon them would begin to recreate a social space within which it would be possible to "live within the truth," not only for themselves, but ultimately for the entire society.

> What else are those initial attempts at social self-organization than the efforts of a certain part of society to live—as a society—within the truth, to rid itself of the self-sustaining aspects of totalitarianism and, thus, to extricate itself radically from its involvement in the post-totalitarian system? What else is it but a non-violent attempt by people to negate the system within themselves and to establish their lives on a new basis, that of their own proper identity? . . . it would be quite wrong to understand the parallel structures and the parallel polis as a retreat into a ghetto and as an act of isolation, addressing itself only to those who had decided on such a course, and who are indifferent to the rest. . . . the parallel polis points beyond itself and only makes sense as an act of deepening one's responsibility to and for the whole. . . . Independent initiatives . . . demonstrate that living within the truth is a human and social alternative and they struggle to expand the space available for that life.[22]

This phenomenon of a gradual reanimation and organization of civil society by voluntary efforts "from below" has been described "as 'the social self-organization of society' in Poland, a 'parallel' or 'independent society' in Czechoslovakia, or a 'second society' in Hungary."[23] Even if this reorganization proves to be more than a transitory phenomenon of political dissent, the question remains whether it can occur only in those nations of Central Europe with an experience of civic culture before the Communist takeover. Some question whether Russia, in particular, has inherited patterns of behavior from its pre-Soviet past that will prevent the implementation of fundamental reforms.

> These enduring constancies in Russian and Soviet political life impose severe limits on the possibilities for the completion of a true cultural revolution: the creation of a novel form of social life informed by a new set of values. Rather, once institutionalized, habits originating in an older tradition are passed on to young generations as part of their socialization experiences. . . . Soviet cultural revolutionaries cannot escape their past, the collective history and traditions of their people.[24]

Similarly, social anthropologist Ernest Gellner asks whether economic pluralism can be

> reborn where it has been abolished? . . . [particularly] in a larger society in which 70 years of Sovietization—a good part of it being years of total terror—have all but eradicated any genuine alternative traditions. The consciously intended re-inauguration of free enterprise may perhaps engender only an opportunist lumpenbourgeoisie, devoid of those virtues which perhaps accompanied the slow emergence of the entrepreneurial class during the first and spontaneous, unintended birth of capitalism.[25]

Whether a true civil society can emerge in the former Soviet Union or whether Russia, Ukraine, and other successor states will slip back into authoritarian modes of political and social organization is obviously of consequence not only to their own citizens but also to the democratic nations of the West.

Just as educational systems were for several generations deeply implicated in efforts to reshape human nature into obedience to the Communist Party/state by eliminating independent thinking and competing loyalties, so today are the same systems on the front lines of the revival of civil society in Eastern and Central Europe.

This process is occurring in two distinct ways. The first is through the renewal of the curriculum to eliminate explicit and informal indoctrination and to teach the civic and social virtues considered necessary for responsible citizenship in the free societies that are struggling to be born. There is great interest in Western models of education, and particularly in developing, with the help of Western specialists, curriculum stressing democracy and free markets, and in training teachers to present this curriculum in a nonauthoritarian manner.

The other aspect of the process of renewal of education systems is that adumbrated by Václav Havel in 1978, when he predicted that

> the official structures—as agencies of the post-totalitarian system, existing only to serve its automatism and constructed in the spirit of that role—simply begin withering away and dying off, to be replaced by new structures that have evolved from "below" and are put together in a fundamentally different way.

These new structures would be

> held together more by a commonly shared feeling of the importance of certain communities than by commonly shared expansionist ambitions directed "outward." There can and must be structures that are open, dynamic and small; beyond a certain point, human ties like personal trust and personal responsibility cannot work.[26]

Havel was not referring primarily to schools in his 1978 essay (though he mentions, as an example of the "independent life of society," "teachers who privately teach young people things that are kept from them in the state schools"[27]), but in fact new and transformed schools have been among the most common "new structures" emerging during the last years of Communist rule and in a flood since its collapse.

Groups of parents and teachers have begun to recreate education through school-level initiatives to serve their children more honestly and more effectively, and education policy debates have focused, even more than in the United States, on whether such initiatives

8

should be merely tolerated as an expression of freedom or welcomed and supported in the interest of society as a whole.

Even more than in the West, such initiatives are an essential aspect of educational reform in the formerly Communist nations, where "a rich network of independent institutions and organizations has to be formed, that are neither state-directed nor state-controlled, that are autonomous social, political, and cultural entities. . . . Seeking and constituting such social, cultural, political forces, capable of attaining such independence and balance, is the process which will decide whether a postcommunist regime is successful in its efforts to achieve democracy."[28] Schools are ideally situated to foster new habits of cooperation, to develop trust as adults work together in the interest of their children.

The Perennial Debate over Educational Freedom

Freedom is essential to full human development. Only as individuals exercise their freedom actively in responsible decisionmaking do they (and thus their societies) grow morally into full humanity. Responsible freedom is thus unavoidably a concern of education, not in the form of indifference to the choices that pupils will make, but in recognition of the heavy moral significance of such choices.

For parents, the desire to raise children capable of exercising freedom within a context of responsibility includes the sense, whether articulate or not, that such responsible decisionmaking requires an effective mastery of an inheritance of convictions and loyalties. All parents, it is safe to say, hope that their children will value and live by the convictions by which the parents have directed and given meaning to their own lives.

Thus it is a fundamental anomaly and injustice when the state sets itself up as a rival to parents in shaping the beliefs and loyalties of children. Responsible decisionmaking by individuals in these societies is not permitted in the sphere of education, the sphere that parents perceive has the greatest moral weight.

It is no accident that education is where the state is most tempted to seek to extend its influence over its citizens. The extension of popular education through government initiatives has, throughout the 19th and 20th centuries, been marked by conflict over the extent to which the state has sought to define and impose a single world-view through its schools. That such conflicts have occurred in almost

9

every modernizing society is by no means accidental: creating state-controlled schooling has in almost every case been a primary means of carrying out the essential tasks of nation building—"breaking through and political integration." Jowitt has described "breaking through" as the "decisive alteration or destruction of values, structures, and behaviors which are perceived by a revolutionary elite as comprising or contributing to the actual or potential existence of alternative centers of political power."[29]

It would be natural to assume that the totalitarian project of creating a new consciousness, a "new Soviet man," through universal compulsory schooling was invented by regimes in which the state has attempted to swallow up all of society.

For a totalitarian regime, indeed, control of popular education is a fundamental means of seeking to impose uniformity and adherence to the regime. In this view, children belong to the state rather than to their families. That parents might seek to nurture in their children commitment to a religious tradition, to distinctive values, or indeed to any entity in the civil society that could be a source of competing values is seen as a direct threat to the state's authority.

Although the opposition between communism and religion is inherent and unavoidable in the claims that each makes upon the human spirit, it should be noted that Marx and Engels themselves did not call for the sort of attacks on religion that became characteristic of all the regimes calling themselves Marxist. To Marx and Engels, religion was the product of unjust social and economic relationships, and would wither away when those relationships did.

For Lenin and his successors, however, religion was an intolerable rival for the total loyalty of the masses and a dangerous source of alternative ways of understanding and living in the world.

The true scope of the educational programs of the totalitarian regimes can be understood only as comparable to those of religious communities toward their adherents. A study of Poland notes that "planned secularization and anti-religious policy, key features of atheist totalitarianism, are themselves a secular version of the millennial fantasy: planned secularization is typically described by its proponents as a means to the realization of those values which Christianity itself postulates but is unable or unwilling to implement."[30]

There is nothing accidental about this quasi-religious emphasis upon winning the hearts and souls of the rising generation. "One important characteristic of a totalitarian regime is that it is not satisfied with simple obedience from its subjects but also tries to obtain their enthusiastic support." It is of central importance to such regimes that "the people actively want what their rulers want them to want" and there is "enthusiastic unanimity throughout the whole of society."[31]

While an authoritarian regime may be satisfied with obedience, a totalitarian regime seeks devotion that will be self-perpetuating. "Anyone seizing power wishes to keep it for a certain length of time; it is however a special feature of people's revolutions to set their goals on the prospect of a boundless future" through "cultivating revolutionary successors."[32]

The project of using popular education to impose a single set of values and loyalties upon an entire rising generation, in the interest of the state and its ruling elite, was not invented in our own age, however, nor was the Communist regime in the Soviet Union the first to seek to implement it.

The French Jacobins of 1792 articulated this ambition as clearly as it has ever been stated. "It is in national schools," Danton told the National Convention, "that children must suck republican milk. The Republic is one and indivisible; public instruction must also be related to this center of unity." Only in this way could the "total regeneration" of the French people called for by Robespierre and his allies be accomplished. But this could be accomplished only through resolute denial of the claims of parents. As the Jacobin orator Billaud-Varenne warned his colleagues,

> You will lose the younger generation in abandoning it to parents with prejudices and ignorance who give it the defective tint which they have themselves. Therefore, let the Fatherland take hold of children who are born for it alone.[33]

While the Jacobin program did not prevail, the nation-building elites who made popular education a priority in the United States and other industrializing nations throughout the 19th century had something similar in mind. Without intending to suggest a "moral equivalence" between the educational goals of totalitarian regimes and those of liberal democracies, it is appropriate to recognize that few political leaders in times of rapid social change can resist the temptation to seek to promote their own agenda through schooling—regardless of what parents want for their children.

In making education a primary concern of government, Horace Mann and his allies were convinced that society could not afford to allow parents to determine who would educate their children. The "prejudices and ignorance" of parents would lead them to favor schools and teachers sharing their benighted views, and thus the grand project of creating a new humanity through schooling would be frustrated.

Indeed, every liberal democracy has experienced the tension between its educational mission and that of the family, and this tension has often been the source of major conflict, as in the early 1980s in France and Spain.[34]

An educational program by and for the state poses an almost irresistible temptation for the state's educators to see themselves as knowing better than parents what is good for their children. Sooner or later, such a *pédagogie d'état* poses severe problems for a democratic society that, through the process of modernization, has become increasingly diverse in values. "Even the well-intentioned state," writes legal philosopher John Robinson, "tends to homogenize its citizens, delegitimizing all loyalties except those that bind the individual to the state. . . . The family is a natural antidote to the state's totalitarian tendencies. As does a church, it generates loyalties that rival in intensity those that the state evokes, and it conveys beliefs that can undermine the ideology that the state is purveying."[35]

As Richard Baer has pointed out, "A government monopoly school system with a captive student audience—a system which in significant curricular matters is no longer locally controlled, and which, especially at the pre-college levels, is no genuine market-place of ideas—will almost always be experienced as coercive and oppressive by various dissenting minorities."[36]

While the educator-state is always tempted to set its goals above and in opposition to those of parents, the Jacobin program has been adopted with special enthusiasm by contemporary Marxist-Leninist regimes. Fidel Castro, for example, has insisted that Cuba can manage its economy without material incentives by creating a "new man" who will respond sufficiently to moral incentives, the desire to serve the Revolution. Cuba, according to Castro, "cannot encourage or even permit selfish attitudes. . . . The concept of socialism and communism, the concept of a higher society, implies a man devoid of those feelings."[37] "From an early age" children "must be discouraged from every egotistical feeling in the enjoyment of material things, such as the sense of individual property, and be encouraged toward the greatest possible common effort."[38]

The totalitarian educational program has been attempted on the largest scale in China, where a major preoccupation of the regime since 1949 has been creating a "totally mobilized society" through a "radical transformation of man."[39] This agenda grew out of the experience of the leaders during the Yenan period of resistance to Japan and gathered strength and power nationwide. Cut off from the urban proletariat on whom they had counted, the Communists were forced to base their growing power upon the peasants of a backward rural area. "Particularly after 1943, there was frenetic experimentation on the basis of the primitive human and natural resources available, and a determined effort to crack the powerful psychological barrier of peasant fatalism."[40]

It is characteristic of totalitarian regimes to dismiss dissent as a relic of the "prejudices and ignorance" associated with the older generation. After all, "All right-minded people are unanimous and enthusiastic about the building of a new social order and support the rulers because they provide inspiration and leadership for this common purpose. Disagreement comes only from a minority who have been corrupted by evil influences of the old society . . . which implies that opposition will fade away as the new society develops."[41]

But opposition does not fade away; the instinct of parents to pass on to their children what has shaped and given meaning to their own lives cannot be eradicated so easily. As totalitarian political control has slipped in Central and Eastern Europe, one of the focal points of dissatisfaction in each nation has been the educational system. Alternative schools have been established or revived, proposals to end the government monopoly of schooling have been advanced as part of the agenda of political reform, and parents have been drawn into the educational process in ways that are fundamentally different from the "mobilizations" that were a basic tactic of Marxist-Leninist regimes. Through this grassroots process, the deliberately suppressed civil society has begun to reassert itself.

The chapters that follow tell this story of education as a tool of totalitarian oppression and then as a vehicle to reanimate civil society

13

in the nations of Eastern and Central Europe that were under Communist rule. The evidence available in the West is scattered and incomplete, and the situation was continually evolving during the two years in which this study was conducted.

The first draft of this study provided a description of the goals and methods of Communist education, illustrated from a number of nations, but several readers of the draft from Eastern and Central Europe complained that it failed to do justice to the distinctive ways in which the educational program was carried out in their own countries, and that recent developments did not make sense without presentation of the background. The Communist program for schooling has therefore been told again for each of the nations covered in this study, even at the cost of covering much the same ground from a somewhat different angle.

As a result, chapter 2 describes at some length the educational strategies of the Communists in power in the **Soviet Union** after 1917, as they sought to create the *Homo sovieticus* absolutely loyal to their rule and program. How the regime dealt with its two major rivals, religion and nationality, helps to explain the strategies employed by the satellite regimes of Eastern Europe after World War II.

The following chapters deal with both the background and the recent developments in schooling in **Bulgaria** and **Romania**, nations in which civil society was substantially suppressed under Communist rule and has not yet fully emerged from that trauma.

Poland, the East-bloc nation where the civil society survived most intact and independent schooling emerged with the greatest vigor after the fall of the Communist government, is described next, followed by the **Czech** and **Slovak** republics and **Hungary**, which share with Poland a relatively healthy and diversified society and educational system.

Recent developments in **Russia** and the **Baltic Republics** are described in the eighth chapter, followed by a discussion of the former **East Germany**. This "case" is purposely described last: its development has not followed a course parallel to that of the other countries because of its absorption into the Federal Republic of Germany and the swift adoption of education statutes modeled upon those of the western *Länder*. The German example is useful, *inter alia*, because it illustrates how even well-meaning state regulation of schooling can, despite explicit constitutional guarantees, severely inhibit the development of a range of educational alternatives.

References

1. Quoted in Zbigniew Rau, "Human Nature, Social Engineering, and the Reemergence of Civil Society," in *The Reemergence of Civil Society in Eastern Europe and the Soviet Union*, ed. Zbigniew Rau (Boulder, Colo.: Westview Press, 1991), p. 31.

2. Quoted from the Introduction to Marx's *Contribution to the Critique of Political Economy* (1859) in Frank E. Manuel, "A Requiem for Karl Marx," *Daedalus: The Exit from Communism* 121, no. 2 (Spring 1992): 7.

3. Timothy Edward O'Connor, *The Politics of Soviet Culture: Anatolii Lunacharskii* (Ann Arbor, Mich.: UMI Research Press, 1983), p. 14.

4. O'Connor, p. 15.

5. Alexander Zinoviev, *The Reality of Communism*, trans. Charles Janson (New York: Schocken Books, 1984), pp. 216–17.

6. Zbigniew Rau, "Introduction," in *The Reemergence of Civil Society*, p. 1.

7. Zbigniew Rau, "Human Nature, Social Engineering, and the Reemergence of Civil Society," pp. 27, 32, 36; Alexander Zinoviev, *Homo Sovieticus*, trans. Charles Janson (Boston: Atlantic Monthly Press, 1985), p. 197.

8. Zinoviev, *Homo Sovieticus*, p. 197.

9. Zinoviev, *The Reality of Communism*, pp. 230–31.

10. Ibid., pp. 246, 186.

11. Václav Havel, *Living in Truth* (London: Faber and Faber, 1987), pp. 50, 84–85.

12. Jacques Maritain, *Man and the State* (1951), excerpted in *Political Order and the Plural Structure of Society*, ed. James W. Skillen and Rockne M. McCarthy (Atlanta: Scholars Press, 1991), p. 185.

13. Ernest Gellner, "Civil Society in Historical Context," *International Social Science Journal* 43 (August 1991): 495.

14. Michael Walzer, "The Idea of Civil Society," *Dissent* 38 (Spring 1991): 293.

15. Zbigniew Rau, "Introduction," p. 2.

16. Ibid., pp. 9–10.

17. S. N. Eisenstadt, "The Breakdown of Communist Regimes and the Vicissitudes of Modernity," *Daedalus: The Exit from Communism* 121, no. 2 (Spring 1992): 30.

18. Martin Malia, "Leninist Endgame," *Daedalus: The Exit from Communism* 121, no. 2 (Spring 1992): 60.

19. Victor Zaslavsky, "Nationalism and Democratic Transition in Postcommunist Societies," *Daedalus: The Exit from Communism* 121, no. 2 (Spring 1992): 116.

20. Malia, p. 71.

21. Havel, pp. 60, 71.

22. Ibid., pp. 102–106.

23. Václav Benda, Milan Šimečka, Ivan M. Jirous, Jiří Dienstbier, Václav Havel, Ladislav Hejdánek, and Jan Šimsa, "Parallel Polis, or An Independent Society in Central and Eastern Europe: An Inquiry," *Social Research* 55, nos. 1–2 (Spring/Summer 1988): 211.

24. Stephen R. Burant, "The Influence of Russian Tradition on the Political Style of the Soviet Elite," *Political Science Quarterly* 102, no. 2 (Summer 1987): 292–93.

25. Gellner, pp. 502–503.

26. Havel, pp. 108, 118.

27. Ibid., p. 87.

28. Jiří Musil, "Czechoslovakia in the Middle of Transition," *Daedalus: The Exit from Communism* 121, no. 2 (Spring 1992): 189–90.

29. Kenneth Jowitt, *Revolutionary Breakthroughs and National Development: The Case of Romania, 1944–1965* (Berkeley: University of California Press, 1971), p. 7.

30. Maciej Pomian-Srzednicki, *Religious Change in Contemporary Poland: Secularization and Politics* (London: Routledge & Kegan Paul, 1982), p. 185.

31. Michael Lindsay, "Contradictions in a Totalitarian Society," *China Quarterly* 39 (July/September 1969): 31–33.

32. Marianne Bastid, "Economic Necessity and Political Ideals in Educational Reform During the Cultural Revolution," *China Quarterly* 42 (April/June 1970): 16.

33. References for Danton, Robespierre, and Billaud-Varenne in Charles L. Glenn, *The Myth of the Common School* (Amherst: University of Massachusetts Press, 1988), pp. 291–92.

34. Charles L. Glenn, *Choice of Schools in Six Nations* (Washington, D.C.: U.S. Department of Education, 1989); Gerard Leclerc, *La bataille d'école: 15 siècles d'histoire, 3 ans de combat* (Paris: Denoël, 1985).

35. John H. Robinson, "Why Schooling Is So Controversial in America Today," *Notre Dame Journal of Law, Ethics and Public Policy* 3, no. 4 (1988): 519–33.

36. Richard A. Baer Jr., "Censorship and the Public Schools," typescript (Cornell University), 1984.

37. Quoted in Joseph A. Kahl, "The Moral Economy of a Revolutionary Society," in *Cuban Communism*, ed. Irving Louis Horowitz (New Brunswick, N.J.: Transaction Books, 1970), p. 100.

38. Quoted in Lee Lockwood, *Castro's Cuba, Cuba's Fidel* (New York: Random House, 1969), p. 110.

39. Tang Tsou, "The Cultural Revolution and the Chinese Political System," *China Quarterly* 38 (April/June 1969): 64.

40. Mark Selden, "Yenan Legacy: The Mass Line," in *Chinese Communist Politics in Action*, ed. A. Doak Barnett (Seattle: University of Washington Press, 1969), p. 140.

41. Lindsay, p. 32.

2. The Soviet Union

The Model of Communist Education

A few years after the Bolshevik Revolution, a leading Soviet educator told a visiting American that "the overall task of Soviet education was to 'change the character of the Russian people.'" Six decades later, his successors continued to insist that "the basic aim of Soviet education is to produce a new type of person."[1]

As Bukharin and Preobrazhensky wrote in 1919 for the triumphant Bolsheviks,

> The task of the new communist schools is to impose upon bourgeois and petty-bourgeois children a proletarian mentality. In the realm of the mind, in the psychological sphere, the communist school must effect the same revolutionary overthrow of society, must effect the same expropriation, that the Soviet Power has effected in the economic sphere by the nationalization of the means of production. The minds of men must be made ready for the new social relationships. ... It is the task of the new school to train up a younger generation whose whole ideology shall be deeply rooted in the soil of the new communist society.[2]

Similarly, a *Pravda* editorial of 1928 attributed to Bukharin emphasized the need to change not only individual attitudes and ways of thinking but the very culture in which human consciousness is rooted. Despite a decade of absolute rule by the Communist elite, the proletariat in whose name they ruled had not yet come to understand and appreciate fully the benefits that they were enjoying. It was thus necessary to create an "armor of proletarian culture" to protect them from "alien class influences, bourgeois degeneration, petty-bourgeois waverings, dulling of revolutionary vigilance in the face of the more cultured class enemy."[3]

Soviet psychologists and pedagogical theorists had considerable difficulty defining in operational terms the virtues of the "new Soviet man." This should not be surprising, since the central characteristic

17

that schools sought to develop was a lack of independent judgment and self-direction, a willingness to be guided by the Party in all things.

From one perspective, every modernizing nation has created and used a system of popular education to develop in the children of its rural population, its immigrants, and its industrial workers the skills and even more importantly the attitudes considered by the governing elite essential to "progress." In every case there has been an orthodox worldview that these schools have sought to impose.[4] What was distinctive about Soviet education, however, was the single-minded purpose with which this program was carried out and the insistence of the regime upon an absolute monopoly of the means of information and values formation. Never before—except for the brief interlude of Jacobin control at the height of the French Revolution—had a modern state outlawed even private religious instruction of children or proposed to enroll all children in boarding schools to remove them completely from the influence of their families and communities.

The ferocity of this campaign cannot be understood as simply an effort "to inculcate the values needed for the population to adjust to industrial society and to accept the legitimacy of the political system."[5] Doing so would banalize an assault upon human freedom and the social and cultural institutions that sustain freedom unprecedented in its thoroughness. The peculiarity of Communist rule was the thoroughness and tenacity of its determination to condition the people so that they would be morally incapable of opposing the leadership of the Party. Milovan Djilas, after his break with communism, insisted that "Communist power is more complete than that of the Jacobins [at the height of the French Revolution]. . . . No religion or dictatorship has been able to aspire to such all-around and all-inclusive power as that of the Communist systems."[6]

One historian has described as "weird" the "Bolshevik effort to push Russia into the fragmented culture of modern times while [at the same time] reviving the ancient subordination of culture to the unifying creed of an established church."[7] It would be more accurate, however, to describe this effort as perfectly consistent with the socialist conviction, with roots deep in the Enlightenment, of the "makeability" of human nature and the obligation of the elite to use its superior wisdom to enlighten the common people for their own good and to make them faithful instruments of state power.

Molding the "new Soviet man" was seen from the start as essential to achieving the goal of a fully Communist society. In turn, the transformation of society would help to produce "a new man in whom spiritual wealth, moral purity, and physical perfection will be harmoniously combined."[8] This required "a rigorous and comprehensive process of nurture, tuition, and mind control."[9]

While the concept of an eternal and unchanging human nature had been under attack in the advanced nations of the West for several centuries, it was blown asunder by the Communist determination to use education as a means of radical change.

> The future Soviet citizen whom we are training must be a stalwart and healthy proletarian, a class and a revolutionary fighter, a scientifically conscious and organized builder of the new socialist state. He must be a dialectical materialist, armed to the teeth with the necessary ability to oppose exploitation and mysticism [i.e., religion] in all its forms. He must be a collectivist in all economic and social activities, in order steadfastly to oppose private property and individualistic aims, on which the class of exploiters has built up its power.[10]

Moral education (*vospitanie*) consisted above all in teaching children not unchanging principles, but "Party-mindedness" (*partiinost'**), to think and act as instructed by the Communist party and to be able to change direction without question as the Party itself determined. As Lenin put it, "Everything that contributes to the building of a Communist society is moral, everything that hinders this is immoral and amoral."[11]

To this end, the Soviet teacher was "expected to arouse in students a highly emotional, passionate conviction about the correctness of any . . . answer. It is not enough, for example, to teach that communists are good and capitalists are bad. The teacher must use the powers of persuasion and moral conviction to instill in students a hatred for capitalists and a love for communists. Students must also be taught how to defend their communist beliefs, because students lacking this ability are subject to the 'pernicious influences' of capitalist propaganda."[12] John Dewey, a generally sympathetic observer, put it plainly when he noted that, in Soviet Russia, "propaganda is

---

*"Party spirit, Party principle, Communist ideology as an integral part of one's activity." *Russian-English Dictionary* (Moscow: Russky Yazyk, 1987).

19

education and education is propaganda. They are more than confounded; they are identified." As a result of "an enormous constructive effort taking place in the creation of a new collective mentality," Dewey concluded, "the final significance of what is taking place in Russia is not to be grasped in political or economic terms, but is found in change, of incalculable importance, in the mental and moral disposition of a people."[13]

There was a clear inconsistency in the Communist position. All the vices that afflicted prerevolutionary Russian society were blamed upon the institution of private property and capitalist exploitation. Establishment of socialism and abolition of private property should have led, with historical inevitability, to the automatic emergence of a new socialist humanity. Why, then, was state intervention to change attitudes and values—indeed, a state monopoly on all public forms of information and socialization—essential?

Lenin himself warned that the creation of a new socialist humanity would not occur spontaneously as a result of social and economic changes, but that propaganda "in the ranks of broad masses of all sorts of cultural, scientific, antireligious . . . knowledge and achievements" would be "of overwhelming importance."[14] The Young Communist League (Komsomol) was instructed in 1920 that it was their job "to educate communists. The whole purpose of training, educating and teaching young people today is to imbue them with communist ethics."[15] The Soviet school "must become a weapon of the dictatorship of the proletariat . . . the conductor of the ideological, organizational, and educational influence of the proletariat on the . . . toiling masses for the purpose of shaping a generation capable of finally establishing Communism." Or, as Stalin put it more bluntly in 1934, "Education is a weapon . . . whose effect depends on who holds it in his hands and who is struck with it."[16]

Lenin's widow, Nadezhda Krupskaya, stressed that "building socialism is not just creating a new economic basis, not just setting up and consolidating Soviet rule, but also bringing up a new generation who will tackle every problem in a new way . . . remolding our psychology, reshaping our relationships."[17] This program of fundamental change through schooling required that teachers come to see their work as fundamentally political. Thus, a resolution adopted at the first congress of Soviet teachers in 1925 confessed the mistakes the teachers had made when still "romanticists deceived by

20

the slogans of democracy and freedom, and the unconscious weapons of the class interests of the bourgeoisie by believing in the democratic harmony of classes."[18]

The most influential Soviet educator after Krupskaya was Anton Makarenko, whose emphasis on creating group solidarity as a means of moral education and discipline grew out of work with youth without families during and after the upheavals of the civil war in the 1920s. "For Makarenko," Bowen writes, "the individual personality was an obstruction to the attainment of the communist state, and he directed his efforts at the primary construction of the collective." This pedagogical theme served as the basis for the subsequent, and more sinister, use of group pressures to suppress individualism and unorthodox beliefs.[19]

Makarenko's work had a precedent in Soviet education, since it had been a premise of the Bolsheviks that the traditional family was, as John Dewey summarized their position, "exclusive and isolating in effect and hence ... hostile to a truly communal life." After all, the first Soviet commissar of social welfare argued that

> the family is ceasing to be a necessity of the State, as it was in the past. ... Nor is it any longer necessary to the members of the family themselves, since the task of bringing up the children ... is passing more and more into the hands of the collectivity. ... Henceforth the worker-mother, who is conscious of her social function, will rise to a point where she no longer differentiates between yours and mine, she must remember that there are henceforth only our children, those of the communist State, the common possession of all the workers.[20]

Similarly, the director of the Petrograd* education department told a conference in 1918 that

> we must exempt children from the pernicious influence of the family. We have to take account of every child, we candidly say that we must nationalize them. From the first days of their life they will be under the beneficial influence of communistic kindergartens and schools. Here they shall assume the ABC of Communism. Here they shall grow up as real Communists. Our practical problem is to

*Subsequently Leningrad; now again St. Petersburg.

compel mothers to hand over their children to the Soviet Government.[21]

Bukharin and Preobrazhensky stressed the same point the next year, in their *ABC of Communism*. "When parents say, 'My daughter,' 'My son,' " they wrote, "the words do not simply imply the existence of a parental relationship, they also give expression to the parents' view that they have a right to educate their own children. From the socialist outlook, no such right exists. . . . The parents' claim to bring up their own children and thereby to impress upon the children's psychology their own limitations, must not merely be rejected, but must be absolutely laughed out of court. . . . Of one hundred mothers, we shall perhaps find one or two who are competent educators. The future belongs to social education."[22]

The heavy stress that Soviet education placed upon using the influence of peer groups represented an effort to find a replacement for family loyalties as the primary determinant of beliefs and values. Dewey noted in the 1920s that "a most interesting sociological experimentation is taking place, the effect of which should do something to determine how far the bonds that hold the traditional family together are intrinsic and how far due to extraneous causes [which were being removed by the Communists]; and how far the family in its accustomed form is a truly socializing agency [that is, teaches children to conform to the norms of society] and how far a breeder of non-social interests." Although "it would be too much to say that [Soviet schools and summer camps] are deliberately planned with sole reference to their disintegrating effect upon family life," it was evident to Dewey that they were having such an impact.[23]

The stress on molding a new form of humanity might well have faded after the first decades of Communist rule. So long as the majority of adults had been socialized under the old regime and in rural isolation, there was a justified fear among Party leaders of counterrevolution against the dictatorship of the proletariat through its vanguard, the Communist party. Although the great landowners and aristocrats who had been the mainstay of the old regime had been killed or were in exile, the Communists felt threatened by the continuing presence of the new middle class that had been growing rapidly in the last decades before the 1914 revolution and possessed skills making them indispensable in the short run. "It was they who, like a vast corrosive, infiltrated all areas of society and, with the doctrines of self-help and free enterprise, destroyed the formation of a social cement that would bind together the workers of society into a united, solidaristic common purpose." This required that the "first task of education [be] the eradication from the consciousness of the people [of] all traces of capitalist, neutralist, and anti-Bolshevik mentality."[24]

After an early flirtation with various forms of progressive education, a period of "bold creativity ... of passionate arguments,"[25] Soviet school policy in the 1930s returned to highly conventional methods of instruction, with a heavy stress upon political conformity. In 1931, the central committee directed that Communist party organizations "strengthen their guidance of the school and take under their immediate supervision the setting-up of the teaching of political-social discipline."[26]

By the end of Stalin's long rule, the majority of the active population had received such a Communist education and a third Soviet generation was entering the schools. Despite 40 years of monopoly of all forms of information and socialization, however, the Party was as urgent as ever to "activize and improve to the utmost every means of influencing the masses ideologically." This was a special responsibility of the schools, where "all teachers, no matter what their subjects, are obliged to make their contribution to instilling a Communist world outlook in the youth."[27]

Khrushchev's "Theses on Educational Reform" (1958) sought to harness the school system even more explicitly to the task of creating the "new socialist man," through a stress on relating education to work and also on developing a thoroughly materialistic worldview to eliminate all religious influence on the minds of youth. "Under Khrushchev, perhaps for the last time, the attempt was made to activate the revolutionary/utopian potential of the ideological long-term goal and to make the vision of Communism into a direct and practically motivating political power. ... Education was given a key role" in this endeavor.[28]

A Conference on Problems of Ideological Work, convened by the Party in the wake of the dramatic 22nd Party Congress, when Khrushchev made his celebrated attack on Stalin, stressed, "The school is not simply an educational establishment. It is an ideological institution" whose Party cells were responsible for helping teachers "make their contribution to the great cause of building communism by educating the new man." The "struggle against bourgeois ideology" was an urgent task for schools, since "sometimes survivals of the past, the corrupt ideology and morality of capitalism, make their imprint on school-age children too. . . . Members of religious sects and church people try to draw children into their meshes, and . . . there are still backward, uncultured parents who push their sons and daughters into religion."[29]

It might seem strange that vestiges of capitalist thinking should be perceived as such a threat, given that only a small minority of the Russian and subject peoples were in any sense bourgeois at the time of the revolution. But the Communist leadership was continually warning teachers and other "ideological workers" that the struggle would be a prolonged one, since "the survivals of capitalism in the minds of the people are preserved for a long time even after the socialist system is established." Despite Marx's insistence that it was "not the consciousness of men that determines their existence, but, on the contrary, their social existence determines their consciousness,"[30] his successors also pointed out that "the consciousness of people lags behind economic development."[31]

But what were these threatening "survivals"? Surely not the desire to lend money at interest or to exploit wage-slaves, but rather the insistence upon retaining that personal freedom, at least in the mind and heart, which was continually condemned as antisocial and inconsistent with being a "builder of communism." Religious beliefs, unsanctioned political ideas, the desire to retain some private and family life that was not mobilized to serve the purposes of the regime were inconsistent with the qualities demanded of "Soviet man—his communist consciousness, love of work, patriotism, humaneness and feeling of internationalism" celebrated by Brezhnev and other Communist leaders, who spoke of achieving a "cultural revolution . . . a genuine revolution in our society's spiritual life."[32]

To supplement and reinforce the message provided by the Party-dominated school, the Party established youth organizations to which a large proportion of young people belonged—though confessed religious believers were not eligible. The Octobrists (Oktyabryata) enrolled children aged 6 through 9, the Pioneers (Pionery) aged 10 through 15, and the Communist Youth League (Komsomol), which was more selective, aged 16 through 28.

These organizations, in addition to helping school officials with social control and political surveillance of teachers as well as pupils, sought "to harness the energies and loyalties of young people to communist ideology and to steel them against bourgeois ideas and morality."[33] A recommendation from Komsomol was needed for admission to higher education and the more desirable forms of employment; it is not surprising that in 1981 there were 40 million members.[34]

Lest the combined effect of teachers and peer group not prove sufficient to mold the "new Soviet man," single-heartedly devoted to following the Party, the Supreme Soviet, on Khrushchev's initiative, resolved in 1958 to create a great network of boarding schools where the distracting influence of family and religious organizations could be minimized and a consistent discipline imposed. Such schools would create "the most favorable conditions . . . for the instruction and Communist rearing of the younger generation," filling them with a "spirit of irreconcilability with bourgeois ideology and all manifestations of revisionism."[35]

Such schools were a logical extension of the goal of establishing an absolute state/Party monopoly of socialization and the formation of values and opinions to train "well rounded, educated builders of communism."[36] Indeed, the idea was not a new one; as early as 1920 education officials had proposed boarding schools for all children under 14 or 15 to minimize the influence of families, with their individualistic orientation, but the resources of the regime did not make it possible to provide for more than the minority of pupils whose unacceptable behavior or family circumstances made a regular school assignment inappropriate. Khrushchev's plans, by contrast, called for an enrollment of 1 million pupils by 1960 and 2.5 million by 1965; he wished to see boarding schools become the standard form of Soviet education.[37]

The fall of Khrushchev, the immense cost required to establish dormitories and support facilities for millions of boarding pupils, and the resistance of parents combined to limit this effort to a fraction of its intended scale. Emphasis soon shifted to establishing extended-day schools, which could have something like the same intense effect upon pupils without the expense and disruption of establishing boarding schools.[38] The insistence upon ideological indoctrination and upon "the complete overcoming of remnants of bourgeois opinions and morals" continued to be the highest priority of the Party, to "raise the consciousness" of the rising generation.[39]

Thus Leonid Brezhnev emphasized the importance of "raising young people in the spirit of the new communist morality" and his future successor Yuri Andropov insisted, in 1977, that formation of the new man was an essential dimension of the international political-ideological struggle.[40] In 1983 Andropov and Konstantin Chernenko spoke at length at the plenary session of the central committee on the problem of forming future citizens. General Secretary Andropov instructed Party members to ensure that schools educated children "not merely as vessels containing a certain amount of knowledge but above all as citizens of a socialist society and active builders of communism."[41] The following year, in his first public address as its general secretary, Chernenko affirmed that the goal of the Communist party was "to construct a new world" through "constant concern for the development (*formirovanie*) of the man of the new world, for his ideological and moral growth."[42]

The central committee, in turn, stressed that "the further improvement of ideological activity and the raising of its effectiveness is one of the most important tasks of the Party" and noted with sorrow that "a section of the people still remain under the influence of religion, and, to be blunt, not all that small a section either."[43] The Party resolved "more actively to conduct the propagation of scientific-materialist views among the population and to devote more attention to atheistic education."[44]

The slogan under which this campaign of ideological formation was to be carried out had been formulated in 1977 as "the unified educational front" of schools, youth organizations, the media, employing organizations, and society in general, all following the leadership of the Communist party. Families were expected to play their part, though there was always an undercurrent of concern lest they prove an impediment to the campaign. The training of teachers devoted more time to ideological studies than to "teaching methods, psychology, and educational theory put together," stressing the politically correct approach to every subject.[45]

Teaching of geography, for example, was presented in a 1979 text for teachers as a perfect opportunity to instill "Soviet patriotism and proletarian internationalism, a Communist attitude toward nature, labor, and the products of labor, [and] a total rejection of bourgeois morality and such relics of the past as religion."[46]

In short, the Communist educational program in the Soviet Union was intended to thoroughly penetrate the entire population with a Marxist-Leninist worldview that precluded any form of independent thinking or social organization. It was part of a "unique process of state-guided social transformation, for the state did much more than just 'guiding': it substituted itself for society, to become the sole initiator of action and controller of all important spheres of life . . . with the whole social structure being, so to speak, sucked into the state mechanism, as if entirely assimilated by it."[47] There was no place for an independent civil society—or for the independent schools that would help to sustain it—in this strategy of social transformation.

In many respects, the "cultural revolution" sought by the Communist elite swept all before it. After the disruptions of the twenties and the Stalinist terror of the thirties, few spheres of life continued to hold out an alternative set of values, a different way of understanding the world. The social elites in whose wisdom and benign guidance the 19th century had placed so much confidence—scientists, university professors, members of the professions, businessmen—all accommodated themselves to the new order or were swept away.

However, two spheres of life, rooted in older realities, resisted with some success the Communist drive to remake human nature and to substitute a Marxist-Leninist worldview that permitted no shadow of deviation. Religion and nationality, though swallowed up by the Soviet regime, proved indigestible.

The Great Rival: Religion

There was from the start a fundamental opposition between the Bolsheviks who seized power in 1917 and the Christian churches, based not only upon the close alliance between the Orthodox church and the old order but also upon the absolute claims made by communism upon all aspects of life, including its spiritual dimension. All religions, no matter how reformed, were considered by the Bolsheviks "systems of ideas . . . profoundly hostile to the ideology of . . . socialism."[48] The Party was "committed to the destruction of all autonomous social institutions and groups—that is, to the eradication of all focal points for alternative loyalties."[49]

27

While the first Soviet constitution (adopted in July 1918) was being developed, religious freedom was one of the few issues on which there was real disagreement. The original version declared that "religion is a private affair of the citizens," but Lenin insisted on substituting a provision guaranteeing freedom of religious and anti-religious propaganda.[50] There was no room, in the Communist scheme of things, for a sphere of privacy in the lives of citizens where the state and Party had no right to seek to advance their agenda.

While the constitution guaranteed freedom of religious expression, it did not provide protection for freedom of religious association. Article 52 declared, "Citizens of the USSR are guaranteed freedom of conscience . . . [and] the right to profess or not to profess any religion," but article 51 limited the right of association to that which is "in accordance with the aims of building communism."[51] As a result, communities of practicing Christian, Jewish, and Muslim believers and the institutions supporting their religious practices were never assured of more than a toleration that could be withdrawn at any time for political reasons. A decree earlier in 1918 had seized all property owned by churches and forbidden them to own property in the future; congregations could use the nationalized property (church buildings, vestments and chalices, books used in the liturgy) only with the permission of local soviets, and church buildings could also be used by nonchurch groups for concerts, films, and other activities.[52]

Although Marxism postulates that religion will die out of its own accord as the social and economic conditions of exploitation that create it are removed, the Soviet regime was vigilant to stamp out relics of "bourgeois thinking," among them religious beliefs and worldviews. Particular dangers were seen in allowing religious communities to carry out catechetical activities for the children of believers, since this would impede the effort of the state's schools to educate children away from the "superstitions" of their parents. A 1929 law regulating religious associations forbade "religious propaganda," while explicitly allowing "atheistic propaganda," and this distinction was maintained in the 1936 and 1977 constitutions.[53]

Lenin himself was by no means merely indifferent to or scornful of religion, like earlier Russian radicals. In contrast with Marx and Engels, who saw religion as the invention of humanity to ease the pain of its wretchedness, Lenin described it as a means invented by the ruling class to keep the masses docile. Rather than a byproduct of oppression, religion was thus one of the principal means of oppression from Lenin's perspective.[54] He saw it, therefore, as a major and very dangerous enemy of communism and launched "a systematic, aggressive and uncompromising movement of atheistic agitation, organized and fully supported by" the Communist party.[55]

The program adopted at the Eighth Party Congress in 1919 was explicit that the Party would not be satisfied with "separation of Church and State," but aimed at "assisting the actual liberation of the working masses from religious prejudices and organizing the broadest possible scientific-educational and anti-religious propaganda." The Tenth Party Congress in 1921 identified the battle against religion as a primary aspect of the Party's work.[56]

Perhaps the fundamental issue in the hostility of the Communist party to religion was that Marxism-Leninism itself had many of the earmarks of a religious belief-system. Thus British philosopher Bertrand Russell, who was otherwise sympathetic to the revolution, pointed out in 1920, "Bolshevism is not merely a political doctrine; it is also a religion, with elaborate dogmas and inspired scriptures," while an American visitor observed that "the church is recognized as a rival . . . [and] loyalty to the Revolution is emphasized and promoted in ways that often suggest . . . the attitudes and methods of a religious movement." John Dewey agreed that "the movement in Russia is intrinsically religious. . . . Never having previously witnessed a widespread and moving religious reality [despite his years in the Chicago of Dwight L. Moody!] . . . I feel as if for the first time I might have some inkling of what may have been the moving spirit and force of primitive Christianity."[57]

Not that this parallel was ever openly avowed by the Communists, as it was, in contrast, by the Jacobins during the most radical phase of the French Revolution in 1792. Lenin reacted angrily when his Bolshevik colleague (and later commissar of education) Anatoly Lunacharsky made the religious nature of Marxism-Leninism explicit, and later reprimanded even Maxim Gorky for a similar suggestion, writing that "any religious idea . . . is the most dangerous foulness, the most shameful 'infection.' " Building the "new socialist man" required, in his opinion, a conscious rejection of any sort of religious faith; no compromise was possible. Unlike Trotsky, Lenin did not believe that the process of modernization that the Communists were pushing forward on all fronts would of itself lead to the

29

secularization of the people in short order, or that cinema would soon replace liturgy as the preferred entertainment of the masses.[58]

Nevertheless, over time the similarity of the Communist party to an established church, with its dogmas, rituals, and hierarchy, grew ever more apparent. Lunacharsky had proposed that the Party engage in "god-building" (*bogostroitel'stvo*), replacing the supernatural God with the deified humanity that would evolve under Communist leadership, as a way of using the emotional power of religion and the values that it cultivated for the Party's purposes.

> It is not necessary to search for god, . . . it is necessary to give him to the world. He is not in the world, but he may be. The path of struggle for socialism, that is, for the triumph of man in nature, that is *bogostroitel'stvo*.[59]

Belief in a transcendent deity persisted, according to Lunacharsky, because people had not become convinced of the possibility of human "perfection through socialist enlightenment." The necessary psychological transformation could be furthered by practices borrowed from traditional religion. Prayer should be addressed to "progress, humanity, the nation, and to the human genius," and rituals should be developed to support the struggle to build communism, creating "a mystical link between the people and the promised Communist society of the future."[60] Secular holidays and ceremonies were devised, Wedding Palaces established, "to compete with and supplant religious holy days and rituals."[61]

Such efforts to "deflect the urges of citizens for expressive gratification onto an official 'political religion,' "[62] while continuing to suffer from ideological discomfort under a regime committed to the strictest dialectical materialism, became an important aspect of Soviet life. These ranged from the ubiquity of icons of Lenin* (and, until he fell from favor, of Stalin) to ceremonies developed to substitute for church weddings and funerals.

One of the first steps of the new Communist-controlled regime was to destroy the ability of its primary rival for the hearts and minds of the Russian people to provide an alternative set of values and interpretations of reality. Lenin declared that the Communist

---

*The heading in a third-grade reading book, "Lenin Lived, Lenin Lives, Lenin Will Live," is unavoidably reminiscent of the proclamation in the Christian liturgy, "Christ has died, Christ is risen, Christ will come again!"

party's "object is to completely destroy . . . organised religious propaganda and [thereby] really liberate the working people from religious prejudices," and on December 11, 1917, he decreed that "all control of educational matters shall be handed over to the Commissariat of Education from all religious organizations. All church/ parish schools, teachers colleges, religious colleges and seminaries . . . all missionary schools . . . with all their property . . . buildings . . . libraries . . . valuables, capital . . . shall likewise be handed over."[63]

The regime set up a Communist-dominated union of teachers within weeks of its seizure of power because of the resistance of the All-Russian Teachers' Union to removal of religious instruction from schools. This did not resolve the problem at once; several years later, Lunacharsky complained that the majority of teachers were still practicing believers, and in 1925 the first congress of Soviet teachers urged that religious instruction be included in the curriculum.[64]

In January 1918, the Soviet government ordered that "the teaching of religious doctrines in all state and public schools, or in private educational institutions where general subjects are taught, is prohibited," and two days later Lenin issued a decree forbidding the Orthodox church to teach religion in state or private schools or to any minors. The education law enacted in October 1918 confirmed that all instruction must be secular and free of religious instruction, while permitting the existence of secular private schools as a concession to the government's inability to provide schooling for all in the short term—a concession that was revoked in 1923.[65] As Bukharin and Preobrazhensky wrote the next year, the Communist school "forcibly expels religion from within its walls, under whatever guise it seeks entry and in whatever diluted form reactionary groups of parents may desire to drag it back again."[66]

In 1921 a penalty of forced labor was decreed for providing religious education to children and youth below the age of 18.[67] "As the Soviet Government is responsible for the children of the country," a township that petitioned for the restoration of religious instruction was told, "it must prevent the minds of these children from being darkened by religious superstition."[68]

This was followed by countless exhortations and orders over the next two decades to form "groups of the Young Godless" in schools and to be sure not to allow school holidays to coincide with religious feast days; there was even an attempt (similar to that under the

Jacobins in France in 1792) to abolish the seven-day week to make it impossible for believers to attend church on Sunday.[69]

Historians have pointed out that Communist efforts to root out religion went beyond any rational calculus of costs and benefits and in fact—as Stalin would eventually recognize—threatened to alienate the people (especially those in rural areas) from the regime during a period when great efforts and sacrifices were demanded of them. It was "an act of incredible folly" that "the strains caused by forcing upon a conservative and mostly illiterate people an abrupt change of age-old life patterns were compounded by an attack on their religion."[70] That this folly was committed by a leadership that on other matters was capable of considerable flexibility suggests how central to the Communist program was the elimination of all competing beliefs.

When Orthodox believers in one industrial town resisted the confiscation of religious articles from their church, Lenin ordered that they be crushed relentlessly, writing in a secret instruction that "it is precisely now that we must wage a merciless battle against the reactionary clergy and suppress its resistance with such cruelty that it may remember it for several decades."[71] The first years of Communist rule, in fact, saw the arrest and murder of dozens of bishops and thousands of other clergy, and sermons were subjected to censorship in 1922.[72]

Some of the Protestant churches enjoyed a certain easing of their situation after the fall of the tsar, whose regime was closely allied with the established Orthodox church, and well into the 1920s, in part because the Communists hoped that "sectarianism" would undercut loyalty to Orthodoxy. The evangelization efforts of these churches proved all too successful, however, and they were included in the crackdown on all religious activity during the "cultural revolution" of the First Five-Year Plan. In 1929, religious associations were forbidden to carry out youth work or to hold meetings or events of any kind apart from regularly scheduled worship, and the earlier antireligious measures were codified in a decree that, among other provisions, ordered that "the teaching of any kind of religious belief whatsoever is forbidden in . . . schools."[73] The League of the Militant Godless, by contrast, organized the same year a junior branch for children aged 8 to 14, the League of the Young Militant Godless.[74]

In order to raise an entire generation free from "superstition and religious prejudices," the Party hoped, the educational system was expected to stress anti-religious instruction. While the education statute enacted in 1918 had required that all schools (state and private alike) be secular, the statute of 1923 disavowed neutrality toward religion and prescribed "the propagating of atheism as an official doctrine in all schools." Since the constitution required parents to raise their children as "worthy members of the socialist society," the school was justified in intervening when, as a result of the home environment, "children are the victims of religious fanaticism."[75]

After a few years of relative toleration of religion, in the interest of national unity during and immediately after World War II, the Communist party renewed its efforts to eliminate religious belief and practice as a dangerous competitor. Believers could not be members of the Young Communist League (Komsomol), it was announced in 1947, while the official newspaper for teachers said that teachers should not be believers and called for a struggle against the idea that education could be merely nonreligious rather than actively anti-religious.[76]

Several years later, the paper reported deplorable conditions in the schools of Yaroslavl', where "many teachers do not conduct a struggle against the penetration into the midst of the children of religious survivals and superstitions." Although "some pupils participate in religious ceremonies and are infected with all sorts of superstitions," going so far as to wear crucifixes, attend church regularly, and pray, there were teachers who "knowing these things, tolerate them and look on them with indifference" or even went so far as to "observe church rites and holidays" themselves. Only "systematic" anti-religious instruction marked by a "militant and offensive spirit" would be adequate to the dangerous situation in Yaroslavl'.[77]

It was under Khrushchev, perceived in the West as a liberalizer, that the attack on religion was escalated; the regime "sought to prevent religion from filling the ideological vacuum that developed in the wake of de-Stalinization by radically reducing the points of contact between the clergy and the population." Half of the Orthodox, Baptist, Lutheran, and Catholic churches were closed, and the number of synagogues was reduced from 400 to fewer than 100.[78]

Even during the period of relative détente between the Communist authorities and the Orthodox and Protestant churches after World War II, Catholic clergy in Lithuania had been subject to imprisonment, deportation, and even execution as Soviet authorities sought to remove all barriers to the reabsorption of the Baltic states into the Russian empire. The harassment of Catholics resumed in the late 1950s under Khrushchev, and "severe sanctions were applied against the clergy for religious instruction of children and for allowing active participation of the youth in religious ceremonies."[79]

The Ministry of Education ordered in February 1959 that all Soviet schools take measures to make education effectively anti-religious,[80] and in the program adopted at its celebrated 22nd Congress, in 1961, the Communist party stressed the importance of overcoming, through patient but insistent education and propaganda, the vestiges of the past, including individualism and superstition. Schools must employ a "comprehensive scientific-atheistic propaganda" to make clear that the worldview of the "new Socialist man" had no place for the "fantastic chimeras of religion."[81]

Children under 18 were forbidden in 1961 to attend Baptist worship services, and two years later this was extended to Orthodox services, thus extending the long-standing ban on religious instruction for minors. In justification, the Young Communist League argued that "freedom of conscience does not apply to children, and no parent should be allowed to cripple a child spiritually." After all, the leading legal journal added, the rights of parents in relation to their children were granted by the state, which could take them away at any time.[82] Or, as a leading ideologist insisted,

> We cannot and we must not remain indifferent to the fate of the children on whom parents, fanatical believers, are in reality inflicting an act of spiritual violence. We cannot allow blind and ignorant parents to bring up their children like themselves and so deform them.[83]

The criminal code of the Russian republic made it illegal for a group, "under the guise of preaching religious beliefs and performing religious ceremonies," to harm the health of citizens or to induce "citizens to refuse social activity or the performance of civic duties." The effect of this statute was that "circumcision, baptism by immersion, fasting, refusal to let a child wear the Pioneer red neckerchief, and a host of other acts [were] criminal offenses."[84]

An article in *Pravda* (January 12, 1967) stressed that "the struggle against religion is not a campaign, not an isolated phenomenon, not a self-contained entity; it is an inseparable component part of the entire ideological activity of Party organizations, an essential link and necessary element in the complex of communist education."[85]

To this end, anti-religious themes were worked into all areas of the curriculum. Biology and other science courses, for example, were expected to contribute by "exposing the anti-scientific character" of religious belief; teaching should be "saturated with atheistic contents."[86] It was essential, a Soviet educator (and later Russian Republic minister of education) wrote, that the pupil "be assisted in ridding himself of prejudices and superstitions through the dissemination and strengthening of materialistic views of all the phenomena of nature and society."[87]

Simply ridding the school of religious instruction and stressing a materialistic worldview, the strategy adopted in 1925, had proved inadequate; experience showed that, in schools that were only nonreligious, "manifestations of various religious superstitions were observed even in the upper grades." No, instruction must have a "clear antireligious purpose" to be effective. This required a subtle approach: "Objective descriptions of and comparative differences between creeds must be avoided in teaching, since this could produce the contrary effect; that is, it could propagate religion" by arousing the interest of the pupils.[88] One cautionary tale told of a teacher who explained to her second-grade class that the cosmonauts had not seen God when so high above the earth, and asked whether they did not find this convincing evidence; one child responded, "I do not know if 300 kilometers is very much, but I know that only those who are pure of heart will behold God."[89]

Teachers were urged not to rely upon lectures and readings alone in carrying out atheistic education, but to assess the situation of individual children who might be under religious influence. "To find out which pupils came from religious families, the teacher will ask: 'Who will tell me something about the origins of religion?'"[90] With those from Baptist families outside the government-recognized association, it would be a waste of time to rely upon arguments, since they would have been well-trained at home to respond and classmates might receive the wrong impression from hearing their answers and confessions of faith; instead, such children should be drawn into interesting activities within which peer influence could come between them and their families.[91] When busy with group activities, as Lenin's widow Krupskaya stressed, "the child will not feel alone, and he will not have any need of religion."[92]

35

A natural result of the systematic denouncing of religion in Soviet schools was that children of practicing Muslim and Christian believers would frequently keep quiet in the classroom and among their peers about their own beliefs; "parents who are quietly religious rarely wish their sons and daughters friction in school and so encourage them to be overt Pioneers and secret believers."[93] Other parents would conceal their own religious (and political) views from their children to avoid drawing trouble upon the family "or simply because they [did] not want to burden the others with the responsibility of sharing these opinions."[94] This subterfuge led to yet another charge against religion, that of "turning young Soviet citizens into hypocrites."[95]

One typical case was that of two brothers in the eighth and ninth grades who "read the Holy Scripture, regularly went to church, and performed religious rites." Though they were well-read and earned excellent grades, "it was not difficult to detect the pernicious effect of religious morality in their behavior: their superficial good breeding concealed such negative traits as individualism, insincerity, and hypocrisy. The brothers fulfilled unquestioningly the social tasks they were asked to perform, but without manifesting any initiative or interest." In other words, they complied in every way with external demands, but the goals of Communist education could not be satisfied without an inner compliance, a remolding of the heart and mind of these adolescents. Finally, after a concerted effort over many months by teachers and classmates, and "many private talks in an unconstrained atmosphere" [!] with the school principal, the Party secretary, and the classroom teachers, "the boys succeeded in freeing themselves from the religious impressions of their childhood."[96] Or at least they said they did.

In another case, it was sufficient for the classroom teacher to have some "warm, friendly talks" with Valya to bring her to understand "that for many years the church had dulled the mind of her mother." Galina was encouraged by her teacher not to tell her mother (a "confirmed Baptist") that she had joined the Komsomol. For some children from believing families like Alik, however, it was more effective to assign to classmates "the task of helping him to overcome his religious prejudices," by extending invitations to extracurricular, athletic, and social events that conflicted with church attendance. The decisive point was reached when "the Komsomol members of his class invited him to the birthday party of Liuda K. Though he had intended to go to church on that day, he gave in to his comrades and spent the evening in their friendly circle." As such activities increasingly "occupied his free time and attention . . . the affairs of the collective became so important for him that in the end he broke with religion."[97]

A careful study of incidents reported in the *Chronicle of the Catholic Church in Lithuania* from 1974 to 1983 found a persistent pattern of harassment of pupils from religious homes. Of 1,012 incidents analyzed, 38 percent involved threats,* ridicule, scolding, and insults; 17 percent some form of administrative punishment; and more than 12 percent an attempt to bribe or force children into denying their faith.

> The incidents rarely arise because of active provocation or challenge by Catholic children or parents. . . . In the vast majority of cases Catholic children do not exhibit their faith in school, but some school officials try to ferret out their students' Catholic activities outside the school, or they purposely assign directly anti-Catholic essay topics which provoke resistance.[98]

In addition to bringing various forms of pressure to bear upon the children, teachers were advised to "direct their efforts toward showing the parents what harm they are causing their children by rearing them in a religious spirit. It is necessary to convince the parents that they are crippling their children, that they are instilling hypocrisy, deceitfulness, and slavish morals, and that they are impeding the children's learning."[99]

For those pupils free of religious influence at home, the goal of the teacher was to develop in them a solid conviction "of the worthlessness of the religious-idealistic world-view" and also to persuade them to give this inner conviction expression in aggressively conducting atheistic propaganda among their peers and neighbors.[100] Nowhere is the resemblance between communism and a religion clearer than in this concern that even its youngest adherents become active evangelists!

---

*For example, that "all believers would be transferred to the retarded children's boarding school."

The effect of three generations of anti-religious teaching in the schools and anti-religious propaganda through associations and the media appears to have been modest. Religious beliefs and practices have indeed declined, so far as these can be assessed by surveys and other sociological studies,[101] but probably no more than would have occurred through the modernization process which, in the Soviet Union as in Western Europe, detached a large part of the population from traditional ways. Although what Marxism-Leninism considers the "social and economic roots of religion" have long since been destroyed in the Soviet Union, there is ample evidence that religious belief and practice have persisted.

There are even some indications that the focus of the regime on attacking religion had the effect of attributing to it more power and vitality than it might otherwise have exhibited. To the extent that religion was continually presented as the great enemy of communism, those seeking an alternative to the regime were encouraged to take it more seriously than they might have done had it been ignored, as in American schools. Religious practices, religious beliefs became a form of protest and the basis for identities other than the "new Soviet man."

The association of religion with cultural and national identity was evident not only among Lithuanian Catholics, German Mennonites, Estonian and Latvian Lutherans, and, above all, Central Asian Muslims, but also, and to a growing extent, among Russians, for whom the Orthodox church, according to an observer in 1988, was "slowly recapturing the role in which it has often been cast by both well-wishers and enemies—that of the only authentically Russian national institution."[102]

"National in Form but Socialist in Content"*

As its sudden collapse in 1991 revealed to the world, the Soviet Union was a multinational state whose minority peoples were never effectively acculturated into a common Soviet identity. Although the Uzbek anthem began, "Hail Russian brother, great is your people," and as recently as September 1989, the Communist party described Russia as "the consolidating principle of our nation,"[103]

*Stalin, 1925.

the swiftness with which the Soviet Union fell apart shows how feebly the Soviet identity had taken root.

This massive reality was concealed from many observers by a constant insistence that the Soviet Union had finally resolved the age-old problem of ethnic coexistence based on cultural diversity with common loyalties and citizenship. Even opponents of the regime like Alexander Zinoviev believed that the Communist system had been able to eliminate ethnic differences and create a new Soviet people that was "beyond nationality."[104]

It had been Lenin's eventual goal that the diverse Russian empire be transformed, as a concomitant of the process of building socialism, "into a national state, in which the minorities would assimilate and adopt the Russian tongue." But, he warned, this goal could be "brought about only voluntarily. . . . In time, the greatness of Russian culture and the material advantages accruing to those who had mastered its language would bring about cultural and linguistic assimilation."[105]

Soviet policy toward the hundred and more national groups within the Soviet Union took three primary forms that may be summarized as "cultural development (*raztsvet* or blossoming), drawing together (*sbizhenie*), and merging (*sliyanie*)."[106] While the first was consistently stressed as one of the proudest accomplishments of communism, a recurrent theme in Soviet policy discussions was the desirability of merging the nationalities into a Soviet national identity, as an aspect of the creation of the "new socialist man." For the non-Russian nationalities, however, such calls were often perceived as being another form of the Russian cultural imperialism they had experienced under the tsars.

Seventy years of "building socialism" did not have the anticipated effect of creating a new Soviet identity, nor did all peoples share equally in whatever measure of prosperity was achieved. Economists have pointed out the "persistence of substantial development gaps and disparities in living standards among national groups," with the level of consumption relative to that of the Soviet Union as a whole varying, in 1985, from 28 percent above in Estonia to 41 percent below in Tajikistan.*[107]

---

*Spelling of the names of (former) republics has been conformed to the form adopted by the Associated Press in December 1991.

Nor, despite a highly integrated economy and centralized political apparatus, did linguistic assimilation penetrate the masses of the subject nationalities to the extent expected. The proportion of the non-Russian population of the Soviet Union claiming to speak Russian fluently varied greatly among the nationalities, and with the rise of separatist sentiment, that proportion actually declined in some areas. In Estonia, for example, 29 percent of the population claimed to be fluent in Russian in 1970, but only 24.2 percent did so in 1979.[108]

Despite constant efforts to make Russian the unifying language of the Soviet Union, studies in the early 1980s found that "more than half of the population of the southeastern [i.e., Central Asian] republics could not speak Russian and that, indeed, fewer young people there knew Russian than their fathers did."[109]

There was even less inclination on the part of Russians to learn the other languages of the Soviet Union. Despite an official commitment to bilingualism as the norm, "only 3 percent of all Russians have bothered to learn to speak a language of one of the non-Russian nationalities, despite the fact that some 20 percent of all Russians live in the non-Russian republics."[110] Of those surveyed in 1979 who lived and worked in the Turkic republics of Central Asia, only 1 to 6 percent declared themselves fluent in the local language.[111] Indeed, a report by leading Soviet linguists defined bilingualism only as "the cultivation of the Russian language among non-Russian populations of the Soviet Union."[112]

Russian terminology refers not to "ethnic groups" but to "nationalities" (*natsional'nost'*), and these are distinguished not by language used but by self-identification on the internal passport that every citizen was required to carry.[113] It is significant that when the format of these documents (first required in 1932) was modified in 1974, the classification by social class was eliminated but that by nationality was retained. Individuals were not free to choose with what nationality they would be identified, except in the case of children of mixed marriages, who were required to make an irrevocable choice at 16.[114]

The relative strength of personal identification with the minority nationalities in the 1960s may be assessed by the selections that such young people made. Children of mixed Estonian/Russian parentage selected Estonian nationality by a 62:38 margin, while those of mixed

Belarussian/Russian parentage identified themselves as Russian by 66:24. Russian nationality was chosen in eastern Ukraine, in Moldova, and in the Tatar, Chuvash, and Mordvin autonomous regions within Russia, while the other nationality was chosen in Lithuania, Latvia, and (by a 98:2 margin) Turkmenistan. It was thus possible to say, even before the dramatic changes of the last several years, that "ethnic identification is a pervasive reality in the Soviet Union."[115]

The facade of unity, under which ethnic distinctions had supposedly been reduced to folkloric remnants, was cracked in 1986 as nationality-based environmental and cultural movements in the republics began to protest against Russian hegemony and the policies of the Soviet regime. Protest demonstrations—almost unknown before—attracted broad participation in Ukraine and Belarus, in the Baltic republics of Estonia, Latvia, and Lithuania, and in the Caucasian republics of Georgia, Armenia, and Azerbaijan. Although Chernobyl and other environmental problems provided the immediate impetus for these grassroots movements, they had their roots in dissatisfactions over Soviet language and cultural policies. "AN END TO RUSSIFICATION!" demanded the Tbilisi, Georgia, mass demonstration of November 1988.[116]

Such protest was not entirely unprecedented; 10 years earlier, thousands of Georgians had demonstrated to demand—successfully—that their new constitution maintain Georgian as the official state language.[117]

The breakup of the Soviet Union into independent nations—evidence of the failure of the effort to create a "new Soviet man"—was possible in part because of the geographical basis of nationality. In the Soviet Union, despite vast displacements of populations like the Crimean Tatars and the Volga Germans, as in the earlier Russian empire of the tsars, ethnicity was tied to geography. With the exception of the Jews and of some nomadic groups, each of the hundred and more peoples who made up the population identified with a territory with at least some degree of self-government.

Although committed to the insignificance of nationality, the prerevolutionary Bolsheviks had identified themselves with the demands of national minorities as a tactic for undermining the tsarist regime, calling in 1903 for the "introduction of the native language on a par with the state language in all local public and state institutions, [and] the abolition of a compulsory state language."[118]

At a crucial moment in the struggle for power, in November 1917 the Bolsheviks issued their celebrated Declaration of the Rights of the Peoples of Russia. Communist victory, they promised, would lead to "the suppression of all restrictions and privileges in the area of religion or nationality" and "the free development of national minorities and ethnic groups."[119]

The following month, Stalin's "Appeal to All the Muslims of Russia and the Orient" sought to gain their support by promising unprecedented freedoms:

> Muslims of Russia, Tatars of the Volga region and the Crimea
> ... all those whose mosques and places of worship were
> destroyed, whose beliefs and customs were trampled under-
> foot by the Tsars and oppressors of Russia! Henceforth your
> beliefs and customs, your national and cultural institutions
> are proclaimed free and inviolable. Build your own national
> life freely and unhindered. You have the right to do so.[120]

When the Russian empire collapsed during World War I, independent states were able to emerge, however briefly, in the Caucasus, Ukraine, and Central Asia, and the Baltic nations retained their independence for two decades. Other portions of the former empire were incorporated into the new Soviet Union, established by the Union Treaty of 1922. In the Union's first constitution (January 1924) the bold claim was made that "it was only under the conditions of the dictatorship of the proletariat that has grouped around itself the majority of the people, that it has been possible to eliminate the oppression of nationalities." This was only the first step "towards the union of workers of all countries in one World-Wide Socialist Soviet Republic."[121]

The actual formation of the Soviet Union was anything but voluntary, however. While Lenin and his colleagues had correctly perceived that the separatist tendencies of the national minorities could help to bring down the tsarist government, and promised an absolute right of secession from the new Soviet Union, they suppressed with military force the efforts of Central Asian, Georgian, Ukrainian, and other nationalities to set up independent nations. Stalin explained this apparent contradiction to the Tenth Party Congress in 1921:

> We are for the secession of India, Arabia, Egypt, etc., because
> this would mean liberation of those oppressed countries from
> imperialism. We are against the secession of the border

regions of Russia, because secession in that case would mean
. . . a weakening of the revolutionary might of Russia.[122]

The main supporters of Communist rule over predominantly rural and conservative populations in several of the subject nations were industrial workers concentrated in the cities. A high proportion of these workers were Russians, and they had no desire to be subject to the rule of the Azerbaijani, Crimean Tatar, or Georgian majority in the name of national self-determination.[123] As Stalin told the Twelfth Party Congress in 1923, "There are times when the right to self-determination is in contradiction with another, higher right—the right of the working class, having come to power, to strengthen its authority."[124]

After consolidating their rule over the subject peoples of the former Russian empire (with the exception of Poland and the Baltic nations), the Communists implemented liberal policies toward indigenous languages to persuade the peoples of Asia and other colonial subjects of their Western enemies of the benevolent intentions of the new Soviet power.

The survival of distinctive nationalities within the Soviet Union was furthered by these policies, which supported language and cultural diversity more than had the prerevolutionary regime, whose slogan had been "one tsar, one religion, one language." It was not that the national cultures were valued in and for themselves, but it was considered important to use them to ensure that the subject peoples would acquire the "common proletarian culture" essential to their mobilization under the leadership of the Communist party. "Proletarian internationalism," in the name of which the Party expected to stimulate worldwide revolution, implied that national differences were ultimately unimportant compared with the common interest of exploited peoples to rise against their capitalist oppressors.

Although the Red Army put down separatist movements in non-Slavic areas, the resistance of Russian and Ukrainian peasants was perceived as a greater threat to the goals of the Communist regime. Breaking the power of the Orthodox church was thus a higher priority than rooting out Islamic beliefs and practices; Islam had been able to develop little institutional power under Russian rule before the 1917 revolution. On the other hand, Lenin and his colleagues misjudged, initially, the extent to which nationalism had developed among the Muslims of the empire.

During the decades before 1917, an emerging intelligentsia among the Central Asian peoples had already sought to build their "own national life" through a pan-Turkic movement. This educated elite, known as Jadids,* sought unity across differences of clan and dialect through popular education in "new method" schools that taught secular knowledge and a revitalized form of Islam. Although these schools continued to be greatly outnumbered by traditional Koran schools (*mäktäb*), they had a great influence in popularizing the Jadids' "concept of a modern nationality: heterogeneous, encompassing the entire community undivided by ethnic or class stratification, and permeated with a spirit of Muslim equality and brotherhood."[125]

By contrast, class stratification and class conflict were fundamental to the Communist view of society, and pan-Turkic unity was perceived as a serious threat to Russian hegemony. Although the various Turkic peoples of Central Asia were mixed together through the dynamic of their nomadic history, it became Soviet policy to divide them into distinctive "nationalities" and to stress differences rather than similarities in their languages and cultures. The Communists placed a heavy stress upon creating separate republics and autonomous regions based upon nuances of dialect and ethnicity. Muslim peoples "were divided into some 36 separate nations, and literary languages were established—and sometimes invented— for each."[126]

The Soviet regime referred to these peoples as "Soviet Muslims"— ironically, in light of its repeated antireligious campaigns. An identity based upon religion had less potential to nurture political separatism, the Communists believed, than one based upon membership in a transnational Turkish people. This is not to suggest that the religious elements of the Muslim identity were fostered; indeed, the new "national literatures" developed for each of the Central Asian peoples "drew more on folklore than on the largely religious prerevolutionary written legacy of the people."[127]

Once Communist power had been consolidated, the administration "worked to focus and raise the subgroups' ethnocentricity rather

*From Jädidlär (reformers).

than continue their integration" and "beat down Central Asian efforts to form new heterogeneous states based on existing relationships among local subgroups."[128] Over time, the "nomad or peasant who prior to the revolution had considered himself above all a Muslim now began to think of himself for the first time as a member of a nation, be it Azerbaijani, Kazakh-Kyrgyz, Volga Tatar, Bashkir, Crimean Tatar, Uzbek, or some other."[129]

This strategy persisted until the end of Communist rule; "the Soviets have taken strong exception," a Western scholar wrote in the mid-1980s, "to the argument that the Muslim umma (community) is a nation; they argue that the Central Asian clergy give their people a false consciousness that reduces their loyalty to their 'true' nations (that is, to the Kazakhs, Kyrgyz, Uzbeks, and so forth)."[130]

Soviet support for minority language schooling must be understood in the context of the "policy of dismantling the religious and cultural unity . . . [of] Russian Islam before the Revolution and of developing separate nations with their own languages, cultures and traditions,"[131] as a means of giving institutional support to ethnic segregation, isolating Uzbeks from Kazakhs and other Turkic peoples. While instruction through Turkic languages—some given standardized form for the first time—was provided in newly established state schools, the authorities abolished both the traditional Koran schools and the "new method" schools established by the Jadid reformers, even in areas where state schools were not yet available. Islamic teaching, in either a traditional or an updated form, was completely unacceptable.[132]

The languages themselves were transformed to serve the purposes of the new regime. By imposing the Latin (and subsequently the Cyrillic) alphabet in place of the Arabic alphabet for writing the Turkic languages, all prerevolutionary publications were made essentially inaccessible for Muslim children who learned to read in Soviet schools, and the vocabulary was purged of words with religious associations, while many new politically correct words were invented.* The same process occurred with Buddhist elements in the Mongolian languages of the Soviet Union.[133]

---

*It should be noted that the government of Kemal Atatürk in Turkey was contemporaneously carrying out a purge of Arabic elements in the Turkish language and an introduction of strongly political elements.

In what was one of their greater miscalculations, the Communist rulers underestimated the extent to which their policies would stimulate national sentiment on the part of peoples with little previous history of independent statehood.

> Whatever the ultimate aims of Soviet nationalities policy—acculturation and bilingualism, assimilation [to Russian language and culture], or the creation of a multinational 'Soviet people'—the dominant process in Transcaucasia has been the ethnic consolidation and growing internal cohesion of the major nationalities. . . . One hundred years earlier Erevan [in Armenia] had a Muslim majority, while in the early years of Soviet rule Tbilisi [in Georgia] and Baku [in Azerbaijan] were largely Russian and Armenian cities. As the Soviet Union entered its seventh decade, these cities had become in the full ethnic sense the capitals of national states.[134]

Soviet education treated non-Russian languages much more generously than it did non-Communist worldviews. Elementary schooling, in fact, was provided primarily in the languages of each of the nationalities, though ambitious parents were encouraged to enroll their children in schools providing instruction through Russian as an advantage in obtaining secondary and higher education.

Tsarist decrees had banned languages other than Russian for publishing and education, especially in Belarus and Ukraine, whose Slavic peoples were to be totally assimilated with their Russian "elder brothers." The Union of Secondary School Teachers, before the revolution, concluded that the school had taken "upon itself to become the tool of Russification and has aroused deep hatred of the Russian language and Russian culture in outlying areas" and thus had alienated the non-Russian nationalities rather than reconciling them to Russian rule. On the other hand, support for minority languages was opposed by those who saw this as a threat to the unity of the empire. The Minister of Internal Affairs described the "systematic striving by the aliens, under the pretext of satisfying their religious and educational needs, to seize into their own hands the primary and even secondary education of the youth and to imbue it with a narrowly nationalistic and more or less vividly expressed anti-government character."[135]

As a result of such forebodings, minority languages under tsarist policies were limited to a supportive role, except in Muslim and Jewish schools that were financially supported by those communities.

The generous policy of the Soviet government toward minority languages was stressed by Stalin, in addressing the Twelfth Party Congress in 1923, when he insisted that "not only the schools but also all institutions, all organs—both Party and government—should become national step by step . . . should operate in the language understood by the masses."[136]

By allowing and even encouraging the preservation of selected language and cultural elements of the subordinate nations—and governing them to a large extent through loyal non-Russian cadres— the Communist leaders believed that the process of history would inevitably lead to the elimination of nationality as a factor in Soviet life. Stalin had gone so far as to predict that "after the victory of socialism on a world scale" the various languages spoken by humanity would "fuse into one common international language."[137] Once Communist power had been consolidated beyond effective challenge, the emphasis shifted from national development to creation of a single Soviet identity.[138]

Although non-Russian parents were free to choose elementary schools that instructed primarily through the Russian language, they had long been guaranteed by the constitution the right of instruction through their national languages (though with Russian as a required subject). The zeal with which such instruction was provided to relatively small language groups peaked in the 1930s, when more than 60 languages were used in Soviet schools. Over time, it was primarily the national minorities with their own republics or autonomous regions that were able to maintain schooling in non-Russian languages.[139]

Soviet policies on language use in schools changed repeatedly, and there were significant variations among the republics, though instruction through the major official languages was always available. One Western observer noted, in 1976, that

> the legal policy toward Ukrainian and Armenian is identical, and in both Republics the indigenous language is in conspicuous official use; yet one rarely hears Ukrainian spoken in the streets of Kiev or Russian in the streets of Erevan. About 80 percent of the schools in the Ukraine use Ukrainian as the medium of instruction, and teach Russian as a second

47

language, but in Kiev itself the position is reversed, and most
of the inhabitants speak Russian with a Ukrainian accent. In
Armenia, by contrast, only some 3 percent of the schools use
Russian as the medium, though children are taught it.[140]

The overall picture is too complex to describe here, but it is helpful
to distinguish among three types of schools in the non-Russian parts
of the former Soviet Union. "The first includes schools where Russian
is the primary medium of instruction and the local languages are
not studied. . . . The second includes schools where Russian is the
medium of instruction but the language of a non-Russian nationality
is studied as a subject. . . . The third type comprises schools where
a non-Russian language serves as the medium of instruction for
almost all subjects (except Russian and foreign languages) while
Russian language and literature are studied only as subjects."[141]

In theory, at least, and depending upon local availability, parents
could choose among these three types of instruction for their children. The situation was never so simple, however, owing to the
ethnic mixing that occurred over the centuries but especially in the
Soviet drive for industrialization. For example, "People belonging
to more than 100 nationalities live in the Georgian Republic, and
there are schools where the instruction is organized in separate tracks
to provide for Armenian, Azerbaydzhan, Greek or Osset speaking
children, and the different groups all learn Georgian and Russian.
In 1974 there were 317 such multi-national schools in Kyrgyzstan.
All the schools in the cities of Daghestan recruit children from five
to twenty-five nationalities."[142] Only Russian parents could count
on finding, wherever in the Soviet Union they might live, schools
using their language as the primary medium of instruction; for other
parents, this choice was available only if they continued to live in
the territory where their language had official status.[143]

While use of non-Russian languages for instruction, based upon
parental demand, continued to be official policy, there were continuing (and irritating) vestiges of the "Great-Russian chauvinism"
deplored by Lenin.[144] Soviet leaders had a tendency to identify Soviet
hegemony with the Russian language and to portray efforts to maintain minority languages as a relic of "bourgeois nationalism." Thus
Nikita Khrushchev, when first secretary of the Communist party of
Ukraine, charged in a 1938 speech that "the enemies of the people—
the bourgeois nationalists—knew the power and the influence of

the Russian language, of Russian culture. They knew what influence Bolshevism ... [and] the teachings of Lenin and Stalin had on the minds of the Ukrainian people, the Ukrainian workers and peasants. Therefore they wiped the Russian language out of the schools." In a resolution responding to his speech, the Ukrainian Party Congress accused nationalists of aiming, through their emphasis on the Ukrainian language, at "separating the Ukrainian people from brotherly friendship with the Great Russian people, at separating the Soviet Ukraine from the Union of Soviet Socialist Republics and at restoring capitalist enslavement."[145]*

Language use in schools and other official settings became a very sensitive issue in several republics, with a tug-of-war between local activists and the Soviet regime over the extent to which Russian should become the norm. There were protests in Ukraine, for example, over the 1959 law that gave parents a choice of the language in which their children would receive instruction, which many defenders of linguistic and cultural autonomy "regarded as a measure of linguistic Russification."[146] There had in fact been heated debates in the Supreme Soviet in December 1958 before this provision was enacted.[147]

The controversy became heated again when the 1973 education reform legislation again gave "parents or guardians . . . the right to select for the children, according to their wishes, the school with the appropriate language of instruction."[148] Making the language of instruction a matter of choice for national minority parents, rather than enrolling their children automatically in schools using primarily a language other than Russian, was correctly perceived as designed to persuade those parents that the interests of their children would be advanced by education through the dominant language of the Soviet Union. As one Soviet critic described the choice process:

> Instead of asking about the desired language of instruction, [educators] usually ask, "Do you want your children to know Russian?" Having received a positive response—and in the overwhelming majority of cases it naturally would be positive—the questioner concludes the conversation: "This means that you want your children to attend a Russian school."[149]

*Apart from the "capitalist enslavement"—Ukraine today would appreciate more capitalism—the Communists seem for once to have gotten their prophecies right!

A powerful disincentive to selecting a school that taught in a language other than Russian was the unavailability of higher and even secondary education in most of the languages in which primary instruction was provided. Parents whose ambitions for their children extended to technical or university training were thus inclined to select the option of early schooling in Russian.

The effect of parent choice of the language of instruction was especially clear in Ukraine, where only 12 percent of the schools of Kiev, the (Russified) capital city, used Ukrainian as the primary language in 1988. Ukrainian nationalists agitated to give the power to designate the language of instruction to the education authorities, thus limiting the rights of parents in the name of language maintenance; they charged that "the practice of parental free choice in the language of education . . . leads to national nihilism."[150]

Such pressures toward the use of Russian for schooling made it possible to conclude quite recently that "the status of non-Russian languages in education is being increasingly reduced to the level of a subject of study in Russian-language schools."[151] Nevertheless, the continuing power of nationalism worked to preserve the non-Russian languages as symbols and vehicles of the drive for autonomy. This occurred despite the fact that children from better-educated Kazakh and other national minority families were likely to be schooled in Russian by the choice of their parents, while maintaining and developing their first languages.

Indirect evidence that Soviet language policies contributed to the maintenance of separatist tendencies is provided by the fact that, as shown in the 1979 census, members of nationality groups without their own republics (and thus native-language schooling) were considerably more likely to consider Russian their first language than were those who did have their own republics. Thus 42.6 percent of Germans, 82.3 percent of Jews, 26.2 percent of Poles, and 44.4 percent of Koreans in the Soviet Union regarded Russian as their first language, contrasted with 17 percent of Ukrainians, 8.4 percent of Armenians, 6 percent of Moldavians, and 1.7 percent of Georgians and Lithuanians.[152]

The Continuing Resistance

A fundamental anomaly of Soviet education was that it combined the most radical break with the past in a single generation ever contemplated (with the exception of the brief episode of Jacobin rule during the French Revolution) with pedagogical conservatism. The remaking of human consciousness was intended to be a one-time change. Once the "new Soviet man" was created, it would be the task of schools to maintain the model unchanged for all future generations. The educational system created to serve this agenda had no room for ongoing change or for deviations from the norm; the actual practice of Soviet education was in that sense highly conservative, based upon the conviction that the principles upon which education should rest had been discovered and would remain forever valid.[153]

How successful was the Communists' united educational front of schools and other institutions at molding a "new Soviet man"? Many accounts by Western observers since the 1920s have accepted at face value the claims made by Soviet officials, whether applauding or deploring their success at creating a new model of humanity. Typical, after the launching of Sputnik, was the following comment:

> The Soviet leaders attribute their achievements in the field of education to the "superiority" of the socialist system over capitalism. In all justice, we must admit that this assertion contains a grain of truth. Soviet experience shows that, with all other factors equal, a totalitarian regime, having at its unlimited command both the material resources and the human energies of a vast country enormously rich in natural resources, can achieve much more than any democratic state.[154]

It is now abundantly clear, however, that Soviet education was not successful at winning the unquestioning and enthusiastic obedience of the generations subjected to its determined efforts. Although generally obedient, accepting the regime with little outward sign of resistance, the great majority of Soviet citizens appear to have held back from the full commitment, the "mobilization," that Marxist ideology demanded.

Based upon interviews with Soviet refugees conducted in the early 1950s, Moore concluded that "a prominent reaction to the incessant demands of the totalitarian state takes the form of flight into a variety of efforts to keep one's personal identity by discovering some tolerable niche within the system. If anything, ordinary Soviet citizens may display in their actual behavior more concern with private and family affairs than is the case in societies with a looser form of political organization."[155]

The family, in particular, was a focal point of silent resistance, even in the face of deliberate efforts to undermine its authority. Although the Communist theory of society did not allot to the family any privileged sphere of private values that could legitimately deviate from those of the Party—and in fact Soviet families came under enormous pressures as a result of displacements, work, housing conditions, and the betrayals encouraged during periods of terror— even Trotsky eventually was forced to concede that "it proved impossible to take the old family by storm."[156]

"In many respects," postwar refugees reported, "the family is most immune to the pressures of the regime. It thus constitutes the single most significant seedbed for the generation, preservation, and transmission of antiregime attitudes and information which the regime would like to suppress." Religious belief was nurtured in the family—many Orthodox households continued to maintain a little shrine with icon and candles—as were the cultural heritages of the Soviet Union's many peoples. Thus family life set a limit to the socializing power of the Soviet school and formal institutions.[157]

Families are in turn nourished by wider communities, and it was the religious and ethnic/cultural communities (to the extent that it is possible to distinguish between the two types of communities) of the Soviet Union that sustained alternative forms of belief and loyalty. Religious communities refused to play the dying role assigned to them by Marxist theory, while nationality groups took advantage of the Soviet regime's hypocritical patronage of their languages and folklore to maintain a core of spiritual independence.

The regime *was* able to impose its monopoly on formal schooling, though this did not become effective until more than a decade after the Revolution. In some areas during the 1920s the peasants, "discontented with the official schools, began to found their own . . . which activity the Government was forced to permit. At first these free schools were built and organized illegally, but they were erected in such numbers that the Government thought best to legalize this movement by imposing certain conditions. Thus the peasants were allowed to erect the school building and to choose a teacher, but the latter had to be approved by the authorities and the school had to submit to the supervision of governmental inspectors. The

Commissariat of Public Instruction was very much perturbed by these spontaneous activities of the peasant population," but was not in a position, for some years, to provide state schools for all.[158]

Similarly, the number and vitality of Muslim religious schools rebounded during the mid 1920s, especially in areas where they were the only schools available, until they were suppressed in a fierce crackdown during the "cultural revolution" of 1929–33; thus in 1929 the Georgian Communist party resolved to close all "Muslim, Jewish and sectarian [Christian] religious schools."[159]

Although children from working-class and peasant homes were more likely to be enrolled in schools using minority languages for instruction, recent events have made it clear that the fully bilingual elites in the republics developed a strong commitment to linguistic and cultural distinctiveness. It was *not* true that "nationality policy has thus, unintentionally, come to mean the Russification of the socially mobile." A more perceptive observer pointed out that the local elites, developed as a bridge to conform their traditional cultures to a Soviet international culture, had in fact come to identify themselves with a revived version of their national traditions; the attempt, through political socialization, to create a unified Soviet society had failed.[160]

Similarly, the explicitly anti-religious character of Soviet schooling may prove to have sheltered the peoples of the former Soviet Union from the full effect of the secularization that modernization wrought in Western Europe, where religious instruction is routinely provided in state schools. Imposition of a Marxist-Leninist orthodoxy of thinking and behavior inevitably conflicted with the "acids of modernity," as the regime sought to adapt the children of a predominantly peasant population to the demands of a modern industrial economy.[161]

Ironically, one effect of the rootlessness produced by forced modernization appears to be an enhanced interest in ways of understanding the world and of giving meaning and purpose to life that offered alternatives to a Communist belief system that lacks credibility. Thus there has been a revival of interest in traditional religion—Orthodoxy, Islam, Catholicism—that, arguably, retained a certain freshness and power as a result of its persistent condemnation by the state school. There was also notably a strong undercurrent of evangelical Protestantism, both in officially tolerated churches and in illegal churches that rejected all co-optation by the regime. Various forms of New Age belief and occult practices have also attracted wide interest in recent years.

Resistance to the Soviet regime and in particular to its efforts to use compulsory schooling to mold a generation whose loyalties would be to the state and Party alone was based, for some, on religious convictions; for others, on a sense of national distinctiveness. For Lithuanian Catholics and for Central Asian Muslims, and for Armenians, Georgians, and other groups, the religious and national motivations merged to a considerable extent. Catholic resistance in Lithuania, for example, was by no means primarily a clerical movement; the church provided a framework, both intellectual and social, for developing a coherent alternative to the dominant Russian communism.

> In a way, in Soviet conditions, where religion has remained the only, however combatted, legally existing alternative to the official Weltanschauung, and the church the only, however restricted and watched, relatively autonomous institution outside the Party's regular ideological, institutional, and personnel controls—in these conditions religious dissent may provide an ideological and organizational framework for the articulation and mobilization of those non-religious interests and social forces that, lacking channels and means in the existing system for their expression and self-realization, have accumulated a massive revolutionary potential.[162]

The anti-religious propaganda of the Soviet regime seems to have had very little effect among Christian or Muslim populations. Although in Uzbekistan, with fewer than 10 million Muslims, there were 42,000 conferences and presentations on "scientific atheism" in 1969–70 alone, the level of Islamic practice in this and other Central Asian republics remained high and even increased. In recent decades, indeed, there have been many indications of a revival of Islam in a more traditional form than was characteristic of the period of reform earlier in the 20th century. "The bold and modern character of the Islam of the Tatars and the Azeris at the beginning of the twentieth century, far in advance of the Islam of the Arabs, Turks, and Iranians, is no longer apparent."[163]

The vitality of Islam, like that of Christianity, in the Soviet Union was largely sustained by unofficial groups rather than by the government-recognized religious authorities. In Azerbaijan, for example, there were 300 places of pilgrimage but only 16 official mosques in 1967. All mosques in the Chechen-Ingush Autonomous Republic of the North Caucasus were destroyed in 1944 and none was authorized until 1978, but Islam flourished through the activities of two Sufi brotherhoods; a survey conducted on one state farm in 1976 found that "35.2 percent of the young men prayed five times a day." Teachers in rural areas were reported to "hide their atheist opinions even from their own pupils, for fear that they will denounce them to their parents." Even worse, from the Soviet perspective, the area gained a reputation as "the most violently anti-Russian territory of the entire USSR."[164]

In clandestine Koran schools across Soviet Central Asia, unregistered mullahs taught the elementary Arabic necessary for participation in worship, and religious knowledge. "Soviet authors describe so-called self-styled Mullahs as illegal, anti-social, fanatic and extremist elements of Muslim society. But in fact they are the people who preserve Muslim education among the sixty million Muslims in the Soviet Union."[165]

Despite all efforts, the Soviet regime was never able to stamp out religious belief and practice; again and again the Party and its press complained of "a rise in the number of citizens observing religious holy days . . . as well as an increase in pilgrimages to holy places."[166] There was a religious revival in the late 1920s, including the organization of an Orthodox Youth Movement or "Christomol" in distinction to Komsomol, the Communist organization. "Two million young people were said to be enrolled in religious youth organizations in 1928, and the Baptist 'Bapsomol' and Mennonite 'Mensomol' supposedly had more members together than the Soviet Komsomol."[167]

Anti-religious propagandists were in some cases killed by the enraged "masses" whom they had come to set free from the bonds of superstition, and by 1937 the leader of the League of the Militant Godless was forced to concede that a third of the urban and two-thirds of the rural population were still practicing believers.[168] In those parts of the Soviet Union occupied by the German army during World War II, church attendance and other religious practices revived.

The Communist party central committee noted with alarm in 1954 that both the Orthodox church and other churches "were successfully attracting the younger generation by the high quality of their sermons, charity work (illegal since the 1929 legislation), individual indoctrination, and the [underground] religious press," resulting in an increase in those attending church services.[169]

Religious practice was particularly strong in Lithuania, where the Roman Catholic Church served as a focus of nationalistic as well as religious resistance to the Soviet regime. The ability of the church to gather 148,000 signatures to a petition to reopen a cathedral in 1980 was an early sign of the ferment that would lead to successful secession from the Soviet Union a decade later.[170]

Secularization was more extensive in predominantly Lutheran Estonia, but despite a sharp decline in religious practice under Soviet pressure, there was also "evidence of the substantial strength of religious sentiments"[171] before the collapse of Communist power in Estonia.

A survey of Russian students reported in 1970 found that "only just over 40 percent of tenth-graders (then aged 16–17) were convinced atheists. . . . It is quite possible that this figure was artificially inflated by those who felt it advisable to give the approved response."[172]

Of course, indifference to atheism may be as significant as interest in religion. Despite the best efforts of Komsomol, many members were anything but zealous "builders of communism." The leaders had to struggle against "attitudes of passivity, indifference, and alienation," and often were constrained to settle for nominal participation.[173]

As recently as 1986, the new premier Mikhail Gorbachev gave a major speech stressing the need to carry on a "resolute and uncompromising struggle against religious manifestations . . . [including] stepping up of mass political work and atheistic propaganda." A strong attack on the Orthodox church, its adherents, and party members showing a "conciliatory attitude toward religion" appeared in *Pravda* in September 1986.[174]

Despite the efforts of the Communist party through a "united educational front" to monopolize all forms of social organization, a vigorous growth of associations and interest groups of all sorts began in the 1970s; by 1988, it was estimated that there were some 60,000 informal groups in the Soviet Union.[175]

Whether religious, cultural, ecological, or drawn together on some other basis, such groups provided the soil out of which a civil culture could begin to develop. Less and less was it true to say, as a Soviet civil rights activist did in 1981, that "one of the peculiarities of the Soviet system is an impotent society which faces an omnipotent state or, to be more precise, the absence of civil society."[176]

The most powerful political force was nationalism in the various republics of the Soviet Union. While many former Communists cloaked themselves in nationalist rhetoric during the period of collapse of Soviet unity, and to some extent maintained command economies in the subsequent months, it is clear that revival of civil society is on the agenda of the post-Soviet nations. The Ukrainian movement Rukh, for example, adopted at its 1989 Founding Congress a commitment to "reduction to the minimum of the paternalistic functions of the state vis-à-vis the people [since] the state is to serve the people and restructure itself under their full control."[177]

The Soviet assumption that the languages and cultures of non-Russian peoples could be co-opted to transmit the doctrines of proletarian internationalism, and thus serve as their own gravediggers, was a miscalculation of immense proportions. Shaking off the ideological content that they served so long, the languages and cultures of the former Soviet empire have in effect declared their independence of Russian cultural hegemony.

Ironically, the policy of developing Communist cadres in each of the Union republics may have done much to create the nationalistic surge that swept away the Soviet Union. This policy of "nativization" (*korenizatsia*) stimulated national consciousness and created an elite increasingly impatient with the need to respond to the orders of Moscow; "the knowledgeable professional classes provide much of the intellectual leadership for the national movements."[178]

Many Russians, in turn, began to see that their interests as a people might be better served by dissolution of the Union.[179] Some began to call for a national (and even nationalist) revival, calling on fellow Russians to

> relearn those things that our ancestors knew very well: to sacrifice one's personal interests and pride for the common good, laboriously, with small steps, without fearing failures, [to] create a Russian movement, mutual understanding and unanimity, renewing the Russian spirit.[180]

The emerging nationalism of the former Soviet peoples is undoubtedly a volatile and dangerous phenomenon, but it is difficult to see how it could have been avoided. After all, a peaceful, open nationalism comes only later, when certainty that the nation can flourish has been guaranteed by time. If we forget this and imagine that these peoples, experiencing a rebirth of their own life, might become modernized and thus accede to democracy while bypassing the nation and its consolidation around powerful national feeling, we are once again reasoning like Lenin, thinking that in the name of a simple postulate we can dispense with certain stages of social development.[181]

These stages are sure to be difficult and perhaps even tragic, but they offer also the opportunity to release creative energies that have been long suppressed—not least in education.

With the weakening and then final collapse of Communist rule, the hubristic illusion that a single model of humanity could and should be created through heavily politicized schooling collapsed as well. It became possible to think of extending freedom even to the school, and to accept that legitimate differences could exist on how children should be educated, and to what end.

The purpose of this chapter has been to describe the Soviet system of education before perestroika, as essential to understanding the Communist-imposed educational systems of eastern and central Europe. Both in its uncompromising hostility toward religion and in its ambivalent treatment of national and ethnic distinctions within the framework of "proletarian internationalism," the Soviet school was the model that client regimes followed.

References

1. Albert P. Pinkevich (1927), quoted in George S. Counts, *The Challenge of Soviet Education* (New York: McGraw-Hill, 1957), pp. 44–45; V. Mitina (1985), quoted in James Muckle, "The New Soviet Child: Moral Education in Soviet Schools," in *The Making of the Soviet Citizen: Character Formation and Civic Training in Soviet Education*, ed. George Avis (London: Croom Helm, 1987), p. 1; Soviet philosopher Zis (1948), quoted in Counts, p. 114.

2. Nikolai Bukharin and Evgenii Preobrazhensky, *The ABC of Communism*, trans. Eden and Cedar Paul (Harmondsworth, England: Penguin Books, 1969), p. 284.

3. Quoted in Sheila Fitzpatrick, "Cultural Revolution as Class War," *Cultural Revolution in Russia, 1928–1931* (Bloomington: Indiana University Press, 1978), p. 14.

4. See Charles L. Glenn, *The Myth of the Common School* (Amherst: University of Massachusetts Press, 1988).

5. Jerry F. Hough, "The Cultural Revolution and Western Understanding of the Soviet System," in *Cultural Revolution in Russia*, p. 247.

6. Milovan Djilas, *The New Class: An Analysis of the Communist System* (New York: Praeger, 1957), p. 131.

7. David Joravsky, "The Construction of the Stalinist Psyche," in *Cultural Revolution in Russia*, p. 107.

8. "Resolution of the Plenum of the Central Committee of the Communist Party adopted November 12, 1958," in George S. Counts, *Khrushchev and the Central Committee Speak on Education* (Pittsburgh: University of Pittsburgh Press, 1959), p. 33.

9. Counts, *Challenge*, p. 45; see Gail Warshofsky Lapidus, "Educational Strategies and Cultural Revolution: The Politics of Soviet Development," in *Cultural Revolution in Russia*, pp. 78–104.

10. Samuel Northrup Harper, *Civic Training in Soviet Russia* (Chicago: University of Chicago Press, 1929), p. 268.

11. Quoted in Counts, *Challenge*, p. 112.

12. Long (332).

13. John Dewey, *Impressions of Soviet Russia and the Revolutionary World: Mexico—China—Turkey: 1929* (New York: Teacher's College, 1964), pp. 71–74.

14. Dimitry Pospielovsky, *A History of Marxist-Leninist Atheism and Soviet Antireligious Policies* (New York: St. Martin's Press, 1987).

15. Jim Riordan, "The Role of Youth Organizations in Communist Upbringing in the Soviet School," in *The Making of the Soviet Citizen*, p. 137.

16. Counts, *Challenge*, p. 47.

17. N. K. Krupskaya, "Four Lines of Work Among Young Pioneers (1926)," in *On Education: Selected Articles and Speeches* (Moscow: Foreign Languages Publishing House, 1957), p. 112.

18. Quoted in Harper, p. 264.

19. James Bowen, *Soviet Education: Anton Makarenko and the Years of Experiment* (Madison and Milwaukee: University of Wisconsin, 1965), p. 141.

20. Alexandra Kollontai (1920), excerpted in *A Documentary History of Communism, vol. 1, Communism in Russia* rev., ed. Robert V. Daniels (Hanover, N.H.: University Press of New England, 1984), pp. 130–31.

21. Bowen, p. 36.

22. Bukharin and Preobrazhensky, pp. 284–85.

23. Dewey, pp. 84–85.

24. Bowen, p. 35; Counts, *Challenge*, p. 45.

25. P. V. Rudnev, quoted in Roy A. Medvedev, *Let History Judge: The Origins and Consequences of Stalinism* (New York: Knopf, 1971), p. 504.

26. From "Decision of the Central Committee of the All-Union Communist Party on the Primary and Secondary School, September 5, 1931," excerpted in *A Documentary History of Communism*, vol. 1, p. 238.

27. "The School—An Ideological Institution," *Uchitel'Skaia Gazeta* (Teachers Gazette), December 30, 1961, in *Education in the USSR: A Collection of Readings from Soviet Journals*, vol. 1, ed. Fred Ablin (White Plains, N.Y.: International Arts and Sciences Press, 1963), p. 33; *Uchitel'Skaia Gazeta* 1961, quoted in Seymour M. Rosen, *Education and Modernization in the USSR* (Reading, Mass.: Addison-Wesley, 1971), p. 132.

28. Oskar Anweiler, Friedrich Kuebart, and Klaus Meyer, *Die sowjetische Bildungspolitik von 1958 bis 1973: Dokumente und Texte* (Berlin: Quelle & Meyer Verlag, 1976), p. 2.

29. "The School—An Ideological Institution," p. 34.

30. Quoted from the Introduction to Marx's *Contribution to the Critique of Political Economy* (1859) in Frank E. Manuel, "A Requiem for Karl Marx," *Daedalus: The Exit from Communism*, 121, no. 2 (Spring 1992), p. 9.

31. M. I. Kalinin (1945), quoted in Counts, *Challenge*, p. 111; E. I. Monoszon, "On Teaching the Course on the Principles of Political Knowledge," in *Sovetskaia pedagogika* (1961): 5, in *Education in the USSR*, vol. 1, p. 158.

32. Leonid I. Brezhnev, *To Educate Our Young: Speech at the All-Union Congress of Teachers on July 4, 1968* (Moscow: Novosti Press Agency, 1968), pp. 4–5.

33. Riordan, pp. 150–51.

34. Frederick C. Barghoorn and Thomas Remington, "Politics in the U.S.S.R.," in *Soviet Politics and Education*, ed. Frank M. Sorrentino and Frances R. Curcio (Lanham, Md.: University Press of America, 1986), p. 164.

35. "Resolution . . . November 12, 1958," 44, 64; "Über Maßnahmen zur Entwicklung der Internatsschulen in den Jahren 1959–1965" (May 26, 1959) in *Die sowjetische Bildungspolitik*, p. 42.

36. Mervyn Matthews, *Education in the Soviet Union: Policies and Institutions since Stalin* (London: George Allen & Unwin, 1982), p. 13.

37. John Dunstan, "Die sowjetische Internatserziehung: Entstehung, Zielsetzungen, Probleme und Ergebnisse," in *Erziehungs- und Sozialisationsprobleme in der Sowjetunion, der DDR und Polen*, ed. Oskar Anweiler (Hannover, Germany: Hermann Schroedel Verlag, 1978), pp. 49, 72.

38. "Über die Einrichtung von Ganztagsschulen" (February 15, 1960), in *Die sowjetische Bildungspolitik*, p. 47.

39. "Programm der Kommunistischen Partei der Sowjetunion" (October 31, 1961) in *Die sowjetische Bildungspolitik*, pp. 69–70.

40. Leonid Novikov, "Erziehungsprobleme in der pädagogischen Forschung der Sowjetunion," in *Erziehungs- und Sozialisationsprobleme*, p. 93.

41. Long, p. 469.

42. Quoted in Stephen R. Burant, "The Influence of Russian Tradition on the Political Style of the Soviet Elite," *Political Science Quarterly* 102, no. 2 (Summer 1987): 273.

43. John Morison, "Recent Developments in Political Education in the Soviet Union," in *The Making of the Soviet Citizen: Character Formation and Civic Training in Soviet Education*, ed. George Avis (London: Croom Helm, 1987), p. 23.

44. John Dunstan, "Atheistic Education in the USSR," in *The Making of the Soviet Citizen*, p. 50.

45. Oskar Anweiler, "Die 'entwickelte sozialistische Gesellschaft' als Lern- und Erziehungsgesellschaft," in *Erziehungs- und Sozialisationsprobleme*, pp. 16–18; Nigel Grant, *Soviet Education*, 4th ed. (Harmondsworth: Penguin Books, 1979), pp. 27–28.

46. Quoted in Joachim Barth, "Wesentlicher Wandel im in sowjetischen Geographieunterricht in den 80er Jahren?" in *Systemswandel im Bildungs- und Erziehungswesen in Mittel- und Osteuropa*, ed. Oskar Anweiler (Berlin: Arno Spitz, 1992), p. 69.

47. Moshe Lewin, "Society, State, and Ideology during the First Five-Year Plan," in *Cultural Revolution in Russia*, p. 41.

48. Yaroslavsky, quoted in Pospielovsky, p. 55.

49. Jeremy Azrael, quoted in David E. Powell, *Antireligious Propaganda in the Soviet Union: A Study of Mass Persuasion* (Cambridge, Mass.: MIT Press, 1975), p. 7.

50. N. S. Timasheff, *Religion in Soviet Russia, 1917–1942* (Westport, Conn.: Greenwood Press, 1942), p. 22.

51. Pospielovsky, p. 2.

52. Timasheff, p. 24.

53. Pospielovsky, p. 2.

54. Dunstan, "Atheistic Education," p. 53.

55. Pospielovsky, p. 19.

56. Pospielovsky, p. 28; Powell, p. 34.

57. Russell, quoted in Djilas, p. 127; Harper, pp. 373–74; Dewey, p. 105.

58. Pospielovsky, pp. 4, 25, 31.

59. Quoted in Timothy Edward O'Connor, *The Politics of Soviet Culture: Anatolii Lunacharskii* (Ann Arbor, Mich.: UMI Research Press, 1983), p. 11.

60. Pospielovsky, pp. 20, 94–95.

61. Powell, p. 17.

62. Barghoorn and Remington, p. 167.

63. Lenin quoted in Md. M. A. Khan, "Muslim Education in Tsarist and Soviet Russia," *Muslim Education Quarterly* 5, no. 4 (1988): 13; Pospielovsky, p. 132.

64. Pospielovsky, pp. 29, 45.

65. Nicholas Hans and Sergius Hessen, *Educational Policy in Soviet Russia* (London: P. S. King, 1930), p. 31.

66. Pospielovsky, pp. 134, 27; Hans and Hessen, p. 20; Bukharin and Preobrazhensky, p. 283.

67. George Z. F. Bereday, William W. Brickman, and Gerald H. Read, *The Changing Soviet School* (Cambridge, Mass.: Riverside Press, 1960), p. 60.

68. Timasheff, p. 27.

69. Pospielovsky, pp. 56–57.

70. Lewin, p. 63.

71. Pospielovsky, p. 35.

72. Powell, p. 28.

73. Dunstan, "Atheistic Education," p. 51; Bereday, Brickman, and Read, p. 61.

74. Counts, *Challenge*, p. 106.

75. Hans and Hessen, p. 33; Long, p. 333.

76. Pospielovsky, p. 70.

77. Counts, *Challenge*, pp. 107–8.

78. Bohdan R. Bociurkiw, "Nationalities and Soviet Religious Policies," in *The Nationalities Factor in Soviet Politics and Society*, ed. Lubomyr Hajda and Mark Beissinger (Boulder, Colo.: Westview Press, 1990), p. 152; Powell, p. 19; Michael Bourdeaux, "The Black Quinquennium: The Russian Orthodox Church 1959–1964," *Religion in Communist Lands* 9, nos. 1–2 (Spring 1981): 18–23.

79. Bohdan R. Bociurkiw, "Religious Dissent in the U.S.S.R.: Lithuanian Catholics," in *Marxism and Religion in Eastern Europe*, ed. Richard T. DeGeorge and James P. Scanlan (Dordrecht, the Netherlands: D. Reidel, 1976), p. 148.

80. Pospielovsky, p. 79.

81. "Programm der Kommunistischen Partei der Sowjetunion" (October 31, 1961), in *Die sowjetische Bildungspolitik*, p. 73.

82. Pospielovsky, pp. 86–87.

83. Quoted in Powell, p. 43.

84. Powell, p. 43.

85. Quoted in Powell, p. 1.

86. Muckle, p. 5; V. Kalinin, "On Fanatical Atheists and the Freedom of Conscience," *Izvestiya*, March 6, 1991.

87. I. A. Kairov (1948), quoted in Counts, *Challenge*, p. 93.

88. Alessio U. Floridi, "Antireligious Education of Soviet Youth," in *The Politics of Soviet Education*, ed. George Z. F. Bereday and Jaan Pennar (Westport, Conn.: Greenwood Press, 1976), p. 91.

89. Powell, p. 54.

90. Floridi, p. 90.

91. Dunstan, "Atheistic Education," p. 60.

92. Quoted in A. M. Netylko, "Concerning an Individual Approach in the Atheistic Upbringing of Pupils," in *Contemporary Soviet Education*, ed. Fred Ablin (White Plains, N.Y.: International Arts and Sciences Press, 1969), p. 256.

93. Shipler, 287.

94. Raymond A. Bauer, Alex Inkeles, and Clyde Kluckhohn, *How the Soviet System Works* (New York: Vintage Books, 1960), p. 125.

95. Dunstan, "Atheistic Education," p. 56.

96. Netylko, pp. 257–58.

97. Ibid., pp. 258–60.

98. David Kinsella and Rein Taagepera, "Religious Incident Statistics for Soviet Lithuanian Schools," *Journal of Baltic Studies* 15, no. 1 (Spring 1984): 46.

99. Netylko, p. 261.

100. Dunstan, "Atheistic Education," p. 62.

101. See data reported in Powell, pp. 11–12.

102. Edward L. Keenan, quoted in Roman Szporluk, "The Imperial Legacy and the Soviet Nationalities Problem," *The Nationalities Factor*, p. 13.

103. Quoted in Nadia Diuk and Adrian Karatnycky, *The Hidden Nations: The People Challenge the Soviet Union* (New York: William Morrow, 1990), pp. 28, 194.

104. Alexander Zinoviev, *The Reality of Communism*, trans. Charles Janson (New York: Schocken Books, 1984), p. 186.

105. Richard Pipes, *The Formation of the Soviet Union: Communism and Nationalism, 1917–1923* (Cambridge, Mass.: Harvard University Press, 1964), pp. 45–46.

106. David Lane, *Soviet Society under Perestroika*, rev. ed. (London: Routledge, 1992), p. 188.

107. Gertrude E. Schroeder, "Nationalities and the Soviet Economy," in *The Nationalities Factor*, pp. 65, 51.

108. Nigel Grant, "Multicultural Education in the USSR," in *The Making of the Soviet Citizen*, p. 201.

109. Teresa Rakowska-Harmstone, "Nationalities and the Soviet Military," in *The Nationalities Factor*, pp. 79–80.

110. Diuk and Karatnycky, p. 59.

111. Rasma Karklins, *Ethnic Relations in the USSR* (Boston: Unwin Hyman, 1986), p. 58.

112. Desheriev and associates, quoted in Glyn Lewis, "Bilingualism as Language Planning in the Soviet Union," in *Western Perspectives on Soviet Education in the 1980s*, ed. J. J. Tomiak (New York: St. Martin's Press, 1986), p. 76.

113. Grant, "Multicultural Education," p. 198.

114. Karklins, p. 32.

115. Ibid., pp. 38, 43.

116. Diuk and Karatnycky, p. 21.

117. Karklins, p. 62; Ronald Grigor Suny, *The Making of the Georgian Nation* (Bloomington: Indiana University Press, 1988), p. 309.

118. Jaan Pennar, Ivan I. Bakalo, and George Z. F. Bereday, *Modernization and Diversity in Soviet Education* (New York: Praeger, 1971), p. 164.

119. Quoted in Alan W. Fisher, *The Crimean Tatars* (Stanford, Calif.: Hoover Institution Press, 1978), p. 117.

120. Quoted in Pennar, Bakalo, and Bereday, pp. 168–69.

121. 1924 Constitution of the USSR, excerpted in *A Documentary History of Communism*, vol. 1, pp. 166–67.

122. Fisher, p. 118.

123. Pipes, p. 163.

124. Quoted by Pennar, Bakalo, and Bereday, p. 167.

125. Edward A. Allworth, *The Modern Uzbeks* (Stanford, Calif.: Hoover Institution Press 1990), p. 168; see also Azade-Ayşe Rorlich, *The Volga Tatars: A Profile in National Resilience* (Stanford, Calif.: Hoover Institution Press, 1986), pp. 84–103.

126. Duik and Karatnycky, p. 170.

127. Martha Brill Olcott, "Central Asia: The Reformers Challenge a Traditional Society," in *The Nationalities Factor*, p. 256.

128. Allworth, p. 182.

129. Pipes, p. 191.

130. Martha Brill Olcott, *The Kazakhs* (Stanford, Calif.: Hoover Institution Press, 1987), p. 252.

131. Dunstan, "Atheistic Education," p. 58.

132. Allworth, p. 224.

133. Hélène Carrère d'Encausse, "Politische Bildung in der UDSSR unter besonderer Berücksichtigung der nichtrussischen Nationalitäten," in *Erziehungs- und Sozialisationsprobleme*, p. 36.

134. Ronald Grigor Suny, "Transcaucasia: Cultural Cohesion and Ethnic Revival in a Multinational Society," in *The Nationalities Factor*, p. 234.

135. Quoted in Pennar, Bakalo, and Bereday, pp. 23, 24.

136. Quoted in Karklins, p. 103.

137. Quoted in Diuk and Karatnycky, p. 30.

138. Mikhail Kuzmin, "The Rebirth of the National School in Russia," *Soviet Education Study Bulletin* 10, no. 1 (Spring 1992): 19.

139. Barbara A. Anderson and Brian D. Silver, "Some Factors in the Linguistic and Ethnic Russification of Soviet Nationalities: Is Everyone Becoming Russian?" in *The Nationalities Factor*, p. 103.

140. Nigel Grant, "The Education of Linguistic Minorities in the USSR," in *World Yearbook of Education 1981: Education of Minorities* (New York: Kogan Page, 1981), p. 71.

141. Anderson and Silver, p. 100.

142. Paul G. Lewis, *Democracy and Civil Society in Eastern Europe* (New York: St. Martin's Press, 1992), p. 79.

143. Wolfgang Mitter, "Bilingual and Intercultural Education in Soviet Schools," in *Western Perspectives on Soviet Education in the 1980s*, ed. J. J. Tomiak (New York: St. Martin's Press, 1986), p. 117.

144. Pipes, pp. 283–86.

145. Quoted in Pinnar, Bakalo, and Bereday, pp. 173–74.

146. Barghoorn and Remington, p. 148.

147. Karklins, pp. 60–61, 104.

148. From Article 20, *The Fundamentals of Legislation . . . on Public Education* (July 1973), in Seymour M. Rosen, *Education in the U.S.S.R.: Recent Legislation and Statistics* (Washington, D.C.: Department of Health, Education, and Welfare, 1975).

149. P. A. Avrorin (1972), quoted in Anderson and Silver, p. 101.

150. Geoffrey Hosking, *The Awakening of the Soviet Union*, enlarged edition (Cambridge, Mass.: Harvard University Press, 1991), pp. 102–5.

151. Anderson and Silver, p. 104.

152. Statistics from Lane, pp. 201–2.

153. Carrère d'Encausse, p. 27.

154. Ramazan Karça, "A General View of Soviet Education," in *The Politics of Soviet Education*, ed. George Z. F. Bereday and Jaan Pennar (Westport, Conn.: Greenwood Press, 1976), p. 3.

155. Barrington Moore Jr., *Terror and Progress—USSR* (New York: Harper and Row, 1966), p. 206.

156. Leon Trotsky, *The Revolution Betrayed* (1937), quoted in W. W. Rostow, *The Dynamics of Soviet Society* (New York: W. W. Norton, 1967), p. 108.

157. Bauer, Inkeles, and Kluckhohn, p. 67; Basile Kerblay, "Sozialisations-probleme im sowjetischen ländlichen Milieu," in *Bildung und Erziehung in Osteuropa im 20. Jahrhundert*, ed. Oskar Anweiler (Berlin: Berlin Verlag, 1982), p. 102.

158. Hans and Hessen, pp. 207–8.

159. Stephen Blank, "The Origins of Soviet Language Policy 1917–1921," *Russian History–Histoire Russe* 13, no. 1 (1988): 88; Suny, p. 244.

160. George Z. F. Bereday, "Class Tensions in Soviet Education," in *The Politics of Soviet Education*, p. 77; Carrère d'Encausse, "Politische Bildung," p. 43.

161. Anweiler, "Die 'entwickelte socialistische Gesellschaft'," p. 12.

162. Bociurkiw, "Nationalities," p. 169.

163. Alexandre A. Benningen and S. Enders Wimbush, "Muslim Religious Dissent in the U.S.S.R.," in *Marxism and Religion*, pp. 133–45.

164. Marie Broxup, "Islam and Atheism in the North Caucasus," *Religion in Communist Lands* 9, nos. 1–2 (Spring 1981): 41–47.

165. Dunstan, "Atheistic Education," p. 58; Khan, p. 17.

166. Powell, p. 39.

167. Timasheff, p. 62; Fitzpatrick, p. 20.

168. Pospielovsky, pp. 62, 65.

169. Pospielovsky, p. 73.

170. Hosking, *Awakening*, p. 95.

171. Toivo U. Raun, *Estonia and the Estonians* (Stanford, Calif.: Hoover Institution Press, 1987), p. 219.

172. Dunstan, "Atheistic Education," p. 69.

173. Barghoorn and Remington, p. 166.

174. Bociurkiw (1990), 161–62; Dina Rome Spechler, "Russian Nationalism and Soviet Politics," in *The Nationalities Factor*, p. 304n.

175. Hosking, *Awakening*, p. 70.

176. Quoted in Salvador Giner, "The Withering Away of Civil Society," *Praxis International* (October 1985): 263.

177. Quoted in Mykola Ryabchuk, "Civil Society and National Emancipation: The Ukrainian Case," in *The Reemergence of Civil Society in Eastern Europe and the Soviet Union*, ed. Zbigniew Rau (Boulder, Colo.: Westview Press, 1991), p. 108.

178. Ronald G. Suny, "Nationalities and Nationalism," in *Chronicle of a Revolution*, ed. Abraham Brumberg (New York: Pantheon Books, 1990), p. 117; Lane, p. 204.

179. Geoffrey Hosking, "The Russian National Revival," *Report on the USSR*, November 1, 1991, pp. 5–8.

180. Igor Shafarevich, "Can Russia Still Be Saved?" translated (anonymous typescript) from *Komsomol'skaya Pravda*, October 18, 1990, p. 2.

181. Hélène Carrère d'Encausse, "Springtime of Nations," *New Republic*, January 21, 1991, p. 22.

3. Bulgaria

Communist Goals for Education: The "New Man"

Education in Bulgaria under the Communist regime that seized power in September 1944 was explicitly modeled upon that in the Soviet Union, with an added (and frequently stressed) objective to promote "friendship and brotherhood with the Soviet nation and its peoples."[1] As in Soviet education, ideology was central to the purpose and functioning of the school, and the state claimed a monopoly on the right to educate, as a concomitant to its control of newspapers and other forms of information.[2]

This intention was expressed clearly in a speech to the Fifth Party Congress (December 1948) by Secretary General Vulko Chervenkov of the Communist-dominated "Fatherland Front." Chervenkov, who would become deputy prime minister the following year and prime minister from 1950 to 1956, had gone into exile in Russia after a 1925 terrorist incident, and returned only in 1944 with the Soviet army; he has been described as "one of the Kremlin's chief agents in Bulgaria . . . a chief promoter of the sovietization of Bulgaria."[3] A "devoted Stalinist," he could be relied on by Russia "to be thoroughly dictatorial in Bulgaria but obedient and pliant toward Moscow."[4] As chairman, from 1947, of the Committee of Science, Art, and Culture, he was in a position to insist on the complete subordination of Bulgarian education to ideological objectives, as in the Soviet Union. This was necessary, he stressed in his Party Congress speech, because of "the disruptive attempts, on the part of the enemy, to diffuse decadent and hostile ideas, especially among pupils and students."[5]

Thus the Party should seek to bring about a "complete cultural revolution" to accompany the suppression of the capitalist economy; capitalism must be "suppressed even in human consciousness." Chervenkov quoted with approval the statement of his brother-in-law, Prime Minister Georgi Dimitrov, that "work and struggle on the cultural and political front are of absolute priority, to root out the rottenness inherited from Capitalism." To this end, Chervenkov urged, the Party should devote special care to (Communist) education within its organization for young children, the "Septembrists," and carry out "a cultural and educational campaign among the people, to free them from all retrograde elements, from obscurantism, from clericalism."

The teaching force would have to be purged vigorously because of the "pernicious and reactionary views" held by some of the teachers. As members of the bourgeoisie, they were susceptible to the "brutal" campaign carried out by "obscurantist Anglo-Americans in the name of so-called philosophy" and thus to "the most out-dated mysticism" of the sort promulgated by "certain Bulgarian theologians and certain persons attempting to make a profit from religious feelings, whether Protestant, Catholic, or other." Attachment to religion was intolerable, since teachers had a primary role to play in "the accomplishment of the cultural revolution in our country."

Not that it was the goal of the Communists to exclude the inculcation of belief from the mission of the school; indeed, the only significant change in the curriculum of elementary schools introduced by the new regime, besides the requirement to teach Russian starting in the first grade, was the replacement of the Orthodox Christian course with an equally orthodox Marxist-Leninist course for all pupils.[6]

There was an extensive purge of schoolteachers whose loyalty to the new regime was insufficiently established, even though this left many schools staffed with poorly trained replacements, "ignorant hacks who were hardly qualified even to teach Marxism-Leninism properly."[7] Those who remained knew they would be discharged if they did not "indoctrinate the students in a Communist spirit."[8]

Homeroom teachers were responsible for daily political instruction, along lines laid down by the Party secretary in each school, in addition to the formal periods of instruction in communism. This was to involve informal discussion in the first three grades, becoming more demanding in the upper grades. Even kindergartens, according to a decree issued in 1954, were to play their part in laying the foundations of a Communist education for the 3- to 7-year-old set.[9]

Among the objectives of instruction was solidarity with other nations in the socialist camp: "Their love and gratitude to the Soviet Union must burn within them." In addition, "The atheistic education of the students must become an indivisible part of the work of our teachers in Communist education." The study of carefully selected literature would be an especially effective vehicle for achieving success in "the struggle with powerful religious superstitions and prejudices."[10]

The stress on indoctrination continued in secondary schools. The teaching of geography, for example, was to be marked by "a clearly expressed ideological political purpose. . . . Party partisanship in the teaching of the geography of Bulgaria means that the factual material must be explained in deep and correct Marxist terms—that is, the students must be correctly instructed in the Communist spirit."[11]

The official course of study for the required course "Fundamentals of Communism" reminded secondary school teachers that "the Eighth Congress of the Bulgarian Communist Party [in 1954] emphasized the increasing importance of ideological work in the education of the new man—the builder of Socialism and Communism—and gave [educators] the task of introducing as soon as possible a special course in the middle schools through which the students will become acquainted with the fundamental problems of Marxist-Leninist teachings and the politics of the Party." In carrying out this charge, "the attention [of the students] must especially be focused on the battle against decadent bourgeois morality . . . and likewise also upon the battle for the uprooting of religion and other anachronisms remaining in the consciousness of some people. . . . It is indispensable that the students be convinced that the struggle for Communism is the chief content of Communist morality and that this struggle must become the thought and content of their life and activity."[12]

This exhortation is characteristic of the need of a totalitarian regime to build and maintain a sense of crisis to justify radical measures to overcome the natural human tendency to grow weary of perpetual political mobilization. Chervenkov's successor, Todor Zhivkov, insisted that "the main and safest barrier against the infiltration of foreign ideological influence among youth is to build a Communist outlook on life and a Communist attitude toward all facts and events, all questions and problems."[13]

The educational program of the Bulgarian Communist regime was summarized in the preamble to education legislation enacted in 1959:

> The main task of the school in the People's Republic of Bulgaria is to prepare the young people for life in Socialist and

> Communist society, as it links their training and education
> with social and productive labor, and to educate the young
> generation in respect and devotion to the principles of Com-
> munism, in love of toil, and in the spirit of Socialist patriotism
> and proletarian internationalism.[14]

Similarly, the reorganization of Bulgarian education in 1979 stressed the need to develop a "deep ideological conviction and Socialist consciousness" in pupils, and to ensure that they integrated ideology and personal behavior.[15]

The mission of the school in ideological formation was intensified by a close linkage with the youth organizations for different ages* that were completely subordinated to Party leadership and thus were "considered by the Bulgarian Communist Party to be the great-est help in the Communistic upbringing of the young generation." The Dimitrov Communist Youth League was expected to turn youth into "a fervent, glowing, selfless band," trained "to devote all its energy to the struggle for the triumph of Socialism and Commu-nism." Among the responsibilities of members, predictably, was "to oppose the influences of bourgeois religious prejudices."[16]

The second constitution of postwar Bulgaria, adopted in 1971, was explicit about the ideological monopoly to be exercised by the state, with the Communist party "the leading force in society and the state." Bulgarian youth must be educated in the spirit of commu-nism.[17] The Party program adopted the same year called for creation of a "unified socialist state," with the implication that the remaining elements of diversity in Bulgarian society would be suppressed.[18]

The ultimate goal of education in Communist Bulgaria, as in the Soviet Union, was the creation of a "new man." "This is an insepara-ble, fundamental part of the struggle for Socialism and Communism, without which the victory of the new social order is completely impossible," a standard text for Bulgarian teachers pointed out. "Socialism and Communism cannot be established without a funda-mental change of the consciousness of the people, their viewpoints, habits, traditions, and understandings."[19]

---

*Chavdarcheta for children in grades 1 and 2; Septemvriiche (Dimitrov Pioneer Organization) for children in grades 3 through 7; Komsomol (Dimitrov Communist Youth League) for youth in grades 8 and above.

In seeking to carry out this program of social and, indeed, human transformation, the Communists in Bulgaria, as elsewhere, assumed that success would lie in destroying or neutralizing the institutional expressions of religious and ethnic communities and especially their schools and other culture-maintaining institutions.

The formal and thus highly visible manifestations of the civil society posed little effective resistance to this campaign. The Bulgarian Orthodox Church was long accustomed to a close alliance with government, while the Turkish minority at first experienced Communist rule as liberating. It then found it difficult to resist, at least as far as its most educated elements were concerned, the opportunity to integrate into the modernizing sectors of the Bulgarian economy and society. Only over time did opposition begin to emerge.

Impediments to the New Order: Religion and Ethnicity

The "viewpoints, habits, traditions, and understandings" that the Bulgarian Communist regime sought to change to create the "new man" were rooted in religion and, for some, in minority languages and cultures.

Although the great majority of the Bulgarian people (89 percent in 1952) were officially Orthodox, the Orthodox Church created no significant impediment to the ideological aggression of the Communist-controlled regime. As the state church, it did not operate its own schools before the Communist takeover; Orthodox religious instruction was provided by lay teachers in the state's schools.[20]

Those schools were of great importance to the Bulgarian people, whose literacy over the previous century had risen to a level well above that of their Balkan neighbors.* The creation of a system of popular education was, by the mid-19th century, a primary expression of Bulgarian nationalism over Turkish political domination and, within the Christian community, Greek cultural domination. The first school teaching in the Bulgarian language was established in 1835, and by the 1870s 2,000 schools provided free education to children of the Bulgarian majority, in addition to the schools of the Turkish and other minorities.[21]

---

*In 1912 the literacy rate of the Bulgarian army was "75 percent compared to 70 percent for Greece, 59 percent for Romania and 50 percent for Serbia" (Crampton, p. 78).

Elementary education in Bulgaria before World War II was relatively extensive for a heavily agricultural nation, with some 83 percent of children receiving at least some schooling. "The overall picture of education in Bulgaria [in this period] is a very positive one. Education could be and was a means by which the children of peasants could improve their status. . . . Nowhere else in Eastern Europe did education radiate so directly into the villages."[22]

From the Communist perspective, the deficiencies of the prewar educational system were above all ideological: "The curricula were soaked in the ideology of the fascist bourgeoisie. . . . Religion was included in the curriculum as a priority subject."[23] The new system that the Communists would create would be correspondingly "soaked" in Marxist-Leninist ideology.

The new regime moved swiftly to bring the Orthodox Church under its control through show trials of bishops and clergy who showed any sign of independence, followed by sentences of death or prison. While recognized as "the traditional church of the Bulgarian people," the Orthodox Church was placed under strict control by the civil authorities.[24] The first Constitution of the People's Republic of Bulgaria, adopted in 1947, prohibited "misusing the Church and religion for political ends or forming political organizations with a religious basis."[25] Even as it extensively used a "tame" Orthodox Church for international propaganda, the regime made it clear that religious groups could in no sense claim an independent existence: church/state issues could not arise, since "there was no question of the existence of secular and spiritual powers since there was only one power, that of the State."[26]

The small Roman Catholic and even smaller Protestant groups, with their international connections and minority status, were less subject to manipulation, and leaders of their clergy were put on trial for espionage with sentences of death or prison for many. The schools and charitable institutions operated by these churches were unacceptable to the new regime.* The American and German secondary schools were closed and, as of September 1948, "all existing foreign

---

*American and other Western missionary efforts in the mid-19th century led to formation of a number of Protestant elementary and secondary schools teaching in Western languages, most notably the American secondary school at Simeonovo; these had a significant impact on the Bulgarian elite. There were also Catholic schools operated by international religious orders.

schools at all levels and types of education, set up or supported by foreign governments, by various religious missions and congregations, or individuals" were closed.[27] Churches were forbidden to engage in secular education, though they could (with state approval) operate clergy training institutions if they provided courses in Marxism.[28]

The 1947 constitution provided the basis for this action: "Education is secular, with a democratic and progressive spirit."[29] "Educational establishments are state-owned" and the education provided by the state "is based on the achievements of modern science and the Marxist-Leninist ideology."[30]

Nongovernment schools could be operated only with permission of the state, and the only such school approved was operated by the Soviet embassy for the children of its nationals.

A statute on textbooks had already prohibited "instruction with old textbooks having religious content in primary and secondary schools."[31] The Party-controlled Ministry of Education was determined to seize "from the hands of private speculative initiative the spiritual food of our children—textbooks, teaching aids, and any kind of literature,"[32] and a state educational publishing house was established to provide textbooks and other materials informed by a Marxist-Leninist worldview.

By 1948 religion and Bulgarian church history were removed from the syllabus for all schools.[33] Schools named for the Orthodox saints were renamed after "partisans and anti-fascists."[34]

While Catholic and Protestant schools, supported by a small minority of the population and tainted by foreign connections, were easily suppressed, it was a more complex matter to deal with the schools serving the large Turkish minority, representing about 10 percent of the population in 1952. The new Communist regime was concerned to distance itself from the prewar regime's oppressive actions toward this group in the spirit of the "proletarian internationalism" of which the Soviet Union boasted and initially provided assurances that their educational concerns would be respected. This included, as in the non-Russian republics of the Soviet Union, providing schools in which the minority language was used for instruction.

Some background is important; Turkish schools had been, for decades, the primary issue around which the concerns of the minority community revolved and through which their organizational life developed, and the attitude of successive Bulgarian regimes toward these schools reflected a positive or (in most cases) negative position toward Bulgarian Turks.

With the establishment of Bulgarian independence from the Ottoman empire in 1878, most civil and religious leaders of the Turkish minority had emigrated to Turkey, leaving a largely rural population to find its place in an aggressively nationalistic Bulgaria. There was little real integration over the next 65 years. "Turks lived in closed communities separate and remote from the Bulgarians in every way. Relations between the two peoples were minimal. . . . In communities where Turks and Bulgarians were mixed, the places of business and of entertainment and leisure, educational institutions and of course the places of worship of the Turks were separate from those of the Bulgarians." Nor was this an enforced segregation: "The Turkish-Muslim community was highly sensitive about preserving jealously its way of life and keeping away from the Bulgarians."[35]

Education had developed vigorously among the Turkish population, as in the Bulgarian population, in the quarter century before Bulgarian independence, but the liberation struggle (largely accomplished by a Russian army) had resulted in the closing of most of the Turkish schools and plundering of the endowments that had largely supported them. Many teachers emigrated to Turkey. Despite this setback, by 1894–95 there were 1,300 Turkish schools with 72,582 pupils. These had the status of private schools: "The Turkish community opened, administered, and supported them. The Turkish community also had the power to appoint the teachers." These schools were organized as private rather than state institutions, though subject to state inspection.[36]

Instruction in the primary schools was exclusively in Turkish, with some Bulgarian (3 hours out of 24–30 per week in 1905) added at the upper elementary level. Significantly—and controversially— the Turkish educational system in Bulgaria was modeled closely on Turkey's, with imported textbooks and teachers, and helped to maintain a situation in which many Bulgarian Turks (significantly, Bulgarian Turks and not Turkish Bulgarians) thought of themselves as Ottoman citizens.[37]

Under a 1909 agreement with Turkey, the Bulgarian government undertook to provide financial support "for the preservation and functioning of Muslim schools and of mosques in Bulgaria." The same year, a new education law extended government oversight over local (including Turkish) schools through a system of inspectors. Land was set aside as an endowment for Bulgarian schools but not (even in predominantly Turkish areas) for Turkish schools until reforms were carried out in 1921. A law of that year provided that "Turkish schools which are equivalent to public Bulgarian schools in educational programmes, rules and regulations and quality of education will be given financial aid like the public schools." The minister of education pointed out that finally the government was "fulfilling the State's duty to a coherent mass of Bulgarian citizens which was doing its share in supporting the State like everyone else."[38]

These reforms, which sought to treat the Turkish minority with respect while allowing it to develop its own institutions, were carried out by the postwar agrarian regime of Alexandŭr Stamboliiski; with his overthrow (and assassination) in 1923, a period of reaction set in that was much less favorable to Bulgaria's Turks. This took the form, not of forced integration (as would occur under the Communists), but of seeking to shut the Turkish population off from the modernizing and secularizing tendencies that were then so powerfully at work in the Turkey of Kemal Atatürk. A central element of this modernization was the adoption of a new alphabet based on Latin letters instead of Arabic script, and an extensive purging of vocabulary based on Arabic and its replacement with newly coined Turkish words. Most Turkish schools and newspapers in Bulgaria adopted these reforms with enthusiasm, but the association of the new orthography with Turkish nationalism led the government that seized power in 1934 to order both to return to the Arabic script: "The Bulgarian fascists could not stomach this attempt of the Turks to join Western civilization."[39]

In addition to requiring Arabic script, the regime in power, from 1934 to 1944 (originally under the control of the military but subsequently under personal rule by the king), did much to crush the Turkish educational system that had grown up locally with little government encouragement. "During these ten years, about 75 percent of the Turkish children of school age could not go to school. About 1,250 Turkish primary schools and 12 Turkish junior high schools were closed down. . . . Beginning with the 1937–38 school year, six hours of Bulgarian and six hours of instruction on the

Arabic script and on religion and the Quran were included in the weekly programme of instruction of the Turkish schools beginning with the first grade. The study of Turkish was reduced to six hours per week in primary schools and to five hours per week in junior high schools."[40]

According to a postwar Communist source, documents were found in the ministry of education proving that there had been a deliberate policy to keep the Turks of Bulgaria as ignorant as possible, including instructions that "(a) all legal measures should be taken to keep at the lowest possible level the education of the Turkish minority . . . . (b) the youth of the Turkish minority should be given the most elementary level of knowledge and care should be taken to emphasize religious education more in Turkish schools. (c) Bulgarian teachers should be appointed to private Turkish schools not for educational purposes, but for the sake of intelligence [i.e., spying]."[41]

With this background, many Turks welcomed the Communist-dominated Fatherland Front that took power with the advancing Red Army in 1944, and the Turkish branch of that organization formulated a program including universal compulsory education to be carried out in Turkish, apart from instruction in Bulgarian, using the Latin orthography. The directors of Turkish schools should themselves be Turks, and the salaries of school staff paid by the government.[42]

The period of tolerance and even support for ethnic diversity in education was brief. In February 1946 Prime Minister Georgi Dimitrov insisted that the Communist regime "must ensure that the Slavs have the leading role in the Balkans and that the Balkans will belong only to the people of the Balkans. We must remove all traces left in the Balkans by the Osmanli [Ottoman] Empire." A few months later, all Turkish schools were nationalized under a law that provided that "the state and municipalities open schools of any grade as they are needed for minorities in Bulgaria to meet their educational needs and to provide them with the means of having education in their own languages. The material expenses of these schools are met by the municipalities while the salaries of teachers and of administrative staff are paid by the state." The endowments that many of the private Turkish schools had possessed, and their buildings and equipment, were transferred to the state.[43]

This nationalization was allegedly in response to the demands of the Turkish community but in fact also served to bring them—

along with other private schools—under state control and thereby extended the Communist party's monopoly of formal education. The initial measures toward Turkish schools, however, were benign, and the 1947 constitution provided that "national minorities have the right to be educated in their vernacular and to develop their national culture, while the study of Bulgarian is compulsory."[44]

Some Turkish leaders pointed out, however, that the regime could have provided the same practical support to Turkish education while maintaining its private status, as the agrarian government of Stamboliiski had done in the early 1920s. "Turkish schools should retain their private status," a group of teachers argued, "but their financial matters should be undertaken by the government."[45]

Government efforts to improve the quality of Turkish schools did produce positive results, with significantly increased attendance (especially in comparison with the immediate prewar period) and better training for teachers. The number of Turkish children in school rose from 37,800 during the 1943–44 school year to 113,575 a decade later and 149,555 by 1966–67.[46] As schools (generally very inadequate) that had served Turkish pupils were made a part of the unified educational system, their dismal quality was improved.

Soon enough, the education authorities showed their intention of using Turkish schools to indoctrinate children in a Marxist-Leninist worldview. An important goal of school improvement was "to fight the religious fanaticism among some circles of the Turkish population."[47] Teachers were told that "one of the most important goals of the teaching of the Turkish language is to give [a] Communist formation to Turkish children," and "ten-year-old Turkish children recited loudly: 'The Party, you are a beloved Mother for us.' " The Turkish readers produced in Bulgaria mocked Islam and sought in every way to distance children from the influence of Turkey. To this end, educators from Soviet Azerbaijan were brought to Bulgaria as (presumed) models of the ethnic Turkish embrace of communism.[48]

Although Koranic instruction continued in some Turkish schools until 1952, it was abolished in that year, along with out-of-school Koran lessons. A law enacted in 1949 proclaimed freedom of religion but also provided that "the education of children and of the youth are [sic] specifically reserved for the state and are [sic] outside the abilities [competencies] of the faiths and their ministers." Over the subsequent decades of Communist rule, "Islam was presented as the main obstacle to Turkish-Bulgarian brotherhood."[49]

75

Efforts to reduce the isolation of the Turkish minority were implicit in the goals of a totalitarian regime: as the state swallows up civil society, no competing sources of meaning and social organization can be allowed to persist. "In the conditions of a socialist society," wrote one Bulgarian authority, "the uniform characteristics and the social integration function of education are reinforced."[50] The function of the school in ethnically mixed areas, another authority wrote, is "the complete incorporation of the Bulgarian Turks to the building of Socialism and Communism and their coming closer to the rest of the working people in our country." The influence of the school must be extended and educational settings created that take children out of their families and social circles for extended periods to overcome the improper influence of the home environment and make them true builders of communism.[51]

The period of accommodation of the Turkish language in the Bulgarian educational system was a transitional phenomenon, as the Communist regime consolidated its power and launched its massive program of industrialization. Tolerance of diversity and the claims of the Turkish minority began to end in the 1958–59 school year, when many Turkish-language schools in ethnically mixed areas were merged with Bulgarian-language schools; instruction in the resulting mixed classes was provided only in Bulgarian.[52] The hours of instruction in Bulgarian were increased in the remaining Turkish schools. This was done on the pretext that the parents did not want their children taught in Turkish and that the authorities "gave permission" for all instruction to be conducted in Bulgarian.[53]

This policy was extended the following year; the remaining Turkish schools were closed or converted to Bulgarian-language schools pursuant to a ministerial circular of June 1960. Parents could request supplemental Turkish-language classes for their children through the next decade, until these, too, were ended.[54] In effect, the policy of suppression of Turkish education undertaken by the prewar "fascist" regime was adopted by the Communists 20 years later, but implemented with greater thoroughness. Whereas the prewar regime sought merely to marginalize Bulgaria's Turkish minority, the Communist regime intended to remold them into "new men."

Bulgaria's training institutes for Turkish-language teachers were closed, as were the Turkish departments at Sofia University. During the seventies, the study of the Turkish language was prohibited, with the last academic credit for this subject given during the 1971–72 school year.

The culminating expression of this policy of remolding the Turkish minority was the intensive campaign launched in 1984 to persuade ethnic Turks to adopt Bulgarian names. The government claimed that this was entirely voluntary, and published "spontaneous declarations" by members of the Turkish minority proclaiming:

> We are the children of the Bulgarian nation, we are the masters of this land, for us this is paradise; there is no other paradise for us and there will not be one to come! Yes, we are Bulgarians, we have renounced, of our own accord, with convictions and in full recognition of the cause, our foreign names in favour of our Bulgarian national roots.[55]

Many lost their lives in the ensuing conflict, and there was a massive flight of some 300,000 to Turkey in the summer of 1989. In 1988, it became illegal to speak Turkish in a public place. While these moves were consistent with the Communist program of creating a new man detached from all particularisms of language, religion, and culture, they were also seen as a way to divert popular unrest at the economic situation by arousing traditional Bulgarian antipathy toward the Turks among them.[56]

The formal rights of the Turkish minority were restored in November 1989, with the fall of the Zhivkov government; it should be noted, however, that substantial resistance to these concessions continues among the Bulgarian populace. For example, when speakers at a mass rally of opponents of the Communist regime said in December 1989 that the rights of Turks must be defended, "they were greeted with boos, catcalls and the chanting of anti-Turkish slogans."[57]

By early 1991, the Turkish community in Bulgaria were vigorously demanding that their mother tongue be taught in schools, with up to 20,000 pupils staging a school strike to reinforce this demand.[58] The leading Turkish opposition group, the Movement for Rights and Freedom (reputed to have 120,000 registered members) disclaimed any desire to restore separate schools, however, insisting that "the study of the Turkish language outside the system of Bulgarian schools would be inadequate. We do not want to isolate our children from their Bulgarian peers. They should enjoy equal rights, which would be possible only with an education of equal value."

This instruction, spokesmen for the group insisted, would be organized "without any help from Turkey."[59] Among the specific demands included in the Movement for Rights and Freedom platform adopted in October 1990 were "the optional teaching of Turkish, three to four hours a week, in Bulgarian schools to pupils who are ethnic Turks" and "the optional teaching of Islamic theology in Bulgarian schools to pupils who are ethnic Turks."[60]

This demand—but not the creation of separate Turkish schools—was also supported by the major Bulgarian opposition group, the Union of Democratic Forces.[61] The Agrarian Union supported the teaching of Turkish provided that it was organized and controlled by the state.[62]

The Bulgarian Socialist Party (as the Communist party had renamed itself)[63] joined in this position, though insisting that all school subjects should be taught in Bulgarian and that Turkish should be an optional extra subject. Significantly, though, the BSP opposed allowing groups to teach Turkish outside of the school setting (and thus beyond government control); this would "encourage tendencies toward isolating parts of the population and could be a real future threat for Bulgarian national security."[64]

Representatives of the various political parties reached agreement at the end of January 1991 that Turkish should be reintroduced at selected schools in areas of mixed population, subject to government approval of teachers and textbooks; this was over the objection of nationalists who argued that teaching Turkish would encourage "separatism and Islamic fundamentalism and undermine the unity of the Bulgarian state."[65]

Despite such disclaimers, rumors have been flying among the ethnic Bulgarians that hundreds of Islamic schools have been set up, that mountains of printed material have been imported into the country from Turkey, that Turkish teachers—paid in gold!—have been recruited to help maintain the "Turkish national consciousness" of this Bulgarian minority group.[66] The collapse of communism, some fear, is being used as a pretext by the Turks to reestablish their empire! Or, if that threat is not imminent, what about the Bulgarian mother who complains that her daughter "came home from kindergarten and asked for *ekmek,* bread in Turkish. Next week she'll call me mummy in Turkish."[67]

Why should Bulgarians pay taxes, some ask, to allow the Turks to maintain their despised language? Isn't this an additional educational service, for which they should pay additional taxes? Why should the Turks be in a privileged position?[68] Bulgarian schoolchildren held hunger strikes to protest the optional courses in Turkish, while their parents complained it threatened national security (the Ottoman threat remains alive in Bulgarian consciousness); Turkish parents declared that they would not send their children to school if their home language was not offered.[69]

The Bulgarian Parliament approved the introduction of such courses, three hours a week, effective September 1991.[70] Meanwhile, positive reports were received from Turkish communities where supplemental home language instruction had already been started, though parents and teachers said that it should be made a part of the regular school program; at least four periods a week were needed to produce good results.[71]

Given the level of controversy over something as anodyne as optional study of Turkish (available in most nations of Western Europe), it seems unlikely that much support will develop for independent schools for the only population group that might seek an alternative to the state educational system.

Hints of Educational Freedom

Reforms that focus on greater flexibility in the educational system have been discussed in Bulgaria for several years. A study published in 1986, for example, stressed the importance of offering more elective courses for all pupils, starting with art and music in the fourth grade and permitting older pupils' "interests in a particular field such as science, art, technology, social sciences and employment" to be explored. It was through the acceptance of this principle that the recent inclusion of such previously denied options as religion and Turkish has been possible.[72]

The then minister of education, Assen Hadjiolov, urged in 1989 that the range of options available in secondary education be expanded to include schools specializing in science, art, technology, languages, and other interests, with the government assuring a "unified national minimum of general knowledge."[73]

Public criticism of the state educational system has appeared only very recently. A recent article focused on the "absurdity" of centralized control by a Ministry of Public Education responsible for "conducting the policies of the Party in education." Under such conditions, "there was no soil for civil structures" and the school was isolated from human culture and values, from contact with the social dimensions of life. Parents, teachers, and local officials could do little to bring about change, the author charged, because the schools were "out of their civil control" and thus did not belong to them. "As an utterly state-owned institution, schools become an apologist of the one-man regime. . . . Educational activities and content are seized by a comprehensive politicization and slogan propaganda." The only solution was self-management by each school, based on "realistic cooperation between parents, teachers and pupils."[74]

Another article criticized the educational system for carrying the logic of egalitarianism to the extreme of attempting to standardize human behavior in a denial of human freedom, while rejecting the reality of cultural pluralism, and called for alternative approaches to education.[75]

While the Ministry of Public Education has carried out a variety of pedagogical experiments in recent years, these did not call into question the unitary nature of the educational system. It was not until after the momentous changes that began in November 1989 that Education Minister Matey Mateev suggested that independent schools might appear, and reported that a group of ministry staff was looking into the experience of other nations with nonstate schooling, in consultation with the European Bank for Reconstruction and Development.[76] One observer suggested that private schools would start eventually, given the number of parents willing to pay for a better education for their children, but that the barriers to gaining approvals and finding suitable facilities would impose delays.[77]

An article appeared early in 1991 calling for "real competition" through a new secondary education statute, guaranteeing "demonopolization and pluralism." "Social guarantees [that is, financial support] should be provided for a variety of schools functioning on different principles, independent of the centralized state educational system. These schools have to be financially, methodically, scientifically, etc. provided in a variety of ways according to the different forms of property and the new economic relationships." Private companies might form schools, the author suggested, and there might again be religious, ethnic, and foreign-sponsored schools in Bulgaria. In addition, government-operated schools should become more diverse without central prescription of their programs. "They have to be independent, self-managed, democratically organized, with free choice of textbooks, pedagogical methods, curricula, based on volunteerism and choice." The role of the Ministry of Education should be reduced to "working out unified State standards for education to be used for grading pupils and teachers."[78]

The Ministry of Education described its initiatives to participate in "Bulgaria's transition from the totalitarian system to a democratic society" in a 1990 report to the International Conference on Education. In contrast with the stress of the 1947 constitution and the subsequent development of schooling on inculcating Marxist-Leninist ideology, the watchwords for the 1990 report were "humanization," "democratization," differentiation," and "individualization." "The political and ideological activities in the Bulgarian school have been ended" and the schools would now seek to "develop the spiritual and moral forces of students . . . on the basis of the national and universal human values of world civilization."[79]

An essential feature of democratization, according to the report, would be free choice of schools and academic subjects, "depending on the achievements, interests and strivings of the individual." But choice would have no meaning without an increased differentiation of the schooling available; thus "the former concept of school as a unified structure and system is left behind." Educational research would be redirected to such topics as "the principles of free choice, alternatives, freedom and creativity of schools, teachers and pupils."

The ministry issued new regulations governing elementary and secondary schools on January 18, 1991; these reaffirm the secular character of public education and allow parents to choose between public schools "in accordance with the interests and abilities of the pupils" without limitation on the basis of residence, though secondary-school admissions are governed by rules laid down by the ministry.[80]

A draft Law on Public Education, included in the 1991 Ministry of Public Education report *The School in the Republic of Bulgaria*, provides the following:

> Article 10 (1) Citizens can avail of their right to education in a kind of school or type of education chosen by themselves depending on their personal preferences and faculties.

81

(2) This right with regards to the underaged is exercised by their parents, guardians or trustees.

Article 11 (5) The cooperative, private, firm, shareholding and mixed schools and kindergartens become corporate bodies according to the Law on Persons and Families.

Article 30 (1) Religious entities may open religious schools for children who have completed junior high school education.

(2) Education in the religious schools may be acknowledged as [equivalent to] secular by the Ministry of Public Education provided it corresponds to the state standards valid for the corresponding education stage.

There also appears to be a "voucher" provision proposed:

Article 41 (3) After allocation of the funds [for capital expenses and teacher salaries] the Ministry determines the annual maintenance of a pupil as per the state standards for kind of school and stage of education.

(4) The municipal council issues to each pupil a check, labelled "School," for the amount rated for the corresponding school year.

(5) Pupils are enrolled in school against presentation of the check.

(6) The checks per par. 4 have bank effects only if presented by the school.

Article 43 (1) Besides the state budget checks, schools and kindergartens may procure funds for their maintenance by fees for auxiliary activities, donations, contributions from firms and ministries.

(2) Schools may procure funds by concluding contracts with firms and citizens for leasing of their study and sports facilities, machines, equipment and other school property as well as by doing pedagogical and other services.[81]

The rationale for these proposed changes is stated in the introductory description. The imposed "class-party approach applied through pedagogical pressure led to a strong ideologisation, to disregarding the rights of the individual, to intolerance of other peoples' opinion and even to aggressiveness. The educational system has been managed by a highly bureaucratic administrative management for a long period of time." The way to reform, the ministry suggests, will be through allowing individual schools to select their own "academic plans and programs, textbooks and technical equipment, as well as the kind of school and education [they will provide]" within general achievement standards set by the ministry.[82]

Meanwhile, the draft Law on Secondary Education goes considerably further to guarantee "free choice" of the "kind of school which corresponds to his or her individual preferences." Article 6 would provide that "religious entities can open religious schools to satisfy their own needs." The education offered by such schools could receive official recognition if it met the standards applying to public secondary schools. Under article 10, kindergartens and schools could be opened by employers, presumably to serve the children of their staff. Article 30 would permit the establishment of foreign-sponsored secondary schools.

The curriculum and program for state schools would be stipulated by the minister of education, while those for other schools would, with respect to the compulsory subjects, be "coordinated with the Ministry." While state schools would be funded by the state, and independent schools would "procure by themselves the financial means necessary for their maintenance and salaries," the draft provides for the former to supplement their public subsidies with fees and donations, and for the latter to receive public funds (articles 140, 144).[83]

Real diversity will not emerge unless there are both demand and initiatives to meet that demand at the local level. Permission to provide alternative forms of education, and even public subsidies, which have not yet been offered in Bulgaria, will not lead to a real "market" in schooling unless there is significant demand from parents and a ferment of school creation by teachers.

There are already some signs of such developments. For example, an independent fee-charging school was started in Plovdiv by Paraskeva Shopova and others in the fall of 1991.[84]

In higher education, the founding of the American University in Bulgaria in Blagoevgrad, with the help of the Soros Foundation and in affiliation with the University of Maine, has revealed how eager young Bulgarians are to learn about free-market concepts and practices and also (according to their American teachers) how well prepared they are academically. The program started in September 1991 with 225 students and is expected to expand to 1,000 over four years as resources permit. The fees for tuition, room, and board are expected to amount to the equivalent of a year's salary in Bulgaria.

The facilities, newly built to serve as Communist party headquarters, have been contributed by the municipality.[85]

In addition, the American College (secondary school) of Sofia, founded in 1860 but closed by the Communists in 1948, is expected to reopen. Like the American University, this would serve primarily Bulgarian pupils, unlike the school for the children of American diplomats and other expatriates that has continued to exist in Sofia, like others around the world.[86]

What are the prospects for more extensive diversity in Bulgarian education?

Nothing in Bulgaria corresponds to the role of the Roman Catholic Church in Poland as a rallying point against the claim of the state to define meaning and to educate youth. The Polish situation was shaped by centuries in which the Catholic Church was identified with Polish nationality against Protestant Prussia and Orthodox Russia and, even at its weakest moments, linked with an international religious community. The Bulgarian Orthodox Church, while equally closely identified with the national identity through the centuries of Turkish rule, was long subordinate to a Greek hierarchy and, even over the last century of independence, has never developed a vigorous institutional life or political agenda. It stands in an Orthodox tradition of domination by the secular authorities.

Nor is there a strong tradition of political dissent in Bulgaria, in contrast with its strong tradition of nationalism. Indeed, one historian concluded that "the traditional Bulgarian response to a political system which was not liked was apathy and withdrawal rather than opposition and confrontation."[87] Another observer has noted that "the absence of an opposition tradition in Bulgaria after the war is striking" and that it was only in 1988 that the first "structured dissident organization" emerged.[88] Thus it is perhaps not surprising that the civic culture has been somewhat slow to reemerge, except where it has been reinforced by ethnic minority status and a history of discrimination.

Bulgaria was the only one of the former "captive nations" still governed, until the October 1991 elections, by the former Communist leadership under a new name. The coalition government of Filip Dimitrov depends on the Movement for Rights and Freedom of the Turkish minority for parliamentary support, which guarantees more responsiveness to that group's educational concerns, including the introduction of four hours of Turkish language lessons within the regular program of schools in ethnic Turkish areas. Many Bulgarians continue to resist such demands, which have been backed up by school boycotts by Turkish pupils.[89]

There are some reasons to believe that additional educational alternatives will emerge through local initiatives in the years ahead; certainly that would be in the Bulgarian tradition. An extensive system of popular schooling had emerged by such initiatives during the last century of Turkish rule. An American journalist found in 1878, the year Bulgarian independence was won, that many villages were served by schools "maintained by a voluntary tax, without any [Turkish] government encouragement, but, on the contrary, in spite of innumerable obstacles created by the very state authorities."[90]

By the 1921–22 school year, the Turkish schools were joined by a number of schools serving other communities and independent of the state system:[91]

	Elementary Schools	Intermediate Schools
Bulgarian	7	1
Turkish	1,673	39
Jewish	27	6
Armenian	10	2
French	10	6
German	6	
Italian	2	
American	2	1
Total	1,737	55

There are also signs of pressure for educational experiences that depart from the present unified model imposed by the Communist regime. The agitation for Turkish instruction is the most evident of these, but there is also a growing interest in learning about Christian and other religious traditions in the school program.

Pupils in grades 4 through 8 attending one school in Sofia began studying religion as an optional course in the fall of 1990; their teachers are professors from the Religious Academy.[92] A course on the history of religion was introduced at a secondary school in

Plovdiv at the start of the 1990–91 school year. "Classes are conducted in the form of discussions and seminars three times a week. The pupils are extremely interested to participate. It does not matter whether we are at the moment counting on the curiosity of the pupils or on what fashion dictates. In either case, it is the intellect and the literacy of the Bulgarian pupil that benefits." Religion, one of the organizers is convinced, "can favorably influence one's concept of the world and opinions and can help us become better to one another and live in peace with ourselves and with the people around us."[93]

Bulgarians value education highly, as their history over the past century and a half demonstrates. Will they encourage teachers to bring new energy and creativity to revive their schools, by freeing what occurs in classrooms from close government supervision?

Will they use the opportunities created by new democratic freedoms to create a diverse educational system responding to the concerns of parents and the interests of students? The energies of Bulgaria's reviving civil society will help also to revive education, provided that a framework of law is created in place of the badly outdated education law of 1959, so that decisions can no longer be made by arbitrary ministerial decree.[94] Only within such a framework will educational diversity flourish.

The effort to create a unitary educational system, delivering a single message of loyalty to a Marxist-Leninist worldview, has been thoroughly discredited in Bulgaria. Will the void left by the collapse of this ideology leave the Bulgarian school incoherent, or will parents and teachers create schools that reflect the civic virtue of respect for diversity?

References

Since I do not read Bulgarian, I have depended for much of my information on material gathered and summarized for me by Professor Hristo Hristov and Mrs. Valentina Krusteva of the Ministry of Education; Mrs. Bissera Antikarova translated verbatim those passages I wished to cite.

1. Peter John Georgeoff, *The Social Education of Bulgarian Youth* (Minneapolis: University of Minnesota Press, 1968), p. 40.

2. Nikolai Pavlov, *On Education and Educational Policy in the People's Republic of Bulgaria* (Sofia: Sofia Press, 1980), p. 19; summarized for the author by Bissera Antikarova.

3. V. Todorov, "Biographical Sketches of Leading Communists," in *Bulgaria*, ed. L. A. D. Dellin (New York: Praeger, 1956), p. 388.

4. J. F. Brown, *Bulgaria Under Communist Rule* (New York: Praeger, 1970), p. 24.

5. This and the following passages are translated by the author from Valko Tchervenkov, *L'education marxiste-léniniste et la lutte sur le front idéologique* (Sofia: Ministry of Foreign Affairs, 1949), *passim.*

6. Georgeoff, p. 51.

7. Brown, p. 217.

8. Georgeoff, p. 11; quotation cited in Edith M. Ham, "Religion," in *Bulgaria*, p. 199.

9. Brown, p. 218.

10. Quoted in Georgeoff, pp. 84, 87.

11. Quoted in translation from Pesheva and others, *Sv'rzvane na obuchenieto . . . (Relating the Study of Geography with the Economics of the Place of Birth)*, 1964, in Georgeoff, p. 275.

12. Quoted in translation from the Official Course of Study, "A Course Guide for the Fundamentals of Communism for the General Polytechnical Schools and the Middle Vocational-Professional Schools and Technicums," in Georgeoff, p. 214.

13. Quoted in Brown, p. 236.

14. Quoted in translation from *(Law for Closer Ties between School and Life and for the Further Development of National Education in the People's Republic of Bulgaria)*, 1959, in Georgeoff, p. 169.

15. Miltscho Gawasow, *Das Bildungssytem in der Volksrepublik Bulgarien,* (Sofia: Sofia Press, 1985), p. 10.

16. Quoted in translation from the *(Statutes of the Dimitrov Communist Youth League)*, 1963, in Georgeoff, pp. 177–88.

17. R. J. Crampton, *A Short History of Modern Bulgaria* (Cambridge: Cambridge University Press, 1987), p. 186.

18. Crampton, p. 205.

19. Quoted in translation from Bankovska and others, *Osnovi na komunisticheskoto v'zpitanie (Fundamentals of Communist Education)*, 1964, in Georgeoff, p. 268.

20. Ham, p. 185.

21. Crampton, p. 12.

22. E. Garrison Walters, *The Other Europe: Eastern Europe to 1945* (New York: Dorset Press, 1990), p. 255.

23. Naiden Tchakurov and Zhetcho Atanassov, *History of Bulgarian Education* (Sofia: Narodna Prosveta, 1976); cited by Hristov and Krusteva.

24. Crampton, p. 170.

25. Quoted in L. A. D. Dellin, "The Constitutional System," in *Bulgaria*, p. 95.

26. Ham, p. 187.

27. Regulations of the Ministry of Public Education, *Official Gazette* (1944), p. 287; Decree for the Foreign Schools, *Official Gazette* (1948), p. 180; cited by Hristov and Krusteva in an overview prepared for the author, 1991.

28. Ham, p. 190.

29. Georgeoff, p. 12.

30. Article 45, Sections 2 and 3; cited by Hristov and Krusteva in an overview prepared for the author, 1991.

31. Statute on Introducing New Textbooks, *Official Gazette* (1944), p. 288; cited by Hristov and Krusteva in an overview prepared for the author, 1991.

32. Naiden Tchakurov and Zhetcho Atanassov, *History of Bulgarian Education* (Sofia: Narodna Stopanstvo, 1976); cited by Hristov and Krusteva.

33. Regulations of the Ministry of Public Education, *Official Gazette* (1948), p. 7; cited by Hristov and Krusteva.

34. Regulations of the Ministry of Public Education, *Official Gazette* (1945), p. 233; cited by Hristov and Krusteva.

35. Bilâl N. Şimşir, *The Turks of Bulgaria (1878–1985)* (London: K. Rustem & Brother, 1988), pp. 18, 8; see also Halit Mollahüseyin, "Muslims in Bulgaria: A Status Report," *Journal Institute of Muslim Minority Affairs* 5, no. 1 (January 1984): 138.

36. Şimşir, pp. 9–10; Mollahüseyin, p. 140.

37. Şimşir, pp. 28–29.

38. Ibid., pp. 31–37.

39. Ibid., p. 104.

40. Ibid., p. 113.

41. Quoted from Demir Yanev, "Uspeshite na Narodnoto Obrazovaniye (Successes of National Education)" (Sofia, 1954), in Şimşir, p. 120.

42. Şimşir, p. 136.

43. Ibid., pp. 150–51; Mollahüseyin, p. 140.

44. Georgeoff, p. 12.

45. Quoted in Şimşir, p. 149.

46. Iliya Tatchev, Yankov Yanko, and Lyuben Kutsarov, *Education in Bulgaria 1944–1969* (Sofia: Narodna Prosveta, 1969); cited by Hristov and Krusteva.

47. "A Decision taken by the National Educational Board and the Trade Unions," 1955; cited by Hristov and Krusteva.

48. Şimşir, pp. 184–88, 197.

49. Quoted in Alexandre Popovic, "The Turks of Bulgaria," *Central Asian Survey* 5, no. 2 (1986): 18; Mollahüseyin, pp. 141, 143.

50. Julietta Savova, *Social-Pedagogical Problems of Education* (Sofia: Narodna Prosveta, 1985); cited by Hristov and Krusteva.

51. Shukri Tahirov *(The Bulgarian Turks on the Road to Socialism)* (Sofia Teachers' Front Publishing House, 1979), p. 159ff; translated for the author by Bissera Antikarova.

52. Şimşir, p. 200.

53. Hairie Suleimanova-Memova, "The Mother Tongue," *Prava i Svobodi* 2 (February 18–24, 1991); cited by Hristov and Krusteva.

54. Şimşir, p. 202.

55. Quoted in Popovic, p. 23, from *Le Monde*, August 28, 1985.

56. Misha Glenny, *The Rebirth of History: Eastern Europe in the Age of Democracy* (London: Penguin Books, 1990), p. 171.

57. Glenny, p. 173.

58. Connie Sokoloff Hillen, "English elbows out Engels," *Times Educational Supplement*, March 8, 1991.

59. Yashar Shaban and Hairie Suleimanova-Memova, quoted in Albena Arnaudova, "Together," *Cultura* 3 (1991); translated for the author by Bissera Antikarova.

60. Kjell Engelbrekt, "The Movement for Rights and Freedoms," *Report on Eastern Europe* 2, no. 22 (May 31, 1991): 7.

61. Hristov and Krusteva cite two statements of support appearing in *Democracia* 15 and 33 (1991).

62. "Informational Note of the Permanent Delegation of the Bulgarian Agrarian Union," *Svoboden Narod* 207 (February 4, 1991); translated for the author by Bissera Antikarova.

63. Patrick Brogan, *The Captive Nations: Eastern Europe: 1945–1990* (New York: Avon Books, 1990) p. 205.

64. "Statement of the Chair of the Supreme Council of the Bulgarian Socialist Party Regarding the Study of the Turkish Language," *Duma* 37 (February 4, 1991); translated for the author by Bissera Antikarova.

65. Steven Ashley, "Introducing Turkish Language Teaching in Bulgarian Schools" *Prava i Svobodi* 3 (February 25–March 3, 1991); translated for the author by Bissera Antikarova.

66. Nikolai Panayotov, "Myth and Reality," *Bulgarski Glas* 6 (1991); cited by Hristov and Krusteva.

67. *Economist,* March 23, 1991.

68. Bozhidar Stoyanov, "Advantages and Privileges for the Friends of Everything Turkish in Bulgaria," *Zora* 9 (March 5, 1991); translated for the author by Bissera Antikarova.

69. *Utchitelsko Delo,* the newspaper devoted to education, published many statements pro and con the teaching of Turkish in its issue of March 13, 1991; summarized for the author by Bissera Antikarova.

70. *Decision of the Great National Assembly of the Republic of Bulgaria,* March 8, 1991; translated for the author by Hristov and Krusteva.

71. Muharrem Tahsin, "In Class Again," *Praha i Svobodi* 1 (February 11–17, 1991); translated for the author by Bissera Antikarova.

72. Georgi Mavrov, *Problems of Educational Strategies* (Sofia: Narodna Prosveta 1986), p. 153; summarized by Hristov and Krusteva.

73. Assen A. Hadjiolov, *Restructuring of Education: A Pledge for the Future of Bulgaria* (Sofia, 1989); summarized for the author by Bissera Antikarova.

74. Kolyo Genev, "Self-management of the Schools and the Educational Crisis," *Narodna Prosveta* 9 (1990); summarized by Hristov and Krusteva.

75. Emil Penev, "Education—Today and Tomorrow," *Filosofska Misal,* Bulgarian Academy of Sciences 9 (1990); translated by Hristov and Krusteva.

76. Matei Mateev, "Partner for Everyone," *Utchitelsko Delo* 4 (January 23, 1991); summarized for the author by Bissera Antikarova.

77. Mariana Kostova, "Private Schools?" *Pogled,* January 7, 1991; summarized for the author by Bissera Antikarova.

78. Dimitar Kyulanov, "The Economy for the People, the People for the Economy," *Utchitelsko Delo* 2 (January 9, 1991); translated for the author by Bissera Antikarova.

79. *Development of Education 1988–1990: National Report of the People's Republic of Bulgaria* (Sofia: Ministry of Education, 1990).

80. *Statute of the Schools of General Education,* published by the Ministry of Public Education in the *Official Gazette* (Sofia) 5 (January 18, 1991); translated by Hristov and Krusteva.

81. *The School in the Republic of Bulgaria (General Outline and Trends of Development)* (Sofia: Ministry of Public Education, 1991), pp. 34, 37–40.

82. Ibid., pp. 3, 6.

83. Draft *Law on Secondary Education;* translated by Hristov and Krusteva.

84. Melanie Triend, "Free for All?" *Times Educational Supplement,* September 18, 1992.

85. Louise Branson, "Eastern Europe's First American University Set Up in Bulgaria, With Assistance From the U. of Maine," *Chronicle of Higher Education,* May 8,

1991, A39–40; Letter from Sol Polansky, Chairman of the AUBG Board of Directors, September 18, 1992.

86. News note in *Education Week,* October 9, 1991.

87. J. A. MacGahan, quoted in William F. Russell, *Schools in Bulgaria* (New York: Teachers College 1924), p. 9.

88. Russell, p. 52.

89. Celestine Bohlen, "Bulgaria Vote Gives Key Role to Ethnic Turks," *New York Times,* October 17, 1991; "Hung by the Turks," *Economist,* October 19, 1991; summary of article by Radka Petrova in *Duma* (Sofia) of November 1, 1991, in FBIS-EEU-91-215 of November 6; "In business, just," *Economist,* November 16, 1991.

90. Crampton, p. 188.

91. Glenny, pp. 179–81.

92. Emilia Mateika, "(On Sins and Errors)," *Reflex,* November 14, 1990; summarized for the author by Bissera Antikarova.

93. Slavi Kotorov, "(Back to Traditions, or Shall God Come Down to the Schools?)," *Iskra* (Plovdiv, Bulgaria), November 5, 1990; translated for the author by Hristov and Krusteva and by Bissera Antikarova.

94. Georgi G. Bižkov, "Systemwandel im Bildungs- und Erziehungswesen in Bulgarien," in *Systemswandel im Bildungs- und Erziehungswesen in Mittel- und Osteuropa,* ed. Oskar Anweiler (Berlin: Arno Spitz, 1992), p. 181.

4. Romania

The Communist Party Takes Control

The postwar seizure of power by the Communist party in Romania* went far beyond political control as the new regime extended its domination to all aspects of national life. "Briefly put, the [Communist party] leadership moved aggressively and ruthlessly against the established political parties, the organizations of established religions, the mass organizations of society, and the infrastructure of the civil society."[1]

More than in any other Communist-controlled nation, the Communist party of Romania was given a dominant role in government and society by the very laws and the constitution, which stated that it "directs the activity of the mass and public organizations and of the state bodies." In turn, the absolute power of the state in all spheres of life was affirmed.[2] At every level of Romanian government, the Communist party chairman was also the president of the governing council.[3]

Essential to the Communist strategy was a complete takeover of education by the State and the subordination of instruction to the goals of the Party. Schools under foreign sponsorship were abolished in July 1948, and their staff ordered to leave the country.[4] Other nonstate educational institutions (except seminaries for training clergy of the state-dominated Romanian Orthodox and Catholic churches) were nationalized in August 1948, and the propagation of Marxist-Leninist principles was made a central goal of all schools. "To educate the young," the Party newspaper wrote in 1948, "means to provide them with a [social] class education in the spirit of proletarian morality; that is, of morality subordinated to the interests of the proletarian class [struggle]."[5]

---

*Described by Nelson, p. 27, as "a three-and-a-half year process (from August 1944) during which time an infinitesimal communist party incrementally secured power. Soviet military occupation and blatant political intervention ... gradually turned from pressure to coercion."

91

To this end, many experienced teachers were dismissed as "ideologically deficient" and replaced by reliable Party members without classroom skills.[6] All teachers were subjected to ideological reeducation and required to teach from a completely new syllabus.[7] In the schools in which Michael Croghan did his research in the early 1970s, "More than 80% of the grade school teachers were members of the Party, 84% of the high school teachers were members and 92% of the university faculty were."[8]

The formation of the beliefs and loyalties of the "new [socialist] man" became under the new regime a central part of schooling from kindergarten through university and required that every aspect of that schooling be shaped by ideology. As Nicolae Ceauşescu wrote in 1974, "The molding of the new man, the builder of socialism and Communism, requires that all educational work should be based on the revolutionary, materialistic-dialectical and historical conception of Marxism-Leninism." In "giving birth to a new culture" and creating "a new humanism," the role of the Communist party would be to provide "leadership and immediate guidance" for all education, in school and out.[9]

In such an all-encompassing program of cultural and personal change, the sphere of individual self-determination is altogether suppressed. "What may be categorized in some cultures as pertaining to purely personal morality, motive for example, officially belongs in Romania to social morality, and whatever is social, is political."[10]

Gilberg has described this as a process of forced modernization, in which "the most important achievement of the expanded educational effort will be the mass acquisition of a new outlook on society, nature, and the individual. The modernized citizen will discard traditional ways of thinking, and will use his skills for societal improvement rather than for petty, selfish gain."[11]

There was a contradiction at the heart of this enterprise. After all, as Berger and others have shown, it is a feature of modernization that absolute truths are questioned or relativized, and that communal goals must compete with an increased interest in "petty, selfish gain" on the part of individuals. Efforts to press the pace of modernization could not fail to undermine the basis of a totalitarian regime, and thus required ever-renewed stress on indoctrination. Modernization did not "include the opportunity to question the political order; the current Romanian definition of modernity ... states that personal freedom in the functional sense can only be achieved under the leadership" of the Communist party.[12]

Whereas the process of modernization proceeds unevenly in most developing nations, with pockets of resistance and even counter-modernizing impulses, under a Communist regime like Romania's there was no possibility of "opting out of the modernizing regime, let alone questioning it." It was not simply a matter of ensuring conformity to the orders of the state and Party, but of creating a wholehearted enthusiasm for all their goals, no matter how these might change in response to the exigencies of the moment. Through political mobilization by schools, media, and organizations under the control of the state (and no others were allowed), "old fashioned 'bourgeois' and 'anti-State' views will have disappeared. The modernized citizen will participate [in the efforts demanded by the state and Party] not because he feels a sense of duty or perhaps even compulsion but because he is thoroughly integrated into the new society and enthusiastically endorses it."[13]

"The modern society," so conceived, will differ profoundly from the results of modernization in the West and more recently in the developing nations, in that it will be one "in which the citizenry willingly forsakes privacy, consciously abstains from group formation that might isolate the individual from the political leadership, and enthusiastically undertakes any duty laid upon it by the unquestioned leader."[14]

The degree of intensity with which this goal was pursued varied, as in other Communist-controlled educational systems, and the perceived need of the regime to ensure the fervent loyalty of its people at some cost in time and energy diverted from instruction in academic and vocational areas. Whenever there were indications of diminished fervor or of some threat to the regime, a period of "storming" would follow when all other goals of schooling became secondary to its political mission.[15]

For President Ceauşescu, political education and the inadequate level of ideological formation of the Romanian people was a constant theme in policy speeches. On his return from a visit to China in 1971, he launched a "little cultural revolution" designed to eliminate any remaining resistance to the goals of the state and any groups that might compete with the Party's hegemony over social, cultural, and political life.[16] Schooling, in particular, was reorganized "to imbue education and cultural and artistic training with a spirit of 'loyalty to socialism' and commitment to the 'building of communism.'"[17]

Ceauşescu's strategy included "(1) centralized control of culture, education, and the mass media, to be exercised by the Party and its officials; (2) expansion of agitation and propaganda among the masses, especially the youth . . . ; (3) Ceauşescu's own synthesis of Marxism-Leninism and Romanian nationalism, which would provide content for the propaganda and cultural activities."[18]

As the regime grew more and more single-mindedly totalitarian, seeking "to penetrate an increasingly complex society in order to control it in all its aspects,"[19] the demands upon the educational system to stress indoctrination were correspondingly increased. Political education was "ultimately designed to help create a new set of values . . . that will facilitate political control, ensure decision-making monopoly by the Communist elite, and, finally, help create the New Socialist Man whose values will make the transition into Communism possible."[20]

In 1974, for example, Ceauşescu insisted that "the fulfillment of the leading political role of the Party cannot be achieved by administrative methods, but only by intense political, organizational and educational activity." He appealed to Romania's youth to "place at the foundation of your knowledge the revolutionary outlook on the world—dialectical and historical materialism! Adopt the communist spirit . . . always fight with determination against everything that is obsolete and no longer corresponds to the requirements of social development, unswervingly militate for the promoting of the revolutionary spirit . . . !"[21]

The personal leadership of Ceauşescu and his "clan" was substituted to an increasing extent for that of the Party as the source of all wisdom and guidance, until it had very much "the characteristics of a religious cult with (1) an iconography, (2) inspired scriptures, (3) an infallible leader, and (4) rituals of mass worship."[22] Maintaining this cult required persecution of those with strongly held alternative beliefs, especially Baptists and Uniate or "Greek" Catholics. "There is a steadfast refusal to accept the notion that anyone can believe in anything but the organic unity of the people and the state, the latter represented by Nicolae Ceauşescu and his inner circle. Religion becomes treason in the General Secretary's mind."[23]

At the Romanian Communist party congress in 1984, Ceauşescu called for a further increase in the political/ideological education of the Romanian people; the Marxist-Leninist philosophy, he insisted, must be studied and understood by all. Forming the "new Communist man" *(omul nou)* was essential, as was struggle against obscurantism, foreign influence, and mysticism (i.e., religion).[24]

While the Communist regimes in Poland, Hungary, and Czechoslovakia found themselves forced to allow elements of a civic society to reemerge in an attempt to reverse a growing social and economic stagnation, the Ceauşescu regime in Romania pressed forward with creating "a society of mass atomization and also mass alienation on a scale unknown elsewhere in the region," in its "quest for the fully controlled and synchronized society."[25]

According to the leader of a free teachers' union founded during the December 1989 overthrow of Ceauşescu's régime, most teachers under the Communist system "had to teach three explicitly political classes each week: one on political information, one on political education, and one related to military training. On Christmas Eve and before Easter, the schools were generally required to hold special social or political events, in order to make church attendance difficult."[26]

"This programme has been worked out," one young Romanian researcher writes, "as a sort of a genetic engineering operation on culture .... [The goal was] a one-way oriented citizen 'flying to communism' *(spre comunism în zbor)*."[27]

This program of indoctrination necessarily allowed no scope for teachers to create new alternative forms of schooling or for parents to exercise educational choice. "In that system of compulsion any initiative of that kind was understood as a rebellion."[28]

Every Romanian has two fathers, kindergartners were told, "father at home and our Father, Nicolae Ceauşescu," while in the elementary grades they were required to learn by heart the answers to Communist catechisms and to write essays on such themes as "The Communist Party Is the Only Party of Romanians" and "The Importance of the Five-Year Plan."[29] In the elementary grades, "practically the whole curriculum consisted of poems praising Ceauşescu."[30] Older pupils were exposed to massive doses of Marxism-Leninism, the history of the Communist party, and the writings of Ceauşescu, "all of which are of little interest to the students and result in much boredom and cynicism."[31]

Nor was this effort to shape the young to a single worldview and set of loyalties limited to classroom instruction. Through the "Falcons of the Homeland" *(Şoimii Patriei)*, enrolling children from three to seven, the Pioneers (modeled on the Soviet organization) and, in secondary schools, the Union of Communist Youth, out-of-school time was structured and the young were, in Ceauşescu's words, "formed in the spirit of the revolutionary conception of life."[32] Some 90 percent of the nation's pupils belonged to these organizations as of the early 1980s.[33] "Through the Pioneers organization," a Western observer noted, "the student . . . is first introduced into the ideological mobilization of the adult world."[34]

Although parents were expected to help their children provide the ideologically correct answers on their homework assignments, many did so without real conviction. "As the students mature conceptually, the parents tell them the ideological facts of life; what can be said and what cannot be said unless the student does not care about his or her future or the jobs of parents." A secondary student who did not receive a passing grade in ideological studies failed overall and could not go on to further education.[35]

Students were expected not only to espouse the politically correct beliefs, but also to avoid such negative states of mind as pessimism and "mysticism," including any sort of religious belief or "the positing of any cause outside the framework of material consequences."[36] Schools could not teach about religion, except to criticize the "sects"* and those who belonged to them, since "the 'new man' predicted by communism had to be atheist and to assimilate only the new materialist-dialectical view about life and the world."[37]

Ceauşescu took the cult of personality to unusual lengths, but the fundamental principles on which he required that ideological instruction be based were paralleled in other People's Republics. These were the following:

(1) A person should not pursue individual pleasure, or engage in actions for selfish reasons.
(2) All behavior should serve the Party and the state.

---

*Antohi argues that the criticism of smaller religious groups "was also a service to the obedient Orthodox church; the Orthodox believers had less trouble, since their church was zealously helping the Party-state."

96

(3) Serving the Party and state should be a consequence of a positive internalized attitude toward and enthusiasm for serving the Party and the state.[38]

It is the third principle, of course, which defines the totalitarian project of getting inside the mind of the individual to make him or her a willing extension of the will of the guiding elite.

Sources of Resistance

Resistance to the ideological offensive of state and Party in recent years came primarily from ethnic minority groups, particularly stimulated by the identification, under Ceauşescu, of communism with Romanian nationalism.

From the initial period of consolidation of power until the events of 1989, Romanians themselves did not show a strong disposition to challenge the Communist regime. "Romanians traditionally tend to choose individual, indirect, and non-confrontational methods to avoid, rather than oppose, government demands."[39] There was no strong trade union tradition, nor did the Romanian Orthodox Church provide an effective alternative to the regime, within whose sphere relics of civil society might have persisted. "Although an active and important contributor to the process of nation-building and state-building" in Romania over the past hundred years, "the Church claimed neither political primacy nor parity with 'Caesar.'"[40]

For the Hungarian and German minorities, however, "churches have tended to be regarded as national institutions which have helped to underpin national cultures and ... attacks on religious life have been interpreted in national as much as in religious terms."[41]

Between the world wars, the Romanian government paid the salaries of clergy and other church expenses, not only for the Romanian Orthodox but also for other recognized denominations, including the Calvinist churches of the Hungarian minority and the Lutheran churches of the German minority.[42] These public subsidies were not without a price to the churches, which became to some degree part of the apparatus of state administration—a fact of some significance to their neutralization by the postwar Communist regime.[43] The exception was the Roman Catholic Church, which refused to accept the administrative controls that accompanied state funding.[44]

After an initial period of confusion as it consolidated its power, the Communist regime moved to bring the churches and their associated organization under its direct control by a decree issued in August 1948. Formal recognition was extended to 14 religious communities, contingent upon their subservience to the state.[45] Relations with churches in other countries were forbidden, and the government sought "to pack the upper hierarchy with 'progressive' and reliable elements able to control a subservient lower clergy."

A pro-Communist patriarch was appointed to head the Romanian Orthodox Church, after a murderous purge of those bishops and clergy who showed any signs of resistance, and the government continued to pay the salaries of Orthodox clergy, while making the clergy even more dependent by confiscating church lands and endowments.[46] Revival of monasticism was permitted and even encouraged.[47] Thus it was possible for the state to use the Orthodox Church "both as an instrument for recruiting popular support [for the regime and its campaigns], and as one aimed at propagating a 'liberal' image in the West."[48]

The Roman Catholic Church, characteristically, proved resistant to government control. Bishops were arrested; 55 priests, monks, and nuns were executed and hundreds more imprisoned; all Catholic publications were suppressed; religious orders were dissolved; and church assets were confiscated. Although the great majority of children attended state schools before World War II, the Catholic Church had operated 91 elementary and secondary schools (or, according to another source, 376 schools), which served to maintain Hungarian language and culture as well as to provide religious instruction. These schools were confiscated by the state.[49]

Churches were forbidden, by the 1948 decree, to operate schools and educational programs other than those to train clergy and cantors. The 1948 law on education similarly ordered that "all ecclesiastical and private schools are to be reorganized as state schools."[50] The clergy training institutions were required to add courses on the Communist system and its objectives. All religious instruction was banned from state schools, which now possessed a monopoly on general education.[51]

The clergy were permitted to provide religious instruction in church facilities on Saturdays or Sundays, but "the nature and extent of the catechism are determined by the [government's] Department of Religious Affairs, and church leaders are responsible for any irregularity that may occur."[52]

If the churches were brought under control with relative ease (though note that it would be the protest activities of a Protestant pastor that provided the spark that brought down the Ceaușescu regime in 1989), the resistance of ethnic minority groups to assimilation led to continuing tensions over the state's monopoly of education.

"When the multinational empires broke down after World War I, the new political entities that rose from the ashes inherited many subcultures, which would cause great problems in nation-building. In many ways, today's communist regimes in the region are still engaged in the quest for fully-integrated nations, this time on the basis of a 'socialist' culture." Gilberg notes that "religious heterogeneity worked as long as the leaders of the multinational empires were tolerant on this crucial issue. But once nationalism emerged as a political expression of ethnic and religious particularism,"[53] conflict became inevitable.

The largest ethnic minority group in Romania consists of Hungarians, who represented 7.9 percent of the population in 1930 and continued at the same proportion in 1977, though much more strongly represented in much of Transylvania, which was under Hungarian rule until the aftermath of World War I. The German proportion slipped from 4.1 percent to 1.7 percent of the total over the same period, and continues to fall as Romanians of German descent use their right to immigrate into the Federal Republic. The exercise of this right in the last years of the Ceaușescu regime involved bribes from the German government in the guise of economic aid—reportedly 10,000 marks per ethnic German emigrant from Romania.[54] Most Romanian Jews have also emigrated.[55]

The prewar Romanian government claimed, with some justice, that it pursued far more generous policies toward ethnic minority groups than did the Austro-Hungarian empire toward its Romanian minority population.[56] The perception of the Hungarian and German minorities, no longer in the politically and culturally dominant position, was that the Romanian government was bent on destroying their schools and other separate cultural institutions; "out of the 2,641 Hungarian-language schools in 1918,* there were only 1,040 in all of Romania in 1924, only 875 in 1932, and only 795 in 1938."[57]

*Antohi notes that many of these schools, under Hungarian rule, enrolled Romanian children required to study in Hungarian! "Hungarians passed from hegemony to minority status very abruptly; one can understand their feelings."

The postwar Communist regime followed the Soviet model of asserting that nationality was a false distinction that would lose all significance with the achievement of working-class solidarity. "In strict terms, the interests of a Hungarian worker were congruent with those of a Romanian worker and any differences between them arising from self-perceptions were merely the result of a false consciousness instilled in the working class by the bourgeoisie . . . . In other words, the language in which a particular set of ideas or concepts was expressed was immaterial, as long as what was expressed was socialist."[58]

The government sought to conciliate national minorities by providing guarantees of education in their home languages, while moving against aspects of the minority culture that could serve as a competing focus of loyalty. During its first years, "the state organized a national-minority school network extending to every level of education and gave a free hand to the churches . . . . In 1947–48, there were 2,071 Hungarian-language kindergartens and elementary schools in Romania, with approximately 4,200 teachers; there were 184 Hungarian secondary schools."[59] The curriculum of these schools, though taught in Hungarian, was revised completely to stress the Romanian Communist interpretation of history, culture, and current events.[60]

The Romanian Constitution ratified in April 1948 guaranteed "free use of the mother tongue for all the 'co-inhabiting nationalities,' as well as the organization of education in the mother tongue." The education law enacted a few months later, however, formalized the seizure of all church and private schools and of the endowments that had supported them. A sort of educational freedom would be preserved for language minority groups, and in fact be given more official support than had been the case under the prewar regime, but this would be subject to a government monopoly of schooling. The national minority churches (Roman Catholic, Calvinist, and Lutheran) would no longer be able to serve as sponsors and thus as protectors of the schools serving their communities. "In effect, then, the language of instruction was the only element of nationality education to be preserved, since the entire educational system had been redirected to serve the realization of proletarian internationalism,"[61] as of course it had been for Romanians as well.

During the postwar years, Gheorghe Gheorghiu-Dej proclaimed that the international character of communism and a common commitment to building socialism would make relations among Romania's ethnic minorities "friendly and mutually beneficial."[62] Many of the early Communist leaders, indeed, were Jews or Hungarians, "a reflection of communism's lack of appeal among ethnic Romanians, who had grown used to authoritarian and profoundly xenophobic ideologies."[63] By the early 1960s, however, he was able to take advantage of the Sino-Soviet split to gain a measure of independence from Moscow that prepared the way for assertion of Romanian nationalism. Under Ceauşescu, after 1965, this nationalism became increasingly Romanian, directed against internal minorities as well as against Soviet and other neighbors. The absolute claims of a totalitarian regime made Party leaders impatient with the persistence of cultural distinctiveness.

"Ethnic particularism [was] seen as a 'bourgeois' and consequently old-fashioned value, whereas integration to a common goal of 'Socialist Man' in modern society [was] a progressive process."[64] By 1971, a Party publication would call for "increasingly organic integration" of the national minorities, and the official program adopted by the Eleventh Party Congress in 1974 called for their integration "into the unified mass of working people of a communist society" and predicted that before long "there will be no nationalities, only a socialist nation."[65]

Initially, the Ceauşescu regime was more tolerant toward the ethnic minority groups than that of his predecessor Gheorghiu-Dej, adopting the Soviet formula "National in form, Socialist in content."[66] The constitution adopted in 1965 continued "to guarantee to the minorities education in their mother tongue and use of their language in political organs and cultural institutions."[67]

Instruction in the language of the home—but without reference to elements of ethnic minority culture—was provided in schools where a sufficient number of children whose parents desired such instruction were concentrated; the threshold number of pupils for instruction in minority languages was raised in 1973, however, from 15 in all schools to 25 in elementary schools and to 36 in secondary schools, making it more difficult to arrange such classes. Romanian classes, by contrast, were to be provided if any pupils required them.[68]

Consolidation of minority-language schools with Romanian-language schools and various pressures upon parents, who were told that "insistence on teaching in the mother tongue is a form of nationalism, indicating a lack of loyalty as a citizen and lack of respect for the official language of the state," led to a major decline in opportunities for Hungarian or German parents to obtain the home language instruction for their children that was in theory their right.[69]

Hungarians and Germans, who had a history of political and cultural superiority to the Romanians around them, perceived they were expected to "assimilate 'downwards' to a common socialist culture with strong overtones of Romanian nationalism."[70] The official position was that the problem of "co-inhabitant nationalities" would eventually be solved by their assimilation to Romanian language and culture.[71]

Among both Hungarians and Germans, however, the use of the native language remained very strong and even increased slightly in the period 1956–66; in the latter year, 1,602,259 out of 1,619,592 Hungarians and 372,644 out of 382,595 Germans in Romania reported that they used primarily their mother tongues for communication.[72]

As with the Romanian population, the effect of modernization efforts on the German and Hungarian populations of Romania did not necessarily correspond to the goals of the Communist regime. After all, as Gilberg predicted two decades ago, the demand of an evolving economy for highly skilled workers would increase rather than reduce the social gap between the ethnic groups with a tradition of urbanization and relative modernity, such as the Germans, Jews, and Hungarians, and the more rural Romanian population and socially marginal Gypsies.[73]

After 1980, Ceauşescu's willingness to fund cultural and educational programs for the minority groups declined, and they were excluded to an increasing extent from policymaking and from the economy.[74] As the general situation of Romania degenerated, that of its national minorities grew significantly more difficult, and tensions with the Romanian majority became severe for the first time.[75] Antohi notes that all groups were suffering, but that Hungarians and Germans (while their conditions were no worse than those of Romanians) found economic distress particularly bitter in contrast with the situation of their more prosperous "cousins" in Germany and

Hungary, a bitterness exacerbated by Ceauşescu's "nationalist discourse."

Increasing tension between Romania and Hungary over the treatment of the Hungarian minority led to an unsuccessful intervention by Soviet Premier Gorbachev in May 1987;[76] two years later, it would be the precipitating cause of the overthrow of Ceauşescu, when Hungarians in Timişoara resisted the arrest of Pastor László Tokes (who was subsequently elected one of the bishops of the Reformed [Calvinist] Church and honorary president of the Democratic Association of Hungarians in Romania).

Recent Developments

As we have learned with some relief over the past two years, the Communist project of creating a new humanity through a state monopoly on education and the expression of opinion does not work, at least not reliably or permanently. Even in the early seventies, Gilberg concluded, "the young generation appears to be quite apathetic politically. Adherence to the ideas of Marxism-Leninism is primarily formalistic, with little attempt to relate book learning to real life, and there are disturbing tendencies toward a revival of 'bourgeois-landowner mentality.' "[77] Hale found, also, that the "constant discipline, and the monotony and volume of political training in the school curriculum, created a vast body of politically apathetic students."[78]

Similarly, the relentless atheistic propaganda in schools may paradoxically have led to increased interest in the new Protestant churches that have flourished in Romania in recent years. "At a seminar for Romanian academics involved in atheistic propagandizing, one participant, Georgeta Florea, drew a direct connection between the regime-sponsored 'reversal of religious belief' and the propagation of smaller sects. Increasingly, she noted,

> This reversal of religious belief has created a paradoxical situation. It has only meant loss of confidence in the traditional religions and preservation of the illusion that there must be a better faith. In one way or another, this has brought (disaffected believers) under the influence of the neo-Protestant sects, which are becoming increasingly militant."[79]

Thus it was possible to conclude that "political socialization in Romania has failed to achieve its goal of establishing Socialist Men with a clearcut commitment to the social, political, and economic leadership "of the Communist party." Indeed, the primary result of intensive indoctrination through schools and youth organizations seemed to have been widespread cynicism and indifference to the goals of the regime, which, in turn, has undermined the effort to break down ethnic identities and loyalties.[80] A "dispirited population which is concerned with survival, not progress"[81] grew less and less responsive to the regime's efforts at mobilization to address the economic problems associated with a state-managed command economy.

The Communist regime in Romania was largely successful in its effort to destroy all traces of an independent civil society or "mediating structures" between individuals and the state. The social and psychological consequences were devastating and have in turn done grave damage to the economic system as well. "An atomized society, in which intermediate structures and attachments are destroyed, leaves the individual adrift, personally bereft of support systems that may insulate him or her from the direct exercise of power upon him [or her]. It is much easier to control such a society. It is also much more difficult to get such a society to perform at maximum levels, because there is no discernible common ground, no all-encompassing passion except to stay alive as an individual; there is no collective spirit. Atomized societies maximize power and minimize performance."[82]

Schools were particularly affected by the weariness and cynicism created by decades of mobilization with few concrete results, and by the discongruity between official truth and lived experience. A Western observer found that

> the students in grades V-VIII . . . aged 10–14 begin to distinguish two existences, with two different types of behavior: one, in the institution of the school, and the second, in their family and social life. . . . Students learn what can be said and done with impunity in school. For example, the President is presented as a hero and leader in school; the students at this age level hear their parents' reactions to the President at home where [Ceauşescu] is often addressed in a less than complimentary manner. I have heard adult family members directly instruct children in what not to repeat outside the home.

This insistence upon politically correct speech and writing in all public contexts did not, however, result in a real acceptance of the intended message. "Newspeak on formalized occasions was enough, beliefs were not an issue, with the exception, of course, of Newspeak discourses, carbon-copied all the way down from Ceauşescu's speeches."[83]

Under a totalitarian regime, the only recourse of parents who do not agree with the dominant ideology reflected in the school is to help their children to develop the capacity for ironical detachment and dissimulation. Thus, "what the ideological training achieves is not belief in a group of propositions; through the training students learn how to behave politically within the social system, either for their own benefit or at least without sanction." The project of Marxist-Leninist education, according to this study, had largely failed.

> When the new regime was introduced after World War II, there were . . . only one thousand members of the Communist party in Romania. There is no evidence since 1944 that would indicate any internal commitment to a communist ideology, except those parts of the ideology which are in conformity with traditional Romanian culture.[84]

Habits created by four decades when all initiatives came from the Party or the state are difficult to change, however. "Almost five decades of suffocating bureaucracy cannot be swept [away] overnight. Teachers, parents and pupils are expecting that someone from above, authorities, leaders, eminences [will] change the absurd non-operating school system."[85]

Some things did change, after the great events of mid-December 1989. The Faculty of Pedagogy and Psychology and the Institute for Educational Research were reestablished, and there was a new interest in finding ways to breathe life into Romania's schools. The National Salvation Front government announced that schools could offer moral and religious education on an optional basis. The initial priority, indeed, was upon "giving up the most aberrant forms and means of communist education, mainly by changing school curricula and textbooks."

> The first two years of the transition stage were focused upon [this] objective. Without waiting . . . for a comprehensive reform or a new education law, the first decisions of the new political order were directly focused on eliminating Marxist

ideology, as well as its influence upon the Romanian educational system. There were given up the subjects for communist education or for "shaping the new man," which were formerly omnipresent both as separate school subjects and as diffused contents for all instruction branches and education levels.[86]

Kindergarten staff and others urged that parents be allowed to choose among different types of early childhood education.[87] The International Union of Free Waldorf Schools, in particular, encouraged the establishment of such schools in Romania.

Ethnic minority issues, in particular, have proved complicated once the insistence of the Party/state on uniformity was relaxed. Many of the two million ethnic Hungarians have been calling for their own separate schools, as part of a reversal of Ceaușescu's policy of seeking to deprive them of their language, culture, and identity; this has led to bitter conflicts in the city of Tirgu Mures, in Transylvania.[88] According to Antohi, in at least some schools "all instruction, from kindergarten to high school (3–18 years of age) is done in the minority language, with the exception of, sometimes, History, Geography and some technical subjects, taught in Romanian. Basically, minority schools merely translate the Romanian textbooks, use the same curricula, but learn their mother tongue as a supplement to that curriculum. So, since minority children have to learn everything Romanians learn, they have to stay 3–4 more hours in school (since Romanians don't learn Hungarian)."[89] There is a new openness, in other schools, to providing supplemental (3-4 hours per week) instruction for ethnic minorities in their mother tongues.[90]

The German government has provided financial and other assistance to support German-language schools, in the vain hope that this might slow down the emigration of Romanians of German descent to the Federal Republic. (Yes, Germans loved their distant relatives in the East until they began to "come home" in huge numbers.)

The Ministry of Education and Science adopted comprehensive regulations for the school year 1990–91, while noting that these are transitional "until an essential Education Reform Act comes into force." These regulations make no provision for independent schools,* but do mention the possibility of some forms of choice among state schools. For example, members of national minorities may choose to "attend schools in which the teaching language is their mother tongue."

At the elementary and intermediate levels (grades 1–8), children with unusual artistic or athletic abilities may be served in "schools with a special program of music, fine arts and choreography or schools with [a] sports and physical training program."[91] This is not a new provision for genuine parental choice, however, but a continuation of the practice, on the Soviet pattern, of providing special schools for "gifted mutants, for propaganda reasons."[92]

Although not mentioned in the regulations, the ministry has been supporting one form of alternative education, the Waldorf schools associated with the mystic and progressive educator Rudolf Steiner. A two-week seminar cosponsored by the ministry in September 1990 brought together some 500 Romanian teachers and others to hear Waldorf specialists from four nations of Western Europe and from Hungary stress the spiritual and intellectual development of children according to the theories of anthroposophy, Steiner's New-Age-before-its-time philosophy.[93] A similar seminar was held in 1991, and there are now Waldorf primary schools and kindergartens in many Romanian communities, and a training program at the University of Bucharest.[94]

This event grew out of the energetic missionary work of Steiner's disciples in Central and Eastern Europe since the events of 1989; they moved in effectively to help fill the vacuum left by the discrediting of the belief system on which the People's Republics and their schools had been based. The Waldorf pedagogy, with its stress upon "awakening the child as a spiritual being," is based upon a comprehensive worldview and prescription for living, which also includes elements of holistic medicine and theories of creativity based in Eastern religion.[95] That Waldorf schools were developed, along with other forms of progressive education, in Germany in the wake of World War I and the apparent collapse of Western culture may help to explain its attractiveness to Eastern Europeans going through a similar crisis of meaning.

*"The whole educational system is governed by the Ministry of Education which has the overall responsibility for the organization, content and control of the [educational] process."

The child-centered and noncompetitive classroom practices in Waldorf schools have much to attract liberal middle-class parents (a 1975 study in Germany found that 40 percent of the Waldorf pupils sampled were from academic families) who do not buy into the religious/philosophical beliefs that underlie these practices.[96] There is reason to believe, however, that it is precisely the mystical aspects of Waldorf pedagogy that account for the Romanian interest.

In an interview with a German publication, Professor (of electronics and computer science) George Stefan stressed his own intense interest in exploring spiritual (not explicitly religious, in the traditional sense) dimensions of existence and attributed the similar interest on the part of many of his countrymen as a reaction against decades of Marxist materialism.[97] On the other hand, one of the education officials who encouraged the development of Waldorf schools in Romania in 1990 disclaims interest in the mystical aspects of the Waldorf program and insists that it is "the alternative character of these schools after decades of uniformity [that] is very appealing. . . . I am interested in introducing alternative worldviews, topics, and methods. Besides, the articulation of problem areas in the Waldorf curriculum might inspire Romanian educationalists to design a different, more interdisciplinary curriculum."[98]

Official guidelines were published in September 1990 on providing Waldorf pedagogy to those parents who desired it, as trained Waldorf teachers become available. Under these guidelines, existing schools are permitted to become Waldorf schools through majority votes of the teachers and the parents, provided that enough trained teachers are available and an experienced Waldorf educator is available to advise the school. Parents may transfer their children to a Waldorf school.

New Waldorf schools will be established on the demand of a sufficient number of parents, provided that trained teachers are available. In such schools, the staff may depart from national curriculum guidelines as necessary to implement the Waldorf pedagogy. Each Waldorf school is to be self-governing, with authority to hire and fire staff, admit and expel pupils, and set its own examinations. No teacher can use the word "Waldorf" to describe a program without express permission of the ministry and of the Waldorf Association.[99]

Through what resemble the concordats negotiated between some 19th-century governments and the Vatican, the Romanian Ministry of Education appears to have granted a privileged status to Waldorf schools, within the state system for its resources but completely self-governing in all other respects. Other alternative schools may also emerge, though they are slower off the mark. There are some indications that the rapidly growing Protestant movement in Romania* will establish a network of confessional schools.

> The problem is that the Montessori, Freinet and other alternative schools, invited constantly to "copy" their Waldorf competitors, are less effectively organized. So we had merely a symposium on Montessori and Freinet pedagogy in Timișoara, Sept. '91. The paradox is that Montessori and Freinet can function within "normal" schools, but very few foreigners are interested in that. The success of the Waldorf crusade is partly due to their being taken for German-education apostles (schools in German are very popular among Romanian elites), with all the bonuses imagined (trips to Germany, fellowships, eventually emigration). Besides, the existence of Romanian Waldorf specialists among the emigré community was very important. One of them simply became a full-time Waldorf activist in Romania, others came to teach and organize seminars.[100]

No ready summary of the development of educational freedom in Romania is possible at the time of writing. While there are many indications that new energies released by the fall of the Ceaușescu regime are finding expression in the creation of new schools, as well as in other social spheres, the uncertain political situation and very difficult economic situation have prevented wide-ranging educational reform. Such reform can work only if it is implemented school by school in ways that are beyond the control even of a totalitarian government, much less one with an uncertain mandate. The fact that an extensive public opinion survey published in Bucharest in November 1991 found the morale of 83 percent of the respondents low and that of only 1 percent of them high suggests how difficult it will be to take bold initiatives. The same survey found widespread

*Bugajski and Pollack estimated the number of new Protestants at 450,000. "Almost half of them are Baptists—more than in all other East European countries combined." (page 164)

concern about the persistence of "communist structures and attitudes" resistant to fundamental change, and a "moral and spiritual
crisis" in social life.[101]

Romania is also faced with the difficulty that reform of the education system and of the economic and social order in general depends
upon availability of "competent and motivated human resources
but the society doesn't have the necessary means to secure these
resources. Thus, contrary to appearances, the major problem of the
ex-communist countries is not a political or economic one but an
educational and moral one."[102]

It is difficult to predict the outcome of the ethnic tensions over
schooling, especially those involving the large Hungarian minority.
The pressures of the last years of the Ceauşescu regime for assimilation have largely been abandoned and Hungarian-language schooling is expanding, but the continuing economic and political difficulties faced by Romania create a dangerous potential for scapegoating
Hungarians along with Gypsies and other minorities. In turn, the
relative success of postcommunist Hungary and the tensions sur-
rounding the Hungarian minority in Slovakia seem likely to heighten
ethnic awareness among Hungarians that could lead to further polarization and conflict.

References

1. Trond Gilberg, *Nationalism and Communism in Romania: The Rise and Fall of Ceauşescu's Personal Dictatorship* (Boulder, Colo.: Westview Press, 1991), p. 141; see also the extended discussion by Kenneth Jowitt, *Revolutionary Breakthroughs and National Development: The Case of Romania, 1944–1965* (Berkeley: University of California Press, 1971).

2. Elemér Illyés, *National Minorities in Romania: Change in Transylvania* (Boulder, Colo.: East European Monographs, 1982), pp. 113, 128.

3. Daniel N. Nelson, *Democratic Centralism in Romania: A Study of Local Communist Politics* (New York: Columbia University Press, 1980), p. 40.

4. Illyés, pp. 169, 293.

5. Julian Hale, *Ceauşescu's Romania: A Political Documentary* (London: George Harrap, 1971), p. 134.

6. Stephen Fischer-Galati, *Romania* (New York: Praeger, 1957), p. 162.

7. Illyés, p. 168.

8. Martin J. Croghan and Penelope P. Croghan, *Ideological Training in Communist Education: A Case Study of Romania* (Lanham, Md.: University Press of America, 1980), p. 43.

9. Nicolae Ceauşescu, *Report of the Central Committee on the Activity of the Romanian Communist Party in the Period Between the Tenth and Eleventh Congress, and the Future Tasks of the Party* (Bucharest: Meridiane Publishing House, 1974), pp. 80–82.

10. Croghan and Croghan, p. 95.
11. Gilberg, *Modernization*, p. 20.
12. Gilberg, *Modernization*, p. 20.
13. Ibid., pp. 21, 23.
14. Ibid., p. 24.
15. Ibid., p. 119.
16. Ibid., pp. 79–81.
17. Illyés, p. 183.
18. Mary Ellen Fischer, *Nicolae Ceauşescu: A Study in Political Leadership* (Boulder and London: Lynne Rienner, 1989), p. 180.
19. Gilberg, *Modernization*, p. 248.
20. Ibid., p. 98.
21. Ceauşescu, *Report*, pp. 76–77.
22. Fischer, p. 160.
23. Gilberg, *Nationalism and Communism*, p. 193.
24. Nicolae Ceauşescu, "Activitatea Politico-Ideologică de Ridicare a Conştiinţei Socialiste Şi Formare a Omului Nou," in *Raport la Cel de-al XIII-lea Congres al Partidului Comunist Român* (Bucharest: Editura Političa, 1984), pp. 57–60.
25. Gilberg, *Nationalism and Communism*, p. 142.
26. Catalin Croitoru interviewed in Ruth Wattenberg, "Ceauşescu's Schools," *American Educator* (Fall 1990): 14; Sorin Antohi, in a letter to the author (May 12, 1992), states that Croitoru was never a teacher, founded the organization for opportunistic reasons, and neither represents typical teachers nor is a force for educational reform.
27. Elena Malec, Institute for Educational Research, Bucharest, letter to the author, January 26, 1991.
28. Monica Cuciureanu, Institute of Educational Research, Bucharest, letter to the author, February 1991.
29. Croghan and Croghan, pp. 97, 107–8.
30. Croitoru, p. 14.
31. Gilberg, *Nationalism and Communism*, p. 133.
32. Ceauşescu, "Activitatea," p. 68.
33. Illyés, p. 171.
34. Croghan and Croghan, p. 115.
35. Ibid., pp. 119, 128.
36. Ibid., p. 140.
37. Cuciureanu, letter.
38. Croghan and Croghan, p. 175.
39. Fischer, p. 260.
40. Michael Shafir, *Romania: Politics, Economics and Society: Political Stagnation and Simulated Change* (Boulder, Colo.: Lynne Rienner, 1985), p. 135.
41. George Schöpflin and Hugh Poulton, *Romania's Ethnic Hungarians* (London: The Minority Rights Group, 1990), p. 9.
42. Sylvius Dragomir, *The Ethnical Minorities in Transylvania* (Geneva: Sonor, 1927), p. 78.
43. Illyés, p. 222.
44. Fischer-Galati, p. 135.
45. Shafir, p. 151.
46. Fischer-Galati, p. 138.
47. Letter from Antohi.

48. Shafir, p. 152.
49. Ibid., p. 154; Fischer-Galati, pp. 136, 148; Illyés, p. 227.
50. Illyés, p. 223.
51. Fischer-Galati, pp. 138–47.
52. Illyés, p. 236.
53. Gilberg, p. 3.
54. Ibid., p. 166; Schöpflin and Poulton, p. 18.
55. Letter from Antohi.
56. Dragomir, passim.
57. Illyés, pp. 91, 162.
58. Schöpflin and Poulton, p. 9.
59. Illyés, p. 165.
60. Schöpflin and Poulton, p. 9.
61. Illyés, pp. 167–68.
62. Gilberg, *Modernization*, p. 123.
63. Misha Glenny, *The Rebirth of History: Eastern Europe in the Age of Democracy* (London: Penguin Books, 1990), p. 100.
64. Gilberg, *Modernization*, p. 25.
65. Illyés, pp. 140–41.
66. Gilberg, *Modernization*, pp. 213-14.
67. Fischer, p. 243.
68. Shafir, p. 163; Schöpflin and Poulton, p. 13.
69. Illyés, pp. 175–77.
70. Gilberg, *Modernization*, p. 130.
71. Shafir, p. 164.
72. Trond Gilberg, "Ethnic Minorities in Romania under Socialism," *East European Quarterly* (January 1974): 3.
73. Gilberg, *Modernization*, p. 228.
74. Fischer, p. 248.
75. Schöpflin and Poulton, p. 17.
76. Fischer, p. 248.
77. Gilberg, *Modernization*, p. 135.
78. Hale, p. 138.
79. Janusz Bugajski and Maxine Pollack, *East European Fault Lines: Dissent, Opposition, and Social Activism* (Boulder, Colo.: Westview Press, 1989), p. 165.
80. Gilberg, *Modernization*, pp. 233–35.
81. Gilberg, *Nationalism and Communism*, p. 75.
82. Ibid., p. 145.
83. Letter from Antohi.
84. Croghan and Croghan, pp. 179–84.
85. Malec, letter.
86. Cesar Birzea, "Education Reform and Human Resources Policy in Romania" (paper presented at the Symposium "Stand der Bildungsreformen in Mittel- und Osteuropa: Bilanz und Perspektiven einer gesamteuropaischen Zusammenarbeit," *Loccum*, March 20–22, 1992).
87. Doina Sterescu, "Dialog Colegial," *Tribuna Invatamintului* (Educational Tribune) 13 (1990).
88. Joan Phillips, "Winter Hopes Dashed by Spring of Discontent," *Times Educational Supplement*, May 11, 1990.

89. Antohi, letter.

90. Maria Constantinescu-Condrut, "Învăţămîntul în limba maternă a minorităţilor naţionale" (Education in mother tongues for national minorities), *Tribuna Invatamintului* 46 (1990).

91. *Regulations Concerning the Romanian Educational System in the School Year 1990–1991* (Bucharest: Ministry of Education and Science, Institute of Educational Sciences, 1990).

92. Antohi, letter.

93. "Waldorf-Seminar beendet," *Neuer Weg* (Bucharest), September 18, 1990.

94. Antohi, letter.

95. For a critical but comprehensive account, see Heiner Ullrich, *Waldorfpädagogik und okkulte Weltanschauung* (Weinheim and Munich: Juventa, 1987); see also B. C. J. Lievegoed, "Het kind als geestelijk wezen," *De levende school* (Zeist, Netherlands: Uitgeverij Vrij Geestesleven, 1980).

96. Ullrich, p. 218.

97. Jörg Hermann Schröde, "Interview mit George Stefan, Minister für Erziehung und Wissenschaft in Rumänien," *Crescendo* 2 (1990).

98. Antohi, letter.

99. "Rechtlinien zur Gründung von alternativen Unterrichts-Einheiten, Erziehungsgemeinschaften von Lehrern, Eltern and Schülern," *Neuer Weg* (Bucharest), September 28, 1990; Kevin McCarthy, "Opting for a State of Grace," *Times Educational Supplement*, July 13, 1990.

100. Antohi, letter.

101. *Romania Libera*, November 15, 1991, 5, translated in *JPRS-EER*-91-180, December 17, 59–64.

102. Birzea.

5. Poland

Turning from Bulgaria and Romania to Poland, we find an entirely different response to the Soviet model of using schooling as a primary instrument of state and Communist party domination. In Poland, the persistent efforts of the regime to indoctrinate and to eliminate diversity through its schools seem to have been less vigorous and more successfully resisted by an enduring civil society.

This may in part be explained by Poland's proximity to the West; Poles insist that they are "Central" not "Eastern" Europeans and think pejoratively of the Balkans as almost Asian. But the people of the former German Democratic Republic were even more "Western," less rural, and tied by a common language to neighbors with pluralistic democracies (the Federal Republic, Austria, Switzerland), but did not exhibit the same independence of the Soviet model. So the answer cannot be sought primarily in geography.

A substantial part of the explanation undoubtedly lies in the role of the Roman Catholic Church in Poland. As one observer wrote a decade ago, "If today in Poland the Communist Party is forced to relax its grip on society by the organized pressure of free trade unions and public opinion, this will be due in large measure to the survival and growth of the church."[1]

The stubborn independence of the Polish Catholic Church, rooted in 19th century experience when it became "the mainstay of Polishness," and sustaining national identity under oppression by Protestant Prussia and Orthodox Russia, enabled the church in the postwar era to preserve a space for civil society apart from the totalitarian demands of the state and Communist party. The church "linked religious practices with familial and national elements and provided in this way not only a symbol but in fact a real possibility to experience Polish identity. Family and church were thus the only load-bearing pillars of Polish society during 123 years of statelessness."[2]

The church's resistance to the Nazis during World War II—over a thousand priests died or were shot in concentration camps—protected it to some extent from postwar attacks by the Communists.

Unlike the situation in Czechoslovakia, the clergy of the Polish Catholic Church were not salaried by the government but, in many cases, supported by parochial farms small enough to escape the postwar redistribution of land (the church had lost most of its endowments and large property in the 19th century).[3]

Another contrast with the Soviet Union, Bulgaria, and Romania may be found in the relative absence in postwar Poland of ethnic tensions. While the presence of large Jewish, Ukrainian, Byelorussian, and German minorities that made up some 25 percent of the population was a source of political and social conflict in prewar Poland, the near extermination of the large Jewish minority by the Nazis, followed by a radical reshaping of eastern and western borders after World War II and massive population shifts associated with these changes, made Poland unusually homogeneous ethnically* and more than 90 percent Catholic.

In Bulgaria and Romania the ruling party made the assimilation of the Turkish and Hungarian minority groups a primary task of and justification for suppressing alternatives to the state's monopoly of education. That the schools supported and used by these groups were religious was all the more reason to ban religious schooling in the name of national unity. This pretext did not exist in Poland, and though all but a few Catholic secondary schools were closed, the church was able to provide supplemental educational programs that reduced the state monopoly of schooling.

In this as in other ways, the three groups that came together in the Solidarity movement—workers, intellectual dissidents, and the Church—developed a social resistance when political resistance was impossible, through grassroots organization leading to "the revival of pluralism in Polish society and to the resurfacing of traditional Polish political culture."[4] The result, of course, was a successful political movement that overthrew Communist rule.

With political democratization, a nationwide grassroots effort by parents and teachers has emerged to take control of the education system, both by working with the state schools and by starting

---

*This is not to dismiss the problems experienced by Gypsies that led to establishment in September 1990 of a Commission for National Minority Affairs, but rather to suggest that ethnic and religious diversity has not been a primary concern of postwar Poland and its educational system.

116

independent schools. Four hundred thirty-nine such schools, enrolling more than 31,000 pupils, were operating by September 1991.

Seeking to Follow the Soviet Model

Poland has a long tradition of independent Catholic schooling, and between the wars much innovation was fostered by competition with the developing state system. Like all of Polish life, schools suffered grievously in World War II, but the Catholic system was not allowed to rebuild. In 1946, only one-fourth of 160 surviving private schools were church operated; Catholic schools were refused permits to operate.[5] After 1947 massive confiscations of church land and property, crippling taxation, the abolition of Catholic schools, the closure of theological departments at universities, and general curtailment of the church's pastoral activities and privileges followed. Poland was declared a secular society.[6]

Private and denominational schools were tolerated to a limited extent until 1948, when the Communist-controlled government determined that the time was ripe to establish a state monopoly of education and a thorough politicization of each school through Party cells among the teachers responsible for the ideological content of the instruction. Nonstate schools, with very few exceptions, were eliminated altogether by government decree in 1956.[7]

Katarzyna Skórzyńska of the Ministry of National Education points out that from 1945 to 1988 the "uniformization of all fields of life in Poland embraced the educational system as well."

> The whole education system got crammed into a tight corset of centralized administration and subjected to strict supervision and control. Any private educational initiative was met with suspicion from the side of the communist authorities, and the existing legal regulations left only a very narrow margin for educational activities not administered by the State.[8]

The government's policy was not simply to eliminate a powerful rival in forming the loyalties and worldview of the young, but also to create a state system that would remake the Polish people. Religion was seen as directly inimical to the goals of the Communist regime; as one of the Party's theoreticians wrote, "The function of a religious Weltanschauung (I have Catholicism in mind particularly) consists

117

of weakening the social activity of people in the struggle for real earthly emancipation."[9]

On the other hand, the regime did not feel free to follow the Soviet model of promoting explicitly atheistic instruction, contending that struggling against religion would be less effective than, in the words of a minister of education, "fostering apathy."[10] Thus, "direct attacks on belief in God, on religious dogmas, or even attempts to pour scorn on believers have been virtually unknown in Poland for years."[11] The activities of the Secular School Society and other avowedly antireligious groups have achieved little resonance in Polish public life.[12]

Nevertheless, as in other Communist-controlled nations, "education in Poland in the post-war period was subordinated to ideology and politics. That was reflected in education management structures. The Minister of Education was subordinated to the Central Committee [of the Communist Party], the school superintendent to the provincial Communist governor. The teacher was at the very end of the ladder of official dependence. No wonder then that school favored passive and conformist behavior." "Communism was everywhere— also in schools—in programs, omnipresent boredom, ugliness and poverty of our classrooms."[13]

Four decades of schooling based upon the message that society can function well only with the state taking all initiatives and the Communist party possessing all wisdom have had an inevitable effect on the way Poles think and act.[14]

Sociologist Zbyszko Melosik has described the effect of this system on the classroom experience of children and its function in maintaining Communist hegemony:

> The chief aims of education and schooling were to disseminate communist or socialist ideals and indoctrinate the youth with a belief in the infallibility of Marx and the leaders of the Polish and Soviet Communist parties. Education was to confirm the dominate [sic] role of the Communist party in all spheres of Polish social life and consolidate the communist moral maxim—the only good was that which was good for socialism—in practice it was only that which was good for the Communist party elite. . . . Simultaneously, the schools were to inculcate a conviction that, for their own good, the socialist state should play a dominant role in all spheres of social life. The state was to be ubiquitous, "a part of a citizen's

mind," thereby fulfilling the essence of the communist educational ideal. . . . Such education aimed to create a primitive "adapter," homo sovieticus, who could adapt to all the demands of the communist ruling elite.[15]

In countries with a capitalistic economic structure, Anna Sawis writes, critics often claim to detect a "hidden curriculum" of the educational system that has more importance than the teaching of content and skills, but in Poland as in other socialist nations the political mission of schools was entirely overt: the secretary of the Communist party cell in each school was responsible for ensuring that teachers did not slack off. As recently as 1986 the regime, sensing that its control on the political content of school was slackening, insisted upon a "verification" (*weryfikacja*) process under which teachers were required to explain to their principals and Party representatives how they were meeting the state's requirements on excluding religion and including the Party program in their teaching.[16]

Although the open character of the schools' political goals meant that the goals could be promoted without apology, it also made them easier to recognize and resist, and many Polish pupils did so. The hidden curriculum was demystified. Ironically, the heavily politicized educational system did eventually produce a politically mobilized generation—mobilized in successful opposition to the regime that had thought to mold it to its purposes.[17]

The Resistant Civil Society

Communist hegemony was never complete in Poland, and resistance was more visible than in other East-bloc nations. "Polish historical traditions of fighting for freedom and independence and the exceptional incompetence of Communist rule [had the result] that our nation has never become a Sovietized nation."[18] Although in other Slavic lands Russia had historically been a valued ally against Austro-Hungarian and Ottoman domination—in Bulgaria, the modern nation was won by a Russian army—for Poland Russia had been an oppressor and a threat, and the subservience of the Communist regime to Moscow did not gain it any credit with the Polish people.

Table 5.1
SELF-ASSESSMENT ON A LEFT/RIGHT CONTINUUM

	Left	Center	Right
Czechoslovakia	9	70	21
Hungary	8	74	18
Romania	6	74	20
Bulgaria	18	65	17
All (except Poland)	9	72	19
Poland	3	62	35

Amid the general rejection of communism in Eastern Europe in recent decades, Poland stands out by its strong affinity for conservative positions. A survey conducted between June 1984 and March 1985 among Eastern Europeans visiting in the West but planning to return home found the Poles distinctly more conservative.[19]

The state's policy of separation of church and state, in sharp contrast with the close alliance that marked the prewar years, may in fact have "strengthened the Church by giving it the means to resist state interference in its internal affairs."[20] Although the church had shown itself willing to cooperate—and did not, for example, enforce the Vatican's excommunication of Catholics who actively supported communism[21]—in early 1953 the regime launched an offensive against the church's independence with an assertion of its right to appoint bishops. Later that year, Cardinal Wyszyński was imprisoned, as were other bishops and 900 priests.[22]

With the post-Stalin thaw of 1956, however, the organizational independence of the church was ensured and Gomulka and subsequent Communist leaders sought the support of the hierarchy for the state's economic and social agenda. "The Party does not divide society into believers and non-believers," the Fifth Party Congress was told in 1968, "but assesses a citizen on the basis of his attitude to state interests and the tasks of socialist construction."[23]

While cooperating with the regime on economic development and the maintenance of social peace, the church pressed ahead vigorously with a program of spiritual renewal through celebrations and pilgrimages that placed Christianity in direct competition with the ideological hegemony of communism.[24] Many observers have suggested that Christian faith in fact became more deeply rooted among the Polish people as "a very successful form of defence against the encroachment [of communism] into the innermost recesses of being."[25] Despite the heavy losses experienced during World War II, it is striking that the number of Catholic priests grew from 11,348 in 1937 to 17,986 in 1967, while the number of nuns and lay brothers grew from 19,246 to 31,250.[26]

Nor was the effort to sustain or deepen the Christian commitment of the Polish people unsuccessful. A 1978 survey found that 75.6 percent of urban and 94.2 percent of rural respondents described themselves as "religious." However, despite efforts to inculcate atheism throughout the educational system, only 12.8 percent of urban and 1.9 percent of rural respondents described themselves as nonbelievers. Another survey, the same year, of nearly 9,000 youth in the last year of secondary education found that 77.4 percent described themselves as religious and only 8.4 percent as nonbelievers.[27] Polish intellectuals, according to another study, were markedly more religious than those in the West: 79.7 percent declared themselves to be believers.[28]

It is not that the goals of Polish Communists were less totalitarian than those of their counterparts in other nations. The Polish regime heavily stressed the political mobilization efforts favored by Communist parties in power to force citizens, and especially youth, to acknowledge and, if possible, internalize the legitimacy of one-party rule in all aspects of national life. Periodic rebellions against Communist rule were attributed to the persistence of "outmoded customs, habits and traditions" that reflected failures in the Party's work of ideological socialization of the Polish people.[29]

Creation of a "unified educational front" ("*jednolity front wychowawczy*") of schools, youth organizations,* workplaces, sport and cultural groups, and the media was essential to "unite the entire younger generation for the construction of Socialism." Only in this way could the ideological and cultural level of the Polish people be raised, the close association of the rural population, in particular, with the Catholic Church be broken, and the (unprogressive) influence of families on their children be reduced.[30]

While the school was not expected to bear the whole burden of this task, a commission of experts advised in 1973 that it was in

---

*Braves (7–11), Pioneers (11–18), Rural Youth (16–21), Socialist Youth (15–28).

school that a foundation must be laid for later acceptance of the messages and the interpretation of reality provided by the Party. Only in this way could the most important goal of education be achieved: winning the younger generation for a commitment to socialism and a rejection of bourgeois values by developing a world-view with a rational and materialistic basis.[31]

Although these efforts at ideological indoctrination and political mobilization enjoyed some early successes in the postwar period, their effectiveness dropped sharply after 1956 and, in contrast with other nations under Communist control, "in Poland people who did not join any political organizations did not automatically deprive themselves of any chance of success in their careers and, in a broader sense, in their lives."[32]

Efforts to make education and socialization an instrument of state policy through a "unified educational front" were frustrated by the persistence of the religious and cultural loyalties of the Polish people.[33]

The relative ineffectiveness in Poland of the regime's efforts to achieve ideological hegemony was not reflected in leniency toward religious instruction in state schools. This had been explicitly pro-vided for in a 1950 agreement with the church,* but was abolished by decree in 1955 and partially restored, under a requirement of explicit written request of parents, with the thaw of 1956. Unlike what transpired in Czechoslovakia and Hungary, this requirement that parents request religious instruction did not have the anticipated chilling effect: "ninety-five percent of all parents duly put forward their children's names for the term beginning on January 15, 1957."

Buoyed by this support, the church issued a circular in August 1960 that "with astonishing self-assurance, turned the government's arguments against itself. If the objection to religious teaching in schools, the circular said, is that by being taught simultaneously with materialistic doctrine, confusion is created in the children's minds, the church fully understands this, for neither is it the church's

---

*". . .the government has no intention of limiting the present number of hours allotted to religious instruction. Programs of religious instruction will be prepared by school authorities in conjunction with the representatives of the episcopate, and schools will be equipped with the necessary textbooks. Teachers of religion, lay and clergy, will be treated on the same level [i.e., in pay and benefits] as teachers of other subjects." Text of the full agreement is provided by Stehle, 306–309.

ideal to teach in a school in which materialism is taught. . . . The ideal solution is the confessional school, in which all teachers and all teaching are inspired by the same spirit."[34]

In the face of such a fundamental challenge, the government abolished religious instruction in state schools by the 1961 school law, which declared definitively that schools were "secular" after the central committee of the Communist party adopted a resolution that such instruction "creates a foundation for fanaticism and intolerance."[35] After all, "the main organized antisocialist power in our country—a veritable center consolidating all the currents that are hostile to our system . . .—is the reactionary core of the Episcopate, acting on the strength of the institutional structure of the Roman Catholic Church."[36]

Cardinal Wyszyński and other bishops responded by directing parishes to start after-school catechetical centers and resisting attempts by the state to require registration and inspection to determine that nothing but religion was taught.[37] Although the church would cooperate with the government on matters benefiting the Polish people, Wyszyński announced several years later, it would not compromise on "the indispensable defence of religious life, Catholic education, Catholic culture, and the right of Catholic institutions to develop to meet the demands of the believers."[38] In the face of massive resistance, the government backed away from the attempt to oversee catechetical programs, and their numbers grew from 384 in 1960 to 15,551 in 1964 and 23,000 in 1990.[39]

Banishment of religious instruction from state schools where it could only be an uneasy guest proved to be a blessing for the church: "It not only increased the determination of Catholics to defend their educational role but also stimulated further the process of development of the Church as an autonomous organization with the society."[40] The experience of operating and supporting catechetical centers through local effort helps to explain the ability of parents and others to create hundreds of alternative schools after the political changes of 1989.

The effort of the regime, under the cover of its education reform program of 1973, to undermine catechetical programs by extending the school day so that children could not attend supplemental programs and by (unsuccessfully) demanding lists of children participating in the church's classes only increased popular alienation.

Cardinal Wyszyński counterattacked in a widely noted sermon in which he called for educational freedom and demanded that the regime's attempts to promote atheism be abandoned. In the wake of the workers' riots over food price increases in June 1976, the government sought to patch up its relationship with the church and, the next year, abandoned its efforts to interfere with catechetical programs.[41]

Minister for Religious Affairs Kąkol's statement that "we will never permit the religious upbringing of children" was whistling in the dark, and the election of Cardinal Wojtyla as pope in 1978 meant that the Catholic Church, "once excluded from the public life, was now in everyone's thoughts and people began to talk freely about their faith and their Pope."[42] Studies in three cities found that, among secondary students, 40–50 percent attended Sunday Mass "regularly," 55–72 percent said prayers "often," and 75–80 percent took part in some form of religious instruction.[43]

By the early 1980s, then, the Catholic Church was a major independent force in Polish society offering an alternative worldview to the Party's. With 7,600 parishes, 20,000 priests, 40,000 members of religious orders, and 89 newspapers,[44] the church was a massive presence creating space for the growth of both grassroots and national movements, and its deep concern for education based upon values other than those dominating state schools could not fail to have an influence on many parents, including those for whom Catholic teaching was not a primary concern. In alliance with dissident intellectuals and the independent trade-union movement, the church was able to resist successfully the totalitarian claims of the government to manage all aspects of Polish life and thus preserve a free space for the development of civil society.

During the 1980s, the teachers' branch of Solidarity (*Solidarność*) and underground publications like *Edukacja i Dialog* also kept an alternative vision of education alive. The "Polish school owes much to people who were active in the movement and also to those who were of the same mind but who may not have [had] enough courage to be active in underground structures but who taught following their own conscience. Due to those people, the effectiveness of [the] school as a tool of Communist constraint of the nation was never complete."[45] Although the July 1982 Plenum of the Communist party—after the temporary cursing of *Solidarność* and the imposition of martial law—made the political socialization of youth its primary concern,[46] the battle for the hearts and minds of Polish youth was essentially lost.

Podemski analyzed the discussion of the social crisis of the early 1980s in the Polish press and found a strong emphasis on the need for increased autonomy by social institutions of all kinds. The *Solidarność* weekly in particular stressed *podmiotowość*, defined as "sovereignty, being one's own subject, being an agent in every action one takes part in." While there was interest in vertical decentralization, through relegating decisionmaking authority to lower levels of administration, there was even more interest in horizontal decentralization, or restricting the power of central political institutions over one or more spheres of social life.[47]

Central to the alternative vision of education that evolved from these years of resistance was the formation of freely chosen communities of learning based upon local initiative. Allowing civic activity in lieu of state monopoly from the center is seen as fundamental to a revived Polish society in transition from "real socialism," a euphemism for the totalitarian society, to democracy. *Solidarność* strategist Brownisaw Geremek stressed in debate with a leading Western socialist that the foremost need of Polish society was to learn to exercise freedom after political culture was destroyed by the Communist regime, and this could happen only through a revival of local democracy.[48] Freedom of association was seen by the Polish reformers, as it was by de Tocqueville, as essential to democracy; for what purpose could association be more meaningful than for the education of children according to a shared vision?

As Katarzyna Skórzyńska, who was a parent activist and *Solidarność* supporter before she became part of the new team in the Ministry of National Education, put it, "Democracy in education . . . means primarily the possibility to choose." This freedom, she explains, implies that students will be able to choose their schools and teachers, and their programs and methods of study from among those available, and to influence how education is provided. For parents and teachers, it means the right "to found or choose school[s] in accordance with their own educational and political expectations" and to participate in school governance.[49]

One of the most devastating effects of 40 years of Communist rule on Polish society was the development of a mistrust of participation, a passivity toward conditions and events in the public arena. The system of so-called "democratic centralism," by concentrating all power and authority in the central organs of state and Party, led ordinary citizens to lay responsibility for solving every problem on the authorities and to refuse to take any initiatives without explicit direction.[50] "Withdrawal consists of staying as far away from the state as possible."[51] Families and face-to-face social circles (środowiska) became the focal point of life for most Poles, for whom neither work nor political participation offered rewards. "With the dissolution of autonomous groups [by the Communist regime] came a general suffocation of argument, specialization and initiative."[52]

That the privatization of life did not become as extreme in Poland as, for example, in Romania may be attributed to the aggressive role played by the Catholic Church and, in recent years, by the independent trade-union movement and dissident intellectuals, but these manifestations of civil society underlined the vacuum of public life. As a result, even after the fall of the Communist regime, "people are still accustomed to waiting for directions"; they must learn again to take responsibility for the issues that affect their lives. In particular, they must find a way to overcome the "lack of well-established local communities and local ties that the communists consciously destroyed."[53]

The extreme bureaucratization of the Polish educational system discouraged initiatives to identify and solve problems at the school level, as described in the first-hand accounts of institutional paralysis published regularly. Even when teachers and parents in state schools were able to agree on needed reforms, they encountered delays in obtaining approvals and flexibility in use of resources.[54] Insistence on a highly centralized state monopoly with "an extensive administrative apparatus" led to increased inefficiencies in education as in other social services.[55]

Kaminski sees certain advances to the protracted collapse of Communist rule in Poland, spread over a decade, in contrast with its sudden collapse in other nations of Central and Eastern Europe: "The disintegration of state socialism spread over a longer term allowed the emergence of alternative social arrangements outside the direct reach of the state that have already proved extremely useful in assuring political stability while state socialism is dismantled in Poland."[56]

Against this background, the willingness of thousands of parents and teachers to become involved in establishing and maintaining new independent schools must be seen as an encouraging sign of returning civil society.

> On July 15, 1987 at my house Marek Zieliński . . . my wife and myself began to discuss how good it would be at least to break the monopoly of the communists in education. Marek said, "Well, do it!" And that is how it started. . . . One of the first people I talked to about it was Andrzej Witwicki. Then, among my friends, another dozen or so people were willing to join in. . . . Then we talked to many research workers and activists. Professor Szaniawski almost hugged me saying, "That is exactly my idea, Sir! I had been thinking about the same thing for several months." I answered, "So it is our mutual idea."[57]

Thus Wojciech Starzyński, an intense and bearded veterinary surgeon from Warsaw, describes the grassroots initiative that became Poland's nationwide Civic Educational Association (CEA) [*Społeczne Towarzystwo Oświatowe*], the sponsor of 105 of the 207 independent schools set up before the end of 1990.

In December 1987, 23 individuals signed the petition to city authorities in Warsaw for legal registration of the CEA as an association so that it could sponsor nonstate schools under Polish law. The reasons given were the critical condition of Polish education, the shortage of well-qualified teachers as a result of the low status of the profession and the lack of a personalized approach to the educational process. No claim was made in this initial petition for state support for the efforts of the proposed association. Nevertheless, the petition for registration was rejected by the city in March 1988 on the grounds that other organizations were already seeking to improve Polish schools, a decision sustained by the Ministry of Internal Affairs in May 1988 on the grounds that collecting tuition fees (as CEA proposed) was in conflict with the principle of free education.[58]

Andrzej Witwicki, a robotics engineer by profession and the first CEA secretary general, wrote later that they were "openly claiming the right of parents to choose their child's school, with the right to establish new schools included. It was all consistent with Polish law but hardly anyone believed they would be able to practice their rights." As a sign of the changes occurring in Polish institutional life, however, the CEA was successful, on appeal, in obtaining a ruling on December 29, 1988, permitting its registration as an officially recognized organization.[59]

The CEA has described itself as

> an organization of all those who are interested in developing alternative forms of education in Poland . . . . Our aim is a socially open Polish system of education which would provide a free choice of education patterns for parents and children.
>
> The creation of the Civic Educational Association was inspired by people who are distressed with the condition of the uniform educational system supervised by the state administration, by all those who do not want to accept the hopeless stagnation and deterioration of this system, and who are aware of responsibility for the future of their children.[60]

The impetus behind the CEA had nothing to do with church/state conflicts nor with a desire to reestablish an explicitly religious system of schooling in Poland. While the Catholic press was friendly toward the organization's efforts, church officials took no public position. Nor, although leaders were active in *Solidarność*, did the CEA consider itself part of the opposition to Communist rule in Poland.[61] They sought to work through legal channels to confront the incapacity of the state education system to reform itself and to provide effective alternative schooling.

> The system of education in Poland is inefficient because of the monopoly of state bureaucracy. It is now evident that the decline of learning as well as teaching standards is due to a process of permanent degradation of Polish schools. Schools in Poland cannot provide adequate conditions for a proper development of Polish youth. Programs of far-reaching reform and improvement of this system have often been formulated, but they have never been successfully implemented. We no longer believe in such pledges. We are interested in the immediate future of our children, and for that reason we cannot and will not accept the degradation of our schools.

The CEA was convinced that education could be improved for all Polish children only through creating alternative examples of excellence.

Aware of the limitations of the present system of free schooling we are prepared to meet the cost of our educational projects ourselves, through widespread social participation—even in a period of acute economic crisis. We believe that for many parents a good education of their children is a fundamental need, and can encourage them to undertake extra effort.

The CEA intends to establish various educational institutions in order to provide the best learning conditions for children, as well as good teaching conditions for teachers. We want schools to develop personality, encourage creativity and love of knowledge. We are not putting forward any revolutionary solutions. The principles we advocate are: small groups of pupils, well qualified teachers, close interpersonal relations between children and their tutors, development of creative abilities, encouragement of self-education, attention to health and physical development, respect for pupils so that they can grow up in an atmosphere of security, acceptance and enjoyment.

The CEA does not advocate a [single] clearly-defined model of education. Its final form ought to depend on many factors, including the abilities of the children, the wishes and demands of the parents, and pedagogic ideas of the various experiments based on creative approaches to the processes of teaching and learning.

Our criticism of the present state of education does not indicate our rejection of the existing school systems. We would like to work to improve it through our civic activity; it seems obvious that public involvement will help to develop the whole educational system in Poland, and to change the position of children as well as teachers within it.

But the founders were convinced that the state system could not be reformed without a healthy dose of competition and example.

The state educational system has been criticized for many years. We have decided that the time has come to abandon useless discussions and complaints and to break the state monopoly of education through public activity, aimed at seeking new, alternative solutions.

New educational institutions, founded and supervised by parents and teachers, must be established in the near future to stimulate quick and efficient development of the educational system in Poland. We have to guarantee modern learning conditions, as well as good education for the greatest number of children.

Although parents active in the CEA declared their willingness to raise the funds for new schools themselves (see above), they also made a claim on a share of the public funds provided for education. Their goals of smaller classes and more professional compensation for teachers made alternative schools expensive despite the lack of overhead.

> A system of grants and scholarships must be provided to support the new educational institutions, and we are convinced that we can count on the support of the whole Polish society in our attempts to stimulate widespread civic activity aimed at securing a happy [future?] for our youth.

The CEA, some 8,000 members by mid 1990, was the largest but not the only group working to reform Polish education through mobilizing parents and teachers for real reforms; at least 20 others were active by that point in starting independent schools and seeking to influence state schools.[62] The number continued to grow; a year later, there were 15 more organizations, though the CEA continued to play the leading role as it attempted to adjust to the evolving political situation.

The adjustment included having to learn how to function as part of the educational establishment rather than as a protest movement. Relations between the central office and local chapters—often established by a handful of parents whose energies then became totally absorbed in starting and supporting a school for their own children— raised delicate problems for an organization committed to decentralization.[63]

This issue was discussed heatedly at a "summit meeting" in April 1991 for CEA activists from across Poland. Some proposed that the organization become a federation of essentially autonomous regional groups, to avoid falling into the overcentralization that had been characteristic of the Communist system, and objected to a regulation adopted in January placing local groups and their schools under the general oversight of the nationwide association. Others stressed that local groups were not yet strong enough to stand on their own and that the support of the central organization was still essential. The

latter position prevailed, with the result that the local school commit-
tees have a purely advisory function, though a strong one.[64]

What has been happening in Poland is an awakening of the civil
society that sociologist Melosik reports is a chief casualty of 40
years of Communist rule.[65] Establishing and supporting independent
schools, rather than fighting with the bureaucracy to make an impact
upon state schools, seems to have mobilized a substantial portion
of the Polish middle class to organize concrete local activities.

There is at least some indication that these new energies will be
directed to reforming the public education system as well, with
independent schools adapting teaching methods to the strengths
and needs of each pupil, and overcoming conflicts between the
values presented by the school and those in the society and/or the
family. State schools could become more like the new independent
schools if the role of the bureaucracy is reduced to securing and
overseeing educational funding.[66]

Considerable resistance to such reforms exists particularly to the
increased differentiation of schools. Much of the resistance, predictably, comes from socialists—well ensconced among educators and
bureaucrats, as in other countries—who continue to seek a society
in which schooling will be an instrument of the state to perfect society
by molding the rising generation. Thus an article that appeared in
April 1988 as the petition for official recognition of the CEA aroused
widespread controversy, and gave three reasons for preserving the
state's monopoly on education: it (1) permitted indoctrination of
students in the system of values considered fundamental by the
state, (2) ensured that human resources would be used effectively
for the national economy, and (3) encouraged social mobility. Similarly, a secondary school principal wrote, "I am an out-and-out
Communist, a Party member for the past 20 years, and the very idea
of private schools makes me upset. . . . In our political system there
is no place for private schools. It would be contradictory to the
achievements of socialism and the constitutional right to education."[67] On the other hand, Rostowski points out that public attitudes
toward private-sector activity were growing less hostile during the
last years of Communist rule.[68]

There have also been concerns that many children will be disad-
vantaged by changes benefiting only the children of parents able to
afford tuition. An article appearing in March 1988 predicted that

approval of the CEA would result in groups of well-to-do parents luring the best teachers away from the state schools with promises of smaller class sizes and higher pay, so that "the State schools will deteriorate even more. Many active parents and grandparents, who nowadays still think about working on improving the whole educational system, will turn their backs on the problem."[69]

Of 112 articles in the Polish press about the CEA during 1988 and January 1989, 57 were generally positive in tone and 31 generally negative, while the balance were neutral. The positive articles emphasized most often the poor condition of state schools and the stress that many students experienced from crowded classrooms and an overburdened curriculum. State schools were described as unresponsive to parents; one elementary school in Warsaw was reported to have a sign, "No trespassing in the school corridors by parents." Independent schools, in contrast, could be a "peaceful, safe, friendly, freely chosen alternative to the State schools [which are] based on compulsion." What was wrong, they asked, with parents seeking to create optimal conditions for their children?[70]

> Parents want to have a say in issues associated with the conditions in which their children get their education. They would like to be assured that their children will not be mistreated physically or mentally at school. That a teacher or a maintenance person will not raise his/her voice at the child, that the child will not cry because somebody pushed him in an overcrowded lunchroom and he spilled his soup on the floor. That the child will not give up going to the restroom because the restrooms are dirty. And finally that the child will not be beaten up by the stronger students.[71]

Precisely because such conditions may exist in state schools, opponents of the CEA insisted, the creation of alternative schools "can only become a new open wound on the sick body of our educational system." What kind of equality was it, Starzyński replied, if everyone had the same but it was inadequate for all?[72] The CEA insists that it is committed to creating independent schools that are "public" in the sense of not being limited to the children of the affluent, though financial pressures are making this increasingly difficult, given the present level of public subsidy.

The State Surrenders Its Monopoly

In Poland, the post-Communist government has responded positively to new initiatives to provide schooling outside the government system; indeed, the openness of the Ministry of National Education to educational alternatives has been unusual by any standard, East or West.

The education portfolio was one of those taken by *Solidarność* in the historic coalition government formed in August/September 1989. Education Minister Samsonwicz appointed Katarzyna Skórzyńska to head a new office charged with promoting innovations within the state system and with overseeing nonstate schools.

The 1950 "modus vivendi" agreement between the government and Cardinal Wyszyński provided that "schools run by the Church will be able to enjoy the rights of state schools on the general principles prescribed by appropriate laws and regulations issued by the education authorities,"[73] but only ten Catholic secondary schools (eight of them boarding schools for girls run by religious orders) were able to maintain their existence. The Polish Constitution adopted in 1952 did not guarantee educational freedom; regulations adopted by the ministry on February 26, 1965, provided for approval of schools outside the state system, but the ministry's officials made this exceptionally difficult. Only recognized local organizations that professed socialist ideology were considered eligible.[74]

In June 1988, while the CEA was still trying to negotiate a way through the approval process so that it could sponsor nonstate schools, an individual, Anna Jezioma of Krakow, petitioned the ministry for permission to open an independent elementary school. The petition was refused, but she appealed the decision to the High Administrative Court with the support of a number of organizations, including the CEA. On February 24, 1989, her right to open an independent school was sustained by the court; the ice was beginning to break up.[75]

With the radical political changes later that year, the ministry established on August 25, 1989, new provisions for subsidizing from the state budget kindergarten and other educational programs run by the Catholic Church.

The new team that came to the Ministry of National Education in late 1989 resolved to use the existing provision for approval of nongovernment schools to respond to the growing parent-initiated demand and stimulate new initiatives by teachers. They broadly publicized their willingness to approve applications without endless bureaucratic hassles. Response was overwhelming. "Between April and July 1990, 2 or 3 non-state schools appeared every day in various parts of the country. They appeared primarily in big cities. But not only there. Such schools came to exist also in smaller towns and even in villages. Fortunately, towards the end of the year they multiplied at a more moderate speed. Otherwise we would soon have more private schools than the United States."[76]

Rather than seeing as rivals the CEA and 36 other organizations that—by the end of the 1990–91 school year—had established non-state schools, the ministry has worked closely with them as a source of energy and vision for the reform of the state system as well. As a ministry official has put it, "The transformation of the state educational system will be slower and less efficacious if this system will not have to compete with the newly emerging system of non-state education. Today, one can point out concrete examples which prove that well functioning non-state schools have a positive influence upon the nearby state schools. The state schools are under the necessity of introducing innovations, the parent-teacher-student relations must be changed at these schools."[77]

In addition to approving nonstate schools, the same office in the Ministry of National Education was given authority to approve innovations within public schools. Although such approval had been possible under the Communist regime as well, "the rules of approval were different and they did not stimulate deep changes in the educational system." Under the new rules, issued in November 1989, 244 applications for waivers of requirements were submitted during the first year, of which 198 were approved and implemented for the 1990–91 school year. The innovations had to do with such matters as establishing new elective courses, integrating several school subjects, grouping pupils in different ways (with the approval of their parents), and (in almost half the cases) assessing achievement differently. Although most proposals were initiated by teachers, two-thirds of the schools proposing innovations included a role for parents in selecting teachers. The widespread interest in experimentation is indicated by the fact that proposals were submitted from 84 percent of the provinces in Poland.[78]

The Ministry of National Education issued a report in December 1989 that outlined a number of measures taken to transform the state educational system from an instrument of Communist indoctrination to a democratically oriented and more decentralized model.

For example, a ministerial directive that had prescribed school practices had been replaced by one that gave more stress to human rights—though, as one critic pointed out, the revisers had failed to remove such statements as "the Polish schoolteacher is an employee of a socialist state." Measures had been taken to increase the involvement of parents and students in making decisions, though the same critic noted that evidence was missing that this had had real effects to date.[79]

The next step in the support of educational alternatives was the decision on February 26, 1990, to subsidize non-Church organizations (such as the CEA) that run schools. Subsidies were to be granted for partial costs in accordance with government regulations for schools not administered by the state. The subsidy, which is financed from the central budget, amounts to 50 percent of the current average cost of education of pupils in state schools of the same type in the same area. Educational costs include all current expenditures for school maintenance, staff salaries and benefits, and materials.[80]

Since one of the primary reasons for setting up independent schools has been a desire for smaller classes, the pupil-teacher ratio averages half that of state schools. Thus, the public subsidy really amounts to about 25 percent of costs.

Meanwhile, the effort to improve state schools engaged the efforts of many of the same reformers. Incompetent and time-serving bureaucrats were replaced, and the new administration moved vigorously to find regional superintendents capable of pushing educational reform—though some complained that the new superintendents were surrounded by the same Communist bureaucrats who continued to resist real change.[81]

The Ministry of National Education's system of school inspectors was abolished at the end of May 1990, with full responsibility passing to these regional superintendents. With responsibility for allocating funds and overseeing schools, the superintendents could entrust kindergartens and other schools to independent groups in their communities to the extent that they saw fit, effective 1994. Thus the central approval of new independent schools carried out by the office in the Ministry of National Education would no longer be necessary.[82]*

*The director, Katarzyna Skórzyńska, became Poland's ambassador to Brazil, effective January 1992, and several of her former colleagues, including Jerzy Pomianowski, also left the Ministry for other positions.

This was part of a broader devolution of responsibility for education from the state to the local community. Local government (the commune) was empowered to take over operation of schools from the state, though it is not required to do so. The state's regional school superintendent "continues to oversee educational and pedagogical aspects of the operation of educational institutions taken over by the commune" at least for the present, because there are no local government officials with that assignment, but the commune hires teachers and principals.[83] A similar move toward institutional autonomy has been taking place in higher education.[84]

As a further measure to break up the centralized educational system, the Center for Professional Development of Teachers—with 1,800 employees, of whom 500 had doctorates, in 26 offices across the country—was replaced with organizations that will compete with each other for clients.[85] A well-informed observer of this process suggests, however, that such a structural change will not lead to real changes at the school and classroom levels so long as the personnel remain essentially the same. As a result, there is interest in starting a teacher training institution that would be wholly separate from the state system and would draw on—and serve—teachers in independent schools.[86]

In conjunction with the development of legislation for the overall reform of Polish education, the CEA proposed that attendance districts for state schools be abolished to permit pupils to go to any school, and that education in all schools be financed by vouchers. Such vouchers should cover at least the full cost of teacher salaries, to be supplemented by tax-deductible parent donations, funds raised by the schools, and support from municipalities, enterprises, and foundations.[87]

Drafts of the legislation included strong guarantees of educational freedom, consistent with the 1984 Resolution of the European Parliament and the various international documents on fundamental human rights, but the form in which this emerged from the ministry in the spring of 1991 would have made it more difficult to create new schools because of a reimposition of government requirements. These were justified by the ministry as necessary to ensure the comparability of the diplomas awarded, but the CEA was not convinced and argued that an imposed uniformity would be a step backward from the progress made in the previous two years.[88]

Particular objection was raised to the proposal that all schools be required to become uniform in educational methods and organizational structure. The position of the CEA as expressed by Starzyński in an interview was that, while elementary schools might be held to common standards set by the state, such relative uniformity should not be sought from secondary schools, which should be free to organize themselves in any way satisfactory to the teachers and parents.[89]

The present requirement is that independent schools "in order to issue diplomas and certificates equivalent to government schools' documents, must meet operational standards regarding [the] mandatory curriculum minimum [and] follow the same system of pupils' promotion and assessment as accepted in government schools."[90]

The tension between diversity at the school level and ensurance of essential common outcomes is, of course, fundamental to all systems permitting or encouraging parental choice of schools. As a senior official in the ministry put it, since schools are concerned with educating in the fullest sense, "they should be microworlds rather than cells of a macrostructure." On the other hand, schools do not exist in isolation, and the freedom of teachers to create and to find solutions is necessarily limited by the need for common societal standards. The delicate problem is to ensure that these common standards will be met while creating "empty spaces" that the people who work in each school (including parents) can fill according to their own ideas, so that the school will have its own distinctive identity.[91]

The education law enacted in September 1991 recognizes the "opportunity" to establish and operate schools, but retains the subsidy level from the education ministry at 50 percent of the expenditure of public schools; this was a considerable disappointment for the supporters of independent schooling.[92]

In Poland, then, perhaps uniquely among nations worldwide, the establishment of alternatives to the state system is being encouraged by the state itself, as part of an overall strategy for educational reform. Government officials see these schools as offering an opportunity to test new approaches to education and "observe the reactions of parents, teachers and pupils to the solutions in organization, curricula and finances, knowledge that could be used subsequently in state schools as well." In addition, "non-state schools introduce

Table 5.2
ENROLLMENT OF INDEPENDENT SCHOOLS, 1990–91

Enrollment	Number of Schools
under 20	14
20–39	34
40–59	40
60–79	42
80–99	20
100–149	15
150–199	2
200–250	6
over 250	3
total	176
enrollment	12,009
median	58

SOURCE: Analysis from data provided to the author by Jerzy Pomiarowski of the Ministry of National Education.

an element of competition that is indispensable in the functioning of any system."[93] The CEA reports that "a real educational mass movement" is developing that is having an effect on changing the state system as well as in creating alternative schools, and that state school staff are seeking the CEA's help in implementing changes.[94]

The Shape of Alternative Schooling

Poland's more than 200 new independent schools vary greatly in focus and other characteristics, though most are small: of 176 independent schools on which 1990–91 enrollment data are available, only 26 enroll more than 100 pupils.

The small size of independent schools is explained by the fact that many are serving only the first year of elementary or secondary school, or both, intending to add grades each year. For example, the Zespol Szko Spoecznych in Tarnow reports that it now enrolls 12 elementary and 15 secondary pupils, though eventually it plans to offer 12 years of instruction.[95]

Another limit on size is that many independent schools are functioning in makeshift facilities. The Second Civic Elementary School in Warsaw, for example, functions in two nonadjacent rented rooms:

"their owners blackmail us by frequently raising the rent," the organizers report.[96] In addition, a number of the schools are deliberately
small so they can offer an alternative form of education, especially
for pupils who have experienced difficulty in the state schools.

Each school has gone through a process of self-definition, though
this has differed according to whether the initial impetus was from
parents dissatisfied with their local state school, or from teachers
seeking to provide a new form of education, or even, as in at least one
case, from a university professor with a clearly formulated theory of
learning. The sponsoring organizations vary also, from many that
operate a single school to the CEA, which sponsors (though it does
not control) more than 100.

Few of the schools are formally church affiliated, though many
consider themselves Catholic. About 20 of the 36 sponsoring organizations (though not the CEA, which is the largest) identify themselves as Catholic, but the energies of the Catholic hierarchy have
been devoted more to introducing optional religious instruction in
state schools than to founding a separate system of Catholic schools.

Making a distinction between secular and religious motivations
in the private initiatives creating these new schools is difficult in a
nation where the civil society is as diffusely Catholic as in Poland.
Consider the elementary school in Podkowa Leśna, sponsored by
the Catholic Intelligentsia Club, which also sponsors a school in
Gdynia. This school had its origins in a March 1988 meeting in the
John Paul II Library of the local parish church, organized by the
Parish Committee of Brotherhood Aid with representatives of the
CEA present to explain how to organize an independent school.

> Within less than a month, on April 29, a meeting was held
> in a private house, where 40 people had to fit in. The decision
> was reached: We will do it. Not everybody. Another month
> later 30 people enrolled their children in a new school which
> didn't yet exist.[97]

Problems arose when the club sought government approval to
establish the new school; the club's statute authorized it to carry out
"intellectual and moral activities" but this, the bureaucrats insisted,
had nothing to do with education! When the statute had been suit-
ably amended, the organizers turned to the parish church for space
for classes; though this would not be a "parochial school" in the

American sense, it was natural to turn to the institution that had for years provided part-time education to adults and children as an alternative to the indoctrination provided by state schools.

The parents and other organizers renovated and equipped four rooms to accommodate classes, even though they would be paying tuition: "For several dozen years people were yearning for the chance to take over state property. The parents were doing all this for their own children and so—indirectly—for themselves. Also, they were willing to work toward a sensible end, toward something which would not be wasted, was not just a 'collective action' or a spectacle."[98]

A description of this school stresses that "there are 10–15 children in each class. These children and their teachers should be less unhappy than pupils and teachers in state schools in classes of 40. They should be less tired, less nervous, less collectivized, less stupefied. These children will be brought up according to Christian principles. . . . The teachers, used to crowds of noisy children, are suddenly astonished to find that, within a few days, they know so much about each child that they can work with every one individually. Although they are working according to the state curriculum for elementary schools they will soon have to work out new methods of . . . teaching, not known by a system that must cope with mass instruction. . . . The parents scrutinize their work very carefully, waiting impatiently for results."[99]

The parents who established the First Civic Elementary School in Krakow describe their goals, which could be used by any alternative schools in the United States, in very different terms: to create "a school to which our kids will go with joy, where the pupil's individuality will be respected and his talents developed, where he will not be suppressed by *ex cathedra* authority but convinced to a proper kind of behavior."

The parents go on to strike a distinctively Polish note, reflecting a nation that has been under almost continuous foreign domination for more than two centuries, when they say that they will create a school "where a pupil will be taught not only to speak, write and read in Polish but where he will also be taught to think 'Polish' which shall mean 'human,' wisely, justly, bravely but thoughtfully, where he will learn solidarity in a group, and tolerance for dissimilarity."[100]

The Second Civic Elementary School in Warsaw was started by a group of parents in a new housing development where the state school was running overcrowded classes in triple shifts until eight o'clock at night to accommodate 3,000 pupils in a school built for 800. Apart from size, the parents describe their school as differing from the state school in its willingness to work with and fully integrate pupils with various kinds of special educational needs. "The working conditions, that is the small groups (12–15 children), the truly familial atmosphere, the individual attention on the part of the teacher give these children the opportunity for entirely normal development." The school also provides after-school enrichment of a sort not available in a barren housing development on the outskirts of the city: art and music, gymnastics and swimming, and voluntary religion classes. Parents organize two meals a day at the school for the children.[101]

An independent elementary school in Szczecin was initiated by a psychologist who encouraged the parent of one of his patients to work to create a school that would meet her needs. With others, they organized a branch of the CEA, decided upon a tuition rate that would make the school accessible to all social groups, and began to recruit teachers oriented to a child-centered approach. The school took as its goal to "train both intellects and other areas of spirituality, including transcendental values, self-awareness, and self-knowledge." Soon the school was operating in borrowed space with two kindergartens, two first grades, one second grade, and one third grade, each with about 16 pupils. The oldest pupils had the greatest difficulties, as a result of three years in a state school, according to the psychologist. "Acute headaches, hyperactivity, aggressiveness toward teachers—these were leftovers from state schools." So the school stresses creating a safe environment within which individual attention is provided to each child, where children "will be eager to learn and participate, free from excessive stress and inhibition, seeking partnership with adults."[102]

But all does not go smoothly in the independent schools. In this one, a tired teacher complained to a visitor that "after three months of work she could say that the teacher bore all the burdens. The civic school was to differ from a state school. But this was not as simple as it sounded. Nobody taught teachers at college how to establish a partnership-type of relationship with the children. . . .

The teachers are carrying the burden of experimentation. They are under the constant scrutiny of the parents."[103] Parents had very different expectations, as well; some expected an elitist model of education, while others were most concerned about structure and discipline.[104] The mother of a child in another new independent school described her frustration over the failure of parents, teachers, and administrators to productively discuss how to resolve issues arising in the school.[105]

Reports from another independent school were more positive about the involvement of parents, which included not only monthly meetings to discuss school issues but also practical assistance in meeting the school's needs. Students in this secondary school were said to work much harder than those in state schools because they did not want their parents to have to pay for them to repeat a grade.[106]

Teachers and parents have worked together to devise new types of schools that would not have been possible within the state system. These vary from progressive to highly traditional education. For example, an "ecological school" was organized by a group of parents who had moved to the countryside to live together in an "ecological village." Their school operates without grade levels or divisions among academic disciplines; the curriculum is oriented not only toward a holistic approach to nature but also toward "exploration of the inner world" by each child.[107] Another school is based upon the belief that education should build upon the "natural knowledge" that children bring to school to ensure their active participation in learning, with teachers serving as advisers and sources of information desired by the pupils but not imposing their opinions.[108]

A far more academically oriented reworking of the curriculum is that implemented by the First Civic High School in Warsaw and adopted by a few other independent secondary schools. This school, sponsored by the University of Warsaw and directly overseen by the Ministry of National Education, is notable for its restructured curriculum, under which the traditional subjects are organized into four integrated blocks: humanities, natural sciences, math/physics, and psychological and physical development. Each of these was designed by leading experts working collaboratively with teachers. In addition to between 27 and 30 hours of required classes each week (including four hours of sports and recreation), pupils may take several hours a week of extra language or computer classes.[109]

Each day, pupils concentrate on one of the integrated blocks without interruptions, except for breaks called by the teacher.

A very different sort of education is provided by the secondary school, enrolling 41 youth, started by Aleksander Nalaskowski, a professor of psychology in the Pedagogical Institute of the Copernicus University of Torun. The author of a book on the development of creativity,[110] Nalaskowski founded an "Inventic" secondary school sponsored by a small furniture factory. The emphasis of this school is on the "teacher's inventiveness in his own development and thereby in the development of the students," and the "students' inventiveness in shaping their own lives and relations with others." Nalaskowski insists that "we simply should not admit the thought of uncreative education. . . . Is development without creativity possible?[111] "A traditional school," he writes, "teaches how to use and work for things which already exist. However, true creativity means looking for something that does not exist yet."[112]

This is not the place to attempt to do justice to Nalaskowski's thinking about and practice of pedagogy, but we should stress his concern for real cooperation between school and parents. Most teachers, he has observed, expect parents to facilitate the work of the school but not truly to cooperate. The educational system should permit a variety of forms of schools that differ in approach and in "spirituality." If parents are forced to send a child to a school that is exactly like every other school, they inevitably will not give it their wholehearted support and "their active participation is practically impossible." For education to become truly effective, schools "must be cozy, small and coherent to traditions of home. It is not home which should minister to school; after all home was first. And school shouldn't minister to home because [in that case] it doesn't introduce anything new. Home and school should develop mutually, evolve in a mutual contact. According to [Nalaskowski's] theory of inventiveness, the union of both environments should make [a] completely new [high] quality education."

Nalaskowski describes how a group of parents, all living in one block of apartments in a large housing development, came to him "anxious about their children who are either already or will be in the nearest future attached to wrong and giant school" located in the development. All these parents were, in one way or another, authorized to teach different subjects; together they decided to set up a school in which "each of the parents would fulfill definite tasks and functions" including teaching. "Immediately after taking the decision about founding [a] parental school, I witnessed a real eruption of didactic ideas. Some of them are excellent and new."[113]

As this description implies, most of the active parents in this school are themselves well educated; the same is true of the sponsoring group of the elementary school described above. "Intelligentsia" has the sense, in Eastern Europe, of individuals who work primarily with their minds rather than their hands, though not necessarily as high-status intellectuals. In general, as might indeed be expected given the efforts required, it is this group that places a high value on education that has been the impulse behind the new independent schools in Poland.

How are the independent schools supported? A teacher at one of the CEA-sponsored elementary schools in Warsaw supplied the following information in late 1990:

> The parents of the pupils had to pay a registration fee (about twice the monthly tuition fee) and now pay a monthly tuition fee. This fee is 400,000 z (about $40) which is nearly half the average monthly salary in Poland at the moment. Apart from this, parents are expected to participate, both financially and in the actual labor, in the adaptation to the school's needs of the building we received from the local authorities. The state contributes 92,000 z (about $9) per pupil per month. This sum is half the monthly cost of educating a child in a state school. The school and teachers do not pay any taxes. The local authorities let the school use the building rent-free and pay for the heating. The school has, so far, managed to make ends meet, but only just.
>
> The tuition fee is very high when compared with the average family income. This does not mean that the children in our school all come from relatively wealthy families. Many people are prepared to do without to be able to send their children to the school they think will make their children happy and give them a better chance to gain an education adequate to their needs and ambitions. Parents who have chosen our school consider it extremely important that their children should be taught in a small group (16 children in a class as compared with 25–40 in Warsaw state schools). The parents also expect the children to have regular foreign language lessons, instruction in the arts and a lot of physical exercise—the general opinion being that none of these

receive adequate attention in state schools. We hope that in the future the school will have funds to award scholarships to children from underprivileged families. The teachers' salaries are a little higher than the salaries they would receive in state schools and are roughly equal to the average monthly salary in Poland.[114]

Another new independent high school in Warsaw organizes its program around environmental themes, "to prepare its students regardless of their future profession to become ecologically responsible." The school frequently takes extensive field trips to places of ecological devastation as well as to beautiful state parks.[115]

There are a few educational initiatives influenced by such "new age" worldviews as that of Rudolf Steiner or of Transcendental meditation,[116] but they represent a much smaller share of the independent sector than in Romania or East Germany. Some independent schools are operated by Roman Catholic teaching orders—there is, for example, a new Catholic boarding school for boys in Siedlce,[117] while most are Catholic in at least a general sense.*

The main attention of the church hierarchy, however, has not been devoted to establishing confessional schools but to reintroducing Catholic religious instruction into the curriculum of state schools. This priority was determined at the bishops' conference in April–May 1990, and was urged as a response to the crisis afflicting Polish schools and society and a means for schools to teach the national tradition.[118]

Sociological research 20 years ago found strong support for religious instruction among both rural (97.5 percent) and urban (75.5 percent) respondents;[119] its provision outside of the state school and thus as an expression of an alternative value system may have been healthier for Christian nurture than the rather routine religious instruction in many Western European state schools. Nevertheless, the church made optional Catholic instruction a major demand after the democratization that began in 1989.

---

*"There is hardly any political party or organized public group that would not identify its activities with Catholicism and with the Church. Crosses, religious pictures and other Church symbols are prominently displayed in schools, offices, public buildings, and factories. Major public ceremonies usually revolve around religious services" (Weydenthal, 16).

Minister of Education Samsonowicz issued instructions in June 1990, without parliamentary debate, to begin optional religious instruction in all state elementary and secondary schools in September of that year; nationwide polls in May 1990 and March 1991 found better than two-to-one support from respondents, though there are indications of growing resistance to attempts by the church to shape public policies. Some have expressed outrage at the opposition of the Catholic hierarchy to providing alternative religious instruction for the appreciable numbers of Protestant or Orthodox children in some schools.[120]

Others suggested that it was not in the interest of a vital religious life in Poland for religious instruction to be imposed upon students as an ordinary school subject, one that in many cases would be taught inadequately. Opposition seems to be centered in the intelligentsia, of whom only 25 percent supported religious instruction in schools in the May 1990 poll, contrasted with 74 percent of workers and 80 percent of farmers.[121]

On the other hand, there are those intellectuals who believe that

> we will not get rid of intolerance by excluding religious instruction from schools, or by excluding religion from our lives. It is impossible to eliminate intolerance through the process of homogenization; this will not work. . . . Current educational system accustomed us to doublethink, hypocrisy and the attitude of a slave with a face for every occasion. That is why many of us are afraid of stating our beliefs openly and clearly. . . . We are afraid of everything independent, different, and because of that we are trying to blend everything in, make everything uniform. Elimination of religion in schools does not remove sources of potential intolerance . . . . School has to become the place where ideas and values of European civilization are shaped. It has to happen very soon.[122]

It is not yet clear, in fact, precisely what role the Catholic church will take in the further development of the Polish educational system. During the two decades of Polish independence between the two world wars, the church was by no means an advocate of educational diversity. Though frustrated in its efforts to gain overall control of education, the church succeeded in persuading the government to require religious instruction and participation by all pupils, including Jews, in Catholic religious observances in state schools.[123]

Undoubtedly, the primary contribution of the Catholic Church to educational freedom in Poland has been its long-term efforts to keep civil society alive and resistant to state hegemony. The bishops appear determined to continue this role during the transition to democracy, and have insisted that the new constitution affirm the rights "of individuals and of human and civic communities," with particular reference to the sanctity of life (that is, opposing abortion) and to "the right of parents to ensure that their children are brought up in accordance with the parent's religious convictions."[124]*

Whether the church will be an advocate of real educational diversity, however, remains to be seen; perhaps Adam Michnik, a leader of the democratic "secular left," is correct in charging that the church "learned how to defend itself against communism, but it has not yet learned, because it had no time to learn, how to exist in a democratic state."[125]

According to Nobel Prize-winning author Czeslaw Milosz, the Catholic "Church achieved an unusually high moral position in Poland both during the war and afterward, during the forty-five-year period of atheistic regimes that tried to erase the boundary between good and evil by introducing chaos into language. The Church continually issued reminders about basic values, and thereby defended the simplest and truest distinctions." He sees real dangers, however, in the effort to use the power of the State and its educational system to advance Catholic teaching and warns that "a hollowing-out of religion from the inside will take place, and in a couple of decades Poland will become a country as little Christian as England or France, with a strong dose of anti-clericalism, the passionate intensity of which will be proportionate to the power of the clergy and its program for a theocratic state."[126]

Independent and State Schools

The number of independent schools has continued to grow each year. Whereas during the 1989–90 school year there were only 23, the number increased to nearly 200 in 1990–91 and to about 430 in 1991–92.

The Ministry of National Education commissioned an extensive research study of the perceived characteristics of a sample of 10

*Western media attention, characteristically, has focused on reporting negative responses to the church's position on the abortion issue.

elementary and 10 secondary independent schools and their clientele, in comparison with those of a sample of state schools in the same (largely urban) communities.[127] One of the issues studied was whether the clientele of independent schools differed significantly from that of state schools. The study found that, at the elementary level in particular, the fathers of pupils in independent schools are in higher status occupations than those of pupils in state schools.

It would appear that this may have less to do with income than with the sphere within which fathers work, since independent schools are used more by fathers in "new class" occupations that involve manipulating ideas than by those whose work involves manipulating things: the children of "engineers, designers, management personnel of plants and factories" are not overrepresented in independent schools.

On the other hand, "the largest differences occur in cases of such professions as doctors (the percentage of their children at [independent secondary] schools is 3 times as large as at state schools), scientific workers and university teachers (also almost 3 times as large)." Nevertheless, "parents with higher education predominate" in the new Polish independent schools.[128] Whether these are "elite" schools would therefore depend upon whether that is defined by the education or by the income of parents: Polish state schoolteachers were at that time paid about two-thirds of the salaries of bus drivers and other skilled workers.

The profile of pupils in independent schools has implications for these schools, since children and youth with strong backgrounds and family support are easier to teach: "this creates far-reaching possibilities of constructive cooperation of teachers, parents and youth itself around a goal."[129]

The significance of family background is seen very clearly in comparing the level of education attained by mothers of pupils in state and in independent schools, especially at the elementary level; the mothers of children in independent schools have, on average, far more education than mothers of children in state schools. At the secondary level, the contrast is reduced, since working-class children (despite the former regime's rhetoric of commitment to eliminating social class distinctions) are less likely to pass the examinations required for admission to both state and independent secondary schools.[130]

Table 5.3
PARENTS OF CHILDREN IN POLISH SCHOOLS, 1991

Characteristic	Elementary		Secondary	
	State	Independent	State	Independent
Father's occupation				
Professional/managerial	10.0%	34.8%	34.1%	46.2%
White collar	19.3	9.6	27.3	14.2
Skilled worker	42.4	9.6	19.4	6.6
Unskilled worker	7.2	0.5	1.2	0.5
Farmer	0.5	0.0	1.7	0.9
Private enterprise	20.6	45.5	16.4	31.6
Total respondents	389	198	422	212
Mother's education				
University	9.0%	41.3%	24.6%	37.9%
Vocational	5.1	17.5	9.3	20.1
Other	85.9	41.2	66.1	42.0
Total respondents	434	206	452	214

Table 5.4
CAR OWNERSHIP OF PARENTS OF CHILDREN IN POLISH SCHOOLS

	Elementary		Secondary	
	State	Independent	State	Independent
Do you have a car?				
Yes	54.2%	84.3%	70.4%	78.3%
No	45.8	15.7	29.6	21.7
Total respondents	419	204	449	217

These are the parents described by the first director of the CEA as "middle-budget intelligentsia, people with family traditions where education is treated as a priority value. Education is the basis of their existence so they want their children to have the same experience."[131] This fits the description, by the Ministry of National Education responsible for working with independent schools, of the founders of these schools as "mostly university graduates, whose ambition it was to set up very good schools that might be at the same time cultural centers in the given area."[132] All accounts speak of the high degree of parental involvement in creating these schools.

Table 5.5
FINANCIAL STATUS OF PARENTS OF CHILDREN IN POLISH SCHOOLS

	Elementary		Secondary	
	State	Independent	State	Independent
Wealth/can save money	23.5%	45.1%	27.3%	39.1%
Enough but no extra	50.2	48.5	58.6	53.0
Experiencing difficulty	25.8	6.4	14.1	7.4
Total respondents	422	204	447	217

The same parents whom oxen couldn't budge to join the Parents Committee [of the state schools], who hid beneath the benches at school meetings when classroom representatives had to be elected. They know that the [state] schools belonged to the Ministry, the local superintendent, the director, and that they were only a barely tolerated addition. Now they are becoming the masters of their schools. They must take care of them like they would take care of their own home, arrange everything, but also make all the decisions. And they feel it is worthwhile because the school serves their children. It is subordinated to their welfare and not to the plans, programs, and statistics of officials.[133]

Although most of the new independent schools were by no means created by or for the financial elite of Poland, the pupils are, almost by necessity, from families that are above average in income. Among pupils in elementary schools there is a clear contrast in material possessions (color television, VCR, car) between those in state schools and those in independent schools.

The contrast is not marked, however, between the possessions reported by parents of pupils in state and independent secondary schools, because of the selective nature of secondary education in Poland. That is, the enrollment in state secondary schools is itself skewed toward children of the middle class, despite efforts to give priority to the children of workers.

When asked directly about their level of prosperity, parents with children in independent schools were more likely to be prosperous and less likely to be in need, though the numbers who were just scraping by were equivalent in the two groups.

Table 5.6
REASONS PARENTS GIVE FOR CHOOSING INDEPENDENT SCHOOLS

	Parents of Children in Elementary		Parents of Children in Secondary	
	State Schools	Independent Schools	State Schools	Independent Schools
Small classes	17.2%	37.6%	17.1%	16.3%
Individual attention	16.5	24.8	10.8	10.9
Lack of stress	3.7	24.8	9.1	22.2
Bad experience in state school	0.7	23.8	1.2	9.5
Teaching Western languages	2.7	21.9	2.4	17.2
No double sessions	1.0	16.2	0.5	1.4
High level of instruction	37.4	12.4	36.5	28.5
Affluence of parents	29.7	0.0	24.8	0.0
Snobbery and ambition	17.0	0.0	20.0	0.0

Should we think of these, then, as selective schools, and their establishment as introducing social class differentiation into the Polish educational system? At one level, the answer is obvious: the independent schools do serve a disproportionate share of children whose parents are deeply concerned and effectively mobilized about education, and this seems likely to strengthen the education of these children. To a substantial extent, of course, these children have already had an advantage in the state system, since their parents have supported them at home and advocated for them at school, and most have presumably attended schools (based upon place of residence) with a low proportion of children from working-class families. In short, the creation of independent schools may widen existing gaps in educational outcomes.

On the other hand, it does not appear that the independent schools included in this study are serving simply as exclusive havens for the affluent, though some parents of children in state schools think so, as indicated by their responses when asked their opinions about why some parents choose independent schools instead.

There is a marked contrast between the reasons attributed to independent school parents by state school parents, and the reasons that independent school parents themselves give for their choice of school. The latter are far more likely to cite specific educational features of the school as the basis for their choice, while many state school parents see paying tuition to an independent school as a way of buying quality or social position, as a form of conspicuous consumption.

The perception that independent schools are elitist is undoubtedly reinforced by misinformation about tuition costs. Whereas parents with children in independent elementary schools report tuition fees averaging 277,500 z (roughly $28.00) a month, parents with children in state schools estimate independent school fees as 65 percent higher. At the secondary level the discrepancy is even greater—100 percent overestimation of tuition.

It is certainly true, however, that sending children to independent schools represents a considerable sacrifice for many parents. The fact that pupils are drawn disproportionately from families with above-average education (which does not always mean above-average income) reflects the high value these families place on education more than it does superior resources. One independent school stresses, "This is not a school for the rich, this is a school for the active," since all parents must take a turn on maintenance, supervision of the children, administration, provision of medical care, and other duties.[134]

When asked whether they would enroll their children in independent schools if they could afford the fees, 52.9 percent of parents of children in state elementary schools and 48.3 percent of parents of youth in state secondary schools said that they would. Asked directly whether independent schools were better than state schools, 47.6 percent of state elementary school parents said that they were, while only 13 percent insisted that state schools were better; similar results appeared at the secondary level.

Although independent schools were rated more highly by parents on a number of characteristics, the most salient had to do with the pupil-teacher relationship and the teacher-parent relationship in independent schools. Parents from both types of schools were concerned about learning conditions, which is not surprising given the overcrowding and dilapidation of the state schools and the makeshift facilities of most of the new independent schools.

Teachers and secondary students from state schools were less likely than parents with children in those schools to attribute the preference for independent schools to snobbery, showing off, or excessive ambition. Half of the teachers in elementary state schools, and 30 percent of those in secondary state schools, said that they would send their own children to an independent school. As for secondary pupils themselves, only 8.5 percent of those in state schools reported that they attended their schools "very willingly," contrasted with 46 percent of those attending independent schools.

A poll conducted among parents of pupils in State Elementary School #70 in Warsaw and their children asked them to describe the ideal school. In addition to the usual concern about replacing ineffective teachers, the poll found support for more diversity in the curriculum, even including supplemental classes for which parents would pay fees.[135]

Polish education is showing new signs of life because of these parent and teacher initiatives as the civil society, so long dominated and manipulated by Party and state, regenerates itself through grass-roots activity. Will the benefit of these initiatives accrue only to the children of the most sophisticated and affluent parents? Already there are signs of the emergence of elite schools, including a secondary school in Warsaw claiming—inaccurately—to be organized on the basis of the International Baccalaureate curriculum and charging tuition of around $200 a month, or twice the average salary. "The idea for the school," according to a British observer, "is simple, if depressing. Many parents assume that the future of their children lies outside Poland and want to equip them for success in the cut-throat West. As soon as Poland starts to lay down its first golf course (scheduled for June) golf will be put on the curriculum. Driving courses, with Western cars provided by the parents, are on the curriculum, as are socially indispensable ski and tennis lessons." Only 66 students were admitted to the first class, out of more than 400 who took the entrance exams.[136]

The failure of the new education statute, adopted in mid-1991, to provide funding to support the education of children in independent schools equivalent to that provided in state schools, has increased the likelihood that the vigorous independent sector will grow increasingly elitist as schools are forced to raise their tuition and other fees. This would be directly contrary to the intentions of the CEA and other groups seeking to reform Polish education. But for the CEA, the rapid collapse of the Communist regime has posed a new challenge: how to make a successful transition from the opposition to a part of a pluralistic political system—indeed, in the eyes of many, a privileged part.[137]

The CEA expresses commitment to transformation of the entire educational system, including government schools, even as most of its energies are absorbed in founding and maintaining independent schools with meager resources. In an interview the local CEA president in Szczecin made a point that the Ministry of National Education was funding teacher and parent training for government schools, and that parents with children in those schools could have a major effect on their quality.[138] Whether this is simply wishful thinking or a harbinger of widespread citizen involvement in the reform of state schools remains to be seen. Aleksander Nalaskowski warns that most teachers in state schools are capable only of working "as communist functionaries" receiving directions from above and predicts "a growing tendency to establish new schools and to put aside state schools as unreformable."[139]

Meanwhile, interest in alternative approaches to education continues to grow in Poland. As in Romania, the Waldorf pedagogy of Rudolf Steiner is being actively promoted by leaders in the Polish independent school movement and also by Western European specialists. A house has been obtained in Warsaw, and is being renovated into the first Waldorf school in Poland.[140] However, the Catholic dominance in Poland makes the Waldorf the 500th nonstate school to open, not the first as in Romania.

What are the themes that emerge from this overview of the developing educational freedom in Poland? One is very familiar to education reformers in the West: the conviction that real changes in educational practice must be initiated by those in schools in direct contact with children and their parents. This was the theme of the editorial in CEA's journal, warning against policies that would turn teachers once again into "a group of people managed from outside." Real innovation requires changing the entire system of the school, not merely a few elements, the editors insisted, and only those directly involved can accomplish that. Real education occurs when children see adults acting responsibly, making important decisions, and sharing in the process.[141]

Another is the critical importance of the stress in Poland on "a new concept of politics based on ethical values rather than a social or economic doctrine."[142] As we will see, a similar emphasis upon the political relevance of truth was central to the successful resistance to totalitarianism in Czechoslovakia as well. Can such concerns be set aside, now that political freedom has been achieved? Are they relevant only under an oppressive regime, or do they have something important to say to the reform of education, in particular, in Western democracies?

The revival of civil society in Poland is not yet complete; much passivity and cynicism remain, and the current economic crisis has caused difficulties unanticipated in 1988. Schools have suffered severely, and many teachers are demoralized by salaries well under those of industrial workers and by overcrowded and inadequate facilities. New programs that would have made a difference are in many cases abandoned. There are some signs, indeed, that the independent schools are feeling this pinch less severely because "they were never under the protection of the State. They had to struggle and organize everything for themselves."[143] Over the long term, it is schools in which teachers and parents and pupils struggle and organize everything for themselves that will be healthy and will teach lessons that go beyond the formal curriculum.

References

Many of the materials used for this study were summarized or translated for the author by Magorzata Radziszewska-Hedderick ("MR-H"); I am grateful for the help and good judgment.

1. Alexander Tomsky, "Poland's Church on the Road to Gdansk," *Religion in Communist Lands* 9, nos. 1–2 (Spring 1981): 28.

2. Suzanne Oster, "Familie und junge Generation in Polen," in *Bildung und Erziehung in Osteuropa im 20. Jahrhundert* ed. Oskar Anweiler (Berlin: Berlin Verlag, 1982), p. 187; Jan Jerschina, "The Catholic Church, the Community State and the Polish People," in *Polish Paradoxes*, ed. Stanislaw Gomulka and Antony Polonsky (London: Routledge, 1990), p. 78.

3. Ludwik Dembinski, "The Catholics and Politics in Poland," in *Gierek's Poland*, ed. Adam Bromke and John W. Strong (New York: Praeger, 1973), p. 177.

4. Jacques Rupnik, "Dissent in Poland, 1968–78: The End of Revisionism and the Rebirth of the Civil Society," in *Opposition in Eastern Europe*, ed. Rudolf L. Tokes (Baltimore: Johns Hopkins University Press, 1979), p. 61.

5. Richard F. Staar, *Poland 1944–62: The Sovietization of a Captive People* (Baton Rouge: Louisiana State University Press, 1962), p. 266.

6. Maciej Pomian-Srzednicki, *Religious Change in Contemporary Poland: Secularization and Politics* (London: Routledge & Kegan Paul, 1982), p. 59.

7. Anna Sawisz, " 'Nowa Socjologia oswiaty' a polski system edukacji (The 'new sociology of education' and the Polish educational system)" *Edukacja i Dialog*, September 1989, pp. 12–28; summarized for the author by MR-H.

8. Katarzyna Skórzyńska, "Legal/Financial Aspects of the Educational System Not Administered by the State in Poland" (Warsaw: Ministerswo Edukacji Narodowej, 1990), p.1.

9. Tadeusz Jaroszewski, quoted in *Religious Change in Contemporary Poland*, p. 49.

10. Wladysaw Bienkowski, quoted in Hansjakob Stehle, *The Independent Satellite: Society and Politics in Poland Since 1945* (New York: Praeger, 1965), p. 68.

11. Stehle, p. 74.

12. Staar, pp. 266–69.

13. Katarzyna Skórzyńska, Lecture in São Paulo, Brazil, typescript July 1989.

14. Jan Kopycinski, "Szkola spoleczna—droga do demokracji (Independent school—way toward democracy) *Edukacja i Dialog*, June 1990, pp. 2–7; summarized for the author by MR-H.

15. Zbyszko Melosik, "Poland in the 1990s: The Role of Education in Creating a Participatory Society," *Social Education*, March 1991, p. 191.

16. Sawisz, p. 23.

17. Ibid., p. 14.

18. Skórzyńska, Lecture in São Paulo.

19. Maria Hirszowicz, "The Polish Intelligentsia in a Crisis-Ridden Society," in *Polish Paradoxes*, 1990, p. 151.

20. Pomian-Srzednicki, p. 60.

21. Staar, p. 244.

22. Bogdan Szajkowski, *Next to God . . . Poland: Politics and Religion in Contemporary Poland* (New York: St. Martin's Press, 1983), p. 16.

23. Ray Taras, *Ideology in a Socialist State: Poland 1956–1983* (Cambridge: Cambridge University Press, 1984), p. 95.

24. Tomsky, p. 33.

25. Pomian-Srzednicki, p. 124.

26. Stanislaw Staron, "The State and the Church," in *Gierek's Poland*, p. 159n.

27. Research cited in Wadysaw Piwowarski, "Polish Catholicism as an Expression of National Identity," in *The Polish Dilemma: Views from Within*, ed. Lawrence S. Graham and Maria K. Ciechocinska (Boulder, Colo.: Westview Press, 1987), pp. 85, 87.

28. Hirszowicz, p. 147.

29. Taras, p. 97.

30. Ilse Renate Wompel, "Schule und gesellschaftliche Umwelt: Das Konzept der offensen Schule in Polen," in *Erziehungs- und Sozialisationsprobleme in der Sowjetunion, der DDR und Polen* (Hannover, Germany: Hermann Schroedel Verlag, 1978), pp. 213, 228.

31. Janusz J. Tomiak, "Die Determinanten der Bildungspolitik und die theoretischen Grundlagen der intergrierten Erziehungskonzeption in dem Bericht uber den Stand des Bildungswesens in der Volksrepublik Polen von 1973," in *Bildungsforschung und Bildungspolitik*, pp. 77–78.

32. Jerzy J. Wiatr, "The Party System, Involvement in Politics, and Political Leadership," in *The Polish Dilemma*, p. 22.

33. Oskar Anweiler, "Die 'entwickelte sozialistische Gesellschaft' als Lern- und Erziehungsgesellschaft," in *Erziehungs- und Sozialisationsprobleme*, p. 24.

34. Stehle, p. 91.

35. Staar, p. 251.

36. Jan Szydlak, quoted in Rupnik, p. 88.

37. Tomsky, p. 32.

38. Cardinal Wyszyński quoted in Rupnik, p. 87.

39. Stehle, pp. 95, 100; Ewelina Lawecka, "Za i przeciw religii w szkole (For and against religion in school)," *Edukacja i Dialog*, July–August 1990, p. 15.

40. Szajkowski, p. 20.

41. Ibid., p. 38.

42. Tomsky, pp. 36, 38.

43. Piwowarski, p. 91.

44. Taras, p. 226.

45. Skórzyńska, Lecture in São Paulo.

46. Taras, p. 231.

47. Krzysztof Podemski, "The Nature of Society and Social Conflict as Depicted in the Polish Press in 1981," in *The Reemergence of Civil Society in Eastern Europe and the Soviet Union*, ed. Zbigniew Rau (Boulder, Colo.: Westview Press, 1991), pp. 70, 67.

48. "Soares-Geremek: notre Europe," *L'Express*, April 6, 1990, p. 54.

49. Skórzyńska, Lecture in São Paulo.

50. Janusz Reykowski, "Sociopsychological Aspects of the Polish Crisis," *The Polish Dilemma*, p. 183; the same point was made by Deputy Minister of Education (and former Solidarność leader) Wiktor Kulerski in an interview published by *Education Week*, April 4, 1990.

51. Bartlomiej Kaminski, *The Collapse of State Socialism: The Case of Poland* (Princeton, N.J.: Princeton University Press, 1991), p. 166.

52. Mira Marody, "Contradictions in the Subconscious of the Poles," in *Polish Paradoxes*, pp. 240–41.

53. Melosik, pp. 192–93.

54. Teresa Bochwic, "Szkolny torcik (A school layer-cake)," *Edukacja i Dialog*, May 1990, pp. 3–6; Anna Paciorek, "Bez szarych klas (Without gray classrooms)," *Edukacja i Dialog*, June 1990, pp. 10–13; "(Sisyphean labors)," *Educational Review* 1 (December 1, 1990), p. 5, summarized for the author by MR-H.

55. Maria K. Ciechocińska, "Problems in the Development of Social Infrastructure in Poland," in *The Polish Dilemma*, pp. 161–62.

56. Kaminski, p. 12.

57. Bogdan Krawczyk, "Breaking the Monopoly" (Interview with Wojciech Starzyński), *Education and Dialogue*, December 1990, pp. 5–6.

58. Anna Sawisz, "Szkoa i Monopol. Powstanie Spoecznego towarzystwa Oświatowego (School and Monopoly: The Establishment of the Civic Educational Association)" in *studia nad Ruchami Spoleczynymi* 3, ed. Jolanty Supińskiej and Wojciencha Modzeiewskiego (Warsaw: University of Warsaw, 1990), pp. 6–10.

59. Andrzej Witwicki, "The Avalanche Has Started," *Education and Dialogue*, December 1990, p. 13; Sawisz, p. 10.

60. This and the following passages cited are from a *DECLARATION* of the Civic Education Association, accepted by the First General Meeting on January 22, 1989; English wording slightly revised.

61. Sawisz, pp. 1–56.

62. Interview with Katarzyna Skórzyńska reprinted in *Edukacja i Dialog*, June 1990, pp. 53–54; summarized for the author by MR-H.

63. A. W. [Andrzej Witwicki], "O ksztalt oświaty spolecznej (About the shape of civic education)" *Edukacja i Dialog*, January 1991, pp. 2–3; summarized for the author by MR-H.

64. Andrzej Wrede, "Skromnie, ale owocnie (Humble, but fruitful)" *Edukacja i Dialog*, March–April 1991, pp. 2–6; summarized for the author by MR-H.

65. Melosik, pp. 192–93.

66. Kopycinski, pp. 2–7.

67. K. Kruszewski and an unidentified principal, quoted in Sawisz, pp. 22–24.

68. Jacek Rostowski, "The decay of socialism and the growth of private enterprise in Poland," in *Polish Paradoxes*, p. 211.

69. Jan Zubelewicz, "Klasy elitarne w szkole podstawowej (Elitist classes in elementary schools)," *Edukacja i Dialog*, April 1990, pp. 20–26; summarized for the author by MR-H; A. Bieniak, quoted in Sawisz, p. 21.

70. Sawisz, pp. 19–20; summarized for the author by MR-H.

71. T. Stylinska, quoted in Sawisz, translated for the author by MR-H.

72. A reader's letter in *Gazeta Mlodych* (May 6, 1988) and interview with Starzyński.

73. Stehle, p. 307.

74. Beata Bugaj, "New Ideas of Education in Poland." Paper given at a conference in Oslo, November 1991, p. 3.

75. Anna Paciorek, "Those will survive who can fend for themselves," *Education and Dialogue*, December 1990, p. 10.

76. Jerzy Pomianowski. Presentation at the annual meeting, American Educational Research Association, Chicago, April 1991.

77. Ibid.

78. Ministry of Education, Committee on Innovations. Data from "Raport o innowacjach w sckolach państwowych w roku szkolnym 1990/1991 (Report on innovations in public schools for the school year 1990–91)"; summarized for the author by MR-H.

79. Anna Paciorek, "Oswiatowe saldo (Educational balance)," *Edukacja i Dialog*, April 1990, pp. 11–13; summarized for the author by MR-H.

80. Ibid.

81. Interview with Katarzyna Skórzyśnka, pp. 53–54; complaint from "(Clean-up in educational system in Radom)," *Education Review* 11 (December 1, 1990): 4; summarized for the author by MR-H.

82. Bogdan Krawczyk, "Interview with Jolanta Szpakowska," *Edukacja i Dialog* July–August 1990, pp. 11–12; summarized for the author by MR-H.

83. "Szkola samorzadowa—Prawna analiza obowiązków i uprawnień (Autonomous school—Legal analysis of its responsibilities and rights)," *Edukacja i Dialog*, December 1990, pp. 40–43; summarized for the author by MR-H.

84. Karen Sorensen, "Poland's 1990 Law on Higher Education: Departures, Debates and Dilemmas." Conference paper, Oslo, November 1991, p. 4.

85. Notices in *Edukacja i Dialog*, May 1990, pp. 55, 56; summarized by MR-H.

86. Katarzyna Skórzyńska, interview with the author, October 1991.

87. "(Dilemmas in education—attempts to find solutions)," *Rzeczpospolita*, March 16, 1992; summarized for the author by MR-H.

88. "Oświata kontrolowana? (Controlled education?)," *Gazeta Wyborcza*, April 25, 1991; summarized for the author by MR-H.

89. "Wolności dla szkoly (Freedom for school)," *Edukacja i Dialog*, May 1991, pp. 3–5; summarized for the author by MR-H.

90. Miroslaw Szymanski, letter to the author, November 20, 1992.

91. Bogdan Krawczyk, "Limits to School Independence: Interview with Deputy Minister of Education Anna Radziwill," *Education and Dialogue*, December 1990, pp. 18–20 (appeared originally in April 1990 *Edukacja i Dialog*).

92. Bogdan Krawczyk, "Edukacji—bilans dwuletni (Education—a summing-up after two years)"; summarized for the author by MR-H.

93. Interview with Katarzyna Skózyńska, 1990.

94. Witwicki, "Avalanche Has Started," p. 15.

95. Letter to the author, January 1991.

96. From an untitled document prepared (in French) by the school.

97. Julian Radziewicz, "Finding a Place for the Children," *Education and Dialogue*, December 1990, p. 7.

98. Ibid., p. 8.

99. Ibid., p. 9.

100. Jerzy Giza, letter to the author, October 20, 1990.

101. From an untitled document (in French) by the school.

102. Aleksandra Ciechanowicz-Sarata, "A School Which Does Not Terrify," *Education and Dialogue*, December 1990, p. 24; Robert Ryss, "Zerwać z belferstwem (To break away from school teaching)," *Edukacja i Dialog*, May 1990, pp. 11–13; summarized for the author by MR-H.

103. Ciechanowicz-Sarata, p. 25.

104. Ryss, p. 12.

105. Hanna Mierzejewska, "Zebranie (The meeting)," *Edukacja i Dialog*, May 1990, p. 15; summarized for the author by MR-H.

106. Hanna Mierzejewska, "Lekcja za kotara (Classes behind the curtain)," *Edukacja i Dialog*, May 1990, pp. 7–10; summarized for the author by MR-H.

107. Katarzyna Stemplewska-Żakowicz, "Koncepcja skoy ekologicznej (Mission of the ecological school)," *Edukacja i Dialog*, November 1990, pp. 36–40; summarized for the author by MR-H.

108. Marzena Otys, "Wiedza naturalna a naukowa (Natural versus scientific knowledge)," *Edukacja i Dialog*, August 1991, pp. 10–15; summarized for the author by MR-H.

109. "Curriculum of the First Civic High School in Warsaw," *Education and Dialogue*, December 1990, pp. 29–35.

110. *Spoeczne Uwarunkowania Tworczego Rozwoju Jednostki* (Social Preconditions for the Creative Development of the Individual) (Toruń, Poland: Uniwersytet Mikolaja Kopernika, 1989); see also the description by Wanda Koscia, "Elite Guinea-Pigs Line Up for a Mould-Breaking Experiment," *Times Educational Supplement*, July 21, 1989.

111. Aleksander Nalaskowski, "Inventic School," typescript, no date.

112. Aleksander Nalaskowski, "Towards the Inventic School," *Education Now* (UK) 7, (January/February 1990): 13.

113. Nalaskowski, "Inventic School."

114. Elżbieta Tomasińska, "The Financial Status of Primary School nr XV in Warsaw and Its Implications Pertaining to Parent Choice and the Teachers' Work," (Warsaw: no date; received by author December 1990).

115. "Program wychowania i edukacji ekologicznej (Curriculum for ecological education in the independent high school of the Wrocaw Educational Association)," *Edukacja i Dialog*, July–August 1990, pp. 51–53; summarized for the author by MR-H.

116. Tadeusz Doktor, "Ruchy parareligijne o motywach edukacyjnych (Parareligious movements with educational elements)," *Edukacja i Dialog*, June 1990, pp. 20–25; summarized for the author by MR-H.

117. "Speech of Father Ryszard Borkowski" at the Meeting of the European Catholic Education Committee, Dublin, May 1991; printed in *QIEC Bulletin* (Brussels) 118 (November–December 1991).

118. Lawecka, p. 15.

119. Research of H. Kubiak (1972), cited Pomian-Srzednicki, p. 126.

120. Jan B. de Weydenthal, "Catholic Bishops Call for Cooperation between Church and State," *Report on Eastern Europe* 2, no. 20 (May 17, 1991): 15–17; Vera Rich, " 'Intolerant' bishops may preach to empty seats," *Times Educational Supplement*, November 9, 1990.

121. Lawecka, p. 17.

122. Stanislaw Czachorowski, "Splasczenai: Rzecs o modelu oswiaty (Oversimplification: about the model of education)," *Poslaniec Warminski* 24, no. 9 (November 18, 1990); translated for the author by MR-H.

123. Edward D. Wynot, Jr., "Reluctant Bedfellows: The Catholic Church and the Polish State, 1918–1939," in *Marxism and Religion in Eastern Europe*, ed. Richard T. De George and James P. Scanlan (Dordrecht, the Netherlands: D. Reidel, 1976–89).

124. Weydenthal, p. 16.

125. Adam Michnik, "The Two Faces of Eastern Europe," trans. Anna Husarska, *New Republic*, November 12, 1990, p. 24.

126. Czeslaw Milosz, "A Theocratic State?" trans. Madeline G. Levine, *New Republic*, July 8, 1991, pp. 27–32.

127. *Szloly spoleczne na tle szkót panstwowych: Raport z badania ankietowego (Independent schools against the background of state schools: A report on survey research)* (Warsaw: Ministry of National Education, [Innovation and Independent School Department]). The study was directed by Zbigniew Sawinski and Marta Zahorska of the Institute of Sociology, University of Warsaw. The sponsor provided the author with a copy and a rough translation ("Public Schools in View of State Schools: A Report on Poll Studies") in April 1991. All figures that follow are from this extremely useful draft.

128. Ibid., part 2, p. 2.

129. Ibid., part 2, p. 5.

130. "Republik Polen," *Halbjahresbericht zur Bildungspolitik und Padagogischen Entwicklung in der DDR, der UdSSR, der VR Polen, der CSSR under der VR China* (Bochum, Germany: Ruhr-Universität, 1989), pp. 2, 79.

131. Witwicki, p. 14.

132. Interview with Katarzyna Skórzyńska, 1990, p. 4.

133. Witwicki, p. 14.

134. Anna Paciorek, "Marzenia o szkole idealnej (A dream about an ideal school)," *Edukacja i Dialog* (May 1990), pp. 15–19; summarized for the author by MR-H.

135. Paciorek, "Oswiatowe saldo," p. 12.

136. Roger Boyes, "Priestly Power Brings Pupils to Their Knees," *Times Educational Supplement*, March 1, 1991; Wojciech Dorosz, article in *Rzeczpospolita*, October 3, 1990, trans. in JPRS-EES, December 27, 1990.

137. Micha J. Kawecki, "Educational Changes in Poland" (Warsaw: Civil Educational Association, no date); A.W., "O ksztalt oświaty spolecznej (The shape of civic education)," *Edukacja i Dialog*, January 1991, pp. 2–3; summarized for the author by MR-H.

138. Ryss, p. 13.

139. Aleksander Nalaskowski, "The Revitalization of Polish Education," Lecture in Madrid, typescript, February 1991.

140. Bogdan Krawczyk, Letter to the author, May 27, 1992.

141. [Bogdan Krawczyk and Julian Radziewica], "Kilkanaście zdań (Few sentences)," *Edukacja i Dialog*, October 1990, p. 2; summarized for the author by MR-H.

142. Rupnik, p. 91.

143. Hanna Budzisz, "Sposob na kryzys (Dealing with the crisis)," *Edukacja i Dialog*, November 1991, pp. 8–11; summarized for the author by MR-H.

6. The Czech and Slovak Republics

"Communism was overthrown by life, by thought, by human dignity."

Václav Havel[1]

Two Nations with a Shared History

Any discussion of educational policy in Czechoslovakia* must come to terms with the differences between the Czech lands—Bohemia and Moravia—and Slovakia. These differences are rooted in very different historical experiences over a thousand years during which these regions "never experienced common administration, still less common self-government."[2]

The population of Czechoslovakia was made up almost exclusively of Czechs (64 percent in 1980) and Slovaks (31 percent in 1980), in contrast with the prewar situation, when Bohemia was 40 percent and Moravia 30 percent German with a large Polish minority as well. As a result, ethnic tensions were primarily interregional, between Slovaks and Czechs, though there have been ugly incidents of discrimination and violence against the Romany (Gypsy) minority.[3]

Bohemia, with strong communications to Germany and the West by the Elbe River, has participated in European cultural affairs since the Middle Ages: Prague's Charles University has been distinguished since its founding in 1348. Moravia (leading city: Brno) is a prosperous agricultural and industrial area stretching across the center of the country from Poland to Austria.

Slovakia (capital: Bratislava), more rural and cut off by difficult terrain, was long dominated by Hungary to the south and is poorly integrated with the two Czech regions. The Magyar (Hungarian)

*Until the end of 1992, officially the Czech and Slovak Federated Republic or Česko-Slovensko Federativní Republika. This account does not attempt to deal with the events associated with the breakup of Czechoslovakia, nor to predict the future development of the two educational systems.

invasion in the late ninth century separated what is now Slovakia from "Greater Moravia" and inaugurated 10 centuries of separate development as an integral part of Hungary, so that not even a province of that country was designated as Slovakia.

Czech (the predominant language in Bohemia and Moravia) and Slovak are mutually intelligible members of the West Slavic family of languages, of which the other prominent language is Polish. It is indicative of the extreme sensitivity of Slovaks about their distinctiveness within the Federation that the status of Slovak as a distinct language rather than a dialect of Czech was a major controversy in the 1930s. Language, in this case, "stood proxy for the character of the overall Slovak relationships to Czechs," raising the question, "how much of an independent identity could the Slovaks claim for themselves? Could their interests be subsumed under Czech interests? Did they speak the same language, linguistically, morally, or politically?"[4]

When Czechoslovakia was created in the wake of World War I out of relics of the Austrian and Hungarian portions of the Habsburg empire, "no successor state save Yugoslavia harbored so much national confusion. Most troublesome were the sizable German and Hungarian groupings, transformed overnight in 1918 from ruling nations to distrusted minorities."[5] But tensions already existed between the Czechs, who saw themselves as enlighteners and benefactors of their Slovak cousins, perceived as "a sort of Tatra Mountains [hillbilly] variant of the Czechs,"[6] and the emerging generation of Slovak leaders.

Under Habsburg rule, the Czech majority in Bohemia and Moravia was subject to German cultural and political domination that became more grievous as a Czech-speaking middle class emerged. "The political history of the Czech lands from 1620 to 1800 is largely written in German, so complete had been the defeat of the Czechs. . . . For many years only the peasants were truly Czech, but an economic upturn and consequent rise in population in the mid- to late-eighteenth century helped to revive a Czech middle class and weaken the German dominance of the towns and cities. . . . The new Czech middle class developed a strong interest in education and thus became the nucleus of a renascent national movement."[7]

The history of education in what became Czechoslovakia is justly celebrated, with the reformer Comenius and the Charles University in Prague its most celebrated landmarks. Less well known is the vitality of educational reform and experimentation during the brief life of Czechoslovakian democracy, between the world wars, building upon the major role played by schooling—and schoolteachers—in reviving Czech national awareness during the 19th century.[8]

Although they struggled with the cultural domination of German, the Czechs were allowed to provide education and to publish in their own language; the Slovaks, under Hungarian rule, were given little scope to develop their own forms of cultural expression above the level of peasant folkways. "The Hungarians were adamant: the minorities were to use the Magyar language or they were to be silent. This implacable stand was probably a consequence both of the fact that the Hungarians were a minority in their own country and of their relative insecurity with a recently revived language and culture."[9] It was exacerbated by Slovak support for the Habsburg monarchy when Hungary sought to break away, in 1848; the settlement of that controversy with creation of the Dual Monarchy in 1867 "in effect licensed Magyar control over their Slavic subjects," and all Slovak secondary schools were closed, along with other cultural institutions.[10]

Professional advancement under Hungarian rule required assimilation to Magyar culture as well as language, in contrast with the development of a Czech-speaking civil service and professional class in Bohemia and Moravia. As late as 1920, many Slovak respondents to the census "were still prone to offer regionally or religiously defined self-identifications to the census-takers" rather than to identify themselves as Slovak, and "even those who spoke Slovak at home were apt to have little written facility with the language."[11]

Slovakia remained a predominantly agricultural area under Hungarian rule and did not develop a nationalist intelligentsia until relatively late, but when such a group did emerge "Magyar [Hungarian] persecution from 1867 on increased national consciousness and stiffened the resolve of those who considered the Slovaks to be a separate entity from the Czechs."[12] Thus Hungarian cultural policies created an attitude among Slovaks that "nationalism was the touchstone for analyzing every ill."[13]

The Slovak nationalism and separatism of recent years, which has split the Federation apart, reflects the sensitivity of an ethnic group that has always been subordinate in a state dominated politically and culturally by another group, first the Hungarians and then the more numerous and politically and economically advanced Czechs within the republic established in 1918. If anything, this sense that Slovak distinctiveness must be guarded at all costs grew more rather than less insistent over the six decades of Czechoslovakia. Even in recent years, "whereas Czechs have always blamed the Communists for their ills, Slovaks tend to blame the Czechs."[14]

Although most Czechs are officially Catholic, the long identification of Catholicism with Austrian German domination has made them less enthusiastically so than the Slovaks, and there is a relatively high rate of secularization. "In the Czech lands, Catholic institutions symbolised the destruction of the nation and its forced incorporation into the Austrian Empire. The 're-catholization' carried out during the Counter-Reformation to root out the Hussite spirit, in which German-speaking Jesuits were notable for arranging auto-da-fes, made the church, in the popular mind, an instrument of foreigners."[15] It was only in 1781 that Catholicism ceased to be the only officially permitted religion in Bohemia and Moravia, and even then Protestants could build their churches only outside of community boundaries.[16]

It was in Prague, in 1968, that the foredoomed project of creating "communism with a human face" was crushed by East-bloc forces, dealing a fatal blow to communism in Europe as an ideology able to seduce the idealistic. This was not the first time that a renewal movement on Bohemian soil was destroyed by outside intervention: Bohemia became one of the cradles of Protestantism around 1400, when Jan Hus called for reforms to make the church more faithful to Scripture and his followers fought to maintain a measure of religious freedom.

Two centuries later, the devastating Thirty Years' War grew out of unsuccessful Bohemian Protestant resistance to the policies of the Austrian Habsburgs, who had ruled Bohemia since 1526; their forces were crushed by Catholic Germany in 1620. Many Czech Protestant leaders, including the celebrated educator Komensky (Comenius), emigrated to the West, while their churches reestablished themselves under more religiously tolerant Hungarian rule in Slovakia, where they continue to use Czech as a liturgical language. Under Austrian rule, "the combination of political and religious absolutism produced in the Czech people a tendency toward religious lassitude and a strong anti-clerical sentiment masked by a veneer of conformity."[17]

On the other hand, Hungarian religious toleration and even a measure of competition resulted in far more vital churches in Slovakia, both Catholic and Protestant, than in the Czech lands. In the 1980s, "51 percent of the Slovak population identified themselves as believers, in comparison with only 30 percent of the Czechs."[18]

In both the Czech lands and Slovakia, under Austrian and Hungarian rule, the "recognized" churches were "public corporations, supervised, supported, and protected by the state, enjoying full autonomy in internal matters." This arrangement continued after 1918 under the republic, though some anti-Catholic elite sentiment in Bohemia manifested itself in unsuccessful calls for eliminating state support of the churches.[19]

The situation of the Czech Catholic church under the postwar Communist regime is in many respects the mirror image of that of the Polish church. Whereas the latter is a primary expression of Polish national identity, the Czech church enjoys no such position, while the Catholic church in Slovakia, though more vital, has suffered from its identification with the wartime Nazi puppet regime of Msgr. Joseph Tiso. Thus in neither the Czech lands or Slovakia did the Catholic church or the smaller Protestant churches serve as such a dynamic alternative to the Communist party and the state as did the Catholic church in Poland. The development of elements of a civil society independent of and in opposition to the hegemony of the state has therefore, in Czechoslovakia, been more limited to urban intellectuals than was the case in Poland.

Even before the anti-religious campaigns of the Communist era, this reserve toward institutional Catholicism "was often translated into a hostile view of church participation in educational, cultural, and political affairs."[20] With the collapse of Austrian sovereignty in 1918, many Catholic clergy and laity joined the newly established "Czechoslovak church," while others became Protestant or unchurched.[21] The proportion of Catholics in the total population of Bohemia fell from 95.7 to 76.3 percent between 1910 and 1921.[22]

The 1920 constitution of the Czechoslovak republic made the supervision of education the exclusive responsibility of the state.[23] Confessional schools were permitted but not encouraged in the Czech lands, and they were subject to state regulation that included standards and policies for all levels of private as well as public schooling. Crucifixes were removed from public schools, causing much hard feeling in Slovakia toward the Czech-dominated republic.[24]

Only 32 private schools operated in Bohemia and Moravia in 1921, compared with 9,700 state schools. In Slovakia, by contrast, while there were only 26 private schools, there were also 2,386 confessional schools and only 797 state schools in 1921.[25] In addition to the predominant Catholic educational system, "many denominational schools were maintained by the 'accepted' Protestant churches.* The state was obligated [by a Hungarian law still in force in the successor state of Slovakia] to contribute to the maintenance of these schools."[26]

"The Soviet Union is our model" (Sovětský svaz náš vzor)

Postwar Communist rule in Czechoslovakia enjoyed more potential for popular support—38 percent of a free vote in 1946—than in other nations of Eastern Europe. This support was largely limited to the highly industrialized Czech lands, where Socialists and Communists together won a majority of the votes. In Slovakia, the majority was won by Christian Democrats.

In other nations of what became the Soviet bloc, "The Communist regimes were installed by the Red Army or emerged from the chaos of wartime resistance. In Czechoslovakia, a democratic regime of unquestioned legality was overthrown by the Communist party, aided by street demonstrations and the moral and political collapse of the 'bourgeois' parties."[27]

The Communist regime that consolidated its power in 1948 moved immediately to eliminate all possible competition for the loyalty of the people. The most widespread and dangerous influences of bourgeois ideology, Party secretary Novotný would say several years later, were "Bourgeois Nationalism, Social Democratism, Masarykism [that is, support for the liberal values represented by the former president], and religious obscurantism."[28] The first three could be attacked by eliminating competing elites, but the fourth also had deep roots among the people and in ramifying institutions.

---

*A Catholic source (Zubek, 131) claims that all elementary schools in Slovakia were in a sense confessional, since "elementary schools with the name of national schools remained only in the villages where both religions, Catholic and Lutheran, were about equal in numbers and the number of children was not enough to maintain two schools, Catholic and Lutheran."

The Czech and Slovak Republics

These institutions could not be allowed to continue their independent existence. As a Slovak critic of the regime wrote,

> The attitude of the Communist Party to religious societies is, as a matter of principle, immutably negative. . . . In actual practice the Party is more opportunist: it seeks to dominate those religious societies which let themselves be dominated, and at a propitious moment, to render harmless those which resist.[29]

The new regime suppressed the religious press and seized Catholic and other confessional schools. "Abuse of spiritual office for statements hostile to the People's Democratic system" was outlawed and, in 1949, the clergy were brought firmly under state control by the nationalization of all church property and endowments; henceforth, they would receive salaries directly from the state, limiting their capacity for independence. Meetings of clergy without prior government approval and publication of pastoral letters were forbidden. Opponents of the regime would not be allowed "to misuse religion and the Church for the dark game of reaction."[30] Indeed, Communist Party General Secretary Rudolf Slánský proclaimed that "the struggle against the reactionary clergy is the key sector in the battle against reaction today."[31]

As civil servants, priests and ministers were required to take an oath of loyalty to the government or be barred from exercising their ministry.[32] After an initial resistance to this and other measures that had its heroic moments, most—including six of the twelve Catholic bishops—took the oath, and the churches became in many respects instruments of the government's policies, both domestic and international.[33] Protestant theologian Josef Hromadka, indeed, became widely admired in progressive church circles in the West for his contention that there was no essential difference between communism and Christianity.* It should be noted, however, that Hromadka was repudiated by his denomination, and that seven Protestant ministers and one Catholic priest were among the courageous signers of "Charter 77," the 1977 protest that crystallized opposition to the Communist regime.[34]

---

*A phenomenon to which I can personally attest from my divinity school days in the early 1960s.

A State Office for Church Affairs was established in 1949 and given control over all church staff and financial matters, as well as "religious instruction in public schools, including the subject matter."[35] Among its powers were appointing and removing priests and ministers, and censoring the content of sermons.[36]

Special concern was expressed by Communist leaders about members and even officials of the Party who were still "captives of religious obscurantism" and needed to be helped "to free themselves from it and accept the Marxist-Leninist world outlook."[37] Despite official respect for religious freedom, in other words, there was a strong expectation that those in positions of any responsibility—which virtually required Party membership—would be atheists.

During the period of political liberalization, in 1968, the churches were given much more freedom, but there was another crackdown during the period of restoration of hard-line Communist domination on the Soviet model, or "normalization." This included the arrest of about a hundred clergy. After all, the Party insisted, "religion was reactionary and offered false guidance to man."[38]

Thus from its first days the Communist regime made the struggle against "the forces of reaction"—prominent among them, the churches—an absolute priority. The result of severe restrictions on the activities of the institutional churches was not, however, the withering away of religion but, at least to some extent, a revitalization of private belief and practice. Church attendance rose, by some accounts, in areas where the population had become largely disaffected from religious practice, with young people in particular attracted to "catacomb churches," illegal and clandestine services in apartments.[39] As the exiled Cardinal Beran said at Vatican II, "In my country, the Catholic Church seems to be expiating its mistakes and the sins committed in its name against religious liberty in times past," and thus gaining a new authenticity.[40]

The essence of the Stalinist regime in Czechoslovakia—its craving to subjugate minds as well as bodies—was expressed in the show trials of Slánský and his associates (most of them Jews) among the initial Communist leaders who were judged insufficiently subservient to Moscow. Nothing would satisfy the regime but the "voluntary" confessions of these erstwhile colleagues to a series of improbable charges.

Proclaiming the necessity of completing "the socialist revolution in the field of ideology and culture," without which "the construction of a socialist society is unthinkable," the Communist leaders sought to anchor education "fully on the foundations of Marxism-Leninism and . . . lead it decisively in the communist spirit."[41] As Minister of Information and Culture Václav Kopecký insisted, "Every citizen must be imbued with a new worldview—a new ideology, a new morality. The goal is to educate every citizen to thinking with all his energy and intensity of the realisation of Socialism; to the determination to defend it; to ardent love for the Soviet Union and Stalin. . . ."[42] As another Communist leader put it, the school "must become a powerful instrument of the socialistic, communist transformation of society and must rid itself quickly of the last [traces] that remain from the bourgeois school. . . . There must be firmness in keeping the Marxist-Leninist principles and in fighting the bourgeois remnants, especially superstitions and darkness. . . . Therefore our school must be deeply political."[43]

This required creation of a single state-dominated school system (private schools were prohibited in 1948) with a strong orientation toward ideological indoctrination. The structure of the system was changed to conform to the Soviet model in many respects by the Education Act of 1953, including reducing the number of years of compulsory schooling from nine to eight years. References in the earlier statute to "ideals of humanity," "national traditions," and "independent thinking" as goals of education were dropped in favor of the training of "new socialist citizens."[44]

Courses on Marxism-Leninism and the history of the Communist parties of the Soviet Union and of Czechoslovakia were compulsory.[45] Children should learn "boundless love for the Soviet Union, the protector of our freedom, independence and socialist development" and "limitless love for the Great Stalin who leads all the working people of the world toward the victory of communism."[46] Teaching about the Soviet Union was the primary objective of third-grade civics, according to a 1951 directive, and study of the Russian language was required from the fourth grade.[47] In Slovakia as recently as 1989, fifth graders were required to devote 4 out of 29 school periods a week to studying Russian, and the Russian requirement continued each year through secondary schooling.[48]

An official government publication in 1989 continued to stress that "Soviet pedagogics and organisation of the school system had

171

been at the cradle of the first legal measures and steps taken to build the new socialist school in our country. Also at present we have been drawing on the vast experience from the restructuring of the school system, education and instruction in the Soviet Union and other socialist countries."[49] This is in marked contrast to the prewar Czech and Slovak perception of Russia as being at a primitive level of development compared with their own westernized sophistication.

Subordination of schools to the political objectives of the state was relatively easy because years of Nazi rule in Bohemia and Moravia and of the Nazi puppet state in Slovakia had already destroyed much of their independence. All Catholic schools in Slovakia had been nationalized by the Tiso government, losing their independence though not their Catholic character; under the Communist regime, the latter was lost as well. "Parochial and private schools were abolished and a single public school was established in towns and villages."[50]

On the other hand, initial resistance on the part of secondary students—their schools were described in 1949 as "the hotbed of reaction"—may perhaps be explained by the earlier experience of the postwar generation of students, a generation that had "attended school during the [German] Protectorate and witnessed the re-education and the transformation of the education system by Naziism, the personnel changes in the teaching staffs, the substitution of textbooks, commanded celebrations, double-talk in teaching and examining, [and thus] recognized in the communist reforms characteristics it had seen in the era of the German occupants and therefore was not only immune to them, but revolted by them." This resistance "was to be stamped out by the joint influence of the teachers and of the textbooks supplemented by elimination of the students' leisure time and by tying them up in the uniform youth organization."[51]

Thus with the establishment of a state monopoly, the content of schooling was changed from the earliest grades, with the avowed intent "to educate pupils to become new citizens of our land, liberated from the last vestige of the old capitalistic morality; to enable boys and girls to enjoy great happiness in this Socialist and Communist epoch of our homeland."[52] The Communist state wanted "its children singing hymns about their happy lives, reciting verses about the Party and their love for the Soviet Union, learning by heart meaningless texts for their political education, and always ready to agree with the teacher's every word."[53]

The role of teachers in this process was essential, and any teacher who pretended to objectivity in presenting the subject matter (thus "fawning upon the bourgeois culture") would not be coddled by the authorities or permitted to be "apolitical and without any ideology."[54] A definitive Communist handbook for teachers stressed that if their

> work has the correct ideological and political foundations and is organized systematically, it can fully prevail over the reactionary influences of the family and any other nonscholastic factor [such as the churches]. . . . The teacher's work in educating the growing generation has a militant character: the teachers, to whom belongs the main role in education in the spirit of socialism and communism, must lead the fight not only for the creation of a new, higher socialist morality of the young generation, but also against the survivals which manifest themselves in the minds of the children and youth through the influence of adults. That is why the . . . Communist Party of Czechoslovakia directed us to fight for the soul of the youth against those who would like to lead it away from the road to socialism.[55]

To ensure that every teacher was sufficiently committed to this mission, the Communist party organization in each school had a direct responsibility, overlapping with that of the school administration, for the work of staff and the ideological education of students. Loyal "communists—even if the youngest members of the staffs—controlled the work of the principal as well as of their colleagues."[56] To this end, they were "instructed to gather information from selected communist students in the Pioneer and Youth Union organizations who bring them 'a view from below' regarding the teacher's work."[57]

As the handbook for teachers makes clear, the influence of parents was seen as potentially negative. The journal of the Communist Youth Movement pointed out, "Our youth often lives under the impact of the contradictions between the influences of the school and the family. It wavers, and lets itself be influenced by the mystic and solemn character of church services."[58] A Party representative at the annual Teachers' Conference in 1950 threatened those who would seek "in any way to distort the souls of our children, whether they be reactionary parents or teachers."[59]

To counteract family and church influences, then, each school was expected to have an Association of Parents and Friends of the School; the "friends" would be local Communist militants whose role included persuading parents not to interfere with the ideological indoctrination of their children, lest this harm their future prospects for education and employment.[60]

At the end of secondary education, the all-important examinations that gave access to further study must, according to decrees issued by the Ministry of Education, place equal emphasis upon the student's knowledge and his or her "political maturity and ideological dependability."[61] The latter would be judged by how actively the student had joined in the propaganda activities of the Communist youth organization; such evidence of commitment, the ministry ruled, should excuse "minor gaps and slight insufficiencies in his erudition."[62]

The Czech government in its 1960 Education Act followed the lead of the Soviet Union by flirting with the idea that boarding schools would be the ideal way to create future citizens with no loyalties other than to state and Party.[63]

Religious instruction, seen as supporting "the moral educational aims of the school," had been a regular and indeed (unless parents requested an exemption) compulsory part of the curriculum in state schools under the prewar democratic regime. Each of the seven recognized denominations had a right to such instruction for its children at public expense; the existence of separate schools for each of the ethnic minority groups facilitated the provision of religious instruction, since Ruthenians were generally Orthodox, Hungarians Calvinist or Catholic, and Germans Lutheran or Catholic.[64]

The Communist regime did not drive religious instruction out of state schools, as eventually occurred in Poland, but perhaps more astutely placed it under the control of school officials. Religious instruction was provided as a supplemental course on school premises after school hours, though only to children under 12, at the request of both parents in writing.[65] Such requests, naturally, were discouraged and could lead to later denial of the upper levels of secondary education. Appointment of teachers for these classes was completely in the hands of state officials, with the role of the churches limited to making suggestions; only those who had given evidence of their "higher political ability" could be appointed to teach religion.[66]

Zubek comments dryly that "few Catholic laymen felt the vocation to teach religion under communist supervision."[67]

While religious instruction was available, the school was also expected to stress "anti-religious education, i.e., the training of conscious and militant unbelievers," according to the president of the Slovak Academy of Sciences, and "should not be satisfied with making people indifferent to religion but should transform them . . . into militant atheists."[68] At the Ninth Party Congress in 1949 the education minister said, "There still exist among us remnants, actually old feudal remnants, of religious education. . . . We must endeavor to radicalize everything and to create a new man, a man truly communist."[69]

The Society for the Propagation of Political and Scientific Knowledge was set up in 1952 to lead the "struggle against religious obscurantism."[70] Children must learn to reject "all the remnants of bourgeois thinking and behavior" and especially "religious survivals and superstitions."[71]

During the period of liberalization in 1968, the churches were again given control of religious instruction, but state control was reasserted and intensified during the period of "normalization" after the Soviet Union in 1968 crushed the efforts of the Czechoslovak regime to liberalize to a limited extent.[72]

The ideological mission of schooling was also advanced with renewed vigor during normalization, coupled with concerted atheistic propaganda. The regime insisted on "introduction of a surfeit of ideology into even improbable subjects in the centrally controlled curriculum." This was necessary because, as one Party spokesman stated, "we have learned that there is no science without communist party-mindedness."[73] Kindergartners were to be taught such key concepts as "Lenin," "party," "Red Army," and "October Revolution," while the instruction of older children was permeated with political messages.[74]

Teachers were blamed for ineffective indoctrination because students were among the most enthusiastic supporters of reforms. Only one-fifth of secondary students, the regime complained, were leaving school having fully rejected religious belief.[75] The Czech Ministry of Education issued "Principles of Scientific-Atheist Education" to all schools, spelling out six aspects of religion against which teachers should struggle: "as an idealist look at the world, as an ethical set of directives, as ideology of the [bourgeoisie], as a component of man's emotional life, as a cult, and as an institution."[76]

Many teachers were removed from their positions or reassigned "in order to destroy any undesirable ideological bonds they may have established with their students."[77] "It was the duty of the educational authorities," wrote the Party's newspaper for educators, "to ensure that only teachers who brought up the children in a socialist spirit could stay in the profession."[78] After all, an official report pointed out as recently as 1984, "as a publicly political worker [the teacher] actively enforces the policy of the Czechoslovak Communist Party and is constantly active in the socio-political sphere." Teacher training stressed "ideologically political" themes in all subjects, throughout the course of study, including "history of international movement of working class and history of the Czechoslovak Communist Party, political economy, marxist philosophy and scientific communism. [The sequence] is finished with lectures and seminars on scientific atheism."[79]

All teachers were required to take an oath:

> I swear that I shall always work for the interest of the working class and implement the policy of the Czechoslovak Communist Party. ... I shall teach [the children] respect for the working class and the Czechoslovak Communist Party. I shall educate them in the spirit of the Marxist-Leninist *Weltanschauung*. ... I am aware of the consequences which would transpire [sic] for me from a failure to stand by this oath.[80]

Secondary schools and higher education institutions were instructed to deny admission to students whose class origins or parents' activities during the "thaw" might make them ideologically unreliable; no student should be admitted to the upper sections of secondary education (at age 15) without determining "the family's attitude to [the] political interest of the state."[81] In this way, anti-regime political activists could be punished and deterred from making trouble by the threat to their children, while the influence on schools of parents with alternate values was minimized.

As described retrospectively by a leading Czech education researcher, "The universal aim [was] to educate an increasing number of high-quality builders of the socialist society. They should be developed in an all-round and harmonious way; have a communist approach to work. ... Finally, they should be ready to defend selflessly the socialist homeland and the community of socialist countries."[82]

To accomplish the objective of molding a rising generation totally committed to the system and its goals, a strict centralization was imposed. "All types of schooling and all curricula were strictly governed by the party apparatus. Schools and local authorities had a very limited responsibility for education. Teachers had practically no space for their own initiative or experimentation. The same textbooks were obligatory for all pupils of a certain grade."[83] The organizers of a new independent school justified their effort by the "devastating" effect of the Communist system under which "all schools shared the same curriculum and inadequate textbooks; and, furthermore, teachers were chosen according to their loyalties and not according to their knowledge and abilities."[84]

This harnessing of the entire educational system to a political agenda was fundamental to all nations in which the Communist party became dominant. As an official publication put it in 1984, "The school system is an inseparable part of revolutionary changes that are carried out by the working class together with the other working people under the leadership of the Czechoslovak Communist Party." To this end, the school system must be uniform, with no room for a diversity of schools reflecting varied philosophies and approaches to education. The Czech and Slovak ministries of education established "the rules for the ideological and pedagogical management of schools."[85]

The mission of the school was frequently described as "forming a personality with a communist morality," a "class fighter," "a militant," "a collectivist." This required developing a hatred toward people living under capitalist systems and even toward the history of one's own nation before Communist rule. Schools were expected to foster "an absolute atheism and absolute intolerance to any religious thinking or feeling."[86]

Demand for Truth and Freedom

Among the charges brought by the "Charter 77" group against the Communist regime was the violation of the "International Covenant of Economic, Social and Cultural Rights," to which Czechoslovakia had agreed in 1976. "Countless young people are prevented from studying because of their own views or even their parents'.

Innumerable citizens live in fear of their own, or their children's right to education being withdrawn if they should ever speak up in accordance with their convictions."[87] Communist education was based upon the teaching of lies by schools but also the "voluntary" suppression of truth by parents. After all, as a Slovak critic wrote several decades ago, "the ideological corruption of the masses is the very foundation of the rule of the managers. . . . The Party concentrates its corruption efforts on those whose views are not crystalized or are in the process of crystalization: youth, especially children."[88]

The emphasis of Václav Havel on truth as an essential dimension of true freedom reflects the burden of the decades in which lying and blind obedience were fundamental principles of statecraft. "Our country is not flourishing," he told the Czech and Slovak people in his first major address as president in January 1990. "The enormous creative and spiritual potential of our nations is not being used sensibly." The economy and the educational system were a shambles; the environment was terribly polluted. "But all this is still not the main problem," he said. "The worst thing is that we live in a contaminated moral environment. We fell morally ill because we became used to saying something different from what we thought. We learned not to believe in anything, to ignore each other, to care only about ourselves.[89]

Historian Misha Glenny wrote,

> The moral devastation of which Czechs and Slovaks speak includes the development of obedience towards authority and the readiness to execute any task, however absurd, provided it has been requested by a superior. In this way the "normalizers" [under the Communist regime] were able to build upon the Habsburgian traditions of Czechoslovakia. . . . Although German-speaking and Jewish, Kafka's grotesque visions were inspired by Habsburgian Prague.[90]

Havel professed himself puzzled (in 1987) that "foreign journalists and Western visitors" seemed to find his emphasis upon truth to be "stuffy, moralistic and old-fashioned." For him and others living under totalitarian regimes, to the contrary, it was an essential step toward reclaiming their freedom.[91]

The motto of the Czechoslovak republic founded in 1918 was that of the Hussites five centuries earlier, "The Truth Prevails," and by all accounts it was through holding to a concern for truth that the opposition movement sustained itself under the pressure of deception and hypocrisy imposed by the Communist regime.

Deception and hypocrisy were learned in the schools, as Havel wrote in his celebrated "Letter to Dr. Gustáv Husák, General Secretary of the Czechoslovak Communist Party" (1975): "For fear of losing his job, the schoolteacher teaches things he does not believe; fearing for his future, the pupil repeats them after him."[92]

Prague teachers talked with a reporter after the "velvet revolution" of 1989. 'Jesus, it's an enormous relief,' said the principal. 'You can see it in the children; they were under enormous stress,' according to a teacher. 'They were exposed to daily lies. They heard one thing at home and were taught the opposite in school.' Teachers 'had to attend compulsory ideological lessons, given by the party members [among the faculty] for nonparty teachers.'[93]

According to many observers, one effect of the relentless barrage of ideological indoctrination, in school and out, was that "large segments of the public have developed immunity to official propaganda."[94] The state's very insistence upon a test of family political loyalties for admission to advanced secondary and higher education, one Czech critic of the regime pointed out, was an admission of "the powerlessness of its educational system to counteract parental influence in a child's upbringing."[95]

With the almost miraculous rebirth of political freedom in late 1989, Havel and others became concerned with how Czechs and Slovaks could be drawn out of their cynical withdrawal and into a broad-based effort to rebuild democratic institutions. While there might be, as Havel claimed, "enormous human, moral, and spiritual potential and civic culture that slumbered in our society under the enforced mask of apathy," the habits of the previous 40 years were difficult to change. Unlike the regime in Romania, which continued mass mobilization campaigns until the fall of Ceauşescu, the Communist regime in Czechoslovakia had been quite content to encourage citizens to "escape from the public sphere of activity" into the refuge of private preoccupations.[96]

In Poland, the intense organizational life of the Catholic church, including thousands of after-school catechism centers, had helped to sustain the civil society, the ability of people to work together outside the frameworks provided by the state. Such experience was not as widespread in Czechoslovakia, beyond the largely intellectual circles of those involved in the illegal political and cultural opposition. In those circles, however, the concept of a "parallel polis"—coined by Catholic philosopher Václav Benda in 1978—crystallized the idea of developing an entire cultural life over that imposed by the Communist authorities. In Benda's concept, this would include "an uncensored information system, popular music, unofficial education and scholarship, and the so-called second or black-market economy."[97]

While the story of the dissident cultural life that emerged has been told repeatedly since the "velvet revolution" of 1989, it is notable that Benda himself lamented in 1988 that "in one area we failed catastrophically: independent education. There were and still are various attempts to do something about it, but all of them have been marred by an excessive exclusivity (not only regarding the circle of participants, but chiefly in the form and content of the courses of study), considerable vulnerability to repressions, and a lack of clear-sighted, responsible generosity." This was a critical omission, because the greatest threat under communism, Benda wrote, was "a decline into barbarism, the abandonment of reason and learning, the loss of traditions and memory." To prevent such a catastrophe, "the aim of independent citizens' movements that try to create a parallel polis must be precisely the opposite: we must not be discouraged by previous failures, and we must consider the area of schooling and education as one of our main priorities."[98]

What could possibly be the significance of the inevitably small-scale results that could be achieved in alternative schooling and higher education, in the face of monopoly by the Party/state of the entire system of formal education? Benda insisted on the vulnerability of totalitarian systems in the face of such spontaneous developments in the civil society.

> Totalitarianism, concentrating all its efforts on this struggle for power, must always win. . . . There is no systematic doctrine capable of liquidating totalitarian power from within or of replacing it. That power, however, works consciously at the outer limits of its own possibilities: a single loose pebble can cause an avalanche: an accidental outburst of discontent in a factory, at a football match, in a village pub. The important thing is the chance factor: totalitarian power is capable of successfully blocking any apparent adversary, but it is almost helpless against its own subjects who foolishly

and infectiously start working to bring about in practice the
notion that they need not go on being mere subjects.[99]

His fellow dissident Milan Šimečka, while conceding that the civil
society was more highly developed in Poland or Hungary than in
Czechoslovakia, argued similarly that activities outside the apparatus of state control, with its pretensions to monopoly, had the potential for "creation of islands of plurality that may become a prefigura-
tion of a pluralistic society."[100] The parallel polis does so, another
dissident stressed, because it "establishes, or rather renews, relationships that, in return, give its members the dignity of participating
in decisions that concern the community, and in creating that community's structures."[101] Indeed, "the regeneration of our cultural
and intellectual life," a fourth dissident wrote, "is possible only in
the form of free initiatives undertaken by individuals and small
groups who are willing to sacrifice something in the interest of
higher aims and values, especially in the name of truth."[102]

Although, as Benda lamented, alternative schools for children did
not emerge formally as part of the dissident program of reviving
the civil society, a climate of thinking was created that stressed what
we would call "grassroots" efforts parallel with and in place of state-
controlled structures. It is thus not surprising that the recognition
of and support for nonstate schools figured in the programs of civic
and political groups after the fall of the Communist regime.

Perhaps the most explicit statement of such a program was by the
Slovak Christian Democrats. The Christian Democratic Movement
(KDH) seeks "to realize revival and prosperity of Slovakia upon the
values of Christianity . . . to create a spiritually healthy society, filled
with love and justice, prospering and living in a healthy life environment." It calls for "radical economic reform, which it has generally
understood and accepted as a program of strengthening freedom and
democracy and the transition of the economy to a market basis."[103]

Educational reform is important to the KDH, which seeks the
removal of ideological indoctrination from state schools, "the
renewal of church schools, and the advancement of moral instruction." The party does not seek to substitute Catholic for Marxist
teaching as a prescription for all pupils, but "recognizes the primacy
of the family in education and favors educational choice in accordance with different families' respective worldviews."[104]

The Christian Democratic election program of May 1990 called for fundamental changes in Slovakia's educational system, declaring (in an awkward translation):

> Our educational system passed through many reforms, whereby it was always one-sidedly ideologized and politically deformed.
>
> In view of this situation, the Christian Democratic Movement will encourage:
>
> —To renew, simultaneously with restoring the position of families in the society, the Christian instruction structures.
>
> —The instruction system in schools, safeguarding the possibility of choice according to the world-opinion orientation of the families.
>
> —The foundation of Christian pre-school institutions and schools according to the wishes of parents.
>
> —De-ideologization of the instruction in current pre-school institutions, where the parents cannot choose the [ideological content] of education. . . .
>
> —A system of cooperation between pedagogues and parents in forming the content of education and instruction in schools of all degrees. . . .
>
> —To develop, in the process of education, not only the intellectual, but also moral qualities of each individual.
>
> —To return the teachers and educators discriminated in the past [because of their disagreements with the Marxist content of schooling].
>
> —The renewal of ecclesiastic [denominational] schools.
>
> —To staff pedagogical places with believer teachers. . . .[105]

Laws and Policies Change, Free Schools Emerge

Even before the political events of November 1989, there was a growing realization among Czech and Slovak educators that the framework of laws and regulations within which their school functioned was based upon a "misunderstood uniformity" that failed to take into account the "disrespected diverse demands of pupils."[106]

Oldrich Botlik, an adviser to the Czech Ministry of Education, suggested that the problem of centralized uniformity began before the Communist takeover, with the establishment of national education systems as state monopolies before World War I and their subsequent employment by successive regimes. "Instead of creating a free educational market, the monarchies of the past formed a hierarchy of rigid institutions. The pupils (or their parents) and the teachers—potential buyers and sellers on the hypothetical educational market—never acquired the rights of free customers and independent suppliers. The disciplined centralization and uniformity of the public educational system was conceived in analogy to that of the army—then the dominant element of the public sector. This influence extended into the short democratic period after 1918 and needed cosmetic changes only in order to make the ideological pressures on teachers and pupils during the wartime period of Nazi control and during the postwar period possible; the repressive campaign after 1968 just completed the disaster."[107]

"As a result," Botlik argues, "the roles of pupils and teachers in the contemporary system can best be described in terms of a military unit in training, forced to obey, unconditionally, commands of unspecified origin and date which do not always make much sense. The commanding bureaucratic machinery produces a web of detailed regulations and constraints which have to be honored even though no one can remember their purpose. The condition is aggravated by the fact that bureaucratic supervision over the teachers' work is based on irrelevant criteria. The philosophy of the system allows these officials to perform their functions without any interest in understanding the real problems or in assisting the teachers to find the appropriate solutions. This chain-of-command has effectively frightened away just about all of the most talented potential teachers. And since the State claims an absolute monopoly over all education in the country, the qualified and committed individuals must abandon the educational system altogether so as to avoid the bitter frustration of bureaucracy. . . . In essence, the contemporary public educational system undermines the individual and creative nature of both learning and teaching and dramatically contradicts it. Like any other victory in the sphere of human conflicts, this victory of bureaucracy is a Pyrrhic one. The cost of its petty triumphs is a failing educational system."

The federal government and the Slovak and Czech governments elected in 1990 "made a vow to create conditions for the education system to return to the good traditions of Czech and Slovak education and at the same time to approximate education systems of nations with the highest economic and cultural levels." Among the reforms to which they were committed were decentralizing the rigid system of educational management, encouraging "independent and free thinking in schools," and creating "conditions for the establishment of private and church-run schools," while retaining the State's role as "guarantor to assure that every capable applicant is able to receive education in public schools which will remain the basis of the education system."[108]

Repeal of Article 4 of the constitution, which provided for the "leading role" of the Communist party, forced immediate changes in the teaching of civics and history. Until a new curriculum could be developed, marking was abolished in civics (the correct answers were no longer obvious!), and teaching of post-1918 history was temporarily suspended. Time previously devoted to the required study of Russian could be reallocated by schools to other subjects. Under the new education law amendments that came into effect in June 1990, "all ideological parts of teaching matter which supported the totalitarian regime were abolished," and elementary schools were to stress "patriotism, humanity and democracy." In secondary gymnasia, "the content of all subjects is being re-estimated with the aim to deideologize it, to reduce [the amount of] factual knowledge [required] and to update it. The educational aspects of the subject matter are being strengthened (democracy, active patriotism, humanity, charity, ethics, aesthetic feeling, ecological thinking, family education, survey of world religions, etc.)."[109]

Effective October 1 of the same year, private and church schools could be started, with the stipulation that the education provided be "equivalent to education obtained at other schools."[110] In addition, public schools were given the opportunity to select among several choices of compulsory and elective courses.

Religious instruction was not brought back into the regular curriculum, but headmasters in Slovakia were instructed to arrange convenient times when it could be provided by the local church to children whose parents requested it. In a significant change from practice under the Communist regime, "neither the headmaster nor any body of state administration will inspect it."[111]

With the collapse of the Communist party's monopolistic youth organizations, a variety of sponsors—church organizations, cooperative, and private associations—began to provide after-school activities of all kinds, reflecting a "plurality of views."[112]

The Parliament approved in January 1991 a "Document of Basic Human Rights and Freedoms" that guarantees in section 33 the right to establish independent schools. The procedure requires the person or organization seeking approval to operate such a school to prepare a description of its goals and approach. This may differ from the state schools as to curriculum, methods of teaching and learning, length of school day and year, and other aspects of organization, provided that the independent school will be equivalent to state schools in its standards. Once an independent school has been established, parents are free to choose it over the local state schools.[113]

Parents in larger communities may also exercise a certain amount of choice among state schools. At the elementary level, a few schools offer intensive instruction in foreign languages starting in the third grade. Others offer intensive math instruction starting in the fifth, and yet others offer intensive sports instruction, also starting in the fifth grade. At the secondary level, as elsewhere in Europe, there are choices related to career preparation.

As of September 1990, there were four independent secondary schools, two of them in the Czech republic and two in the Slovak republic, with a combined total of 322 pupils, but others were starting up during the school year or were planned for the next.[114] For example, there was an advertisement in the newspaper *Lidová Democracie* in March 1991 for pupils and teachers for an independent secondary school with a Christian character to open in the fall.

The independent school initiatives in Czechoslovakia appeared to be more academically elitist in their emphasis than most of those in Poland; some stress admissions standards, though leaders take care to point out that these schools also intend to meet the needs of pupils who have been experiencing difficulty in the state schools. As one put it, bluntly, "These schools base their activities on the principle that he or she who pays for his or her education should get more than the standard education offered by state schools."[115]

Considerable attention was attracted by the first independent secondary school, known by its initials as PORG, which opened in Prague in the fall of 1990. "We are mainly motivated," Principal Ondrej Steffl wrote, "by the fact that the education in our country was devastated by forty years of communist rule and we would like to contribute to its new development." The emphasis of the new school would be on new ways of organizing instruction and of relating to pupils.

There were 535 applications for 100 places in the first form (sixth grade), despite a tuition charge equivalent to about 2.5 months of an average salary.* Applicants were selected based on psychological tests and interviews, with particular stress on determining how motivated they were and how much family support they enjoyed. Ten teachers (some part time) were selected from two hundred who applied. The fact that the minister of education attended the formal opening of this school reflects the relatively favorable official attitude toward such new initiatives.[116]

The school's budget for 1990–91 included $20,000 from the tuition for 100 pupils, a state subsidy of $15,667, and private donations of $5,000; offsetting salary costs of $23,333, rent of $2,667, and other expenses up to a $40,667 balanced budget. The state subsidy corresponded to 70 percent of the support for pupils at a state secondary school, but represented only 38 percent of the expenditures of PORG in 1990–91.[117]

Five 45-minute classes were held each weekday and four on Saturday; state schools have no Saturday classes. English (taught by an American) was required for all eight years, along with another living foreign language for three years. "The pupils get acquainted with the fundamentals of European culture, with classical, Christian and Jewish sources of our contemporary culture and with biblical history."[118]

Changes took place in public schools as well. As the grasp of ideology was lifted from the classroom and pupils, teachers and parents demanded more school-level autonomy. Within weeks of the fall of the Communist regime, pupils and parents joined teachers in demonstrations calling for more school-level autonomy in curriculum and schedule. Elections were held to replace principals who alienated their colleagues by vigorous adherence to the party line; according to one report, 9 out of 10 were not reappointed. One told a Western reporter, "Education was always the issue people were most angry about. No one liked their children learning un-truths. I know; I am a mother too."[119]

In preparation for the first school year after the fall of the Communist regime, school authorities were faced with the challenge of providing millions of new school textbooks, especially for history, national literature, and civics, the most heavily politicized subjects.[120]

*This contrasts with average annual tuition at church schools in 1990, which was equivalent to about 2.5 weeks of the salary of a secretary, making them generally affordable.

Prospects for Fundamental Reform

"We shall change human nature in accordance with our needs," a leading Czech Communist intellectual and minister of education proclaimed after the war. "We shall not be satisfied with the innate gifts of man."[121] Convinced of the "makeability" of human nature, the Communist regime was confident that it could create a "new man" committed, without admixture of selfish individualism, to following the leadership of the Party in building the Communist future.[122]

If this program of creating a new humanity and thus a fundamentally different social reality could have succeeded anywhere in postwar Central and Eastern Europe, it was perhaps in the Czech lands, which "corresponded more closely than any other country in history to Marx's vision in which a mature proletariat would articulate its considered hostility to capitalism. . . . In relation to the size of the population, the CPCz was the largest and most influential Communist party outside the Soviet Union."[123] The sophistication of Bohemia's industrial base and work force could have led to a high degree of postwar prosperity and thus a satisfied citizenry, while the extensive secularization of the Czech population and relative lack of influence of its churches removed one of the main barriers to ideological as well as political hegemony by the state and the Communist party.

The project of molding a new humanity failed. Part of the failure must be attributed to the devastating effect of a socialist command economy on a nation that had been one of the most economically advanced in Europe before World War II. "While the [Communist Party] had spent four decades busily trying to persuade Czechs and Slovaks that they were heading steadily towards a Communist utopia, the Czechoslovak economy was marching with equal resolution backwards from tenth position in the world to around fortieth. According to some individual indicators, the jewel in the socialist community's crown now lies behind Nepal and Sri Lanka."[124]

As a result of the manifest failure of the regime to deliver on its economic and social promises, fewer and fewer Czechs outside the ruling apparat remained believers in communism—and relatively few Slovaks had ever been. "In 1948 there existed a much higher number of those who held a bona fide belief in the communist chimera of a humanitarian society free of conflict."[125] Forty years later, this illusion was unrevivable.

187

Despite four decades of indoctrination through schools and the media, the regime turned out to have had very little real support. As Havel predicted in 1975, "The system that seemed likely to reign unchanged, world without end, since nothing could call its power in question amid all those unanimous votes and elections, is shattered without warning. And, to our amazement, we find that everything was quite otherwise than we had thought."[126]

One sphere of society in which the socialist command system manifestly did not work was education. "Almost every parent, teacher, scientist, politician and employer," wrote Botlik, "agrees that the performance of the educational system is no longer tolerable. Unfortunately, most proposals for remedies do not address the surviving constraints that were imposed over two hundred years ago. Since the 'velvet revolution' some actors have been replaced, but in education the play remains the same as before. . . . Two phenomena are really painful: the drastic inefficiency of the system and the consequences of the system's hostility towards inventive and creative teachers who are sensitive to the learning needs of the children."[127]

If the problem with the education system is indeed so fundamental, and not simply a matter of mismanagement or lack of resources, then radical solutions are needed, measures that go well beyond those adopted to date by the governments. According to Botlik, the only solution is to abandon the present system of bureaucratic state control in favor of a system of vouchers, by which he means "*any* system in which the money from the State follows pupils."[128] "We could subsidize directly those individuals who seek education and not the educational institutions themselves. At the same time, we could release all of the constraints currently imposed on each school, thereby guaranteeing their relative autonomy, and leave the assessment of the teachers' competence up to the schools and their administrative bodies."[129]

The Czech Ministry of Education gave Botlik a grant to elaborate on his idea of an alternate system of financing education, working with Deputy Minister Jan Koucky to advance specific legislation to provide public funding to schools through a voucher mechanism, based upon the number of pupils selecting each school.[130] "The administrative procedure necessary to start and register a school" eligible to receive these vouchers "would be so simple and flexible that anybody interested in teaching could establish a new school based only on the demands of the population and the educational ideas which he or she seeks to promote. In the registration procedure the State would not require teacher certificates, since it is widely believed they very often guarantee exactly the opposite of what they claim. This flexible attitude should also be used as an incentive for outsiders to become teachers. Each school which exists now would be registered automatically. Absolutely all educational and administrative issues would be the responsibility of each registered school."[131]

Botlik argues that

> the difference between the proposed system and the existing directive "military" structure in education is similar to the difference between a market economy and a centralized planned economic system. Its influence on the behavior of people who participate in it and the evolution of a more competitive academic environment should be similar as well. Schools would be forced to compete for vouchers, since they would represent an important contribution to the school budget (supplemented by other resources available, not excluding the parents involved). . . . Changes in both the content and the methods of education would be motivated initially by the interests of the teachers. Then the parents would start to inquire about the options available and to compare their particular advantages and disadvantages. Some of them would decide to be involved directly in the education of their children, at least in the lower grades.

As a result, teaching—reestablished as a creative and highly exciting profession again—would attract a new kind of candidate. Educational research would be forced to cooperate more closely with particular teachers as well as with parents. The inhuman pedagogical/bureaucratic experiments conducted anonymously on whole generations of children would no longer be possible. And here is the most important result: bureaucratic involvement would be reduced, roughly speaking, to the monetary evaluation of the vouchers. Bureaucrats would no longer be able to pretend to have pedagogical expertise, and their influence would be paralyzed. An infrastructure would grow step by step, providing the schools as well as the parents and children with services of all kinds. Thus, over the next several decades we would witness the development of and experimentation with an altogether different network of publicly supported schools. Its functions will rely on local efforts and intelligence, not on directive control. These schools would employ very different means of achieving educational results.

> Public education organized in the traditional way has reached its limits and is facing a dead end. Since it cannot respect the individuality of the children or the changing nature of the world, it forces pupils to adhere to the uniformity and rigidity of the system. Teachers as well as children are prevented from independent creative work, which is the essence of any reasonable education. Instead of proposing any particular improvement within the existing framework, my proposal is to change the very philosophy of the system: to accept as a basic axiom the heterogeneous nature of educational needs, and the heterogeneous nature of the means which can be designed to satisfy them. Autonomy for individual schools is just a natural consequence. A system in which money follows students is one way to design a self-generating public educational system not hindered by government controls but advanced by the mutual needs, interests and concerns of teachers and students.[132]

The Slovak Ministry of Education, Youth and Sport issued a discussion paper in 1991 that boldly suggested that each school (including church schools) should have individual legal standing.[133] A subsequent proposal would encourage the development of alternative types of secondary schools based upon local interests.[134] On the other hand, the decrees of October 30, 1990, and February 1, 1991, that, respectively, permitted the recognition of church and private schools insisted that these be tied in with the state system, and the scope of their autonomy is still at issue. It should be noted, however, that by a decree of March 5, 1991, the Slovak government has provided for public funding of private schools.[135]

Do real school-level autonomy and distinctiveness and parental choice in schools have any prospect of success in the Czech and Slovak republics? Much depends upon political developments. Many Czechs and Slovaks find it difficult to conceive of educational systems without a high degree of government supervision, and a recent survey of 1,216 Czech respondents selected to be representative of parents with children in elementary and lower secondary schools found that fundamental dissatisfaction with the schools was generally limited to those with higher cultural and economic levels. On the other hand, the same survey found a general belief that, despite the commitment of the previous regime to uniformity, there are significant differences among schools. Higher-status parents tended to assess diversity in schooling positively. More than half of these respondents said that they would rather have their children attend an independent school, though voters on the left expressed preference for "the traditional system with centralized control."[136]

One proposal to begin to change the present system, as well as to deal with the fiscal crises facing Czech and Slovak education, is to reduce by 20 percent the teaching load for which teachers are paid their present salaries, and allow them to offer additional lessons in school facilities at parental expense. The assumption is that this would force many teachers to become more effective in order to persuade parents to make the sacrifice, and that new supplemental programs would be created to attract pupils. The recent survey found that 63 percent of parents would be willing to pay more for education if the quality were improved, and another 23 percent would consider it, depending on cost. This seems to indicate at least the potential for market pressures.[137]

A similar approach has been proposed for higher education, which was implemented in the 1992–93 academic year. The goal is "to turn universities and colleges into self-standing active entities which will be influenced primarily by the economic market, professional and public control" rather than by the last alone, as before. Departments would receive funding from the ministry for particular courses based upon the number of students who enrolled in them, thus reducing the control of administrators over which courses would be offered. "Let the students themselves—not older faculty members—take the risk of deciding which courses are best for the future," a ministry official argues.[138]

As the Czech and Slovak republics struggle with dismantling the inheritance of 40 years of Communist rule, including command economies and overcentralized educational systems, it is clear that there will be an active debate over allowing parents and students to make educational choices for themselves.

To what extent this will include alternatives outside the public system, or even the total dismantling of the continuing semimonopoly on schooling by the state (as conceived by Botlik), is still unclear in the aftermath of Czechoslovakia's breakup. In March 1992 there were reported to be 130 new private schools, mostly at the secondary level, and 22 new church schools since the fall of the Communist regime. Does this merely reflect demand by the more affluent parents for selective and demanding schools, or is there a broader interest in permitting every school to function with a significant degree of autonomy? After all, the Czech economy in particular is undergoing extensive privatization of more than a thousand state-owned firms with a book value of $9.3 billion to millions of citizen-shareholders. Is it possible that schooling will move in the same direction?

One sign that the civil society is indeed coming alive in part through the creation of new schools is the spontaneous organization of groups that intend to start alternative schools. The Christian Teachers' Movement started in Slovakia in January 1991, and the various alternative schools that have been organized in many communities reflect educational objectives that have less to do with elite schooling than with new ways of thinking about education or a recovery of older values and goals.

The spirit that animates such efforts has much in common with Václav Havel's eloquent words at the World Economic Forum in Geneva, in early 1992:

> Things must once more be given a chance to present themselves as they are, to be perceived in their individuality. We must see the pluralism of the world, and not bind it by seeking common denominators or reducing everything to a single common equation. . . . The way forward is not in the mere construction of universal systematic solutions, to be applied to reality from the outside; it is also in seeking to get to the heart of reality through personal experience. Such an approach promotes an atmosphere of tolerant solidarity and unity in diversity based on mutual respect, genuine pluralism and parallelism. In a word, human uniqueness, human action and the human spirit must be rehabilitated.

Havel had suggested, five years earlier, that this was a problem for the free societies of the West as well as for those living under Communist rule.

> I believe the world is losing its human dimension. Self-propelling mega-machines, juggernauts of impersonal power such as large-scale enterprises and faceless governments,

represent the greatest threat to our present-day world. In the final analysis, totalitarianism is no more than an extreme expression of this threat. . . . It has something to do with the fact that we live in the first atheist civilization in human history. . . . As soon as humanity declared itself to be the supreme ruler of the universe—at that moment, the world began to lose its human dimensions.[139]

Restoration of that human dimension, and thus of a civil society capable of nurturing human life in freedom, is perhaps the most significant aspect of the creation of new educational alternatives in the Czech and Slovak republics, as in other post-Communist societies . . . and in the West.

References

1. Václav Havel, "Paradise Lost" (translated by Paul Wilson), *New York Review of Books*, April 9, 1992, p. 6.

2. Carol Skalnik Leff, *National Conflict in Czechoslovakia: The Making and Remaking of a State, 1918–1987* (Princeton, N.J.: Princeton University Press, 1988), p. 11.

3. Jiří Pehe, "The Emergence of Right-wing Extremism," *Report on Eastern Europe* 2, no. 26 (June 28, 1991).

4. Leff, p. 7.

5. Ibid., p. 16.

6. Karel Skalický, "The Vicissitudes of the Catholic Church in Czechoslovakia, 1918 to 1988," *Czechoslovakia: Crossroads and Crises, 1918–1988*, ed. Norman Stone and Eduard Strouhal (New York: St. Martin's Press, 1989), p. 308.

7. E. Garrison Walters, *The Other Europe: Eastern Europe to 1945* (New York: Dorset Press, 1990), p. 36.

8. Dagmar Čapková, "Die Schule in den tschechischen Gebieten seit 1774. Österreichische Reformzeit und Nationale Wiedergeburt der Tschechen," in *Revolution des Wissens? Europa und seine Schulen im Zeitalter der Aufklärung (1750–1825)* (Bochum, Germany: Verlag Dr. Dieter Winkler, 1991), pp. 297–319.

9. Walters, p. 36.

10. Leff, p. 28.

11. Ibid., p. 18.

12. Walters, p. 82.

13. Leff, p. 32.

14. "The danger of delinquency," *Economist*, March 16, 1991.

15. Walters, p. 192.

16. Čapková, p. 303.

17. Vratislav Busek, "Church and State," in *Czechoslovakia*, ed. Vratislav Busek and Nicolas Spulber (New York: Praeger, 1957), p. 132.

18. Leff, p. 294.

19. Busek, pp. 133–34.

20. Walters, p. 196.

21. Busek, pp. 137–38.

22. Leff, p. 22.
23. Busek, p. 136.
24. Skalický, p. 298.
25. Ivo Duchacek, "Education," *Czechoslovakia*, p. 156.
26. Busek, p. 136.
27. Patrick Brogan, *The Captive Nations: Eastern Europe: 1945–1990* (New York: Avon Books, 1990), p. 84.
28. Vladimir Reisky de Dubnic, *Communist Propaganda Methods: A Case Study on Czechoslovakia* (New York: Praeger, 1960), p. 184.
29. V. Chalupa, *Rise and Development of a Totalitarian State* (Leiden, the Netherlands: H. E. Stenfert Kroese N. V., 1959), p. 135.
30. Ibid., pp. 139–40.
31. Quoted in Skalický, p. 315.
32. Eugene K. Keefe et al., *Area Handbook for Czechoslovakia* (Washington: U.S. Government Printing Office, 1972), p. 93.
33. Busek, pp. 148–50.
34. "David W. Paul, *Czechoslovakia: Profile of a Socialist Republic at the Crossroads of Europe* (Boulder, Colo.: Westview Press, 1981), p. 137.
35. Busek, p. 144.
36. Dubnic, p. 201.
37. Ibid., pp. 201–2.
38. Quoted from *Rudé právo* in Vladimir V. Kusin, *From Dubček to Charter 77: A Study of 'Normalization' in Czechoslovakia, 1968–1978* (New York: St. Martin's Press, 1978), p. 218.
39. Paul, p. 138.
40. Keppel, p. 129.
41. President Antonín Novotný to the Eleventh Party Congress (1958), quoted in Edward Taborsky, *Communism in Czechoslovakia, 1948–1960* (Princeton, N.J.: Princeton University Press, 1961), p. 506.
42. Paraphrased in Chalupa, p. 144.
43. Ernest Sykora, quoted in Theodoric J. Zubek, *The Church of Silence in Slovakia* (n.p.: Lach, 1956), p. 144.
44. Taborsky, p. 513.
45. Keefe et al., p. 73.
46. Quoted in Taborsky, p. 507.
47. Duchacek, p. 164.
48. *The Development of the Czechoslovak Educational and Instructive System under the Period 1981–1983* (Bratislava: Slovak Educational Library and Institute of Educational Development, 1984), pp. 42, 68.
49. Július Lihocký et al., *The Forty Years of Slovak Educational System in the Socialist Czechoslovakia* (Bratislava: Slovak Pedagogical Publishing House, 1989), p. 43.
50. Ibid., p. 43.
51. Chalupa, pp. 156–57.
52. Quoted from *Mlada Fronta* (Young Front), August 16, 1951, in Duchacek, p. 162.
53. Milan Šimečka, *The Restoration of Order: The Normalization of Czechoslovakia, 1969–1976*, trans. A. G. Brain (Verso, 1984), p. 108. The kindergarten curriculum described was not new; a 1953 source cited in Taborsky, p. 524, mentions "little poems, songs, and nursery rhymes about Stalin, Gottwald, and the Party."
54. Ernest Sykora, quoted in Zubek, p. 144.

55. Quoted in Taborsky, p. 536.
56. Chalupa, p. 158.
57. Taborsky, p. 542.
58. *Mladá Fronta*, quoted in Dubnic, p. 209.
59. Gustav Bareš, quoted in Chalupa, p. 159.
60. Taborsky, p. 539.
61. Quoted in Taborsky, p. 528.
62. Zdenek Krystufek, *The Soviet Regime in Czechoslovakia* (Boulder, Colo.: East European Monographs, 1981), p. 97.
63. Taborsky, pp. 517–18.
64. Duchacek, pp. 156, 158.
65. Kusin, p. 218.
66. Busek, p. 147.
67. Zubek, p. 140.
68. Andrej Pavlik, quoted in Duchacek, p. 165.
69. Zdenek Nejedly, quoted in Zubek, p. 133.
70. Václav Kopecky, quoted in Busek, p. 153.
71. Quoted in Taborsky, p. 507.
72. Keefe et al., p. 94.
73. Kusin, p. 96.
74. Ibid., p. 204.
75. Ibid., p. 109.
76. Ibid., p. 218.
77. Keefe et al., p. 74.
78. Quoted from *Učitelské noviny* (Teachers' Gazette) in Kusin, p. 98.
79. *Development . . . 1981–1983*, p. 93.
80. Quoted in Kusin, pp. 98–99.
81. Quoted in Ibid., p. 98.
82. S. Petrácek, "Czechoslovakia," *The Encyclopedia of Comparative Education and National Systems of Education* (New York: Pergamon Press, 1988), p. 225.
83. Jan Prucha, "Political Changes and Their Impact on Education: A Case of Czechoslovakia" (Prague: Institute of Educational and Psychological Research, 1990).
84. Miroslav Burger, "The first private school in Czechoslovakia" (Prague: První Obnovené Reálné Gymnázium, January 25, 1991).
85. *Development . . . 1981–1983*, p. 5.
86. Prucha.
87. Complete text, in an anonymous translation, in *Czechoslovakia: A Country Study*, ed. Richard F. Nyrop (Washington: U.S. Government Printing Office, 1982), pp. 309–13.
88. Chalupa, p. 12.
89. Václav Havel, "New Year's Address," in *Open Letters: Selected Writings 1965–1990* (New York: Knopf, 1991), pp. 390–91.
90. Misha Glenny, *The Rebirth of History: Eastern Europe in the Age of Democracy*, (London: Penguin Books, 1990), p. 31.
91. "Doing without utopias: An interview with Václav Havel," (London) *Times Literary Supplement*, January 23, 1987, pp. 81–83.
92. Václav Havel, *Living in Truth* (London: Faber and Faber, 1987), p. 4.
93. Henry Kamm, "Teachers Relish New Lessons at Prague School," *New York Times*, November 13, 1990.

94. Kusin, p. 203.

95. Šimečka, p. 112.

96. Havel, *Living in Truth*, p. 12.

97. H. Gordon Skilling, "Introduction" to "Parallel Polis, or An Independent Society in Central and Eastern Europe: An Inquiry," *Social Research* 55, nos. 1–2 (Spring/Summer 1988): 212.

98. Václav Benda, "Parallel Polis, or An Independent Society in Central and Eastern Europe: An Inquiry," trans. Paul Wilson, *Social Research* 55, nos. 1–2 (Spring/Summer 1988): 215–16.

99. Ibid., p. 221.

100. Milan Šimečka, "Parallel Polis, or An Independent Society in Central and Eastern Europe: An Inquiry," trans. Paul Wilson, *Social Research* 55, nos. 1–2 (Spring/Summer 1988): 222, 225.

101. Ivan M. Jirous, "Parallel Polis, or An Independent Society in Central and Eastern Europe: An Inquiry," trans. Paul Wilson, *Social Research* 55, nos. 1–2 (Spring/Summer 1988): 227.

102. Ladislav Hejdánek, "Parallel Polis, or An Independent Society in Central and Eastern Europe: An Inquiry," trans. Paul Wilson, *Social Research* 55, nos. 1–2 (Spring/Summer 1988): 242.

103. "KDH Economic Reform Proposal Text Published" (translation of article that appeared in *Hospodasrske noviny*, March 19, 1991), *JPRS-EER*, April 2, 1991.

104. David T. Koyzis, "The Christian Democratic Movement of Slovakia," *Public Justice Report*, March 1991.

105. "Election Program 1990" (Bratislava: Christian Democratic Movement, May 1990).

106. *Development of Education 1989–1990, Czech and Slovak Federal Republic* (Bratislava: Institute of Information and Prognoses of Education, Youth and Sports, 1990), p. 13.

107. Oldrich Botlik, "A New Paradigm for Considerations about Public Educational Systems," Prague, typescript, 1990; an edited version was published as "Proposing a New Paradigm for Public Education in Czechoslovakia," *T. H. E. Journal* (January 1992): 59–61.

108. *Development . . . 1989–1990*, pp. 14–15.

109. Ibid., pp. 14–15, 17.

110. Ibid., p. 26.

111. Ibid., p. 38.

112. Ibid., pp. 69–73.

113. Information gathered for the author by Hana Nováková of the Research Institute of Pedagogy, Prague, 1991.

114. Information gathered for the author by Nováková; an article by Helena Hartl in the (London) *Times Educational Supplement*, of September 28, 1990, states that there were then nine private schools and seven church schools in Czechoslovakia.

115. Article by Dr. Karel Neuman in *Učitelské noviny* (Teachers' Gazette), December 21, 1990, cited by Nováková.

116. Ondrej Steffl, "The first private school in Czechoslovakia" (Prague: První Obnovené Reálné Gymnázium, September 9, 1990); Burger; Helena Hartl, "Private sector emerges as monolith topples," (London) *Times Educational Supplement*, September 28, 1990.

117. Jana Straková of PORG, letters to the author, January 22 and February 22, 1991.

118. From a summary, by Nováková, of an article by Regina Dokoupilová in *Učitelské noviny* (Teachers' Gazette), December 21, 1990.

119. Paul Flather, "A deluge of change in the wake of upheaval," (London) *Times Educational Supplement* March 2, 1990; Jeremy Sutcliffe, "Now recite this: goodbye dogma," (London) *Times Educational Supplement*, March 6, 1992.

120. Helena Hartl, "Dumped in the dustbin of history," (London) *Times Educational Supplement*, July 20, 1990.

121. Zdeněk Nejedlý, quoted in Taborsky, p. 471.

122. Paul, pp. 76–7.

123. Glenny, p. 29.

124. Ibid., pp. 30–31.

125. Krystufek, p. 195.

126. Havel, *Living in Truth*, p. 30.

127. Botlik, "Proposing a New Paradigm."

128. Oldrich Botlik, letter to the author, May 20, 1991.

129. Botlik, "Proposing a New Paradigm"; his proposals are also laid out in question-and-answer format in "Odpovédi na otázky Asociace pedagogů základních škol (Answers to questions from the Association of Primary School Teachers"); paraphrased for the author by Ivana Mazalkova.

130. Oldrich Botlik, letter to the author, April 22, 1991.

131. Botlik, "Proposing a New Paradigm."

132. Ibid.

133. "The Reform and Development of our Educational System up to 2000," summarized for the author by Ivana Mazalkova from *Učitelské noviny* (Teachers' Gazette) 34, September 26, 1991, p. 3.

134. "Proposal for the Creation of a Regional School Policy"; summarized for the author by Ivana Mazalkova from *Učitelské noviny* (Teachers' Gazette) 44, December 5, 1991, p. 1.

135. Materials and information provided to the author by Štefan Švec of Bratislava.

136. Public opinion poll conducted by AISA (Association for Independent Social Analysis) for the Ministry of Education; as reported in a letter from Oldrich Botlik to the author, August 6, 1991.

137. Ibid.

138. *Chronicles of Higher Education*, June 19, 1991.

139. "Doing without utopias," p. 81.

7. Hungary

The challenges faced by Hungarian educational policy in the post-Communist period are daunting:

> The State must secure new freedoms but—and this is the historically paradoxical task—*almost simultaneously* implement new means of integration. Specifically this means: removal of ideology but at the same time achievement of a new consensus; privatization but also workable means of economic coordination and compensatory social policies; political pluralism without chaos; freedom of establishment, structural pluralism, autonomy of educational institutions, but no loss of equivalency or decline of the system. On the one hand. . . institutional differentiation is the order of the day, but on the other hand and in parallel it is essential to ensure the cohesion of society through liberal methods of coordination.[1]

Complicating this task is the virtual destruction over the past 45 years of the rich associational life, much of it organized along religious and ethnic lines, that flourished in prewar Hungary. Under the Communist regime, those associations that were permitted to exist "functioned only as transmission belts for the central power. Civil society was tied down."[2]

In particular, a long tradition of church-sponsored education came under attack with the postwar Communist takeover in Hungary. In prewar Hungary, the state operated less than half of the secondary schools, and only one elementary school in five. Teacher training institutions showed the same pattern: 32 were Roman Catholic, 11 state-operated, 10 Protestant, and 2 Jewish.

Before World War II (1937–38), regular elementary schools operated under the following sponsorship:[3]

Roman Catholic	2,856	41%
State	1,287	19
Calvinist	1,079	16

Local Government	826	12%
Lutheran	395	6
Jewish	145	2
Eastern Rite Catholic	131	2
Private	112	2
Other	68	1
Total	6,899	

Sponsorship of secondary schools was as follows:

State	61	37%
Roman Catholic	45	27
Calvinist	24	15
Lutheran	11	7
Private	8	5
State-sponsored Roman Catholic	6	4
Local Government	5	3
Associations	4	2
Jewish	1	1
Total	165[4]	

The nonstate schools became an immediate target of the new regime, which saw them as an impediment to its central project, the formation of the "new Communist man." The regime also targeted village schools in general, justifying this move in the name of raising the quality of education but also seeking "to destroy the closed communities of the villages, taking away their spiritual leaders, i.e., the teacher and the pastor." Indeed, school-level initiatives of all kinds and differences between schools for any reason were suppressed as threatening the objectives of the system.[5]

The assault upon confessional schooling was not the only measure by which the government sought to neutralize the potential of the churches to provide an alternative worldview and social mobilization. The clergy were a particular target: salaries were provided to those who supported Communist policies, while mass arrests of recalcitrant clergy and widely publicized show trials of Roman Catholic, Calvinist, and Lutheran bishops also occurred. As early as spring 1946, Catholic clergy were accused of participating in a "reactionary, Fascist conspiracy."

Divided politically, Protestant church leaders put up little resistance to the nationalization of their schools; indeed, during the same postwar period their counterparts in Canada, West Germany, and elsewhere were willingly surrendering to the state the last relics of their educational systems, convinced that they were thereby contributing to social reconstruction.[6]

Although Protestants are a minority in Hungary, Protestant schooling has an important tradition associated with the preservation of Hungarian language and culture during the period of Turkish domination beginning in 1526,* and with resistance to Austrian Habsburg cultural hegemony in the 18th and 19th centuries. While the Turkish regime was relatively tolerant, the Habsburg regime sought to impose religious and cultural uniformity upon its subject peoples. What had been a largely decentralized educational system run by local initiative was made into a centralized instrument of the Habsburg policy of promoting "a Germanized Hungary under Catholic hegemony." The Hungarian Protestant community came under intense pressure, and saw preserving its schools as vital.[7]

Despite this tradition, those among the Protestant leadership who had long called for the political and economic reforms that the Communists claimed to be instituting and who hesitated to align themselves with their traditional Catholic opponents surrendered most of the Protestant schools in 1948, and "volunteered" those remaining, with one exception, four years later. According to a recent account by Hungarian Protestants,

> In 1952 . . . the Stalinist dictatorial state "suggested" [to] the leaders of the Protestant Churches [that they] abandon the schools, which they did, partly under threat, partly under manipulation, and partly giving in to force. With one exception—the College of Debrecen—all the Protestant schools left in the care of the Lutheran and the Reformed Churches according to the compromise in 1948 were then "offered" to the state with the argument that their financing became impossible (because all the foundations supporting the schools were taken away by the state). The particulars of this "voluntary offer" are still unclear. It is clear, however, that it was done without the knowledge and consent, and against the will of the congregations. The loss of the schools has been a source of bitterness and tension up to the present day.[8]

*As early as 1550 there were six Protestant secondary schools in Hungary.

The Roman Catholic leadership showed much more determination to maintain confessional schooling. In May 1946, Cardinal Mindszenty and the other Catholic bishops issued a pastoral letter linking the right of the church to operate schools with that of parents to control the education of their children. "Parents are prior to the State," they insisted, and "it is their right to demand that their children are educated according to their faith and their religious outlook."

The pastoral letter faced directly the objections brought against confessional schooling: that it was divisive, and that it prevented the use of education as an instrument of government social intervention. Some were asking, the bishops wrote, "Why do you force your children to attend schools which only split the nation and separate Hungarians from one another by denominational divergences—not to mention the fact that a perfect realization of the educational programme of the Government is frustrated by this split?"

But "we know from experience," the bishops wrote, "that the denominational schools do not disturb the peace among the people but, on the contrary, promote tolerance and respect for the beliefs and outlook of other people. In national and civic education the Catholic schools have always fulfilled their task." Denying any intention of criticizing other schools, the bishops pointed out that "the Catholic outlook cannot unfold itself completely" in schools whose pupils included non-Catholics and whose teachers had diverse views, thus preventing "a harmonious education."

Although at this point the state schools had not yet instituted antireligious instruction, the bishops rejected the idea that there could be such a thing as neutral instruction in which "God is passed over in silence, as if He did not exist or did not matter very much in human life," leading to "a gross and harmful indifference." "Religious indifference inoculated into the souls of children in this way is worse than disbelief; for we know from experience that it is much more difficult to convert indifferent people than militant disbelievers." No, Catholic children needed to experience "the whole Christian atmosphere of the school," and their parents were justified in preferring and supporting such schools, "very often at great sacrifice." Why should they be deprived of this choice? What sort of freedom was it "where no schools are acknowledged except the official ones run by the State—those official schools of the State where a small minority wants to impose its masterful will upon the majority of the people? ... Those people ... for whom everything Catholic spells reaction had better look for reaction in those quarters in which all freedom is oppressed."[9]

The immediate crisis passed; the government did not move to take over Catholic schools in 1946, and as late as February 1948 the Communist minister of education praised the role that Catholic schools had played in the development of Hungary, and disclaimed any intention of laying hands on confessional schools. He also acknowledged that many new confessional schools had been opened by the efforts of parents, while others were in better condition than state schools, as a result of similar efforts.[10]

In "one slice at a time" fashion, the government moved first to monopolize the publication of textbooks. Under the prewar authoritarian regime, the staff of individual schools had been free to select for each subject and grade level privately published textbooks that had been reviewed centrally to ensure that they did not contain "precepts, sections, or phrases that are anti-state or anti-constitutional, or which conflict with the spirit of religious moral education."[11] The Communist-dominated postwar regime, by contrast, forbade publishers to issue and teachers to select textbooks; "every subject, in every grade, had to be taught from a single centrally formulated and approved textbook."[12]

The National Association of Catholic Parents protested strongly, promising "ardent resistance ... if some elements try to impose their influence upon the spirit and the mental attitude of our schools."[13] Such protests were in vain, since they conflicted with what Communists considered the "centuries-old demand of the progressive forces of history for a single, comprehensive system of free public education." The "new order of popular education" was intended to transform society through "the incredible momentum of the nation-building work." Its direction was therefore not derived from pedagogical theory nor from the results of "experience gained at experimental schools," but from political imperatives.[14] Education was a weapon in the class struggle, not something of value in itself or a vehicle to respond to psychological or humanistic, much less religious, considerations.

In June 1948 a bill was enacted nationalizing 4,813 Catholic schools together with almost all other nonstate schools, bringing schools enrolling 639,335 pupils under direct state control. This move followed a campaign to create the appearance that nationalization was demanded by teachers and parents. Lay teachers, in particular, were assured that their financial situation would be improved by becoming part of the state system, and many had voluntarily or under pressure signed petitions in favor of nationalization.

In the past, Cardinal Mindszenty lamented, "parents had the possibility of choosing between different types of schools. With their nationalization, however, nothing will save the schools from decaying in materialism, religious indifference and party politics." He described this as a state "monopoly of the schools" that was "incompatible with the principle acknowledged by the State of the equality of rights of the various ideologies." In addition, he and the other Hungarian Catholic bishops wrote to the minister of education, "The State, by claiming every school for itself, violates the rights of parents, based on Natural Law, according to which parents can choose for their children the school which corresponds with their views, free from compulsion or fear of prejudice."[15]

But, of course, the regime did not acknowledge such a right, nor did it have any intention of permitting a free marketplace of ideas and beliefs, despite its formal proclamation of religious freedom. As the chief theoretician of the Communist party put it in a speech as classes started for a new school year under Party control, "Socialism must be built in the sphere of culture as well as in the economy."[16]

A few nonstate secondary schools (*gymnasia*) were permitted to survive under their previous sponsorship: one Jewish, one Protestant, and eight Roman Catholic, enrolling altogether 2,744 students, or just over 1 percent of the national *gymnasium* enrollment.[17]

The state takeover was not to establish educational neutrality, but rather to ensure the active inculcation of Marxist-Leninist perspectives. The national plan for instruction adopted in 1956 had as a central goal for all schools "the communist up-bringing of youth." As under the Habsburgs, one Hungarian researcher has pointed out, the schools were again expected "to serve directly a uniform national ideology" that "required a dramatic conversion on the individual's part and often implied radical re-education."[18]

Religious instruction (previously two periods a week) was made elective, over strong objections from denominational leaders and many parents, who insisted that it should continue to be required in the curriculum in state schools, with parents choosing whether they wished Catholic, Protestant, or Jewish instruction for their children. The bishops rejected the argument that pupils should be allowed to make up their own minds whether they wanted religion or not, arguing that "nobody minds forcing upon a child writing, reading and arithmetic without asking whether it likes it or not." Their objections were unsuccessful, but reports indicate that many parents, as a gesture of defiance toward the government, made a point of requesting that their children participate.[19] With the anti-religion campaign of the early 1950s, however, such gestures became too dangerous and religious instruction atrophied, except as it was provided clandestinely by lay people or by nuns who worked in secular employment.

One of the first measures taken by the Communist party after World War II was to organize a youth movement on the model of those in the Soviet Union and in competition with the Boy Scouts and the Catholic and Protestant youth organizations. The Association of Working Youth, succeeded by the Communist Youth League in 1957, in turn supervised the Association of Hungarian Pioneers, of which a branch was required in every elementary school. Their goal was to train "Little Drummers" (8–10) and "Pioneers" (11–14) to "love the Soviet Union . . . and live and work according to the teachings of the Party."[20]

Almost all upper elementary pupils became members of the Pioneers, since this was essential to admission to a good secondary school. Monthly meetings of the Pioneers in each school were organized by classroom teachers or Communist Youth League members, and were supplemented by "free trips to the Soviet Union or summer camps and other rewards for those who achieve ideological competence."[21]

During the Hungarian revolution of 1956, the Roman Catholic and Protestant youth organizations reemerged briefly, but were quickly suppressed in the wake of the Soviet intervention. There had been signs earlier of youthful dissatisfaction with Communist rule, and the press had criticized the "clericalism" (that is, religious belief and practice) and "nationalism" (that is, anti-Soviet sentiment) of the younger generation. Clearly the schools were failing in their primary mission of educating students to love and trust the Party.[22]

After suppression of the 1956 revolt, Hungarian education officials redoubled their efforts to ensure that schools successfully brought students to internalize a Communist worldview. Although Prime Minister Kádár sought to gain popular support by easing social and economic controls in the 1960s, this relative liberalization was accompanied by an "ideological offensive" to ensure loyalty. Too many students, the minister of culture complained in 1965, continued to "harbor bourgeois and petty bourgeois views."[23] Teachers, in particular, were organized into collectives to impose ideological conformity; their preparation gave particular attention to developing "a deeper knowledge of dialectical materialism, while training them in the practice of communist morality and Bolshevik behavior and will power."[24]

Legislation enacted in 1961 stated that one of the primary goals of the educational system was to "develop and strengthen in the students a Marxist-Leninist concept of life and socialist morality." The minister of education stressed that it was not sufficient that students have an intellectual understanding of the doctrines of Marxism-Leninism; they should be led to embrace them as well.[25] This required, in particular, that the influence of the family be minimized, to the extent that it did not support the objectives of the Communist regime.

"In the past," Cardinal Mindszenty wrote in one of his pastoral letters, "the ideal was that there must not be a gulf between school and family." The Communist regime shared this ideal, but not as a basis for endorsing school choice; to the contrary, the family was expected to refrain from teaching any values in conflict with those advanced by the school. "During the most radical periods of socialist society-building," as Halász notes, "the prevailing educational thinking suggested that parents' influence on their children's education must be reduced to a minimum level and the state should educate all children directly."[26]

The existence of "conflicting influences in the family and at school" was condemned as a "double education" harmful to children and to the new order under construction. "Parents were considered not as partners [of the school] in education but as persons to be educated similarly to their children." The parent organizations at each school held discussions, not on the concrete problems being experienced by the children, but on "general political issues. . . . Their aim was not participation but political mobilization." Parent-teacher conferences, according to one experienced Hungarian educator, had as their real purpose "to try to persuade parents not to confuse their children with ideas and beliefs contrary to the official propaganda."[27]

The primary result of the regime's efforts to use its schools and other instruments of socialization to impose a single, highly politicized worldview was, perhaps inevitably, an ironical detachment on the part of many. This result was precisely the "double education" of sharply contrasting values by home and school that the regime sought to prevent.[28]

This rejection of the worldview represented by the school was most striking among Hungary's large Gypsy population. Although the Communist regime outlawed their customary traveling and required that their children attend school (often in segregated classes), all attempts of teachers to affect the attitudes and values of Gypsy children were in vain. This was true not only of children from socially marginal families, but of those from relatively prosperous families that functioned effectively in Hungarian society. "Gypsy families expect school to provide effective teaching without interfering in socialization."[29]

While this reaction might have been anticipated from an ethnic group that has maintained its separate existence for centuries–and whose younger members appear to be growing more rather than less self-conscious about their cultural distinctiveness—it seems to have been true for ethnic Hungarians as well. By the 1970s, the regime had tacitly accepted compliance as its goal in lieu of conviction.

There were also growing signs of a youth culture that, while quiescent politically, rejected the values advanced by the regime and its schools, as well as by their own parents.[30] Punks, runaways, drug and alcohol abusers were evidence that both sides of the "double education" had failed or, perhaps, that the gap between the message conveyed by the school and that conveyed by the home had had the effect of rendering all values relative.

The state educational system made no effort to overcome this gap through accommodating its schools to the goals and values of parents, as occurs to some extent in the West, through formal and informal arrangements allowing parents to seek out a school with whose educational mission they are in accord. Individual attendance districts were established for each school under the Communist system and, though it was possible for a pupil to attend another school with the permission of its principal, the government sought—until the 1980s—to prevent any differentiation among the elementary/intermediate schools that served pupils to age fourteen.

The reforms attempted in the 1980s are in some respects an exception to a central theme of this book, that the logic of schooling under communist governments was one of uniformity and detailed central control in the interest of the totalitarian project of shaping subjects incapable of withholding a heartfelt obedience to the ruling Party. Hungarian school authorities, though they made no concessions that freedom of school choice was a fundamental right, nevertheless offered several forms of differentiation among schools—this in itself was not unique among communist systems—and also made some gestures in the direction of school autonomy based upon a partial empowerment of teachers to decide about pedagogical matters in their schools.

Differentiation took the form of a well-established system of selection or tracking of pupils into more and less academic courses of study after the completion of elementary/intermediate education. Whether the selection was, as before World War II, designed to favor the propertied (but non-Jewish) classes, or, as during the 1950s, to favor the children of peasants and workers, or again, as subsequently, based upon academic achievement, it was in no real sense a system of parental choice. Nor did it include options based upon differing values, with the exception of the 10 surviving non-state schools.[31]

There were also a few secondary schools with a special vocational emphasis on the fine arts, and special classes for children gifted in foreign languages, mathematics, or physical education; in 1970–71, 5.6 percent of the elementary pupils took part in some form of specialized instruction. At the secondary level, the existence of specialized programs was much more extensive and allowed a second form of selection for pupils who had made it past the initial process of admission to an academic gymnasium. Contrary to the ideology of the regime, these programs enrolled relatively few children of workers and peasants, who in turn filled the catch-all classes of those gymnasium pupils not in a specialized class.[32]

A measure of choice also existed with respect to the language of instruction. Under a 1946 decree, "the parents or guardians of at least 10 children of compulsory school age have the right to request that they be assigned to a special school for the particular nationality." By 1963–64, 1.9 percent of the elementary pupils attended schools in which the primary language of instruction was not Hungarian (Magyar). There were 21 schools that catered exclusively to a particular language minority group: eight Serbo-Croatian, six Romanian, six Slovak, and one German. Five other schools provided separate sections for language minority pupils. Another 290 schools offered supplementary instruction in minority languages. In all cases, the curriculum was parallel with that in Hungarian: these schools might be "national in form," but they were required to be "socialist in content."[33]

What was not permitted to emerge, until the last years of the communist regime, was educational differentiation based upon different pedagogies or ways of understanding the goals of education. The postwar interest in alternative schools (mostly representing variations on progressive education) was quickly suppressed,[34] nor was there the slightest possibility—apart from the 10 confessional schools that were allowed to exist—of ideological diversity in Hungarian education.

Despite the best efforts of the educational system, however, religious belief remained widespread among the Hungarian people, especially in rural areas; over 60 percent of the rural Catholic population attended Sunday mass in the 1970s.[35] The Communist leadership deplored the fact that "a significant part of the masses . . . is still not unified in its world outlook. This is linked to the fact that there remain traces of the old system's ideology." In confirmation of this concern, a survey among older adolescents found that "over half adhered to a traditional value system, one third also admitted to religious faith, and only 14 percent appeared to espouse Marxist values."[36]

The fundamental dilemma of communist education was expressed well by Ilona Paul soon after the 1956 revolt and long before any sign of liberalization in Hungary, when she asked how it could "expect to train and educate leaders and scientists in the complexities of twentieth century technology without awakening the beginnings of creative and independent thought which has for all time been the nemesis of tyranny and dictatorship?"[37]

The stagnation of the Hungarian economy—despite two decades of "goulash socialism" permitting a certain liberalization of social and economic life in exchange for political passivity—led, in the early 1980s, to demands for changes in the institutions of communist rule. In response to the perception that a stagnant educational system was part of the problem, there were efforts to remake and revitalize it by changing a top-down command structure to one driven by local decisionmaking within a framework of school autonomy. Innovation in the interest of improved schooling, it was recognized, "is inconceivable in a situation where a firmly centralized control is invariable maintained." The Communist Party decided, in 1982, to stimulate school-level response to the diverse needs of pupils. This fundamental shift of emphasis was one of many based upon a new faith in local problem-solving.[38]

A new education law adopted in 1985 stressed local autonomy and teacher initiative, including the selection of textbooks, and released teachers from the obligation to take part in the Pioneer movement and other forms of political socialization. The official role of parent organizations was to be changed from that of mobilizing parents politically to that of exerting parental influence on the school.[39]

While the cynical suggested that the government was offering autonomy because it could not provide adequate funding, there was also a growing recognition that this reform was essential. Schools were charged with developing individual organizational structures and approaches to education through extensive involvement of teachers, and the latter were given substantial decisionmaking authority in school management. Appointment of principals became subject to veto by a majority of teachers in a school.

This was an authority that many teachers were not eager to accept. After all, increased autonomy "meant more responsibility, extra amount[s] of work, more staff meetings etc. A minority which were full of ideas and initiatives excepted, teachers were not enthusiastic about all these consequences. As . . . a headmaster put it, 'teachers preferred criticizing inadequate central programs to preparing something of their own.'"[40]

There was also resistance to the idea that schools should be held accountable for educational outcomes, while enjoying increased freedom in how to organize instruction. Like many of their counterparts in the United States, Hungarian teachers "refused a system which they thought to emphasize [sic] measurable intellectual achievement at the expense of emotional and other non-intellectual qualities."[41]

Accepting accountability for such results, from this perspective, is a devil's bargain that should be refused.

In theory, at least, parents were to be brought into decisionmaking, though in fact teachers often successfully resisted this as well; nor were parents strongly inclined to participate.[42] After all, as efforts to encourage parental participation in American urban school systems have demonstrated, the fact that parents have been alienated by their dealings with a bureaucratic educational system does not mean that they are eager to abandon their passivity and engage on unequal terms with teachers in efforts to take advantage of a measure of school-based decisionmaking.

The idea of educational diversity itself was resisted by many educators, for whom a primary function of the school was to transmit a uniform national culture. "A great number of educational administrators came into their posts either directly from the ideological apparatus of the party or they were helped by references from it. For them, the existing plurality of values in society means something which cries out for change rather than something with which one should learn to live. In their eyes, autonomy of schools endangers the unity of national culture and a homogeneous system of social values."[43]

Critics also noted that the new law gave more authority over schools to local authorities, which might in fact interfere more with school operations than had the more distant central government. While teachers could now select textbooks, the monopoly of the state in the publication of textbooks remained![44]

> The (relative) autonomy of state schools, under which each would be free to determine how to achieve its curriculum objectives within a framework of accountability assured by a system of external examinations, produced mixed results: the emergence and strengthening of some really well functioning local systems on the one hand, with several abortive, dilettantish attempts on the other; a burst of enthusiasm from schools and teachers with an innovative spirit, passivity and bewilderment in the great majority."[45]

In some schools whose teachers were energetic and shared a vision from new forms of pedagogy, real changes occurred. Most moved away from an emphasis on transmission of knowledge toward a more pupil-centered emphasis on development of a broad range of competencies. There was some interest in the pedagogy of Rudolf Steiner, and a Waldorf kindergarten and school were founded.[46] On balance, however, the impact of the intended reforms was disappointing, suggesting that significant changes at the school level cannot take place without fundamental reform of the system in which schools are embedded. This may be seen as a confirmation of the contention of some American educational reformers that a state-operated system of schooling inevitably becomes static and ineffective over time. However necessary and efficient it may appear when the provision of schooling must be rapidly expanded, state operation of schools (in this view) cannot do justice to the demands of a complex and rapidly changing economy and society.

Building a Post-Communist Educational System

The policy of relative liberalization followed by the government of Janos Kadar had the effect of permitting moderate criticism of technical aspects of public policy while largely forestalling the fundamental criticism of the Communist system that emerged from dissenters in Poland, Czechoslovakia, and the Soviet Union. In Hungary, "the political limits of intellectual activity, of the expression of criticism and thus of exerting some pressure on the functioning of the system from within appear to be sufficiently wide to permit the continued existence of . . . [an] opposition that does not overtly question the ideological bases of the system."[47] Perhaps as a result, there was a more vigorous discussion of educational reform in Hungary than elsewhere in Central and Eastern Europe before the fall of the Communist regime, but without calling into question directly the role of the school as an instrument of political socialization.

With the collapse of Communist hegemony, however, the state monopoly on education has itself been challenged. One of the leading demands of the opposition groups which orchestrated a mass demonstration on March 15, 1988, for example, was for "freedom of speech, the press, conscience and education."[48]

In addition to demands for educational freedom for its own sake, there has been an intense questioning whether the state educational system is able to provide adequately for the needs of Hungarian society. Scarcely had the Communist regime fallen than reformers were insisting that "the monopolistic position of [the] state in education must be terminated" and replaced with a mixed system.[49]

The concerns are of two kinds. First, questions whether the state school, even when purged of Marxist-Leninist indoctrination, can find a basis on which to provide a coherent moral framework within which real education can take place.[50] As a group seeking to reestablish Reformed (Calvinist) secondary schools wrote,

> Today, the whole of Hungarian public education is in a very deep moral and financial crisis due to the disclosure of so far hidden facts about the recent history of the socialist world and to the disastrous economic state of the country. In this situation, the loss of the Protestant schools of great tradition is even more painful. We are convinced that it is of essential importance for both our church and our country that Protestant education should be revived. The primary reasons are as follows:
>
> Suicide, abortion, alcoholism, birth, divorce, and mortality statistics . . . show that the lack of perspectives of normal social and economic life . . . have caused self-destructive tendencies which, by now, have reached a limit that threatens the survival of the Hungarian population in Central Europe. In such a situation, it is a very important mission of the Church to educate people who live for others rather than for themselves and are able to move the forces of hope in their fellow men.
>
> Congregational life and youth work (impoverished in the past decades anyway) are insufficient in educating people for Christian responsibility paired with social and intellectual competence. A solid institutional basis cannot be dispensed with. Unlike in fully developed democracies where a rich network of communities and institutions socializ[ing] for Christian morality and altruism is available, within the distorted and insufficient system of social institutions in our country, it is still the school that has the best conditions for educating children for a life with higher principles.
>
> During the past 40 years, the values of life to be pursued as well as the preferred ways of seeking success were, by force of power and "law," prescribed for society including all schools (except for the 10 existing church schools) by the dominant ideology of militant atheism and egoism sugarcoated in socialist-collectivist phraseology. The erosion of humanism and morality within and outside the school was, for a long time, counteracted by the generations of parents and teachers who had been educated in the Christian spirit and who transferred some of this spirit to succeeding generations.

> Now that the last of these generations has left the school,
> the moral collapse of the school system is so obvious that it
> warns society and the government of the dangers of concen-
> trating the school on a materialist world view lacking any
> articulate moral principles.
> Realizing the problems caused by insufficient moral educa-
> tion (e.g. the increase of your delinquency, increase of your
> drug addiction, deterioration of work skills and morals,
> increase of aggressive tendencies in schools and in society),
> the Churches requested the government to allow them to act
> on a wider scale in the sphere of caring, social, and educa-
> tional activities. Their request was not turned down immedi-
> ately, which gives hope that the re-establishment of the aban-
> doned schools is not impossible and the school building
> taken away in 1952 will be given back to the Reformed
> Church.[51]

The priority for the Calvinist (Reformed) Church, with its urgent
need to form a new generation of Christian leadership, is to reestablish its academic secondary schools (*gymnasia*) rather than elementary or vocational schools. The smaller Lutheran church, meanwhile,
is struggling to support its two *gymnasia* and eight elementary
schools, while seeking the return of other confiscated schools.[52] The
headmaster of one historically significant Calvinist gymnasium has
warned, in fact, that the churches should not seek to respond to all
of the demand for Christian schooling until resources and appropriate staff are available.[53]

Second, there are those who question whether the provision of
schooling would be more effective if entirely deregulated and "mar-
ketized," with schools operated by entrepreneurs on a for-profit
basis. The state, under one proposal, would determine standards,
exercise general oversight, and provide vouchers with which individuals would purchase schooling.[54]

Thus the April 1989 election program of the Free Democrats called
for freeing the educational system "from the power of monopolizing
ideology" and, significantly, also "from the power of scientific and
pedagogical interest groups." Educational freedom, they insisted,
required the freedom to establish and to choose schools and financial
autonomy at the school level. Accountability should be exercised
through measuring the outcomes of schooling rather than administrative controls, and schools should be funded on the basis of their

enrollment, whether directly or through giving vouchers to parents. This reform program was also generally supported by the Young Democrats (FIDESZ) and the Democratic Trade Union of Educators (*Pedagógusok Demokratikus Szakszervezetének*).[55]

Under another proposal, the basic instructional program of schools would continue to be provided free, but a variety of supplemental services, including after-school care (intended primarily for children experiencing difficulties) and enrichment programs would be assigned a price based upon actual cost. Parents would be provided with partial vouchers to purchase these services, with the amount of the voucher based upon need. This would "enable parents to influence the quality of the services through their payments, through 'acting as customers.' "[56]

A less drastic proposal would further the free choice of schools by abolishing centralized determination of the number of pupils to be admitted to each school, assure accountability through outcomes rather than the prescription of curriculum, and finance education on the basis of differentiated per-pupil payments to state and independent schools alike. With school-level financial autonomy controlling budgets dependent upon the enrollment attracted, school staff would become "interested in improving the quality of teaching in order to keep their pupils."[57]

It proved difficult for government, even when democratically elected, to give up the habit of seeking to prescribe in detail for the educational system. The government's Program for National Renewal, issued in September 1990, adopted the principles of outcome measures and of per-pupil financing, but also specified in detail many aspects of the program of individual schools. The actions of this new government betrayed at many points a confusion of centralizing and liberalizing tendencies.[58]

Faced with a growing crisis in education—and concerned to address this and other sources of popular dissatisfaction before reforms (as in neighboring countries) were demanded by mass demonstrations in the streets—the Ministry appointed a blue-ribbon committee, headed by former Deputy Minister Ferenc Gazso (a sociologist, not an educator), to make recommendations for fundamental changes. The plan presented by this committee in February 1991 urged that the society-wide trend to renounce state monopoly be extended to education, with a fundamental right to establish and operate schools independent of the state system. Public funds would be provided on an equal per-pupil basis to all schools that met certain yet-to-be-defined standards. Compulsory ideology would be excluded from the state schools; children should not be forced to accept teaching contrary to the beliefs of their parents.[59]

The developments in the direction of diversity and autonomy under communist rule—however imperfectly translated into practice—prepared the way for the comprehensive reforms recommended by the Gazso committee. The new approach is summarized in *Educational Policy for the Nineties*, prepared by the Institute for Educational Research, which is a match for any of the proposals for reform of American education that have come out in recent years— and well ahead of some. "Educational policy," the authors urge, "must shift toward a new paradigm that puts the stress on local and institutional adaptation. . . . The idea of an overall and centrally initiated reform . . . is rejected and a system of continuous development based primarily [on] local initiatives is suggested."

> The new state educational policy has to start from the cultural and ideological variety of the Hungarian society and the presence in it of groups with differing interests; it must be in conformity with the principles of political pluralism, and it must guarantee . . . individuals and . . . minorities their freedom as stipulated in the Constitution . . . special regard must be given to. . . . The aim at all levels should be this: individuals, families and communities should be free to choose for themselves the form of education that they think is most appropriate to them.

To translate this principle into practice, the authors declare, the "State's monopoly control of schools must be ended. The present monolithic state system must be transformed into a mixed system involving state schools, local council schools, and schools owned by other proprietors. . . . The principles of financing, from public resources, schools run by economic units, foundations, cooperative, private and church schools, must be formulated."[60]

Hungarian policymakers are thus debating issues that are central to debates in the United States as well: "where we should and where we should not have central regulation; which are the areas where it is desirable to have alternativity and pluralism, and which are the areas where they are not desirable." There is growing agreement that whatever national core curriculum is developed "should not impose any single ideology or religion; it should enable the churches and private schools to express their own world views in their detailed curricula. In other words, it should open the way to ideological pluralism."[61]

It is one thing, of course, to tolerate ideological pluralism and alternative ways of teaching and learning, and another to structure the educational system so that diversity is actively encouraged. The Parliament took an important step in this direction in January 1990, when it adopted a law on freedom of conscience, guaranteeing the right to operate nonstate schools and promising a subsidy equal to that provided to state schools for those accepting the national education syllabus. The new education law that came into force in June 1990

> gives the local municipality ... the right to authorize the foundation of non-state schools and to exercise judicial control over them. The legal conditions are that these schools must adapt their programmes to the central programmes of national education and [show evidence of] funds adequate to the proper running of the establishment. The fulfillment of these conditions guarantees both the public status of these schools and official recognition of the certificates they award. The pedagogical direction (definition of educational aims) is [the responsibility of] the juridical persons who run them. The State controls only the school's [legal] conformity to the national education law.[62]

In addition to guaranteeing the freedom to operate schools, the new law promises that pupils and their parents will enjoy educational freedom. "The education provided by the state['s schools] must exclude any compulsory ideology. Pupils cannot be forced to accept teachings that go against the beliefs of their parents. The student has the right to select the school he or she wants to attend. The student also has the right to attend private instruction [that is, nonapproved schooling that is not state-subsidized] and take a test in front of a committee at the end of each school year."[63]

On a distinct but related issue, the government (now dominated by a coalition of Christian Democratic parties) moved to make effective the right to optional religious instruction in state schools, guaranteed by law since 1948 but discouraged in practice. Over vigorous opposition from the Liberal Democrats and Socialists in Parliament, the education ministry established agreements with the churches on the effective implementation of these classes by church-commissioned, publicly funded teachers. By the end of November 1990, the ministry reported there were 17,000 new classes for Catholic instruction, 5,000 for Reformed (Calvinist) instruction, 1,600 for Lutheran instruction, and 37 for Jewish instruction in state schools. Despite early indications that such classes might be compulsory, they are in fact voluntary.[64]

With the fall of the Communist regime, interest was revived in the 10 secondary schools that had been allowed to survive outside of the state system. A supplement to one of the leading daily newspapers carried accounts of a number of these surviving schools. A spokesperson for the Catholic schools reported that parental demand had remained strong, even though graduates experienced problems because they were considered ideologically unreliable. Among the reasons for this popularity was "the experience of belonging to a living community." The same observation was made in an article about the celebrated Calvinist school in Debrecen, a significant part of Hungarian history since 1538. The headmaster stressed that the school did not claim to be better than, but to be different from state schools because of its Christian worldview.[65]

This was not a self-evident truth, given the effects of 40 years of government-sponsored secularization. The same headmaster has warned that many

> of the parents demanding Christian schools have little to do with the church and faith, they are the generation of the atheist decades. They have perhaps an ideal picture about the "good old peaceful times" when everybody received a lesson in religion and young people were more disciplined. Especially in villages and small towns there are many parental groups aiming to reorganize schools on a Christian (ecumenical or confessional) basis. The situation is a great challenge for the churches.[66]

The former headmaster of the Calvinist *gymnasium* in Sárospatak, founded in 1531, taken over by the state in 1951, and restored to the Hungarian Reformed church in 1990, put it more simply: "We must again introduce the students to God. *Deus providebit* (The Lord himself will provide)—but it will take time. I am not pessimistic, but it does not go at once."[67]

At present about 5 percent of Hungary's pupils attend several dozen surviving or refounded church-related schools. Intense activity is going on around these and other proposed schools, with the Calvinist and Lutheran school associations seeking advice as well as financial assistance from Dutch and other Western groups concerned with educational freedom. The Dutch Ministry of Education arranged a special training course for Hungarian school managers.[68]

The teachers working in the eight Catholic secondary schools have been meeting to rethink how to teach history and literature in the wake of "the downfall of the Marxist-Leninist ideology," and to plan for assisting lay teachers who will work in the additional schools that will be opening.

However, according to László Szalay, an official of the Ministry of Education, financial conditions will make it very difficult to start new schools despite the country's recently enacted permissive law.

A survey conducted in May 1990 asked 483 respondents how much they felt they could pay for the education of their children; over 70 percent said they could pay nothing, and only 3.3 percent agreed they could pay 1,000 forints or more per month. Since the state pays between 40,000 and 60,000 forints per year on each school child, some form of state support will be essential if independent schools are to serve a significant proportion of the nation's children.[69]

There are also space problems, since the buildings of Catholic or Protestant schools that were taken over by the state are in general not available for use by their former owners. It is significant, therefore, that the Calvinist secondary school at Sárospatak was able to reopen in September 1990 by simply taking over the entire enrollment and faculty—856 pupils and 70 teachers—of the state school occupying its former building. The refounded Calvinist school in Pápa, however, was forced—at least initially—to share its old building with the state school that had replaced it.[70]

This raises an important question of identity: how can a school be "Lutheran" (or Calvinist or Roman Catholic) if it has not selected its staff and most of its students on the basis of a desire to teach and learn in such an environment?

Many non-Lutheran families in Hungary have a tradition of using Lutheran secondary schools as an elite alternative. According to a history of the Budapest Fasor Lutheran Gymnasium (founded in the 18th century and taken over by the state in 1952), the proportion of pupils from Lutheran families dropped from 60 percent in 1855–56 to 26 percent in 1875–76, largely through the growth of Jewish enroll-ment to 60 percent of the school in the latter year. Jewish enrollment remained strong until (of course) World War II and the Holocaust, while Catholic students also enrolled in significant numbers.[71]

This problem was anticipated in a June 1988 article by a clergyman working at the Budapest Fasor Gymnasium. Before the suppression of most confessional schools by the Communists, he wrote, Lutheran church leaders had seen the mission of their schools in liberal terms, as being "to contribute to Hungarian culture by educating well-trained young people." It was now clear that what the nation needed was "conscious Lutheran intellectuals," capable of thinking and acting on an explicitly Christian basis. While a school must stress free decisions in matters of conscience, it was important that teachers be appointed who were firm believers, and the life of the school should include retreats and other forms of religious observance to mark its character clearly.[72]

In September 1989, the Fasor Gymnasium was able to reclaim its old building (used in the interim as government offices) and to reopen; according to the headmaster, "Young teachers who feel the necessity of finding a way out of our educational crisis and . . . elderly teachers who were taking part in pre-war Lutheran education feel a vocation for reviving a noble tradition." The need for this revival, according to the headmaster, was evident from the fact that pupils seeking admission stressed their desire not only for a high level of education but also for a "coherent moral order"; thus the program includes a "thorough religious education."[73]

A teacher in this (refounded) school reports that its Lutheran identity is expressed by compulsory religious education classes for each group of pupils (Lutheran, Calvinist, Catholic, Jewish, and Unitarian) as well as by a half-hour church service every Monday morning.

> This is not compulsory. The school day starts and finishes with prayers. There are some self-organized Bible circles. Our two American English language teachers have their English Bible session each week. A Bible knowledge competition was organized this term. There is a school retreat every term—

we invite scholars, theologians and priests* to give lectures on moral and religious questions. We attend church services together on the festive occasions of the Lutheran church and at the beginning and end of each term. Teaching literature and history, we deal in particular with the period of Reformation. We plan to start afternoon occasions where students could spontaneously talk about their problems concerning religious and other personal questions. That is an urgent demand, because the mass of students is very heterogeneous: from children of very religious, church-attached families to people who come only to get high-level education and are not much interested, and children who are not sure about themselves and would need advice.[74]

As this account demonstrates, the Marxist-Leninist indoctrination that characterized the old system has not been replaced by a coherent Christian instruction, though certainly this school is seeking to make clear what it stands for without apology.

These examples of confessional schools reclaiming their former buildings are by no means unique. Under a law enacted in June 1991, church organizations that were registered before 1948 may seek to reclaim any properties that had been confiscated without compensation. Nearly 3,000 claims were filed by Roman Catholic groups (including reviving monastic groups), while Calvinist Reformed groups sought almost 2,500 properties, with another 500 claims by 11 smaller churches.[75]

Not all new schools are outside the state system. The Városmajor Secondary School is a state school that, according to headmaster Gyula Kálmán, is politically and confessionally neutral and highly selective, offering an elite education to pupils who have passed a competitive entrance examination.[76]

On the other hand, the Burattino Foundation has developed a plan to provide a high quality of education without selection of pupils. Proponents are concerned that liberalizing the educational system could lead to increased social polarization, with the most favored pupils taught by the most capable teachers, and "at the other pole there would be numerous schools without financial support, with a counter-selection of teachers and students, recreating [an] untrained, socially peripheral generation." The Burattino model

---

*Used, in Hungary, to refer to Lutheran as well as Roman Catholic clergy.

assumes that high-quality education results from the training and talent of teachers, and can occur effectively in heterogeneous groups.[77]

Yet another proposal has sought funding from the Soros Foundation to establish a choir school for members of the Children's Choir of Hungarian Radio. In this case, selection would be based upon musical rather than academic ability, and the curriculum would be enriched with additional music instruction.[78]

Will the emergence of growing diversity and competition in education lead to widespread changes? Reformers were disappointed that the expanded autonomy offered to schools since 1985 did not lead to extensive innovation or real reform, an outcome they attributed in part to teacher apathy and the fact that this generation of teachers has known nothing else in its own education than the "Stalinist" system. It may be, however, that there has been a lack of real competition to jolt teachers out of their comfortable habits. Hungary has been a leader, in Eastern Europe, in market reforms of the economy, but the same dynamic has not been applied to the schools so far.

Indications are that it will be, and some predict that many teachers "will not be happy with the increase in consumer control, the setting of more rigorous criteria of performance, the performance-based remuneration, the right of families to a free choice of school (which has the indirect effect of ranking the work of schools and teachers), the programme-financing systems based on an evaluation of teachers' work" and other proposed reforms.[79]

Privatization of schools is supported by many Hungarian liberals because they believe it will give parents and the nation's minority communities more influence upon individual schools than can be achieved through participatory governance structures.[80]

Experience in the West suggests that organized teachers prefer to deal with decisionmakers in centralized systems where they can use their influence, rather than be accountable to parents at the school level. Some Hungarian teachers have expressed concerns that political parties will seek to interfere in schools through the new parent participation mechanisms. For this and other reasons, ways will no doubt be found to limit the actual influence of parents.

It may be that the most effective influence of parents on schools will not be through governance mechanisms, but through the power to withdraw their children; thus "schools became interested in improving the quality of teaching in order to keep their pupils." Public schools may begin to take advantage of increased financial autonomy and school-level decisionmaking because that funding will depend upon satisfying parents who have other options.[81]

On the other hand, the prospects for a truly diverse educational system, responsive to parental demand and disciplined by competition, remain uncertain. As with the reforms of a decade ago that were aimed at increasing school autonomy in the interest of innovation— "ordering people to act independently"[82]—the proposals for expanded parental choice may produce few results because of the resistance of those who have a stake in the present system. The experience of decades of a centrally planned educational system[83] in which few decisions were within the scope of teachers, much less of parents, has created habits that will be hard to change.

There are ample signs that the privatization of the Hungarian economy has slowed to a crawl because "the long shadow of the communist welfare-state mentality hangs over the parliamentary parties . . . [and] many managers and even many politicians are not completely free of a socialist mentality."[84] Judging by experience in the West, that mentality is likely to be especially strongly entrenched among educators.

On the other hand, as a teacher working in a Lutheran Fasor Gymnasium in Budapest wrote recently, "With the political change great numbers of ambitious and talented teachers have emerged, enthusiastic to put their educational Utopias into practice. . . . I think what we do need is a well-built, consistent network and a system of basic principles, without total centralization, leaving space for responsible creativity and thus creating a realistic choice of schools. . . . So we are struggling with a serious amount of problems in the new situation as well, and I am afraid we need another ten years to be able to judge if we [have] succeeded or not."[85]

The growing demand by parents for schooling that is marked by clear and distinctive values, a demand that the weakened churches are not in a position to satisfy, creates an opportunity that groups of teachers and parents could take advantage of to create new models of schooling. There are some encouraging signs that such school-level initiatives, together with the efforts of the churches, will lead to a renewed diversity and vigor in Hungarian education.

223

References

1. István Bessenyei, "Bildungspolitik zur Zeit der politischen Wende in Ungarn," in *Systemswandel im Bildungs- und Erziehungswesen in Mittel- und Osteuropa*, ed. Oskar Anweiler (Berlin: Arno Spitz, 1992), pp. 152–53.

2. Bessenyei, p. 152.

3. Figures from Randolph L. Braham, *Education in the Hungarian People's Republic* (Washington: U.S. Department of Health, Education, and Welfare, 1970), p. 15.

4. Braham, pp. 18–19.

5. József Gyori, "Educational Developments in Hungary," *EPA Info Bulletin 91*, no. 2: 18; Gábor Halász, "The Efficiency Problem and the Policy of School Autonomy in Hungary," typescript, HIER, no date, p. 2.

6. See Charles L. Glenn, *Choice of Schools in Six Nations* (Washington: U.S. Department of Education, 1989).

7. "The Gönczy Pál Reformed School Fund" (Budapest: Board of Trustees, no date); Gábor Halász, "Local Leadership in Education: The Case of Hungary," typescript, no date, p. 2.

8. "Gönczy Pál."

9. *Four Years Struggle of the Church in Hungary: Facts and Evidence Published by Order of Josef, Cardinal Mindszenty*, trans. Walter C. Breitenfeld (London: Longmans, Green, 1949), pp. 57–63.

10. Gyula Ortutay, quoted in *Four Years Struggle*, pp. 141, 144.

11. Quoted in Géza Sáska, *Centralization and Decentralization in the Hungarian System of Curriculum Policy Making Before 1980* (Budapest: Hungarian Institute for Educational Research, 1991), p. 5.

12. József Nagy and Páter Szebenyi, *Curriculum Policy in Hungary* (Budapest: Hungarian Institute for Educational Research, 1990), p. 6.

13. *Four Years Struggle*, p. 81.

14. Sáska, p. 6.

15. *Four Years Struggle*, pp. 147, 150, 158–59.

16. József Rávay, quoted in Braham, p. 25n.

17. Braham, p. 77; Jozsef Magyar, "The Cross of Religion," *This Is Communist Hungary*, ed. Robert Finley Delaney (Chicago: Henry Regnery, 1988), p. 50.

18. W. E. Westerman and H. H. Wubs, "Christelijk Onderwijs in Hongariji maakt een nieuwe start," *Bulletin* (Amsterdam) (May 1991); Halasz, "Local Leadership," p. 5.

19. *Four Years Struggle*, pp. 60–62, 97–98; Bennett Kovrig, *Communism in Hungary from Kun to Kádár* (Stanford, Calif.: Hoover Institution Press, 1979), p. 251.

20. Braham, pp. 180–81.

21. Peter A. Toma and Ivan Volgyes, *Politics in Hungary* (San Francisco: W. H. Freeman, 1977), p. 97.

22. Braham, pp. 179–84.

23. Ervin Laszlo, *The Communist Ideology in Hungary* (Dordrecht, The Netherlands: D. Reidel, 1966), p. 36; Braham, p. 186.

24. Quoted in Ilona Paul, "The Education Weapon," in *This Is Communist Hungary*, p. 159.

25. Braham, pp. 28–29.

26. Gábor Halász, "Parent Participation and Educational Policy: The Hungarian Case" (Budapest: Hungarian Institute for Educational Research, 1988).

27. *Four Years Struggle*, p. 147; Nagy and Szebenyi, p. 5; Halász, "Parent Participation," p. 8; Gyori, p. 18.

28. Feltamadas.

29. Anna Csongor, "Gypsies—the largest minority in Hungary," undated (post-1989), typescript received from the Hungarian Institute for Educational Research; Katalin R. Forray and András T. Hegedüs, "Hungarian Schools and Gypsies: Children Caught Between Two Cultures," *Ifjúsagi Szemle*, 1988, p. 71.

30. Peter Lukacs and Gyorgy Varhegyi, "At School All Day? Services and Social Policy for School-age Children," *Keziratok Beszamolok Dokumentumok*, 1989, p. 4.

31. Peter Lukacs, "Changes in Selection Policy in Hungary: the case of the admission system in higher education," *Comparative Education* 25, no. 2, 1989, pp. 219–228.

32. Braham, p. 51–77; Gyorgy Agoston, Einheitlichkeit und Differenzierung im Schulwesen sozialistischer Lander. Das Beispiel Ungarn, *"Vergleichende Bildungsforschung: DDR, Osteuropa und interkulturelle Perspektiven*, edited by Bernhard Dilger, Friedrich Kuebart and Hans-Peter Schafer, Berlin Verlag/Arno Spitz 1986, pp. 482–83.

33. Braham, p. 85.

34. Agoston, pp. 480–81.

35. Toma and Volgyes, p. 98.

36. Kovrig, pp. 425–26.

37. Paul, p. 142.

38. Andras Vitanyi, review of *Educational Policy and Educational Control* by Halasz, Lukacs, and Nagy, in *Educational Policy Research Papers* 55, Hungarian Institute for Educational Research (January 1983): 9; Lukacs 1988, pp. 3–4; Peter Lukacs, "Reforms and Reform Proposals—Changes in Hungarian Educational Policy," typescript, 1988, pp. 3–4.

39. Halász, "Parent Participation"; Halász, "The Efficiency Problem," Lukacs, "Reforms and Reform Proposals."

40. Halász, "The Efficiency Problem," p. 5.

41. Ibid.

42. Gábor Halász, "The policy of school autonomy and the reform of educational administration in Hungary," typescript, HIER, no date.

43. Halász, "Local Leadership," pp. 11–12.

44. Bessenyei, pp. 115–56.

45. Nagy and Szebenyi, p. 9.

46. Bessenyei, p. 160.

47. George Schopflin, "Opposition and Para-Opposition: Critical Currents in Hungary, 1968–78," in *Opposition in Eastern Europe*, edited by Rudolf L. Tökés (Baltimore: Johns Hopkins University Press, 1979), p. 142.

48. "What Does the Hungarian Nation Demand?" *Uncaptive Minds*, April–May 1988.

49. Tamas Kozma, "An Educationally Affluent Society? Key Issues of Hungarian Educational Policy," Budapest: Institute for Educational Research, 1989; Katalin R. Forray, "Development of Public Education: A Report for the Blue Ribbon Commission" (Budapest 1989).

50. Ibid.

51. "Gönczy Pál."

52. Judit Borbáthné Bánhegyi, letter to the author, February 7, 1992.

53. Westerman and Wubs, p. 20; Gyori.

54. Gábor Pöcze, Sándor Révész and Viktor Varga, "'Szabad Iskola': Egy reformmodell 1982–böl" ('Free School': A reform model from 1982), *Ifjusagi Szemle* (Youth Review), p. 4, 1986, quoted by Lukacs, "Reforms and Reform Proposals," p. 12.

55. Bessenyei, pp. 153–54.

56. Lukacs and Varhegyi, pp. 41–45.

57. Gabor Halasz, "The Policy of School Autonomy and the Problems of School Management in Hungary," typescript, no date, p. 11; Lukacs.

58. Bessenyei, pp. 154–55.

59. Judith Pataki, "Hungarian Political Changes Turn Education Reform into Necessity," typescript (Munich), April 22, 1991, p. 4.

60. Gábor Halász and Péter Lukacs, *Educational Policy for the Nineties* (Budapest: Hungarian Institute for Educational Research, 1990), p. 11.

61. Nagy and Szebenyi, p. 13.

62. Kemenes Laszlo, "Summary of Events over the Past Few Months in Hungary in the Domain of Catholic Education," *QIEC Bulletin* (Brussels) 111 (September–October 1990).

63. Pataki, p. 6.

64. Laszlo, p. 1; *Keston News Service*, February 7, 1991; Peter Dent, "Outcry Forces U-turn on Religion," *Times Educational Supplement*, September 28, 1990.

65. Articles in *Magyar Nemzet*, May 21, 1990; summarized by Judit Borbáthné Bánhegyi.

66. Györi, p. 19.

67. Kalman Ujszaszy, quoted in Dale Cooper, "In Vino Veritas," *Reformed Journal* (October 1990): 8.

68. *JPRS-EER-91-048*, April 15, 1991, p. 43.

69. Pataki, pp. 4–6.

70. Westerman; article in *Magyar Nemzet*, January 19, 1991, summarized for the author by Judit Borbáthné Bánhegyi.

71. Enrollments calculated from Gábor Gyapay, *A Budapesti Evangélikus Gimnázium* (Budapest: Tankönyvkiadó, 1989), pp. 35, 71, 110.

72. Páter Zászkaliczky, article in *Lelkipásztor*; summarized by Judit Borbáthné Bánhegyi.

73. Summary for the author by Judit Borbáthné Bánhegyi of an article by Gábor Gyapay.

74. Judit Borbáthné Bánhegyi, letter to the author, June 9, 1991.

75. Summarized from *Magyar Hirlap* of November 6, 1991, p. 4, in *JPRS-EER-91-176*, December 6, 1991, pp. 9–10.

76. Source: school publications and summary provided by Judit Borbáthné Bánhegyi.

77. Source: materials provided and summarized by Judit Borbáthné Bánhegyi.

78. Source: proposal and summary provided by Judit Borbáthné Bánhegyi.

79. Halasz and Lukacs.

80. Kozma.

81. Halasz, Gabor, "Higher Education in Hungary," typescript, Oktataskutato Intezet, Budapest, 1989, p. 15.

82. Title of a 1987 article by Mária Nagy, cited in Halász, "Local Leadership," p. 16.

83. See, for example, the painfully detailed discussion by Péter Lukács, "On the central planning of education," *Policy Research Papers* (Budapest Hungarian Institute for Educational Research, September 1983).

84. Karoly Okolicsanyi, "Privatization Drive Slackens," *Report on Eastern Europe* (October 25, 1991): 15.

85. Bánhegyi, February 7, 1992.

8. Russia and the Baltic Republics

It is not possible under the confused conditions of 1992 to present a comprehensive account of educational developments in the nations that have emerged from the Soviet Union since 1990.* This chapter will focus on developments in the Russian Federation, where the author has served as a member of an advisory commission,** with a briefer discussion of Estonia, Latvia, and Lithuania. The information available from the other former Soviet republics is too uneven to permit a useful discussion.

Russia

The political developments that resulted in the breakup of the Soviet Union between August and December 1991 and the establishment of an independent Russian republic could not fail to be reflected in the Russian educational system. A comprehensive education law, containing broad guarantees of educational freedom and of support for nongovernment schools, was enacted in March 1992 and, with some revision, went into effect in August 1992. The new law elects a very different spirit from the one enacted in 1984, which was widely perceived as having been written "by the bureaucrats for the bureaucrats" and thus incapable of stimulating real reform.[1]

The 1992 law was written within a new constitutional framework, created by a series of amendments to the constitution of the Russian Federation. The constitution was originally enacted in 1978 and has been amended frequently in recent years; 87 percent of the articles were modified from the 1987 text. This amendment process is now considered inadequate to place the new democratic system upon

---

*The Union Treaty of 1922, which was considered the legal basis for the Soviet Union, was abrogated in December 1991 with the creation of the Commonwealth of Independent States.

**The non-Russian members are Chairman Jan De Groof and Katlijn Malfliet of Belgium, Oskar Anweiler of Germany, Charles Glenn and John Coons of the United States, and G. van den Berg of the Netherlands; the Russian members are headed by Z. P. Dashchenskaya.

a solid foundation as a state based on the rule of law (*pravovoye gosudarstvo*).[2] Thus, an entirely new constitution has been drafted, which seeks to avoid the internal contradictions of the present version and to secure the right of ownership and other essentials of a free economy and society. While the draft has been approved by the council of deputies, it is subject to further revisions before submission to a referendum.*

The process of constitution writing for the Russian Federation gains urgency from the fact that a number of the 21 republics within the federation are themselves preparing constitutions that need to fit within an overall framework. Among the most critical issues under debate is the relationship between the federal government and the republics and regions within the federation. That this issue has not yet been resolved explains the overlapping authority that characterizes the 1992 education law.**

The constitution of the Russian Federation provides an essential framework for the new education law not only because it establishes a constitutional order that limits the centralizing traditions of the Soviet (and tsarist) states, but also because it guarantees fundamental human rights and freedoms. Such guarantees were also included in the Soviet Constitution, to be sure, but they are given enforcement power in the Russian Federation by establishment, under a law of July 1991, of a constitutional court modeled in part on the United States Supreme Court. Under the aggressive chairmanship of Valerii Zor'kin, the court promises to take seriously its mandate to protect the rights of individuals from arbitrary actions by government authorities.[3]

Creating a political, social, and economic system based on objective laws rather than on governmental decrees has been widely

---

*A new constitution of the Russian Federation was adopted by referendum on December 12, 1993. The text of this constitution and a series of commentaries on its implications for education may be found in *Educational Policy in Russia and Its Constitutional Aspects*, edited by Jan De Groof (Leuven, Belgium: Acco, 1994).

**The author participated in discussions of the international commission with members of the parliamentary committee developing the new constitution, and with the chairman of the Department of Constitutional Law of Moscow University, on September 24, 1992. The version of the existing Constitution cited in the following discussion was compiled by commission member van den Berg under the title *Constitutie (Grondwet) van de russische Federatie—Rusland, zoals laatstelijk gewijzigd op 21 April 1992*, Leiden (the Netherlands), July 1, 1992.

acknowledged to be essential to the effectiveness of the civil society that has been growing over the past several decades.[4]

The existing constitution, as amended in April 1992, provides extensive guarantees of individual rights without regard to race, ethnicity, sex, or other characteristics (article 34), of freedom of thought and expression (article 43), of religious belief and practice (article 44), of use of the individual's mother tongue (article 46), and of free education (article 57). It provides that "generally recognized international norms that apply to human rights have priority over the laws of the Russian Federation" (article 32).

Although the existing constitution also grants a right to form associations (article 50) and to establish enterprises (article 52), van den Berg notes that both this law and the drafts of a new constitution are unclear over the rights of organizations to the protection of their rights. After all, he writes,

> By regulating the legal position of a group of persons, at the same time the rights of persons are regulated. A "civil society" only can exist as a consequence of the acceptance of the idea of human rights by the state. In dealing with groups, a court should always translate the rights of the group into the rights of the persons constituting the group. Otherwise, the state may always provide individuals with certain rights, but effectively revoke them by restricting the rights of the groups created by individuals.[5]

This concern has direct implications for educational freedom. The right to establish schools, to determine the character of those schools, and to manage them independently of intrusive state supervision is essential if the freedom of parents to choose schools is to have any real meaning. In discussing the extensive rights granted under Russia's new education law to those organizing schools, one should keep in mind that these rights are in the state's power to grant, rather than inherent as a fundamental freedom. These provisions, like other recent Russian laws noted by van den Berg, are progressive yet at the same time "dangerous since they were based on the principle that the state had to organize a civil society."[6]

Turning to the education law itself, it is impossible not to admire the generous spirit that informs many of its provisions:

- Education as a fundamental right, "regardless of race, nationality, language, sex, age, health, social status, means, profession, descent, place of residence, religion, beliefs, party membership, criminal record" [article 5 (1)]

- Explicit commitment to "freedom and pluralism in education" [article 2 (e)], supported by public funding of "instruction in private state-accredited institutions" [article 5 (4)] that cannot be "lower than the norms for equivalent state or municipal institutions in the same territory" [article 41 (6)]; those educated in private schools or at home have a right to take state qualifying examinations [article 50 (3)]

- Right to education in the mother tongues of citizens "through the creation of the necessary number of appropriate institutions, classrooms and groups, and the creation of the necessary conditions for their well-functioning" [article 6 (2)]

- Possibility that individual schools—whether "state, municipal or free institutions"—may operate under statutes (we might better employ the term "charters") defining the character and mission of each school, how it will operate, and how it will be accountable for results [articles 12 and 13]; further

    the content of the education in a specific educational institution is defined by the study program (or programs) developed, approved and implemented in full autonomy by that educational institution [article 14 (5)]

    the organization of the educational process . . . is regulated by a curriculum . . . an academic calendar and a school schedule drawn up and ratified autonomously by the educational institution [article 15 (1)]

- The requirement that, as pupils are registered, they and their parents be informed about the nature and organization of the school as defined in its statutes [article 16 (2)]

- Registration of the statutes of new (and changing?) schools after review, by local authorities, through a procedure that must be open and take not more than a month, and the stipulation that the appraisal of a school is to focus on whether the necessary physical and staffing conditions "for the realization of the educational process proposed by the school" exist, but *not* on "the content, the organization and the methodology of the educational process" proposed, with a right of appeal to a court if registration is refused [article 33 (1–15)]

- Establishment of norms for the different types of education [article 7] and a process for "objective control of the quality of the graduates' schooling at any level of education . . . by the . . . State attestation office which operates totally independently of the organs of the administration for education" [article 15 (5)]

- Accreditation of an educational institution, so that it can grant state certificates to its graduates, based on an assessment of "whether the content, the level and quality of the educational programs correspond to the norms," as indicated by the success of students over three years [article 33 (16–23)]
- All types of schools—government, private, church run—are allowed to have their own bank accounts and are encouraged to supplement their income from public funds by providing additional educational services or engaging in other appropriate activities [articles 12 and 13]

A closer reading of the new education law, however, reveals potential difficulties and confusions. The law contains contradictions that could paralyze the intended reforms.

Many detailed prescriptions to be developed at the federal level could have the effect of taking back the freedom granted to regional and local authorities to make the same decisions, while these in turn seem to limit the asserted right of individual schools to make most decisions. The listing of federal, regional/republican, and local responsibilities in articles 28 through 31 is far too comprehensive and overlapping for the system to function flexibly and well.

This overspecificity appears to seek to placate rival levels of authority during a time of uncertainty over how actual power will be divided in the Russian Federation. The ambiguity about decentralization just before the breakup of the Soviet Union continues to exist in the Russian Federation:

> The overall tendency of decentralization is supported by everybody (at least overt utterances to the opposite would certainly sound very unpopular). Nevertheless, the delimitation of responsibilities at different levels of government (the country as a whole, the union republics, the autonomous republics, the cities) is not clear and the uneasy relationship between "the centre" and the republics, as well as national conflicts in several places do not make the task easier.[7]

As a result, the law assigns to each level essentially all the responsibilities it would need to exercise if the other levels did not exist.

The consequence, if officials on each level actually attempted to carry out the tasks assigned to them, would be widespread paralysis of the system and loss of the opportunity for fundamental reform.

The experience with decentralized decisionmaking for other aspects of Soviet and Russian society suggests that it is dangerous to allow the central bureaucracy to continue to make decisions as well.

> Decentralization puts the jobs of officials in the planning bureaucracies at risk. They have every reason to resist it or, failing that, sabotage it. . . . Each layer in the bureaucracy can do its bit to frustrate reform. By the time instructions to enterprise managers have filtered down from Moscow to Irkutsk, say, they may look surprisingly like the instructions they were intended to replace. . . . Central planning, though crazy, is reassuring.[8]

The 1987 Law on State Enterprises bears a certain resemblance to the new education statute in that it sought to move decisionmaking to the level of the individual enterprise while retaining central control. "As a result, the existing channels of ministerial control were left intact. Success or failure rested with ministerial officials, who could neutralize the reform merely by issuing as many state orders as before. . . . The leadership continued to call for drives to improve quality here and raise output there." The result, according to informed observers, was "a near-total failure."[9]

Decentralization of broad responsibilities to the local level—one of the final measures of educational reform before the breakup of the Soviet Union—does not necessarily translate into effective autonomy for each school and thus the professionalization of teachers and the empowerment of parents. Local authorities are now expected to carry out a wide variety of functions for schools that have not been their responsibility over recent decades, so that

> very little is left for the school (or, indeed, other institutions) itself. At least it is open to question that educational establishments do really need "help" in selecting and placing the teaching personnel or that parents will not consider "help" in bringing their children up as meddling in their personal affairs.[10]

While this transfer of functions from central to local government may seem a step toward the democratization of education, it has become increasingly clear in the West that local authority can in fact be even more intrusive than distant national authority. The popularity of Britain's policy of allowing individual schools to "opt out" of the control of local education authorities suggests that Russia should be cautious about expecting local government to supervise schools in detail.

The confusion that these contradictions could cause was very apparent to the members of the commission as we observed two days of discussions between Ministry of Education officials and local education officials on September 22 and 23, 1992. It was apparent that the latter were unclear about their responsibilities and unsure of their authority under the new education act.

A further cause for the overspecificity of this law is the need to balance the right of every individual to an education [article 4 (a)] with the free functioning of schools [article 4 (b)] within a framework of public accountability [article 4 (c)]. The law is loaded with provisions that seek to advance these purposes by balancing other provisions that serve other purposes, with the unfortunate effect that they may tend to cancel out each other's positive effects.

The extremely comprehensive list of responsibilities for each level of government raises a further concern: whether Russian government, at any level, has sufficient highly trained specialists to carry out so many sensitive and complex tasks and, if it does, whether these specialists would not be better employed in improving educational practice and school management. As Anders Åslund has pointed out with respect to the economic systems of post-Communist nations, "Administrative capacity is limited in these new states. The beneficial tasks government absolutely must perform will not be accomplished if these governments are required to involve themselves in the day-to-day management of their nations' industry and commerce."[11] The same warning applies, *mutatis mutandis*, to the temptation to seek to continue to manage rather than give overall policy direction to the educational system.

This is not to deny the critically important role of local efforts to encourage new educational initiatives and to provide ongoing staff development and networking for teachers. An account by Ben Brodinsky of discussions in Nizhni Novgorod shows how important the exchange of ideas can be for school leaders who are faced with making a wide range of decisions that previously were made for them by the government.[12]

Another function that can usefully be carried out by local government is the encouragement of diverse types of schooling so that parents will have authentic choices. Calling for a "free market" in educational services, the vice president of the Leningrad (as it was then) education commission proposed in an article in early 1991 that education districts include several types of schools and preschools, among which parents of all income levels could choose. This, he predicted, would stimulate schools to improve, give parents more control over the education of their children, and allow teachers to select schools that matched their own interests and skills. Even the government would benefit, through an independent and impartial means of assessing the quality of its own educational system.[13]

In brief, the greatest threat to the success of the education reforms intended by the new education law lies in the detailed responsibilities reserved to several levels of government, which threaten to reinforce existing habits of passivity at the school level and of meddling by bureaucrats. On the other hand, government must not become so weakened or inattentive that school staff are not clear about what is expected as the result of their efforts.

Setting clear standards for outcomes is essential if an educational system is to become diverse without falling into chaos. The right of parents to free choice of schools must be balanced with the right of their children to an education that is effective by some generally recognized standard. Thus the effort to develop educational standards is both timely and essential, but the way in which it is being approached causes serious concern.

At the conference that I attended in September 1992, the intention expressed by several speakers in positions of responsibility appeared to be to prescribe in great detail how schools would grade their pupils in many areas at many points in their schooling. This would seem to conflict with article 15 (3), "an educational institution selects its grading system in full autonomy, as well as the form, procedure and frequency of partial/preliminary exams," which I take to mean those examinations that enable the school and parents to monitor pupil progress.

One speaker seemed to propose as an innovation that pupils should be "graded on the curve" with a limit on the number of highest marks. This conflicts with a positive trend in the West that stresses the definition of measurable proficiencies and seeks to have each pupil attain mastery.

234

Setting standards for educational outcomes is only one of many tasks that could absorb the energies of Russian educational leaders for years. Some of these tasks are unavoidable; they should be defined as concretely and narrowly as possible. Those tasks of government that are nonessential should be avoided.

One that should not be avoided is the creation of a framework of educational finance that will be fair to every pupil, whatever his or her family circumstances. The growing practice of relying on tuition payments from parents to make up the budget deficits caused by hyperinflation could quickly undo the past achievement of a relatively equitable system.

The Russian Constitution provides a guarantee of access to education without cost (article 57), as did the Soviet Constitution (article 45), and a decree of the USSR Supreme Soviet in July 1991 criticized and forbade the growing practice in higher education of asking for payment from students. But views on this issue have been changing over the past several years, as reflected in a 1990 interview with the then-chairman of the USSR Supreme Soviet Subcommittee on Public Education, who said, "I don't think that paid education as such is so objectionable, if the fees are reasonable. It is even a good thing. And paid education means additional funds."[14]

Schools that continue to be part of the public system are subject also to the provision of the new education law guaranteeing "free general education" [article 5 (3)], and thus should not charge tuition, but some find ways to get around this prohibition. Parents may be asked to become "sponsors" of the school, or to provide funds in a variety of other ways—a practice not unknown in American public schools, though on a much smaller scale relative to the total costs of schooling. Even before the recent liberalization of education laws, a published account of a newly organized selective secondary *lycée* (a revived form of academic secondary education) mentioned that the director was "glad to accept donations from parents which range between 20 and 50 rubles (£20–50) per month."[15] Independent schools, by contrast, may charge any amount of tuition that the market will bear over and above the funding received from government, which is at the same level as government schools. The result is that parents unable to pay additional tuition will increasingly have unequal access to the superior educational opportunities, unless additional public funds are somehow provided.

Russian educational leaders and policymakers should see themselves as being in the position of emergency-room doctors treating severe injuries: they should concentrate their efforts upon those measures necessary to stabilize their patient and to create the conditions for eventual recovery, even if this means neglecting tasks that, under other conditions, might appropriately be carried out.

Based on the Education Law, the Russian central government (whether federal or regional/republican) should move vigorously to take measures in three critical spheres of its authority:

(1) Setting and Enforcing Standards

Government should lead a process of defining clearly and measurably the goals of education for all pupils at several stages in schooling: for example, before passage from primary to intermediate schooling (grade 4) and after intermediate schooling (grade 9).

These goals should be stated in terms of the proficiencies of which all pupils should demonstrate mastery in a limited number of core subjects regarded as essential for further schooling and for participation in a democratic society.* They should "function as standards for an objective assessment of a graduate's education level and qualifications, regardless of the form of education received" [article 7 (6)].

Setting goals for the outcomes of schooling is not the same as setting detailed requirements for how schools will operate, or as determining the subject matter of study programs [article 7 (1)], except as this is implicit in the setting of goals. As pointed out above, such requirements (though implied by some of the language of the law) would conflict directly with the intention of the law to grant significant discretion to individual schools. The need for school-level accountability will be met sufficiently by the registration and accreditation processes, and by an objective assessment of pupil outcomes.

---

*This will inevitably be a sensitive area, given the strongly ideological character of Soviet schooling. I have some concern, for example, about the precise meaning to assign to the provisions of article 2 with respect to the principles upon which education should be based. What is "the unity of culture and education at the federal level," and does it limit the diversity possible at the school level in response to the demands of parents? Does "the non-religious character of education in the state and municipal educational institutions" preclude voluntary religious instruction of the sort that is already developing in some municipal schools, or does it (more appropriately) refer to the neutrality of the state as to whether such instruction should be provided, in contrast with Poland, where it has been mandated for all schools?

These goals for the schooling of all pupils should be developed through a process that ensures broad support, both among specialists and among parents, teachers, and employers [see article 7 (5)].

If the goals are set at the level of republics and regions, there must be a process at the federal level to ensure general equivalency, as through the organization of education and culture ministers in Germany, so that pupils will have access to nationwide opportunities for further schooling and employment [article 28 (14)].

Establishment of the goals should be followed by development of alternative methods of determining whether the goals have been met by individual pupils and by schools. This is a technical task that can be carried out by university-based groups, by freestanding organizations, by individual schools, or in other ways, but should be subject to verification for comparability by the independent body mentioned in article 15 (5).

Each school should, as contemplated by article 15 (3), be free to select among approved means of measuring pupil achievement, and should be required to report the results to municipal officials and to parents. The "state assessment office" described in article 38 will provide an essential safeguard against schools that fail to serve their pupils adequately; note that it is not a state inspectorate that routinely investigates all schools, but a body that responds to requests from parents, vocational education students, or local authorities who have reasons to believe that a problem exists.

Since the purpose of the educational system is to bring every pupil, so far as possible, to the point of mastery of the essential goals, it should be possible for individual pupils who require additional time to reach proficiency to do so without incurring the stigma of failure. Similarly, schools that place a special emphasis upon serving such pupils effectively should not be judged to have failed if their pupils are able to demonstrate proficiency only after several attempts.

After grade 9, the goals for schooling are so differentiated that common standards would be inappropriate; goals should be set in each of the areas of academic and vocational training by drawing upon the expertise of specialists and employers, as well as educators.

(2) Ensuring Compliance with the Law

A simple but effective process should be established by which parents and others in the Russian Federation may seek enforcement of the educational rights guaranteed to them by the constitution, the education act, and international law, both administratively and in the courts, and without delays.

It is not necessary to detail all the issues that might arise under such a process. One example would be if a parent alleged that a school was not providing the educational services to which it was committed under its statutes. Another would be if local authorities had not ensured that appropriate education was available for all children. Another would be if a female student was denied access to a vocational program from which she would benefit [article 5 (1)]. Yet another would be if authorities refused to register a qualified private school desired and supported by parents.

This is not to suggest that it would be desirable if educational policymaking in Russia became dominated by the conflict of rights, as has occurred to a substantial extent in the United States. On the other hand, the credibility of the new system will depend in large part upon whether "redress of grievances" is generally available.

An important aspect of this process will be the ongoing clarification of the intentions and scope of various provisions of the education act. It is not clear, for example, whether article 16 (1), which "guarantees admission to all citizens living within the territory of the [municipal school] in question," in effect outlaws the long-standing practice of operating selective specialized schools in the public sector.

(3) Supplemental Funding

Primary responsibility for the financial support of schooling in the Russian Federation will apparently rest at the local level. Experience in various American states suggests that a decentralized system of funding leads to serious inequities in the support for schooling pupils who live in more and less wealthy areas. The impact of local responsibility for school support should be mitigated through the following:

(a) Supplemental funding to municipalities that cannot provide support to public and private schools up to national standards.

(b) Supplemental funding to school pupils who are more expensive than the average to serve because of physical, mental, or social handicaps, and to ensure equal access for the children of low-income parents, preferably in the form of incentives to encourage independent as well as public schools to serve these pupils [article 5 (6), article 28 (16) e].

(c) Support for the development of new forms of schooling that are judged essential to the society and the economy if these do not emerge spontaneously through local decisionmaking and new school initiatives.

These three tasks, then, should receive the priority attention of federal or republican/regional authorities. This implies that *government should refrain from undertaking some other tasks that it is authorized to perform.* In some instances, they are simply lower priority, and should wait until the most essential tasks are completed.

Other functions, though authorized by law, should preferably be left to the operation of social processes; it is not, as van den Berg reminds us, the business of the state to organize civil society. "Combining centralized planning and a market is the same as fixing a watch with parts of an hour-glass," as a radical deputy is reported to have pointed out in September 1990. The fine intentions of the new education law could easily be sabotaged, as an American observer noted several years ago: "Changing this system is not a simple matter of issuing a few decrees, for there are entire ministries full of functionaries whose main purpose at the moment seems to be monitoring any such changes and modifying them to the point of irrelevance."[16]

One of the primary reasons to stress school-level autonomy is the expectation that energies and creativity will be freed at the school level to bring about fundamental changes in the educational system; this purpose would be frustrated by excessive bureaucratic regulation, even with the best of intentions.

It is unclear to what extent schools that remain within the state or municipal systems will actually enjoy the degree of autonomy that appears to be promised by article 32. It would be a serious mistake if the real autonomy of these schools did not extend beyond that provided by "school-based management" schemes in many American cities. In that event, these schools would be at an enormous competitive disadvantage in relation to private schools, and an opportunity to fundamentally reform the entire system would be tragically lost.

"The primary lesson that has been learned from the reform process so far," comments a specialist on the Soviet economy, is "that the old system is extremely resilient and stable (if highly wasteful and inefficient), that it must be subject to a more serious shock, to more serious competition, if it is to begin to change fundamentally."[17] The new education law creates a framework within which Russian schooling could receive the serious but beneficial shock that would set it on the road to effectiveness and freedom.

New Educational Initiatives

Despite confusion over the interpretation of the education law that came into force in August 1992, about 300 independent schools had been registered in Russia as of September 1992.* The Ministry of Education had issued regulations in 1991 that, in the course of defining new types of schooling, recognized the existence of nongovernment schools, though without committing public funds to them, and Minister of Education Eduard Dneprov met in October 1991 with school administrators who were organizing an association of independent schools, "each with its own curriculum, its own textbooks, even its own property."[18] This was consistent with his declared commitment to break with the "authoritarian, heavily centralized and bureaucratic" nature of the Russian educational system and promote "a variety of educational structures."[19]

Reportedly, many other schools are somewhere in the process of becoming registered or, in the widespread confusion of the moment, are simply going about their business without seeking registration. A likely result of the economic and political crises experienced by Russia in 1992 is to lessen the value of state funding compared with what can be obtained from parents who have managed to prosper from the new economic opportunities, while weakening the credibility of state authority. Registration may not seem as urgent to those starting new schools as it would under other circumstances and as it will when the Russian economy and government revenues become more solid and the oversight provisions of the new law are effectively in place. At that point, the registration procedures, if kept simple and focused upon essentials, should help to address the reportedly uneven quality of independent schools.[20]

By the estimate of a Ministry of Education official, about 50 percent of the new independent schools serve the primary grades (1–4), and

*A comprehensive report is being compiled, and should become available by the end of 1992.

240

perhaps only one or two grades initially, though many of these may intend to develop intermediate grades 5–9 as circumstances permit. Another 30 percent serve secondary grades 10–11, the level at which Russian pupils specialize after completing compulsory schooling. Perhaps 20 percent serve the full range of grades.[21]

Most attention has been attracted by the new secondary schools, some of which charge high tuition (up to 500,000 rubles, or $2,000, a year at September 1992 rates) and emphasize Western languages and business methods for aspiring entrepreneurs. A number of business enterprises have started schools for the children of their employees, and to ensure well-prepared future employees. In some cases, it is anticipated by the Ministry of Education official, these schools will eventually offer grades 5–9 and even 1–4 to prepare pupils for secondary studies.

Under laws adopted in 1990 to clear the way for new business enterprises, some entrepreneurs perceived the tax exemption for income derived from educational services as a way to shelter income from other sources by declaring an educational purpose to their efforts. It seems likely that this is a transitory phenomenon, though it threatens to confuse the situation for parents and to cloud the debate over educational freedom.

Other new schools have been founded in response to demand for education based upon specific values and beliefs. The first independent Protestant school in Russia opened in September 1990 in Moscow, and soon enrolled 200 pupils, and a Jewish yeshiva has also opened in Moscow. Many public schools have reportedly introduced voluntary Orthodox religious instruction, despite the constitutional and statutory provision for the religious neutrality of public education; there was heated discussion in 1990, in fact, over proposed legislation that would have made that practice legal.[22]

Independent schools have been springing up in all parts of the Russian Federation, even 6,000 miles from Moscow on Sakhalin Island.[23]

In Moscow, around 80 independent primary schools were registered as of September 1992, out of 1,300 primary schools altogether. Most of these schools, according to the Ministry of Education official, were just started by people who loved children and knew some alternative method of teaching; she was uncertain whether the new provisions for funding would bring more profit-making motivations into play.

Of the registered independent primary schools in Moscow in September 1992, five were Protestant, four were Jewish, one is a Waldorf school (and some others using aspects of the Waldorf pedagogy), and one or more were Montessori schools. Others employ a variety of approaches.

A particularly interesting phenomenon is the spread of schools using the Accelerated Christian Education (ACE) program from Texas; 65 ACE schools were operated in Russia, Ukraine, and Estonia as of September 1992, 20 of them in Moscow. The expansion was so rapid that ACE staff expected to reach 100 schools by the end of the year.

I was able to visit an ACE school in the Kuntzevo district of Moscow, where it shares a building with a public early-childhood program. The Kosmos School was started by two women, a kindergarten teacher and a doctor, who were dissatisfied with what the public schools offered to young children. The teacher had heard of ACE from a former classmate at her teacher-training institute, who started an ACE school in Sverdlovsk in September 1990. ACE worked with the two women to develop the curriculum for their school, providing training and individual instruction and assessment materials for a highly structured program.

The organizers of the school have been raising funds to renovate a nearby abandoned building into additional classroom space so that they can admit a second class next fall and gradually develop a full program through at least grade nine; there were 2,000 applications for the 30 places available this year.

The Kosmos School teaches in both English and Russian from the start, admitting children who have already started to read in Russian or have passed a reading readiness test. Despite the highly individualized nature of the ACE program, the children have a considerable amount of group time, including a daily Bible lesson stressing one of 60 character traits identified by ACE. These are taught by a young man who was clearly enthusiastic about the lessons' moral content, while telling me that "we are Orthodox, of course."

The young Canadian ACE consultant working with this school had only recently arrived from helping another school in Kiev (Ukraine), and stressed that he could be in another, even newer, school by Christmas. He explained that the Ukrainian government had asked ACE to provide its program to a number of government schools, and that there were also church-sponsored ACE schools in the former Soviet Union, as well as private schools like Kosmos.

Descriptions of American ACE schools in the professional literature have generally been hostile to what is described as their regimented and individualized nature, so I was pleasantly surprised by the relaxed and cheerful atmosphere of Kosmos. It is very difficult for evangelical schooling to obtain a fair hearing from the American education establishment, but it seems to have struck a chord with Russian parents looking for individualization, English, and positive morals teaching.

The Kosmos School has been registered by the authorities and was slated to receive public funds in January 1993, at the same level as similar public schools, while continuing to charge tuition.[24]

In addition to the independent schools that have started in the past several years, there are many public schools that have taken advantage of their new freedom to modify their programs in significant ways. One such school that I visited in September 1992 attracts pupils from a wide area by offering supplemental instruction in the Tatar language and culture.

Officially still known as "Kindergarten 1076," the Tatar school grew out of a small Saturday program that drew children from several schools for supplemental lessons. After several years, the organizers decided that what was needed could not be accomplished in the time available, and decided to organize a full-week kindergarten drawing Tatar children from anywhere in Moscow. They sorted through 300,000 individual record cards to identify potential pupils, and contacted parents directly and with the help of cultural associations and Moscow's three mosques. In September 1991 a first grade was started, and the following year a second grade was added, with the intention of growing to the full K–9 structure.

There is interest also in reviving the Tatar secondary school that operated before World War II. The building, given by a Tatar merchant, was confiscated by the Ministry of Foreign Affairs in 1940, but there is hope of getting it back or of obtaining another facility.

The children in the Tatar primary school learn through Russian in the mornings, then have Tatar lessons in the afternoons, with the intention of giving children some proficiency in their ancestral language. Some of the children speak primarily Russian at home, while a few are indeed of Russian ancestry; others come to the school speaking primarily Tatar.

The staff are clear that academic skills must be developed primarily in Russian for the sake of the children's future, and that they will need to learn English as well to qualify for higher education, but they are determined that the children will "have something to pass on to their children" of their heritage. Thus they organize summer visits to a Tatar village near Nizhni Novgorod, and are seeking to build ties with Tatarstan, an autonomous republic within the Russian Federation. Tatarstan officials have declined to provide financial assistance, however, pointing out that Russian children in Tatarstan have a right to Russian education and that Russian officials should reciprocate for Tatar children in Moscow.*

Just as Kosmos School provides daily Bible lessons, the Tatar school celebrates Islamic festivals (with extensive help from parents) and is unapologetic about morals instruction. It should be noted that there is a long tradition of respect for schooling among the Tatars; this school no more conforms to Western stereotypes of Islamic schooling than the Kosmos School conforms to stereotypes of "fundamentalist" schooling. The classes that I observed were lively, engaging, and purposeful, and the staff insisted on high expectations for the children.

The Tatar School has not yet taken advantage of the new education law's provision for individual school charters, but the organizers have applied for their own bank account and have relied heavily upon "sponsors" within the Tatar community to improve classroom equipment and purchase Tatar materials.[25]

Among the new school projects is an "international children's complex" under development in Novokosino near Moscow, sponsored jointly by the Moscow Board of Education, the Russian Center for Pedagogical Innovations, and the University and Pedagogical Institute of Amsterdam. Two secondary schools will serve 1,300 pupils each, with a heavy stress on languages and business education.[26]

Other innovative projects grow out of the alternative schools provided under the Soviet system for particularly talented pupils. The Scientific Study Center of Novosibirsk University enrolls 400 boarding pupils from some 10,000 15- and 16-year olds who apply each

*During the conference that the author attended on September 22, 1992, First Deputy Minister of Education Vladimir Novichkov volunteered that instruction was being provided only through three languages, even though other groups were entitled to such native-language instruction.

year, and has taken the lead in allowing pupils to select up to half of their courses outside of the mandatory curriculum.[27]

The Russian Ministry of Education had been actively promoting innovation in public schooling for several years before the new education law was enacted. Plans for experimental approaches to school organization and pedagogy were approved fairly routinely, and by the 1990–91 school year there were 16 *gymnasia* and *lycées* in Moscow alone.[28] The "School of Art, Culture and Freedom," for example, receives 20 percent supplemental funding to support a pupil-centered experiential program; only one of its 30 teachers is certified in the usual manner, and learning is promoted through a wide range of activities outside as well as inside the school. When the school opened in 1991, there were 500 applications for 60 places available; in 1993, the school will expand to grades 5 through 11.[29]

Some Russian public schools are exploring how to "opt out" of their municipal systems. Moscow School 27, for example, sent a delegation to visit an independent school in Cambridge, Massachusetts, to understand how it functions.[30]

According to Victor Firsov, many of the new schools are based upon "romantic" concepts of pedagogy and do not cover the entire curriculum; some may therefore prove to lead to educational dead ends.[31]

New educational initiatives are indeed emerging in bewildering diversity, and without the benefit of policies that would ensure that they contribute to the overall reform of the educational system. This is perhaps a price that, in the short term at least, is necessary to pay to prevent the initiatives from becoming bogged down in a highly centralized system of decisionmaking.

To see the hundreds of new or transformed schools springing up in Russia as primarily the result of the new education law would be to fall into the error of some Western Soviet specialists of attributing too much significance to the actions and declarations of central authority. That law is rather an attempt to provide a framework of legality and accountability for a system that was already beginning to renew itself from the bottom up through spontaneous action by some teachers and parents.

The educational system had undertaken an earlier set of reforms in 1984, intended to revive the energy and effectiveness of classroom teaching, though without making changes in bureaucratic decision-making or in the status of teachers that might have given such reform a prospect of success. In this, Soviet education reform in the 1980s had a more than superficial resemblance to reform in the United States. By starting school one year earlier—at six, as announced in 1984—more time would be devoted to Russian language, computer training, social studies, health and ethics, vocational courses, and other studies. Lest this seem to signal a turning away from the ideological function of Soviet schooling, the Communist Party Program of 1986 reasserted the importance of atheistic education and civic obedience.[32]

The 1984 reforms were motivated by the realization by Party and government leaders that the Soviet educational system was not adequate to the demands upon it. Ordered from the center, like many attempts at reform of American education, the reforms reportedly had little impact upon school and classroom practice. By 1988, highly placed critics of the system were describing its "bankruptcy" as a "mass slaughter of talent."[33]

Parallel with these bureaucratic measures, however, was a more potent pressure for reform by teachers with new educational ideas and parents dissatisfied with the adequacy of schooling. The implementation of mandatory secondary education during the 1970s was intended to create the educated workforce that would permit transition to a sophisticated economy, but it also led to a growing criticism of the rigidity of schools from parents who came to demand something better for their children.[34]

Influential parents had long found ways to manipulate the educational system in the interest of their children. About 10 percent of the 1,300 schools in Moscow, for example, provided specialized programs that required admission on the basis of a selection process, often for first grade.

Although the Soviet educational system officially was deeply opposed to any form of privilege other than giving the children of workers an advantage in admission to the more desirable programs, there is abundant evidence that well-educated parents manipulated successfully to give their children every educational advantage, and that members of the *nomenklatura* had no difficulty in doing so.[35]

The Russian republic issued regulations in 1943 dividing towns and rural areas into residentially based attendance areas for individual schools; "the problem of parental choice was thus ... neatly solved: there was none." Mandatory assignments were in fact far more effective than in American communities because the Soviet system of internal passports made change of residence (and thus of school) out of the reach of most parents.[36]

The determination to impose educational uniformity in pursuit of egalitarian goals weakened in the 1960s, when "in spite of the defeat of that proposal in the text of the school law, the movement to build specialized schools for the gifted" began, on the model of the schools for pupils talented in music, fine arts, and ballet. Up to 100 schools were designated as "experimental," under the aegis of the Academy of Pedagogical Sciences. A network of schools offering instruction through foreign (non-Soviet) languages was created, and the Academy of Sciences and some universities established schools for pupils gifted in math and science.[37]

Soviet émigré Alexander Zinoviev pointed out that there were

> privileged schools which it is not simple for ordinary mortals to enter. There are special schools in which the teaching of certain selected disciplines is far superior to that in ordinary schools. The vast majority of educational establishments attractive to young people are in fact closed to the majority of those who want to go to them. . . . The children of parents with a high social position have a better chance of entry to [higher education] institutes irrespective of their state of preparedness.[38]

With the growth of the educated classes over recent decades, and a "proportionate erosion of [their] faith in the state's ability to organize and micromanage . . . the provision of services,"[39] however, the possibility of accommodating growing parental demand through selective schools faded. As in Poland and Czechoslovakia, much of the early impetus for independent schools in Russia came from groups of well-educated parents who were not satisfied with the options available to their children in the existing state schools.[40]

Articles began to appear in the late 1980s calling for "drawing pupils into the learning process," for "going with the pupil to the subject rather than with the subject to the pupil," for a "pedagogy of cooperation" that would be concerned with developing the personality and not simply intellectual abilities, for protecting the individuality of each pupil from the pressures (long recommended) of "collective education," for a "pedagogy of renewal" and a "humanizing of the school" and against the cultivation of "obedient mediocrity." "When are pupils going to learn to seek the truth, argue with each other, form their opinion and learn to defend it?" a young teacher asked in the pages of the education newspaper.[41]

Nor was this concern limited to the quality of schooling; reform of the education system was seen as fundamental to reform of Soviet society.

> The school ... has found itself unprepared to accept the ideas of *perestroika* and still remains the most conservative, politically backward and materially poor sector. [Organizational reshuffling] has so far created merely a semblance of changes for the benefit of the school, which now needs not reform but revolutionary transformation. . . . It is here, in the sphere of education, upbringing, and enlightenment, that the defeat of *perestroika* will bring about irreversible, catastrophic consequences.[42]

As demand grew for a more differentiated and more democratic educational system, the educational authorities of the Soviet Union issued in September 1989 a new schedule for secondary schools that expanded significantly the number of periods that could be devoted to subjects determined by the various republics, by each school, and by pupils and their parents. The new flexibility was intended to correct an overly centralized policy that "did not take into account the diversity of educational needs of individuals, of society and of the state."

The national government would henceforth determine 41 percent of the course requirements over 11 years of schooling, the individual republics 42 percent, and the schools the remaining 17 percent, the determination of which was the *"exclusive right of the school."*[43] Most of the latter, or 12 percent of the total, would be elective courses.

This modification of curriculum requirements provided welcome elbow room for school staff who were already exploring new approaches to education. Like the 1992 education statute, however, it was not itself the cause of the new diversity that began to develop in Soviet education. Many teachers had already reversed the Stalinist formula that "everything not permitted by law is prohibited,"[44] and were doing what seemed best to them in their classrooms unless it was clearly and *effectively* forbidden by law or regulation.

As democracy began to emerge in Russia, observers noted that it would require radically different behaviors from teachers. "Teachers who are passive, unquestioning champions of the status quo cannot be expected to educate citizens capable of building a new social order."[45]

This is not to suggest that all Russian teachers are enthusiastic about fundamental reform. A sociological study published in 1990 found that between 10 and 15 percent of the teachers surveyed believed that totally new forms of schooling needed to be created, about 25 percent wanted to pursue moderate reforms, and about half wanted education to remain much as it was.[46] This resistance to change has meant that "the government has extended them a freedom that most don't want. When the ministry's history division stopped shipping uniform lesson plans, panicked teachers bombarded it with letters asking what they were supposed to teach." Stephen Kerr estimates that only 10 percent of Russia's 1.4 million teachers have been in contact with the current reforms, and that only 1 percent have changed their classroom practices.[47]

With such a high proportion of teachers oriented toward the status quo, it is not surprising that both parents and teachers wanting schools of a significantly different character began to consider going outside the public educational system, especially as *privatisatsia* became a watchword for economic reform. When encouraged to behave in very different ways in the classroom, some teachers naturally sought to change the institutional framework within which they did their work.

"One reads daily in the educational press," a British expert reported in early 1991,

> of the setting up of lycées and gymnasia, teaching many subjects which were not before available in the general system. These experiments are mostly going on in what were formerly the local area schools, sometimes taking over only a part of the school. Sometimes it is at the instigation of a group of teachers, sometimes it is with the support of the local education authority. If additional funds are needed this [sic] is sought either from the local education authorities, or from some charitable fund or perhaps from one of the cooperative organizations. Less often so far from the parents, although this is now being discussed. At the same time there is a constant movement for change in the methods of teaching and for creating greater choice of subjects within the general school system.[48]

The new flexibility in government schools did not satisfy all of those concerned with the education of their children; "underground" private schools began to develop several years before their existence was permitted by changes in government policy. *Literaturnaya gazeta* of July 15, 1987, carried an interview about efforts to open a secondary school "operating on a cooperative basis." As one of the organizing teachers explained,

> Year after year, each of us sees youngsters (there are a few in every class) whom we would like to teach in a different way. They are ready-made young explorers who are seriously fascinated by some subject or other. . . . Unfortunately, the omnivorous nature of the school curriculum (a little bit about everything) and the equally strict requirements for success in all subjects interferes with the development of these youngsters. They must be taught differently.

The proposed teacher-organized school would be selective (based upon entrance tests and an interview) and fee charging; pupils would spend a significant part of their school day working on elective subjects. The school would not have a principal but would be managed by teachers, parents, and pupils.[49]

In another proposal appearing in *Uchitel'skaia gazeta* in early 1991, the former head of a public school described an initiative to organize an elementary school that would be open for everyone willing to pay (in contrast with the elite group of secondary public schools) and that would be strongly child-centered and innovative.[50]

Around the same time, a professor at the teacher training institute in Sverdlovsk, in the Urals, published an article calling for the organization of an independent and highly diverse educational system parallel to that of the state.[51]

The ferment leading to new independent schools is only one among many expressions of changes in Soviet society that have gathered force over the past 20 years. In the process, "new and polymorphous experiments in opposition to bureaucratic authoritarianism have contributed to the gradual erosion of the prevailing ideological myths and to the coalescence of loosely structured, grassroots groups, associations, organizations, and movements."[52] One observer has pointed out that, when Gorbachev told Moscow writers in 1986 that "Soviet society is ripe for change," he was understating the case: Soviet society was already deeply engaged in change. Some

30,000 grassroots voluntary organizations had already developed outside of the supervision of the Communist party and the government.[53]

Many of those who formed such groups, an article in *Pravda* conceded in 1987, were seeking to isolate themselves from Soviet reality. Independent youth organizations sprang up as a challenge to the former monopoly of the Komsomol, which was "regarded as an instrument for mobilizing the energies of its members to achieve specific goals [of the Party] rather than as a means of giving youth a voice in the political process."[54]

Although it is only one form of self-organization, the development of new models of schooling, whether private or public, has proved to be one of the primary spheres for what Gorbachev described in 1989 as "the emergence of new millions of people into the arena of social activity."[55]

Estonia

Estonia is the northernmost of the three Baltic republics that broke away from the Russian empire in 1918, enjoyed a little more than two decades of precariously independent life, and then were occupied by the Soviet Union under the notorious Molotov-Ribbentrop Pact of August 1939. Independence was restored by all three in 1990.

The Estonian language is related to Finnish and (more distantly) to Hungarian and to Lapp. Estonian-speaking people have lived in the area since the third millenium B.C., though often under foreign domination: German, Danish, Swedish, Polish, or Russian.[56]

Russian rule was imposed stably in 1710, though Baltic German elites continued to dominate economic, cultural, and even administrative affairs until the late 19th century, when Russian authorities, in reaction to the failed Polish rebellion of 1863 against Russian rule, sought to impose cultural Russification in all parts of the tsar's dominions. The Estonian educated class that had been emerging within the German cultural milieu was inspired to undertake a movement of national awakening, seeking to extend schooling to the predominantly rural population and to train teachers. At first, this movement was directed against German cultural hegemony rather than Russian political hegemony, and indeed saw the tsar's government as an ally, but gradually the pressure for Russification alienated Estonian intellectuals, and by the early 20th century they were demanding universal elementary schooling in the Estonian language and control over the educational system.[57]

The collapse of the tsarist regime in 1917 and the ensuing civil war allowed an independent Estonian state to emerge; in 1920, the Soviet regime recognized the independence of Estonia and renounced forever all claims to its territory. Free, compulsory elementary education in Estonian was decreed by the new government, though the system inherited from Russian rule was so deficient that the goal was barely achieved in the short life of independent Estonia.[58]

After it occupied Estonia in 1939, the Soviet regime moved quickly to suppress all possibilities of resistance, executing thousands and deporting to Siberia tens of thousands of leading Estonian citizens. Even in the face of impending war with Germany, the Soviets remodeled Estonian education, deporting or executing all schoolteachers considered unreliable—about 10 percent of the total, initially—and abolishing all private schools and religious instruction in state schools. As was already the practice in the Soviet Union, "all subjects were henceforth to be taught in the spirit of Marxism-Leninism." Books published before 1940 were destroyed in large numbers, including 70,000 volumes of theology.[59]

After World War II and several years of German occupation, the campaign to achieve the complete "sovietization" of Estonian life was resumed; farms were collectivized, landowners and their families were deported to the Gulag (from 8 to 12 percent of the rural population in March 1949), together with many of the clergy, and religious literature was banned.[60]

Resistance to Soviet rule, though largely suppressed during the period of Stalinism and its aftermath, began to emerge in the late 1960s. At first, the protests had to do with abuse of human rights, but gradually Estonian nationalism became the dominant theme. The steady influx of Russian workers into the Baltic republics, the most industrialized section of the Soviet Union, led to fears that the Estonian language and culture would be overwhelmed; "will the nation disappear?" they asked.[61] For example, only 17 percent of the television programming provided in 1980 was in Estonian. There was growing pressure to use Russian, though Estonians were very resistant to making it their first language.[62] As national feeling grew, indeed, the proportion of Estonians claiming to be fluent in Russian declined from 29 percent in 1970 to 24.2 percent in 1979.[63]

Soviet citizens were identified by "nationality" on the internal passports that every citizen was required to carry. Individuals were not free to choose with what nationality they would be identified, except in the case of children of mixed marriages, who were required to make an irrevocable choice at 16. The strength of personal identification with Estonian nationality is apparent from the selections that such young people made as early as the 1960s. Children of mixed Estonian/Russian parentage in Tallinn (where the population was evenly divided) selected Estonian nationality by a 62:38 margin, contrasted with those of mixed Belorussian/Russian parentage in Minsk, who identified themselves as Russian by 66:24.[64]

Despite pressures to use Russian as the unifying language of the Soviet Union, most parents continued to take advantage of their right under Soviet law to send their children to schools using the prevalent language of their republic. This inclination did not change significantly in the second generation to live under Soviet rule, even as the proportion of Estonians in the population of the republic dropped from 74.6 percent in 1959 to 61.5 percent in 1989. In 1956–57, 77 percent of the elementary and secondary schools used Estonian as the primary language of instruction, and the proportion fell only to 73 percent in 1972, rising back to 77 percent in 1988. Although there was strong interest in instruction using Estonian, actual treatment of Russian and Estonian was by no means equitable, especially with the drive that began in 1981 to teach more Russian. The study of Russian began in the first grade of Estonian schools, while that of Estonian began in the third grade of Russian schools in Estonia; moreover, Estonian schools were required to provide nearly three times as many periods of Russian instruction as Russian schools provided of Estonian instruction.[65]

In April 1988, resistance to Soviet and Russian hegemony came to a head with a declaration drawn up by leaders in Estonian cultural organizations, charging that the relationship between the Soviet Union and its republics was responsible for "an unprofitable economy, uncontrolled migration, increased risk of an ecological catastrophe, and failure to satisfy the population's social and cultural needs."[66] A declaration of "sovereignty," the right to veto all Soviet laws, was adopted seven months later. Sixteen months after that, in March 1990, the Estonian Supreme Soviet declared that it was moving toward restoration of the pre-1940 independent status.[67]

Since declaring full independence in 1991, Estonia has been vigorous in asserting its distinctive cultural identity and reducing Russian
influence. Although almost one-third of the population is Russian,
only those whose families lived in the country before the Soviet
takeover were initially granted citizenship. Others had the option
of becoming citizens in 1993, after elections in which they were
not allowed to vote. Language requirements intended to substitute
Estonian for Russian in all public transactions have been especially
galling, and the Russian Federation Parliament has accused Estonia
of violating the rights of Russians on its territory.[68]

Although some sections are still taught in Russian in Estonian
universities, all students must demonstrate proficiency in Estonian
before being awarded a degree.

In addition to concerns about the language of instruction and of
society, many Estonian parents and educators sought fundamental
changes in the nature of schooling. They complained that

> the present centralized school schedule and curriculum plans
> are oriented toward an impersonal, statistically average
> Soviet pupil, giving only second- or third-place consideration
> to his abilities, preferences, interests, his national, matura-
> tional and social particularities. . . . Initiatives by pupils and
> even by teachers in the school have been limited, which has
> had serious effects for the entire society.[69]

As a result of these frustrations, several alternative schools have
been established since 1988 in Estonia. These include

- The Music House of the Old City (*Vanalinna Muusikamaja*) was
  the first of these schools; it seeks, according to one account, to
  unite Roman Catholic teaching with alternative pedagogies,
  including some derived from the Waldorf schools based on the
  ideas of Rudolf Steiner.[70]
- The Kolga School is an "open school" that stresses learning
  through activities, with the major stress on communication and
  on self-knowledge.
- The Rosma Free School in Pölva is a Waldorf school, occupying
  the former home of an Estonian education reformer, renovated
  for this purpose by the local government.
- The Free School of Tartu is another Waldorf school, beginning
  with kindergarten and planning to add the elementary grades.

- The Nömme Free School in Tallinn is another Waldorf school that started with six-year-olds, with the intention of adding additional grades.

Although the Waldorf pedagogy is especially popular for alternative schools, a Finnish school that uses the Freinet pedagogy is helping to establish a similar school in Järve in Estonia.

In Narwa, near the border with Russia, the population is 96 percent Russian and only one out of fourteen schools teaches in Estonian. Russian-speaking parents have organized an alternative school that seeks to develop in children an appreciation of both the Estonian language and culture and also what they consider the authentic, non-Soviet Russian culture.

The University of Tartu is now offering training in the alternative pedagogies popular in educationally progressive circles in western Europe.[71]

Latvia

The Latvian People's Front, organized in the fall of 1988 and victorious in the elections held in late 1989 to early 1990, stressed in its January 1991 program the importance of the "development of an independent system of national education." The educational system would have to be transformed, with "both private instruction and home study a part of it"; licenses would be issued for private schools. Freedom of conscience would be recognized "in all areas of public and personal life," and the educational system would "cease mandatory instruction in atheism and reject the mandatory study of any religion."[72]

Russian would continue to be taught in Latvian schools, but only as one foreign language among others. Ethnic minorities (mostly Russian) would continue to have the opportunity for elementary and secondary schooling in their home languages, but it was "essential that there be strict compliance with the status of Latvian as official language and that a favorable psychological atmosphere be created for use of the Latvian language."

The education statute adopted by independent Latvia on June 19, 1991, was consequently different in several significant respects from the previous Soviet.

The most controversial change in the education laws had to do with the role of the Latvian language. While parents had previously (generally as in other Soviet republics) been entitled to choose either Russian or Latvian as the first language of instruction for their children, and university courses were offered in Latvian as well as in Russian,[73] access to higher-level educational and employment opportunities required a high level of proficiency in Russian, a fact that many Latvians considered discriminatory. Under the 1991 legislation, however, all students seeking higher education will be required after July 1, 1993, to pass an examination in Latvian even if they attended schools in which Russian was the primary language of instruction and Latvian was taught (as Russian parents complain) very badly.[74]

While similar provisions have been adopted in other newly independent states, the issue is particularly sensitive in Latvia, where the native population has been more nearly overwhelmed by immigrants than in other parts of the former Soviet Union, with the exception of Kazakhstan. Of 2.7 million inhabitants in 1989, only 52 percent were Latvian, and a study a decade before found that only 20 percent of the non-Latvian population could speak Latvian. The situation for the Latvian character of the nation is even more grave in urban and industrial areas: the population of Riga is only 27 percent Latvian.[75]

Preservation of the Latvian language and curtailment of immigration from Russia, Belorussia, and Ukraine (attracted by the higher standard of living in the Baltics) had been leading concerns of the protest movement that emerged in Latvia in the 1980s.[76] The official Soviet policy, while allowing instruction through the Latvian language, had been to promote Russian from the earliest grades which, according to the minister of education in 1979,

> safeguards the effectiveness of patriotic internationalist education, promoting the development of high moral and ideological-political qualities among pupils.[77]

The establishment of Latvian as the only official language is therefore an act of cultural self-preservation and also a rejection of the political program associated with the promotion of Russian. This does not make it any easier for the large non-Latvian population, mostly Russian speaking, to accept. Conflict has arisen over the issue of Latvian citizenship:

> Latvians fear that the future of their nation will be endan-
> gered if non-Latvians are granted citizenship too easily, and
> they claim that the Russians were brought into Latvia [by
> the Soviet government] as part of a deliberate policy of Russi-
> fying their country. The Russians, for their part, assert that
> they have a right to remain . . . and that they would be loyal
> to their new homeland, independent Latvia.[78]

The June 1991 education statute also gave permission for the establishment of nongovernment schools and required that national and
local government contribute to their support up to 80 percent of
costs.[79]

Lithuania

Since declaration of Lithuanian independence from the Soviet
Union in March 1990, the educational system has been undergoing
a steady process of reform, which has included measures to promote
educational freedom and to end the ideological hegemony of the
state in schools. These changes have been opposed by former Communists and Social Democrats; the Democratic Labor Party criticized
"new attempts, under cover of depoliticization, to forcefully ideolo-
gize culture, education, creative art" and "the categorical denuncia-
tion and destruction of expressions of yesterday's [that is, Soviet]
culture."[80]

The goals adopted by the Ministry of Culture and Education,
however, include creating "democratic, depoliticized and demilita-
rized Lithuanian schools," "a variety of educational forms and private initiatives in the sphere of education," and "a certification
system for educational institutions of all types, public and private."[81]
Private initiatives are expected to create the diversity that will allow
parents, as one Lithuanian educator put it, to make mistakes and
to correct them.

> There must be applied gradual regulation of relations among
> different kinds of schools and the state. It is a consequent
> [responsible] process. It cannot exist without a variety of
> schools, and without a proper balance between the need of
> the state to assure that the children are prepared for their
> future as citizens and the demands of freedom for parents
> to make decisions about their own children, we won't be
> able to free man's creative abilities and make progress in
> our way.[82]

There is, as this comment suggests, a strong emphasis on the role of the family in Lithuanian policy. In contrast with their counterparts in the United States, Lithuanian education officials predict a decrease in the need for preschool education as new social policies make it more possible for mothers to remain home with their young children, "giving the prerogative of bearing and upbringing of children to families."[83]

Soviet education in Lithuania had alienated many parents because of its stress on debunking religious truth claims and practices. A secondary school principal wrote recently that, until 1988, teachers were not free to express their personal views, nor could parents select schools or the subjects that their children would study. He surveyed 106 pupils in his school, aged 16 to 18, and found 81 percent favored allowing parents and children to choose schools reflecting "their convictions and values," and only 2 percent opposed. Teaching religion in schools was supported by 63 percent of these youth, and opposed by 19 percent. Asked about the education of their own (future) children, only 2 percent of the pupils said they would want them to attend a uniform state school, while 75 percent "would like their children to study in a high school which would provide for a possibility to select different teaching contents and ideas," and 22 percent would like other kinds of schools.[84]

Under the Soviet regime, "atheistic ideas were forcibly spread and because of that parents expressed their reproaches [against the] school. The teachers were forced to make lists of the schoolchildren who believed in God, and speak against religion."[85]

The new education statute adopted in 1991 provided for religious instruction in public schools upon request of parents; during the 1991–92 school year, according to the Ministry of Culture and Education, 67.5 percent of the pupils in Lithuanian-language schools and 91.3 percent of pupils in Polish-language schools, but only 12.2 percent of pupils in Russian-language schools, participated in this (almost exclusively Roman Catholic) religious instruction.[86]

As this description suggests, parallel education systems are provided for children of the different language groups. Although the proportion of schools that instructed primarily in Lithuanian (88 percent) had not changed significantly from the height of Stalinist oppression in 1952–53, when 85 percent of the schools were Lithuanian, or from the prewar independent Lithuania of 1938–40, when

88 percent of primary schools were Lithuanian, these figures fail to do justice to the deep sense among Lithuanians that Soviet rule involved a determined assault upon their cultural distinctiveness through the educational system.

> The Lithuanian language has been used everywhere although the Soviet occupation has been trying to restrict its usage. Attempts were made to curtail its usage in official life ... students majoring in Russian were given higher scholarships, teachers received higher salaries. Russian schools were favored. The Lithuanian community sensed the danger to its language and defended it constantly. . . . In primary and secondary schools, grades 1–12, instruction was in Lithuanian. All textbooks (except foreign language and Russian texts) were written in Lithuanian.[87]

The 1991 education statute provided that language minority groups, primarily Russian and Polish, would, in areas where they lived in significant concentration, continue to have state-supported kindergartens and elementary and secondary schools, based on parent choice "of desirable teaching language." In areas where the concentration was insufficient to provide separate schooling, language minority children could have supplemental classes in the home language. These schools and programs are supervised by an Office of Schools of National Minorities in the Ministry of Culture and Education.

This provision has not eliminated all tensions over the position of these minority populations in the educational system. In March 1992, for example, the Lithuanian government ordered supplementary history textbooks published in Poland removed from Polish-language classrooms. "Warsaw did not respond in kind, but declared that Lithuanian-language schools in Poland would continue to use books published in Lithuania, and expressed the hope that in accordance with the Polish-Lithuanian declaration of January 1992, the Lithuanian side would observe the principle of reciprocity."[88]

Other language minority groups benefit from the same provision. The Jewish community, once so significant in Vilnius and elsewhere in Lithuania, has reemerged to provide sufficient demand for a publicly funded school in Vilnius and a supplemental program in Šiauliai. Ukrainians have supplemental home language programs in

Vilnius and Sniečkus, where there is also a supplemental Belorussian program and supplemental Armenian and Kharaim programs.

In 1990–91, there were 1,801 Lithuanian schools, 85 Russian schools, 44 Polish schools, 1 publicly operated Jewish school and 110 schools that used some combination of languages.[89] As of December 1991, the language use in the different types of schools was as follows:[90]

	Periods a week			
	Lithuanian	Russian	Polish	English
Lithuanian schools	81	20		25
Russian schools	36	78		27
Polish schools	75	16	30	21

Although members of language minority groups represent a much smaller proportion of Lithuania's population than in Estonia and Latvia, there is a continuing potential for conflict around ethnic issues. A substantial part of the country, including the capital, Vilnius, was part of Poland until World War II, and elements in Poland continue to raise issues of the cultural autonomy and human rights of Lithuania's Polish minority. Poland gave strong support to Lithuania's struggle for independence, but the demand that a Polish university be established (again) in Vilnius caused some cooling of relations.[91] Community leader Czeslav Okinczyc has complained that the schools provided for Polish children are inferior to those provided for Lithuanian children, and that very few Polish secondary school graduates are able to go on to university. Poles in Lithuania are sharply underrepresented in higher education, and those who go off to Polish universities do not return to lead the Polish community of Lithuania.[92]

Lithuanians retort that the "national minorities" have not done enough by their own efforts to preserve their cultural heritage, and that the most pressing need is to achieve national unity around a revived Lithuanian identity.

Summary

Russia and the three Baltic republics have each taken steps to revitalize their educational systems by making provision for parent choice, school-level initiatives, and the diversity among schools that is the consequence of both. The results can best be characterized as very uneven, as the habits and institutional structures developed under decades of Communist rule have inevitably proved resistant to the intended changes. The uncertain pace of educational reform in these countries is a reminder that education depends upon a subtle interaction of schools, families, and society, with the effects of explicit governmental policy often muffled and not infrequently producing unanticipated consequences that are the opposite of what was intended.

Fortunately for those who value educational freedom, the new experiences of a free society (however compromised and confused) and the expectations growing out of those experiences seem likely to produce an increasing democratization of schooling. The genie of freedom is out of the bottle, and parents and teachers—and pupils themselves—will continue to transform existing schools and to create new ones.

References

1. Stephen T. Kerr, "Reform in Soviet and American Education: Parallels and Contrasts," *Phi Delta Kappan*, September 1989, p. 21.

2. See the discussion by William E. Butler, "Towards the Rule of Law," in *Chronicle of Revolution*, ed. Abraham Brumberg (New York: Pantheon Books, 1990), pp. 72–87.

3. Ger van den Berg, "Human Rights in the Legislation and the Draft Constitution of the Russian Federation," *Review of Central and East European Law* 18, no. 3 (1992): 202, 230.

4. Mikhail Gorbachev to the 28th Party Congress, July 14, 1990, cited in Detlef Kuchenbecker, "Gegenwärtige Tendenzen im Sowjetischen Bildungsrecht," in *Systemswandel im Bildungs- und Erziehungswesen in Mittel- und Osteuropa*, ed. Oskar Anweiler (Berlin: Arno Spitz, 1992), p. 86.

5. van den Berg, p. 239.

6. Ibid., pp. 237–38.

7. Nikolai D. Nikandrov and Mikhail L. Levitski, "Urbanisation and Education: The USSR Perspective," typescript, 1990, p. 3.

8. Clive Crook, "And Now for the Hard Part," *Economist*, April 28, 1990, p. 11.

9. Crook, p. 12.

10. Nikandrov and Levitski, pp. 4–5.

11. Anders Åslund, "Four Key Reforms," *American Enterprise*, July/August 1991, p. 53.

12. Ben Brodinsky, "The Changing Role of the Soviet Secondary School Principal Under Perestroika," *NASSP Bulletin*, May 1991.

13. Iuri Maleishev, "Six Steps Beyond the Horizon," *Uchitel'skaya gazeta* 6, no. 3 (February 5–12, 1991); summarized for the author by Bissera Antikarova.

14. Alexander Tomasz Massey, "Soviet Institutions' Plan to Charge Fees Is Declared Illegal," *Chronicles of Higher Education*, July 24, 1991; Vladimir Belyayev, "Education, Rebuilding from the Bottom Up," *Soviet Life*, November 1990, p. 2.

15. Jennifer Louis, "A Fresh Start That Echoes Tsarist Times," *Times Educational Supplement*, July 14, 1989, p. 13.

16. Paul Craig Roberts, "Seven Days That Shook the World," *National Review*, October 15, 1990, p. 26; Kerr, pp. 25–26.

17. Richard E. Ericson, "What Is to Be Done?" *New Republic*, March 5, 1990, p. 37.

18. Herbert Buchsbaum, "Coming In from the Cold," *Agenda* (Winter 1992): 54.

19. Huw Richards, "Reforms That Might Delight the British Right," *Times Educational Supplement*, August 17, 1990.

20. Andrea Rutherford, "Soviet Students Learn Some New Lessons," *Wall Street Journal*, February 26, 1991.

21. Interview with Elene Sergeevna Seninskaya, chief specialist of the department of nonstate educational institutions, Moscow, September 25, 1992.

22. Ron Popeski, "Supreme Soviet Passes Law on Freedom," *Boston Globe*, October 2, 1990; Ken Sidey, "New Law Extends Religious Freedom," *Christianity Today*, November 5, 1990, p. 77; Elya Vasilyeva, "Alexis II: New Patriarch of the Russian Orthodox Church," *Soviet Life*, November 1990, p. 49; "For Christian Parents in Moscow: The Beginnings of Educational Choice," *World*, April 1991.

23. Francis X. Clines, "Outsider on a Soviet Island Builds a Free-Market Model," *New York Times*, October 15, 1990.

24. Interview with Jane Simonyan, September 24, 1992.

25. Interview with Larisa Ivanovna Sokolova, September 25, 1992.

26. Jennifer Lewis, "Lessons for the Free Marketeers," *Times Educational Supplement*, February 14, 1992.

27. Jordana Hart, "Soviet Schools Will Change, Russian Educator Says," *Boston Globe*, February 9, 1992.

28. Kirsten Goldberg, "Pedagogical 'Perestroika': Education Reform, Soviet Style," *Education Week*, October 12, 1988, pp. 10–11; Felicity Barringer, "Rigidity Gone, Soviet Schools Learn Dissonance," *New York Times*, September 13, 1991; Gregory Gransden, "Crisis Hits System under Strain," *Times Educational Supplement*, August 23, 1991.

29. Stephanie Simon, "Experimental Moscow School a Lesson in Freedom," *Los Angeles Times*, June 9, 1992.

30. Hart.

31. Victor Firsov, "Educational Reform and the USSR," presentation at the annual meeting, American Educational Research Association, San Francisco, April 1992.

32. Donald W. Treadgold, "Perestroika and Soviet Education," *Issues in Soviet Education*, National Advisory Council on Educational Research and Improvement (March 1988): 40–41.

33. Jennifer Lewis, "Reforms Aim to Release Students' Hidden Talents," *Times Educational Supplement*, September 2, 1988.

34. Oskar Anweiler and Bernhard Schiff, "Krise und Erneuerung von Schule und Erziehung in der Sowjetunion," *Osteuropa: Zeitschrift für Gegenwartsfragen des Ostens* 40, no. 10 (1990): 571; Vasilii G. Razumovskii, "Die Vergleichende Pädagogik und die internationale Zussamenarbeit: Thesen aus Sowjetischer Sicht," in *Systemswandel*, pp. 27–28.

35. David K. Shipler, "The Willing Suspension of Disbelief," in *Soviet Politics and Education*, ed. Frank M. Sorrentino and Frances R. Curcio (Lanham, Md.: University Press of America, 1986), p. 268; *Soviet Education: The Gifted and the Handicapped*, ed. James Riordan (London: Routledge, 1988).

36. Mervyn Matthews, *Education in the Soviet Union: Policies and Institutions since Stalin* (London: George Allen & Unwin, 1982), p. 10.

37. Jaan Pennar, Ivan I. Bakalo, and George Z. F. Bereday, *Modernization and Diversity in Soviet Education* (New York: Praeger, 1971), p. 101.

38. Alexander Zinoviev, *The Reality of Communism* (New York: Schocken, 1984), p. 160.

39. S. Frederick Starr, "Soviet Union: A Civil Society," *Foreign Policy* 70 (Spring 1988): 29.

40. G. Kreidlin, " 'We want to open a school on a cooperative basis,' " *Literaturnaya Gazeta*, July 15, 1987, cited in *Soviet Education Study Bulletin* 7, no. 2 (Summer 1989).

41. A generous sample of such articles is reprinted (some in abbreviated form) in *Osteuropa: Zeitschrift für Gegenwartsfragen des Ostens* 40, no. 10 (1990): 573–606; James Muckle, "*Glasnost* in the Communist Curriculum," *Times Educational Supplement*, September 30, 1988, p. 29.

42. Lyudmila Saraskina (June 1988), quoted in Gerald Howard Read, "Education in the Soviet Union: Has *Perestroika* Met Its Match" *Phi Delta Kappan*, April 1989, p. 608.

43. Official document entitled "Ob utverždenii gosudarstvennogo bazisnogo učebnogo plana srednej obščeobrazovatel'noj školy" (Approval of the State Basic Schedule of Comprehensive Secondary Schools), translated into German in *Osteuropa: Zeitschrift für Gegenwartsfragen des Ostens* 40, no. 10 (1990): 599; emphasis in the original.

44. William E. Butler, "Towards the Rule of Law," in *Chronicle of Revolution*, ed. Abraham Brumberg (New York: Pantheon Books, 1990), p. 80.

45. Stephen T. Kerr, "Ya uchus' v sovetskoi shkole (I Study in a Soviet School)," Seattle: typescript submitted to *Novoe Vremia* (Moscow), February 1991, p. 8.

46. Study by A. Ovsjannikov (1990), cited in Kuchenbecker, p. 82.

47. Buchsbaum, p. 56.

48. Jeanne Sutherland, letter to the author, March 10, 1991.

49. G. Kreidlin, "Private School for Bright Children Asked," *Current Digest of the Soviet Press* 39, no. 38 (1987): 20–21; Simon Solowejtschik, "Underground-Schule," *Neue Zeit* 35 (August 27–September 2): 1990.

50. T. Luban, "Open for Everybody," *Uchitel'skaia gazeta* (Teachers Gazette), no. 11 (1991); summarized for the author by Bissera Antikarova.

51. V. Bezrukova, "Out of the Dead-end Street," *Uchitel'skaia gazeta* (Teachers Gazette), March 5–12, 1991, summarized for the author by Bissera Antikarova.

52. Vladimir Tismaneanu, "Unofficial Peace Activism in the Soviet Union and East-Central Europe," in *In Search of Civil Society*, ed. Vladimir Tismaneanu (New York: Routledge, 1990), p. 1.

53. Starr, p. 27.

54. Eduard Kuznetsov, "The Independent Peace Movement in the USSR," in *In Search of Civil Society*, 55; Alexander Rahr, "Old and New in the Komsomol," *Radio Libert Research* 196/88 (May 6, 1988): 3.

55. Mikhail Gorbachev at the April 25, 1989 meeting of the Central Committee of the Communist Party, quoted in Charles H. Fairbanks Jr., "Gorbachev's Cultural Revolution," *Commentary* (August 1989): 23.

56. Toivo U. Raun, *Estonia and the Estonians* (Stanford, California: Hoover Institution Press, 1987), pp. 3–34.

57. Ibid., pp. 62–95.

58. Ibid., p. 134.

59. Ibid., pp. 154–55.

60. Ibid., pp. 176–88.

61. Riina Kionka, "Who Should Become a Citizen of Estonia?" *Report on the USSR*, September 27, 1991, p. 23.

62. Raun, pp. 195–97, 205.

63. Nigel Grant, "Multicultural Education in the USSR," in *The Making of the Soviet Citizen: Character Formation and Civic Training in Soviet Education*, ed. George Avis (London: Croom Helm, 1987), p. 201.

64. Rasma Karklins, *Ethnic Relations in the USSR* (Boston: Unwin Hyman, 1986), p. 38.

65. Romuald J. Misiunas, "The Baltic Republics: Stagnation and Strivings for Sovereignty," in *The Nationalities Factor in Soviet Politics and Society*, ed. Lubomyr Hajda and Mark Beissinger (Boulder, Colo.: Westview Press, 1990), p. 214; Raun, pp. 211–12; Peter Hilkes, "Bildung und Erziehung im Spannungsfeld nationaler Beziehungen: das Beispiel Estland," in *Systemswandel*, p. 38.

66. Quoted in Geoffrey Hosking, *The Awakening of the Soviet Union* (enlarged ed.) (Cambridge, Mass.: Harvard University Press, 1991), p. 96.

67. Nadia Diuk and Adrian Karatnycky, *The Hidden Nations: The People Challenge the Soviet Union* (New York: William Morrow, 1990), p. 130.

68. Jon Auerbach, "Moscow Says Estonia Violates Rights of Its Russian Residents," *Boston Globe*, July 18, 1992, p. 5.

69. Rein Virkus, "Die Schulerneuerung in Estland," in *Systemswandel*, p. 46.

70. School descriptions are taken from "Zum Stand der freien Schule und der Alternativpädagogik in Estland," typescript prepared by Sirje Priimägi (Tartu University) with Tiiu Bläsi-Käo for a conference in Helsinki, May 1991; provided to the author by Siegfried Jenkner, University of Hannover.

71. Priimägi and Bläsi-Käo.

72. "Program of the Latvian People's Front," translated from *Baltiyskoye Vremya*, January 8, 1991 in *JPRS-UPA-91-016*, March 25, 1991.

73. Karklins, p. 108.

74. Friedrich Kuebart, "Das neue Bildungsgesetz der Lettischen Republik," in *Halbjahresbericht zur Bildungspolitik und pädagogischen Entwicklung in der UdSSR, der Republik Polen, der ČSFR und der Volksrepublik China* 1/1991, ed. Wolfgang Hörner, Ruhr-Universität (Bochum: Arbeitsstelle für vergleichende Bildungsforschung, October 1991), pp. 13–17.

75. Diuk and Karatnycky, p. 117.

76. Romuald J. Misiunas, "The Baltic Republics: Stagnation and Strivings for Sovereignty," in *Nationalities Factor*, pp. 96–99.

77. Mirdza Karklinš, quoted in Misiunas, p. 219.

78. Jan Arveds Trapans, "Latvian Supreme Council Faces Split over Citizenship Law," *Report on the USSR*, September 27, 1991, p. 22.

79. Kuebart, p. 14.

80. "Program Statement: On the Lithuanian Democratic Labor Party's Near-term Activity Goals" (from *Tiesa*, December 15, 1990), *JPRS-UPA-91-018*, April 5, 1991, p. 27.

81. From a documentation package provided to the author by the Ministry, 1991, p. 16.

82. Stanislavas Taišerskis, letter to the author, May 7, 1991.

83. "The Educational System of Lithuania: Aims—Structures—Reforms" (Ministry of Culture and Education, no date), p. 5.

84. Stanislavas Taišerskis, letter to the author, May 7, 1991.

85. Ibid.

86. Zivile Bandorienne, "Some aspects of the educational system of Lithuania," trans. by Judita Junkeryte-Mauersberger, typescript prepared for the author by the Ministry of Culture and Education, December 1991.

87. From a documentation package provided to the author by the Ministry, 1991.

88. Stephen R. Burant, "International Relations in a Regional Context: Poland and Its Eastern Neighbors—Lithuania, Belarus, Ukraine," typescript, 1992, p. 22.

89. From a documentation package provided to the author by the Ministry, 1991.

90. Stanislavas Taišerskis, letter to the author, December 12, 1991.

91. Saulius Girnius, "The Lithuanian Citizenship Law," *Report on the USSR*, September 27, 1991, p. 21.

92. Richard J. Krickus, "Lithuania's Polish Question," *Report on the USSR*, November 29, 1991, p. 21; Stephen R. Burant, "Polish-Lithuanian Relations: Past, Present, and Future," *Problems of Communism*, May–June 1991, p. 79.

9. Eastern Germany

In determining the order of chapters for this study, I found the chapter on the former German Democratic Republic created the most difficulty.* To the extent that the study has focused on the development of a legal and policy framework for the exercise of educational freedom, it seems natural to deal with Germany as the final and culminating point; the people of the eastern *Länder* have inherited a fully elaborated set of laws anchored in the German Constitution and defended by a constitutional court. In a sense, the task of protecting schools and parents from the arbitrary exercise of government power is complete, and Germany can thus serve as a benchmark for the process that is still going on in other post-Communist societies.

To the extent, however, that this study has focused on the contribution of schools that correspond to the educational goals of teachers and parents to the reemergence of civil society, the German example does not serve as a natural culmination to the story. As many Germans themselves have noted, the people of the eastern *Länder* are suffering a sort of hangover from freedom obtained too easily.** Simply taking over models developed in the West, along with massive financial subsidies, has short-circuited the process of learning how to be free and responsible.

The example in another sense is not an altogether happy one with which to conclude. Although educational freedom is explicitly guaranteed by the constitution of unified Germany, its actual exercise has been hedged with such restrictions that there is not the rich

---

*This chapter focuses primarily upon the former German Democratic Republic (East Germany), with as much information about the preunification Federal Republic (West Germany) as is necessary to explain the policies now applicable to the entire nation.

**Although there are some indications that Germans from the western *Länder* are suffering more: according to *The Economist* (August 15, 1992), the proportion from the western *Länder* complaining of headaches or migraines rose from 25 percent to 33 percent between 1989 and 1992, while the proportion of Germans from the eastern *Länder* actually fell from 33 percent to 28 percent!

diversity of educational offerings that might be expected in a country with a strong tradition of alternative pedagogies. One legal specialist charges that German educational policy continues to be "marked by a statist understanding" of the role of the school that continues to be rooted in a "Prussian absolutist tradition of the State's comprehensive authority to determine the shape (*Gestalt*) of the education which occurs in schools." This is in fundamental conflict, he argues, with the present nature of society, marked by a pluralistic understanding of values.[1]

Educational Diversity in Prewar Germany

The people of the eastern *Länder* of Germany have not found the gift of freedom altogether easy to accept. After all, the Communist regime in power for 45 years was particularly insistent on ideological orthodoxy, as its very name (Socialist Unity Party of Germany or SED) suggests. "Of all the East European Communist parties," one observer concluded just before their collapse, "it seems that the SED takes ideological issues most seriously."[2]

The German educational system has long been characterized by a high level of state supervision. Education reformers in other nations in the system-building period of the early 19th century frequently praised the active role of the Prussian government, in particular, in promoting quality improvements and standardization of schooling.[3]

The Enlightenment-inspired rulers of Prussia and Austria during the late 18th century had asserted the authority of the state in education over the churches and individual families. Austrian Empress Maria Theresa decreed that education was a *politicum*, an affair of the state, and began in 1760 to create the administrative structure that would make this a reality. A comprehensive regulation was issued in 1774, with the goal of implementing uniform norms for schooling by gradually incorporating or eliminating the diverse forms of schooling that had developed over the previous centuries. All children whose parents did not provide private tutors were required to attend school from ages 6 to 12, and their teachers were expected to use a standard method of instruction and forbidden to use nonauthorized textbooks.[4]

Adopting a requirement of elementary schooling did not mean, of course, that schools immediately became available for the entire population of the Austrian empire; diversity was even more characteristic of some 1,800 principalities and other political entities into which Germany was still divided. In the areas ruled by Prussia and in other parts of Germany influenced by Enlightenment goals of remaking and "improving" the common people, a process of state intervention and leadership began to create educational systems. It is important to stress that these state efforts were not directed so much at *creating* schools—many existed already, through the efforts of communities, individuals, churches, and organizations of all kinds—but at *organizing them into systems of schooling* that would be responsive to state objectives.[5]

This state dominance did not emerge all at once, it should be noted, and it was tempered by a policy of working through the state-supported Protestant and Catholic churches. One result was that the development of alternative schooling was modest, in contrast with the United States and other countries where parents wishing denominational schools were forced to go outside of the government-sponsored educational system. The desire for religious schooling thus did not lead to really significant alternatives in German education. Government itself provided Catholic and/or Protestant schools in most parts of the emerging Germany of the 19th century. Elementary schools, in particular, were placed under the supervision of local pastors and stressed religious instruction.

The great majority of public elementary schools continued to be either Protestant or Catholic in Prussia and Bavaria until the 1930s. Even the nominally interdenominational schools found in some areas were often de facto confessional, since the population was so overwhelmingly Protestant in some areas and so overwhelmingly Catholic in others that only one form of religious instruction was provided. Children of the other confession might attend nongovernment Catholic or Protestant schools, which received a corresponding subsidy from public funds.[6]

In 1932, just before the takeover by the National Socialists, there were roughly 4,560,000 Protestant elementary schoolchildren in Germany, of whom 3,365,000 (74 percent) attended Protestant public schools, 1,142,000 (25 percent) interdenominational public schools, 24,000 (0.5 percent) Catholic public schools, 29,000 (0.6 percent) secular public schools, and 17,000 (0.4 percent) nongovernment schools.

Catholic students were even more concentrated in confessional schools, with 2,295,000 (85 percent) of 2,702,000 attending Catholic

269

public schools, 337,000 (12 percent) interdenominational public schools, 64,000 (2 percent) Protestant public schools, 6,000 (0.2 percent) secular public schools, and 17,000 (0.6 percent) nongovernment schools.

There were in that year altogether 52,959 publicly supported elementary schools in Germany, of which 29,020 (55 percent) were Protestant, 15,256 (29 percent) Catholic, 8,291 (16 percent) interdenominational, 295 (0.6 percent) secular, and 97 (0.2 percent) Jewish.[7]

German education, although dominated by the state (less than one pupil in 200 attended nongovernment schools) was thus marked by diversity. At the elementary level most public schools were confessional, reflecting the religious makeup of the local community, while secondary education was divided among three types of schools of varying academic difficulty, the *Hauptschule*, *Realschule*, and *Gymnasium*.

Despite this measure of structural diversity, German education was not marked by a commitment to parental choice. It was the rights of the established Catholic and Protestant churches rather than those of individual parents that accounted for diversity in elementary schooling, and it was selection by schools rather than by parents that marked secondary education.

Under the Weimar Republic in the 1920s, conflicts over the confessional character of elementary schools "exceeded in intensity and scope all other conflicts over school policy."[8] The political struggle developed during the writing of a constitution between those supporting confessional schools and those wanting to use education to develop common loyalties to the new political system, or a "school of national unity."

Prussian Minister of Culture Carl Heinrich Becker stated in 1919 that Germany needed a cultural policy consisting of "the conscious employment of spiritual values in the service of the people and of the state to achieve internal consolidation and strength for external competition and struggle with other peoples."[9] The idea of using education as an instrument of state policy was thus an element in the agenda of the postwar liberal democracy.

Although the Social Democrats—opponents of confessional schooling—were the largest party in the National Assembly elected in 1919, they were forced into compromise with the Catholic Center party and Protestant conservatives. The decision about whether schools would be organized on a confessional basis was left up to "those entitled to determine the education of the children," though with a provision that "Christian interdenominational schools" would be the norm unless parents requested otherwise. Article 120 of the Weimar Constitution provided that "the education of their children for physical, intellectual and social efficiency is the highest duty and natural right of parents, whose activities shall be supervised by the political community."

As Helmreich observes, this clause "was directed against the extreme Socialist demand for "community upbringing" (*Gemeinschaftserziehung*), but it was also aimed at the Catholic theory that parents' rights over their children's education were outside the sphere of the state."[10]

Article 146 provided that

> for the admission of a child to a particular school, his gifts and interests, not the economic and social position or the religious confession of his parents, is [sic] decisive. In each community, therefore, elementary schools will be established based upon the confessional or worldview demand of those responsible for education [that is, parents or guardians], provided that a well-organized school system is not affected thereby. The desires of those responsible for education are to be respected so far as possible.[11]

This compromise left room for each group to press for its preferred type of school at the local level. Socialists could seek "secular" schools, liberals could insist that interconfessional schools were the norm unless parents asked for an alternative, and Catholics and Protestants could count on most parents to request continuation of the existing arrangements. In one significant change, clergy supervision of schools—more a burden than a source of real authority for pastors—was abolished.

Nongovernment elementary schools could be established only if "there is in the municipality no public elementary school of their religious type or of their worldview, or if the [public] educational administration recognizes a special pedagogical interest." Schools based on a worldview were those whose distinctiveness was not religious but based on some form of humanistic pedagogy.

The state's control of education was made absolute during the subsequent period of Nazi rule. Although Adolf Hitler's initial statement of his government's policy in 1933 promised that "the national

Government will allow and confirm to the Christian denominations the enjoyment of their due influence in schools and education," the National Socialists moved to eliminate this source of alternative loyalty as soon as they were securely in power. The extension of direct and exclusive state control in education was an important element of the Nazi program of radical centralization and imposed uniformity, in which everything possible was done to eliminate competing sources of opinion and independent thinking. "The influence of uncontrollable or, from a National Socialist perspective, opposed educational forces (such as Family, Church, private schools, residential homes, and alternative pedagogies) was eliminated to the greatest extent possible. In this connection the closing of almost all experimental and private schools was considered a decisive measure of educational policy."[12]

A primary instrument of the Nazi program was the "German Community School" (*Deutsche Gemeinschaftsschule*); the phrase echoes the earlier Socialist demand for *Gemeinschaftserziehung*. In 1937 Hitler insisted that "this Reich will hand over its youth to no one, but will take its education and its formation upon itself."[13] By 1939 Nazi leader Martin Bormann issued a directive that

> the creation of an ideologically objective school system is one of the most important tasks of the Party and the State. . . . Not for nothing have the political Catholics, above all, realized the importance of teaching the young and controlling their spiritual growth and character building. . . . [Thus]
> (a) the State ought to be the basic organizer and controller of the school system. In many cases, the private schools and institutions can be simply transferred from the [teaching] Orders to the State. . . .
> (b) in many cases, particularly where public schools are available, private schools can only be regarded as superfluous, especially those which cannot be regarded as ideologically objective. The pupils should be put in the public school system, and the private schools closed.[14]

And, in a second directive two months later, he ordered that "by the end of the year, no educational institutions should exist which are under denominational influence."[15]

To implement these directives, all government subsidies for non-government school salaries were cancelled, and many religious schools were closed or taken into the state service. Religious instruction in public schools was greatly reduced in its role, and teachers were urged to replace "Christian teaching with a 'germanified' religion" that omitted the (Jewish) Old Testament and inculcated loyalty to the regime. Nazi ideologue Alfred Rosenberg boasted that "the curriculum of all categories in our schools has already been so far reformed in an anti-Christian and anti-Jewish spirit that the generation which is growing up will be protected from the black [i.e., clerical] swindle."

As a young girl wrote in her confirmation class, "In our religious knowledge period we have to speak about our Führer and must learn poems about him. We do not need any poems or sayings about Paul or John."[16]

While of course schooling for acceptance of the Nazi worldview did not survive the collapse of Hitler's regime, the effect of Nazi policies was a long-term weakening of alternative influences upon German education, including those of the churches.[17]

The "Command Pedagogy" of Communist Schooling

The postwar governments in East and West Germany took very different approaches to countering the results of Nazi education policies. "In hardly any other sphere is the division of Germany and the development of two states so clearly expressed as in the functions assigned to political formation and instruction in the educational system."[18]

In the West, the decision was made to exclude from the school all efforts on the part of the state to shape the values and the character of children, and to make it possible, once again, for independent schools to provide a competing approach to education. The goal of political education was to shape a "mature citizen" capable of "understanding political processes and decisions and of acting according to democratic norms and individual interests in his sphere of responsibility and life."[19]

In the East, by contrast, the authorities decided to maintain the ideological control of schools seized by the Nazis and use it "to re-educate the population on the basis of new values, new norms of behavior and a new image of society." They assumed an identity between the interests of the individual and the state that required that schools adapt the former to the latter.[20]

The character of East German schooling was marked until the end by the experience of the 1950s, when its mission was less one of education than of *reeducation* of an entire society, starting with the teachers themselves. Special stress was placed upon creating in each school a Communist party cell for staff and a Communist organization for pupils, and upon orchestrating ceremonies and events of all kinds to ritualize and reinforce commitment to the new order.[21]

Although presented as the only means to undo the legacy of National Socialism, this Communist program in fact essentially continued Nazi education policies. The first East German school law, enacted in May 1946, insisted flatly that "the education of youth in schools is exclusively an affair of the State,"[22] and its successors under the Communist regime were marked to an increasing degree by the monopoly of all decisionmaking power in the central state/Party bureaucracy.

The traditional German dominance by the state of the educational system was, in Communist-controlled East Germany, taken to its logical extreme of "an unlimited and centrally operating state educational monopoly," based on what the preamble to the 1965 law called the "leading cultural and educational function of the state." The goal was the creation of a "unitary Socialist educational system."[23]

The stress on unity extended to an insistence, in the law, on unitary goals, unitary courses of study, and unitary providers of education. No room was left for diversity, with the exception of the kindergartens, which in some cases were under church sponsorship. No possibility of conflict could occur between the views of (good) parents and those of the state on the best interests of children.[24]

Nor was this unitary political education confined to children; the 1968 East German Constitution stipulated that "the unitary Socialist educational system guarantees each citizen a continuity of instruction, education, and adult education," and defined the function of cultural life as "the full development of the Socialist personality." The Communist regime sought in a sense to make society as a whole into an educational system from which there would be no escape.[25]

As late as June 1989, Margot Honecker (wife of the chief of Party and state and the longest-serving minister of education in the world) insisted that there would be no fundamental change in the mission of the system of schooling.

This program was carried out with German thoroughness, so that as a study published in 1987 put it, "The educational system of the GDR [German Democratic Republic] reveals a logic, consistency, and homogeneity that cannot be matched in any Western state. Indeed, in this respect the GDR surpasses its eastern neighbors, Poland and Czechoslovakia, whose communism is reluctantly embraced, as well as the Soviet Union, whose immensity and diversity make homogeneity a virtually unachievable goal. East Germany is a small cohesive state firmly committed to its Marxist-Leninist ideology."[26]

To extend the power of the state and Party to all forms of organized schooling, the few nongovernment alternative schools offering various forms of *Reformpädagogik*, such as those implementing the pedagogical theories of Steiner, Petersen, or Montessori, were suppressed. Their crime was to stress individualism and creativity, which was directly contrary to the educational goals of the regime. They were condemned as providing a form of "late-bourgeois pedagogy" inconsistent with the Soviet models that schools should follow. A single Catholic school for girls in grades nine through twelve was allowed to survive in East Berlin.[27]

As an East German educational authority wrote, in an article on "the optimal development of the personality of each pupil," "It is not being multi-talented or possessing originality that is worthwhile in the expression of individuality, but how this is connected with social orientation, activity and responsibility, with making the potential of the individual useful for society, for the collective." The goals of political education were summarized in the sequence of stages by which it was expected to proceed: "Knowledge—Consciousness—Understanding—Conviction—Action."[28]

The effort to impose the Soviet model of schooling, while not entirely successful, was far more so than the contemporaneous effort by American occupation authorities to persuade West German educators to adopt the comprehensive secondary school. The East German regime obediently declared that Soviet education was the most "progressive" in the world, and that the first priority in school reform was to spread the "progressive scientific knowledge of Marxism/Leninism and of Soviet pedagogy" among teachers.[29]

The campaign to "build Socialism," beginning in the mid-1950s, was less concerned with changing the economy through abolishing free markets and private ownership of enterprises—this was already largely accomplished—than it was with political mobilization to "create a new consciousness among the masses." It was thus to a large extent an educational campaign, in the broadest sense, and placed heavy responsibilities on schools and their teachers to "convey a fundamental knowledge of Marxism/Leninism," as the 1965 education statute put it, so that their pupils could "grasp the Meaning of Life in our times and think, feel and act in a Socialist manner." "Pedagogical guidance," wrote an official journal, "is political guidance toward laying the foundations in pupils for the worldview and morality of the working class."[30]

The Communist party thus undertook an "ideological occupation of the school" that was intended to be a cornerstone of its power; as one of its leaders told an American reporter, "We cannot expect the older ones to change their ways, but the youth, they must be convinced of the superiority of Communism." This became all the more critical as East German youth came increasingly under the influence of the music, clothing, and lifestyle of the Western youth culture, which the Party saw as a deliberate offensive on the part of the enemies of socialism.[31]

The underlying premise of the Communist educational program was the total availability of human beings to serve the purposes of the state rather than to pursue their own purposes. This implied that the school would have to exert an unprecedented influence and would not need to adapt itself in any way to the ways in which children differ. The comprehensive, unitary school could be implemented with no concessions to the interests, aptitudes, or needs of its pupils, "leveling them down to the lowest common denominator, producing formalistic learning and estrangement from reality."[32]

Quite apart from political indoctrination, many came to feel that the insistence of Communist school authorities on uniformity placed serious barriers in the way of meeting the needs of pupils. If East Germany suffered from the effects of a "command economy," its schools suffered also from a "command pedagogy" that sought to make uniform "individual gifts, accomplishments, and interests, that demanded too much of the weaker and reined in those capable of greater achievement," that was centrally controlled and led by the nose by detailed plans.[33]

There was an important exception to this insistence upon the unitary school: children who gave evidence of special talent for sports or for science were identified in the third grade for assignment to specialized schools that promoted these aptitudes intensively, at the cost of a well-rounded education.[34] Thus, despite the frequently expressed formal commitment of the East German regime to a unitary structure of education, alternative provision was in fact made for gifted pupils. This provision produced an opportunity for well-connected parents to manipulate the system to obtain preferential treatment for their children. Special classes and even special schools were created to provide intensive preparation in Russian, math, and science, or sports.[35]

Such exceptions aside, the educational system did not accommodate individual interests or values. Not that this effort was particularly successful in creating the "socialist personality" so constantly discussed in East German pedagogical materials, the personality that united knowledge with enthusiastic conviction in socialist partisanship (*Parteilichkeit*).[36] Sociological studies found that manual workers (in whose name and for whose benefit the system claimed to operate) were far more concerned with their pay and what they could buy with it than they were with "building socialism." East German youth were no less concerned with various forms of diversion, and no more politically mobilized than youth in West Germany.[37]

A 1974 review of empirical studies of East German youth found that the regime "had not yet succeeded in 'integrating' the overwhelming majority of youth to the point that they identified themselves without reservations with the norms and values of the system." A later study noted that secondary school pupils who were active supporters of the Communist youth organization tended to be mistrusted by their classmates and accused of seeking to improve their grades and chances for further study by showing fealty to the regime. One of the "fundamental rights" demanded by a group of East German youth in 1985, in fact, was for access to higher education to be unaffected by religious faith or worldview.[38]

Brämer has suggested that, despite its clear ineffectiveness, the insistent political socialization throughout the East German school program served an important function of legitimizing, in the minds of the ruling elite, their own monopoly of power. Upper-status youth made a distinction between learning to parrot the slogans of Marxism-Leninism and acquiring the technocratic skills necessary to their future careers within the system. Youth of the working-class majority, by contrast, paid little attention to the ideological content of their schooling; they associated "politics" with "a lot of talk." Thus neither group took political education seriously.

On the other hand, according to Brämer, political education functioned for the Communist system independent of its actual results. The Communist party's monopoly of power was justified by its alleged creation of an entirely new society of social justice, peace, and prosperity. Was there widespread political skepticism among the masses toward the regime and Party, "as a result of its stain of collaboration with the unloved and exploitative occupying power [i.e., the Soviet Union], of the establishment of a new hierarchy of privilege, of the intolerable patronizing and propagandistic stupefying of the individual by bureaucracy and the media, and more besides"? All the more reason to take as a principal task of political leadership making a change in the consciousness of the masses, to "substitute for their concrete social experience a fictional image of Socialism."

From this perspective, the leading role of the Party was essential because the masses had not yet shaken off the vestiges of bourgeois mentality, and the heavy stress on political socialization in schools and elsewhere in society was evidence that the Party was doing its job—whatever the actual effect on the attitudes of pupils.[39]

Anweiler suggests, indeed, that the primary characteristic of the Communist educational system in East Germany was its authoritarian character, which directly continued the Prussian and Nazi tradition. From this perspective, the ubiquity of ideological content in East German schooling was a means of justifying the lack of the democracy that was constantly proclaimed as its goal.[40]

Unity and uniformity were constant themes of public discourse in East Germany, and whatever threatened to disturb them was considered the enemy of the regime. For individuals or families to pursue goals different from those of the state and Party was considered a form of sabotage. Thus a commentary on family law stressed that one characteristic of a socialist society was that society, schools, and families had the same educational goal: the total development of the socialist personality of children. That some families might not share this goal could only be an aberration; there was very little room, in a socialist society, for a distinction between public and private, between home and school, between outer and inner conviction.[41]

Although religious belief was formally tolerated, pupils from believing families experienced many difficulties in the schools; they might be singled out in class for mockery by their teachers. Many learned what could be said in school, and what could be said only at home. Their parents might be excluded from participating in parent activities because they were perceived as not being fully loyal to the goals of the school. There was great pressure on pupils to participate in Young Pioneers and in the ceremony of *Jugendweihe*, a school-organized substitute for the churches' sacrament of confirmation, in which adolescents were inducted into the adult community by vowing "their commitment to their socialist homeland," and in other Communist-flavored school ceremonies, or lose the opportunity for further study. In the early years of Communist rule, the strong opposition of evangelical and Roman Catholic leaders to *Jugendweihe* led to low participation, but over time the pressure was too great for all but the firmest Christians to resist, and the opposition of the Protestant churches became muted as a concession to reality. They agreed, for pastoral reasons, to confirm children who had participated in the ceremony.[42]

The annual ceremonies in which youth pledged their loyalty to the "great and noble cause of socialism" were a public expression of daily political indoctrination in the classroom and recreational groups. Through Soviet influence, East German educators adopted Pavlov's theory that conviction developed through repeated verbal expression; by requiring pupils to repeat socialist slogans over and over, according to this theory, they would come to internalize a socialist worldview, and would acquire "political-ideological convictions about the truth and beauty of the revolutionary struggle of the working class for socialism/communism."[43]

In brief, the system of formal schooling in East Germany was completely at the service of the state, seeking, even if unsuccessfully, to develop and enforce complete loyalty to communism and to the separate existence of the German Democratic Republic.

Educational Freedom in West Germany

After World War II, the confessional character of schooling was re-established in much of West Germany, though not without political conflict. In the three zones occupied by the Western Powers, the political left called for "a unitary public school system with clear separation of Church and School."[44] For most Social Democrats, schooling was a key to social reconstruction, and confessional differences represented an impediment to achieving its full effect.

The reaction of Protestant leadership to the excesses of the Nazi regime was one of repentance "in a solidarity of guilt" with the German people. "We condemn ourselves because we did not believe more courageously, did not pray more devotedly, did not believe more joyously, and did not love more deeply," they proclaimed in 1945. In this spirit, they were ready to question the church's traditional understanding of itself as an ally of the state, and thus the extensive cooperation between the two upon which state-supported and state-managed confessional schooling rested. From this perspective, and in line with the general trend of postwar Protestant thinking in Europe, the nonconfessional school could be seen as representing progress away from "churchiness" toward an effective engagement with the world.[45]

By contrast, among Catholic leadership the lesson of the Nazi period was the importance of maintaining their church's independence in providing education. Until about 1960, there was considerable self-congratulation by the Catholic Church on its record of resisting the Nazis; Pope Pius IX cited the struggle to maintain confessional schools as a primary evidence for this resistance. The bishops saw no need to apologize for efforts to protect their flocks from the threats of atheism and Marxism in the postwar world. As political leaders worked to draw up West Germany's constitution in 1948, Catholic leaders pressed for a recognition of the right of parents to demand confessional schooling for their children.[46]

Initially, the Western occupying powers—Britain, France, and the United States—were no more inclined than the Soviet Union to support restoration of the system that had prevailed under the Weimar Republic. In its only official policy statement on the issue, however, the coordinating body of the four military governments stated on December 5, 1945,

> In matters concerning denominational schools drawing on public funds, religious instruction in German schools, and schools which are maintained and directed by various religious organizations, the appropriate allied authority should

> establish in each zone a provisional regulation adapted to
> the local traditions, taking into account the wishes of the
> German population in so far as these wishes can be deter-
> mined . . . . In any case, no school drawing on public funds
> should refuse to children the possibility of receiving religious
> instruction, and no school drawing on public funds should
> make it compulsory for a child to attend classes for religious
> instruction.[47]

While in the Soviet zone, as we have seen, nongovernment schools
were banned and religious instruction in public schools was greatly
restricted though not forbidden, the American, British, and French
authorities, though inclined to take the same position, backed down
in the face of strong opposition from the Catholic Church and permitted confessional schools in areas where referenda showed that they
were desired. When such plebiscites were held in 1946 and 1947,
they showed strong support for confessional schools by Catholics
and for nonconfessional schools by Protestants, except, significantly,
by those Protestants living in Catholic areas.[48]

Demands to restore confessional schooling were successful
because, for many, the churches (for all their weaknesses) were the
only institution in German life to emerge with some honor left from
the period of Nazi rule. They "were tacitly recognized as the sole
institutions above direct military control . . . and as exempt from
'reorientation' into directions determined in Washington, London,
or Paris."[49] This unique position enabled them to resist the desire
of the American (though not the Soviet!) occupation to denazify
Germany through a fundamental reorientation of schooling.

In reaction to Nazi education policy and its equation of "ideological objectivity" or neutrality with a totalitarian state pedagogy, the
West German Constitution adopted in 1949 assigned no authority
for education to the national government. Articles 6 and 7 affirmed
parent rights and provided that religious instruction would be an
integral part of public schooling, though with a right of excusal.
Despite efforts by the Catholic Church, however, the decision of
whether to organize those schools on a confessional basis was left up
to state governments, thus making it likely that only nonconfessional
schools would be provided in predominantly Protestant areas.[50]

Apart from taking advantage of these vestiges of an earlier system,
parents in the postwar Federal Republic (West Germany) were not

able to exercise much influence over the education of their children. The choice of a publicly supported Catholic school, for example, may not have offered real pedagogical differences, given substantial government regulation and pressure for uniformity.

In the Frankfurt-am-Main area (Hesse), with the strongest liberal and nonconfessional tradition of education in Germany, the American "common school" model was followed most closely. This arrangement had two aspects: a continuation of the interdenominational character of elementary education, with a gradually diminishing religious content; and the comprehensive, nonselective model of lower secondary education, or *Gesamtschule*.[51]

The sometimes heavy-handed efforts of American educators working in the occupation government to impose American forms of schooling, in the interest of reeducating an entire nation, aroused strong resistance by many who had also opposed Nazi measures to achieve uniformity. Future chancellor Konrad Adenauer, a Catholic, pointed out in a 1946 speech,

> The resolution of the issue of elementary education led in the past to bitter conflict among the political parties, until [the compromises reached under the Weimar Republic] . . . . The confessional schools based on these compromises were abolished by the National Socialist Government in 1939 through illegal implementation of the so-called German Common School. What should happen now? In every other sphere the illegalities of the National Socialist Government are being abolished. The earlier legal situation is being reestablished. We want that for elementary schools as well. It is unacceptable to validate precisely that illegality of the Nazis experienced as painful by the broadest sections of the population. Therefore we call for the restoration of the confessionally organized elementary schools.[52]

The American model of a common public school, dependent exclusively on state and local government and ignoring confessional differences, seemed to some Germans uncomfortably close to the Nazis' German Community School.

In Bremen, similar to Hesse in its liberal school policies, the draft state constitution stated that the "public schools are community (nonconfessional) schools where an undenominational instruction in Bible history is given." Pressure from Protestant and Catholic leaders, however, led to constitutional guarantees of the rights of confessional schools and of the explicitly Christian character of religious instruction in public schools.[53]

In Bavaria, the *Land* with the most conservative and Catholic influence, an initial effort was made with American support to implement interdenominational *Simultanschulen* in place of restoring confessional schools, but encountered such determined opposition that the attempt was abandoned and the Bavarian Constitution guaranteed a right to confessional education. As recently as 1988, the Bavarian constitutional court confirmed that "reverence for God" was the highest objective of Bavarian schools.[54]

Public confessional schools became the norm in three predominantly Catholic *Länder*: North Rhine-Westphalia, Rhineland-Palatinate, and Bavaria. Baden and the predominantly Protestant *Länder* (including the city of West Berlin) opted for nonconfessional schools, while providing for public funding of nongovernment confessional schools.

The Protestant churches have made much less use than the Catholic Church of the opportunity provided in most West German communities to insist upon confessional schools. In 1965, for example, 17 percent of public elementary schools were Protestant compared with 40 percent that were Catholic and 43 percent nonconfessional or other. (Figures exclude Hamburg, Bremen, and Berlin.) This contrasts with 1911, when 71 percent of the elementary schools in Germany were Protestant, or with 1932, when 55 percent were Protestant, though it should be noted that the heavily Protestant provinces of Imperial Germany were in what became East Germany.[55]

In summary, a diverse situation has emerged since World War II, with five types of schools: public schools with a Catholic character, public schools with a Protestant character, public schools with some other distinctive worldview, nondenominational public schools, and nongovernment schools.

In Berlin, Bremen, Hamburg, Hesse, Schleswig-Holstein, and Lower Saxony (except in Oldenburg) all public schools have been nonconfessional, while in some *Länder* virtually the full cost of maintaining nongoverment Catholic schools has been borne by the state government. In Bavaria, Rhineland-Palatinate, Baden-Württemberg, and Saarland, the picture was mixed. In Saarland schools were only confessional; in Bavaria schools were confessional except in a few large cities; in Rhineland-Palatinate two-thirds and in Baden-Würt-temberg one-fifth of the schools were confessional. Thus, despite the federal arrangement, the large majority of Catholic children were in Catholic public schools and an additional number were in publicly assisted Catholic nongovernment schools.[56]

This accommodation of religious convictions began to weaken during the 1960s, not least because the convictions themselves weakened through growing secularization. The resettlement of some six million German refugees from the East after World War II confused the centuries-old pattern of religiously homogeneous communities, as did the growing movement from rural areas to cities. These events, together with the creation of larger schools in the interest of efficiency and a modern curriculum, had the effect of making confessional schools less practical and less in demand.

Protestant leaders formally supported nonconfessional schools in 1958, and through the next decade many schools gave up their Protestant identity. The Catholic bishops fought a rearguard action, but with declining support from parents. Thus, confessional public schools have faded in significance over the past three decades. A referendum in 1968, for example, overwhelmingly approved an amendment to the Bavarian Constitution that made all public elementary schools "Christian" or interconfessional, with some confessional instruction. Nongovernment confessional schools were assured full public funding.[57]

Where public confessional schools continue to exist (as in North Rhine-Westphalia, the largest *Land*, where they are attended by more than one-third of elementary students), they are operated by local school authorities and are subject to essentially the same controls as nonconfessional public schools. Public confessional schools may indeed represent an alternative for unchurched parents who object for some reason, such as the presence of Turkish and other minority children, to the local nonconfessional school.

The confessional identity of the Catholic and even more of the remaining Protestant public schools may be limited to their periods of religious instruction. Clerical influence, in particular, is strictly limited. Despite the continuing existence of denominational public schools, then, they have tended to become "Christian community schools (*christliche Gemeinschaftsschule*) that differ little if at all from [nondenominational] community schools."[58]

While the role of state-sponsored confessional schooling has faded in postwar West Germany, that of nongovernment independent schools, while still numerically insignificant, has grown.

Article 7 of the constitution guarantees the rights of nongovernment education in language that is close to that of the Weimar Constitution. The first section, in the German tradition, states that "the entire educational system shall be under the supervision of the state." The second section asserts a limited right of parents "to decide whether [the child] shall receive religious instruction," which is offered in most schools, as provided under the third section.

This is as far as the constitution goes in asserting a right of parents to make decisions about the schooling of their children. Nevertheless, some argue that to the extent that the state's own educational system does not provide the various forms of schooling—whether religious or pedagogical or structural, whether extended-day or bilingual—desired by parents, the state is under a constitutional obligation to provide support to independent schools to meet that demand.[59]

Educational freedom, as in the United States since the *Pierce* ruling, is more explicitly guaranteed with respect to the right to operate schools than to the right of individual parents to select schools.

The fourth section of article 7 guarantees "the right to establish non-government schools," but then makes them subject to government approval if they are to replace municipal schools for compulsory attendance. The approval "must be given" if they are equal to public schools "in their educational aims, their facilities and the professional training of their teaching staff." Another requirement is that the operation of the nongovernment school not have the effect of promoting "segregation of pupils according to the means of their parents." Finally, the "economic and legal position of the teaching staff" employed by the nongovernment school must be assured. Thus the right to establish a nongovernment school is in fact highly circumscribed under the German Constitution. While state laws in the United States may require that nongovernment schools provide an education equivalent to that available in local public schools, there are no cases in which their right of existence is limited by considerations of social class integration or the interests of teachers.

Limitations are even more apparent in the fifth section, which specifies that a nongovernment elementary school will be permitted

285

only if the education authority finds that it serves a special pedagogical interest, or if, in the application of persons entitled to bring up children, it is to be established as an interdenominational or denominational or ideological school and a state or municipal elementary school of this type does not exist in the community.

In other words, there must be an explicit educational justification for a nongovernment elementary school, and it would not be sufficient to cite the quality of the instruction provided. The school must have some pedagogical, religious, or ideological specialty that is not available in the local public schools, something comparable to the *caractère propre* that serves as the basis for the autonomy of a nongovernment school in France. These additional conditions applicable to elementary education (grades 1 through 4) are based on "the interest of the state in pupils from all sectors of the population receiving a common basic education."[60]

This provision, by leaving it up to public education authorities to decide whether a particular form of schooling "serves a special pedagogical interest," has had the effect, according to Jach, of reducing significantly the diversity of German education. For example, an independent alternative school might be turned down on the grounds that no experimental justification exists because similar schools exist elsewhere.[61]

While the right to operate independent schools is guaranteed, the process of administrative approval of such schools has created growing pressure upon them to conform to the model of state schools.[62] The very detailed requirements spelled out in the education statutes of the various *Länder* provide many occasions for officials to make it difficult to start and operate nongovernment schools. The requirement of close conformity to the standards set by state schools is a heavy price to pay; "accordingly a state-approved [substitute] school will take care not to risk its privileges by deviating too greatly in its syllabus and method."[63]

Jach charges that "educational diversity in the sense of different forms of schooling that co-exist on an equal basis" doesn't exist in the state educational systems of the western *Länder*, and that independent schools are in an unequal position because of the overregulation and an elaborate approval process. The approval process itself is based on judgments about the purposes of schooling that may conflict with the educational priorities shared by teachers and parents who have created a particular school, and thus with the constitutional guarantee of the free development of personality. The state is required to be neutral, Jach points out, and educational freedom must mean the right of those who operate each school to shape its goals as well as its perspective on the world and its teaching methods. This is not to say that "educational freedom" applies only to teachers, however, since it would be naive to assume that their goals will always accord with those of parents. No, there must be freedom to educate and also freedom to choose schools.[64]

The state's neutrality, Hennecke argues, should forbid the definition of a single set of goals for education and model of personal development (*Bildungsideal und Erziehungsziel*) or of a single model of schooling, even for the public system. Significant groups within the society—perhaps even the majority—who think otherwise are forced by such abuses either to subject themselves to demands with which they do not agree or to leave the public system to which they are entitled and use private schools.[65]

To some critics, then, West German education was not altogether free of pressure for ideological uniformity. Although political education in West Germany had significantly different goals from that of the former DDR, it came under criticism as lending itself too easily to fashionable causes: "for the peace movement, against rearmament, for or against the military, etc." To the extent that the state exercises a virtual monopoly on formal schooling, it should not seek to shape the attitudes of its young citizens in a particular direction.[66]

The Weimar Constitution of 1919 recognized independent alternative schools as a useful stimulus to improve the established schooling, as a standing criticism of a state educational system that was continually expanding its scope and thus in danger of losing its flexibility. Such schools provided forms of education that the state did not wish to offer or was simply unable to provide.[67]

Controversy has arisen in the western *Länder* over the extent to which public funds should subsidize the right of parents to make choices among schooling alternatives for their children. As early as 1955, the argument was made that a right guaranteed by the constitution should be secured by public funding, especially if independent schools were required to be equivalent to state-funded schools.[68]

Initially, the *Länder* education officials agreed among themselves that the language of article 7 of the constitution guaranteeing the right to nongovernment schooling did not create an obligation to provide public funding to nongovernment schools. A federal administrative court ruling in 1966 found, however, that the stringent conditions for approval of nongovernment substitute schools would be impossible to meet without subsidies.[69]

The provision of subsidies did not put the issue to rest, however, since the ruling left it up to the *Länder* to determine how best to meet their obligation to make it possible for nongovernment schooling to survive. The actual practices varied. In some *Länder*, nongovernment schools were reimbursed for their expenditures in certain categories within limits set by the expenditures of public schools; this "involves considerable administrative work and allows the relevant state authorities a great deal of scope for exercising control and influence." In other *Länder*, the amount of public subsidy provided is based upon "the staff costs for a comparable state school pupil based on the average state school class size ... the school retains complete freedom as regards the utilization of the aid."[70] The variation among *Länder* has led to repeated litigation.

> In several of the *Länder* government funding is provided to private schools at some proportion of that provided to public schools. Recent litigation has tested whether this support is a matter of discretion or of right. A 1984 case in North Rhine-Westphalia, for example, was decided by the Federal Administrative Court against a private school which claimed that its 85 percent subsidy was arbitrary since the law would have permitted [the subsidy] to be as high as 98 percent in case of financial need. The Court found that there was no constitutional guarantee for any particular private school but only for private education in general.[71]

In contrast to this narrow ruling, the federal constitutional court issued in April 1987 a ruling based on the constitutional guarantee that "everyone shall have the right to the free development of his personality" (article 2.1) that went further than ever before in asserting a right to publicly funded nongovernment education.

The case was brought by several state-approved nongovernment schools in Hamburg that had been receiving a public subsidy at 25 percent of the costs of comparable public schools. The nongovernment schools pointed out that they were having difficulty surviving with this level of support, and that confessional schools in Hamburg were receiving a 77 percent subsidy. The government responded that "the function of nongovernment schools consists of the widening and enrichment of the public school system through alternative offerings." Experience had shown that the greatest demand for such alternatives was for confessional schools and "reform-pedagogical" schools.

> The higher support for schools with a distinctive worldview rests in the final analysis on their reliance [upon this support], developed through many years of constant demand. Confessional schools have always played a special role in the German educational system. For this reason, but also as a matter of duty, in order to make up for the closing [by the Nazi government] of the confessional schools in 1939, Hamburg gave them a high level of support in the years after the War.[72]

The federal constitutional court concluded that Hamburg could not treat the support of nongovernment schools at its absolute discretion, so as to make them prosper or decline as seemed best to public officials. The constitution recognized a right to found nongovernment schools. The basis for this right was the concern of the constitution for human dignity, for the unfolding of personality in freedom and self-direction, for freedom of religion and conscience, for the neutrality of the government in relation to religion and worldview, and for respect of the natural rights of parents.

It was not enough, the court found, for the government simply to allow nongovernment schools to exist; it must give them the possibility to develop according to their own uniqueness. Without public support, such self-determination would not be possible. Nongovernment schools could not, at present cost levels, meet the requirements for government approval out of their own resources. To expect them to do so, the court ruled, would inevitably force them to become exclusive schools for the upper classes (*Standesoder Plutokratenschulen*). But this was precisely what the constitution, like Weimar Constitution before it, was concerned to avoid by requiring that nongovernment schools could not lead to economic segregation. Nongovernment schools must remain accessible for all, not in the sense that they must accept every qualified student, but in the sense that economic circumstances do not function as a barrier to attendance.[73]

> Only when [nongovernment schooling] is fundamentally available to all citizens without regard to their personal financial situations can the [constitutionally] protected educational freedom actually be realized and claimed on an equal basis by all parents and students .... This constitutional norm must thus be considered as a mandate to lawmakers to protect and promote private schools.[74]

The constitutional right to the free development of personality requires, according to Jach, that the state abstain from defining a single model of maturity that all schools should strive to develop in their pupils. In particular, it should recognize that the goal of individualization does not necessarily point toward the liberal model of the freestanding individual, but may rather require meaningful participation in a community. Simply to proclaim "toleration" as the fundamental principle of public schools does not satisfy the developmental need of children to form secure identities in relation to such communities. The state is thus obligated to make it possible for young citizens to have a variety of types of schooling, based on different concepts of the meaning of "development of personality," and to support independent schools to the extent that public schooling does not include the necessary diversity.[75]

The reality is far different. Independent schools of all kinds, not including Catholic or other confessional public schools, served only 6.2 percent of the pupils in West Germany of compulsory school age in general education in 1989. Of these, 59 percent attended nongovernment Catholic schools, 17 percent nongovernment Lutheran schools, 12 percent nonconfessional independent schools, and 11.2 percent Waldorf schools.

Although the nonstate sector in West German education is relatively small, it has been growing in recent years despite a declining school-age population. While the number of pupils in state *Gymnasien* in 1989 had declined by 19 percent since 1975, the number in nongovernment *Gymnasien* had increased by 5 percent; the enrollment in Waldorf schools had doubled over the same period.[76] Smaller numbers of pupils attended around 30 Montessori schools as of 1987, 6 schools based on the pedagogical ideas of Peter Petersen, 17 rural boarding schools, and some 14 "alternative schools" close to the Green movement. There were applications pending for approval of around 50 additional schools.[77]

Waldorf schools are based on the philosophical and pedagogical ideas of Rudolf Steiner, who founded the first of them in Stuttgart in 1919, though their great expansion began in the 1960s. As of 1990, there were 117 in West Germany, out of a total of 350 altogether in Europe. The Waldorf pedagogy, with its stress upon "awakening the child as a spiritual being" and upon creativity and nonlinear thinking, is based upon Steiner's philosophy of "anthroposophy," a comprehensive worldview and prescription for living, which includes elements of holistic medicine and theories of creativity based in Eastern religion.

The child-centered and noncompetitive classroom practices in Waldorf schools have much to attract liberal middle-class parents (a 1975 study in Germany found that 40 percent of the Waldorf pupils sampled were from academic families) who do not necessarily buy into the religious/philosophical beliefs that underlie these practices.[78]

Waldorf and other forms of schooling were thus not like earlier independent schools, established to fill gaps in the schooling provided by churches and governments, but were a criticism of existing schools. A spokesman for the Waldorf schools described state schools as based on a "materialistic/intellectualizing understanding of humanity" that was anything but neutral. While state schools prepared youth to fit into the world as it is, he claimed, the Waldorf schools developed students' creative capacity to change the world by approaching its new challenges with new ideas.[79]

The growing significance of independent schools was predicted in an important article two decades ago. Anticipating recent policy debates in the United States, Vogel pointed out that the public task of education did not have to be carried out exclusively or even primarily by government-operated schools. It was for that reason that independent schools rejected the label "private" and instead called themselves "free schools"; they were, indeed, "public schools under free sponsorship."[80]

According to Vogel, the German educational system was designed to serve the needs of the state to mobilize its population, and not the needs of individuals or of society, rightly understood to be distinct from the state. Under present conditions, the primary challenge was to create the most flexible and differentiated educational system possible, one that would prepare children to function with initiative and creativity in a complex society. The energy of free initiatives was more important for educational reform, Vogel argued, than the integrative authority of a state that had enjoyed a monopoly for two centuries.

Free schools should not be seen as an educational stop-gap for small groups in the society but as a model for the entire educational system for more school-level autonomy and for more individualized attention to pupils. "In contrast to value-neutral state schools," Vogel wrote, "free schools are a place of education on the basis of clear ethical principles."[81]

This is consistent with the conclusion of Weiss and Mattern, that

> the absence in the state schools of the stable values and unambiguous value orientations sought by many parents and the increasing lack of consensus as regards the educational goals of the schools (as a consequence of the greater pluralism of values) have probably influenced parental decisions in favor of private educational institutions when changing schools. The development in enrollments suggests that those private schools which are more strongly oriented towards values related to "self-fulfillment" (such as, for example, Waldorf schools) have benefited from this, as have to a degree the private church schools, which uphold more traditional values. The church school associations confirm that consensus between home and school on fundamental educational principles, together with parental confidence in the orientation of church schools to values which they consider important, are [sic] often of greater relevance for the choice of a denominational school than membership of a particular religion or the pedagogical concept of the school.[82]

Independent schools are attracting interest from well-educated parents who are "dissatisfied that the assignment to a school occurs almost automatically—some ordinary public school is already there. More parents all the time seek for their children schools that work in accordance with particular pedagogical viewpoints, that employ other methods and seek carefully-chosen goals."[83]

Turning Point in the East

The overthrow of Communist rule in late 1989 has been called "the first successful revolution in the thousand years of German history."[84] This led to a widespread hope, especially among intellectuals, that it would be possible to create distinctive new ways of organizing education and society in general, not simply to take over models prevalent in West Germany, "no matter how democratic and efficient they may be judged to be."[85]

More than simply a political upheaval, these events had the potential, they hoped, to lead to "a renewal of [East German] society 'from below,' "

> beginning as an emancipation from the embrace of ideology, as a shaking-off of political tutelage by a [single] party and its state instruments of control, as a process of deep-reaching spiritual renewal. . . . This emancipation from repression and restriction, from tutelage and dependency, from illusion and errors, from indoctrination and opportunism we had to carry out ourselves—we could not import it with German unification.[86]

Detachment from and even resistance to the Communist system had begun to grow in East Germany in the late 1970s; in its place developed a new respect for pluralism. As one New Forum leader put it in 1989, "we've simply had enough of running after colored banners. Our parents did that, and we've gone along with it for forty years. . . . Now we don't want to make the mistake of waving [new] banners ourselves and seeking to lead others when in fact we know that we don't have the solutions or can offer only fake solutions."[87]

This resistance to political manipulation directed itself with particular force against the regime's efforts to employ schooling and youth organizations to shape wholeheartedly loyal participants. More than a dozen reform groups, in particular those with roots in church circles, began to propose new forms and models of schooling. Youth began to create informal autonomous groups in preference to participation in the Party-controlled organizations.[88]

In October 1989, when hundreds of thousands of protesters took part in the Monday candlelit marches through the old center of Leipzig, one of the demands that appeared on their placards was for educational freedom, for the right to organize independent schools. Two of the many associations that formed to press for democratic reform were the *Initiative Freie Pädagogik* (Initiative for

Educational Freedom) and the *Arbeitsgemeinschaft Freie Pädagogische Einrichtungen* (Working Group for Free Schools).[89]

The educational system was a particular target for reform demands, partly because it had been carefully protected from public criticism, together with the State Security (*Stasi*), military, and police systems. The effect of school reform debates in the Soviet Union created strong pressures to engage in a similar debate when East Germany's Ministry of Popular Education held its Ninth Pedagogical Congress in June 1989. Many teachers and others sent letters to the ministry before the congress, containing suggestions for reforms.[90]

What did the authors of these letters call for? Many urged fundamental reforms, with an emphasis on limiting the influence of the state in education in favor of that of the family and of teachers. The free development of the personality of each pupil should be respected; pupils should not be treated as the objects of educational manipulation. Ethical and moral norms should be taught on the basis of universal values rather than on one-sided ideology.[91]

The theological study group of the League of Evangelical Churches also submitted a paper containing proposals for school reforms. "Christian parents, communities and churches in the GDR," the group wrote, "consider themselves a part of society, even with the separation of State and Church." In order to be a part of the process of shaping questions about education, the group held discussions at all levels. Certain areas of broad agreement emerged. Their concern that Christian children and youth be treated with respect in the schools was one aspect of a fundamental issue about education, which should be characterized by candor, anxiety-free expression of opinion, and dialogue about differing ways of understanding life, values, and the world. Although the unitary nature of the system's comprehensive schools was a protection against inappropriate tracking of pupils based on their social class, the group also felt the system needed to respond to differing interests and capabilities through more optional offerings. In addition, the contribution of religion and the churches in the past and present should be presented fairly.[92]

Recommendations for such changes to a pedagogical congress controlled by the Communist authorities were in vain. After Margot Honecker was removed as minister in November 1989, researchers found several hundred of these letters, marked "No response" followed by initials indicating that copies had been sent to the *Stasi*.

Honecker made it clear that she regarded the discussion of reforms in the Soviet Union as a serious mistake, and called for the recognition and stabilization of the leading role of the Party, with education based firmly on Marxist ideology and increased centralization of decisionmaking to ensure that no schools deviated from this position.[93]

With the sudden collapse of the government of Erich Honecker, the Communist position was accommodated somewhat to the demands for change, though calls continued for "renewal of the socialist school." As late as November 1989, the Action Program of the East German Communist Party (the SED) called for a new educational law that would contribute to the development of youth committed to "a modern socialism in their homeland," while Communist leader and Chief of State Hans Modrow urged that "the renewal of socialism requires a reform of the educational system." The Party did not want pupils to continue to be insincere yes-sayers, he insisted, and schools should become equally hospitable to all religious and philosophical views that contribute to responsible participation in a socialist society.[94]

For some who were not supporters of Communist rule, the remedy to the stagnation of both school and society was nevertheless a renewal of socialism "with a human face." This would mean, for example, more dialogue and free expression within the state schools, but not a diversity of schools. Reformers called for decentralized control, for education centered on learning rather than on teaching, for content more directly related to the lives of pupils, and for an emphasis on criticizing existing social arrangements—in brief, for the sorts of changes that progressive teachers often demand in the West, freedom to use schools to promote a different agenda. By the late 1980s, a democratic, humane school, free from political indoctrination, was among the leading demands of the opposition. Such a school, many believed, would be a place for free formation of opinions and of tolerance.[95]

For others, however, the structure of education itself was part of the problem; they thought it essential that the Party/state relinquish its monopoly on the formation of a worldview rather than simply give it a more humanistic form. With the intense grassroots efforts that developed in the late 1980s, groups of teachers and parents began to seek the right to create a distinctive profile for their schools.[96]

The League of Evangelical Churches had become a major source of criticism of the regime during the 1980s, in quite a different way than had the Roman Catholic Church in Poland.

> The Polish church was a refuge for the Poles' faith and a bastion of the resistance to communist ideology. The Protestant churches in the GDR have rediscovered their Reformation calling. They have taught the East Germans, by no means all of whom have a religious faith, to assert their individual freedom and their free judgment in the face of the state; they have given them the courage not to be afraid of either the authorities or their prohibitions.[97]

The evangelical churches raised five questions about education, including (1) how to present, in the classroom, the diversity in points of view within the German Democratic Republic, in place of the Party line; (2) how to increase the ability of pupils to make ethical judgments; and (3) how to help pupils learn to form their own judgments about history, including a more positive assessment of the role of religion and the churches.[98]

By December 1989, the Christian Democrats in their official position were calling for a diversity of youth organizations, a constitutional guarantee that the role of parents in education is primary, and the freedom for parents or organizations to establish independent schools, which should receive public funding equivalent to that provided to state schools. Parents should be able to choose among the schools in an area, and the schools should be allowed to set admission criteria. The party's electoral platform of March 1990 also provided for publicly funded independent schools.[99]

More surprisingly, the Social Democrats, while asserting the primacy of the state school, left room for the establishment and even the public subsidizing of independent schools.[100]

Other parties confined themselves to calling for purging state schools of ideological indoctrination and encouraging free inquiry, without supporting independent schools. The ceremony of *Jugendweihe* and other Communist-flavored school ceremonies came under frequent attack by critics who insisted that parents should be allowed to decide whether and how nonpartisan ceremonies might have a role in the life of the school.[101]

In the policy debates, there was a growing consensus that new forms of schooling would emerge now that the state monopoly was broken, though it was not clear to what extent the resulting competition for pupils would serve educational reform. Would there be a clearer "profiling" of schools as their staff sought to attract pupils through their educational mission, or would schools lower their requirements to serve as many pupils as possible?[102]

Despite these pressures for change, many were startled when the education minister of the last Communist-dominated government, that of Modrow, called for "a renewed educational system" with an emphasis on allowing each individual to pursue individual interests as well as abilities. Such a system would, H. H. Emons wrote in his March 1990 "Theses for Educational Reform," include both state-sponsored and independent public educational institutions.[103]

After the elections of March 14, 1990, and the assumption of power by a coalition government of non-Communist parties in April 1990, all talk of renewing socialist education was abandoned. Chief of State Lothar de Maizière spoke, in his declaration of policy direction (*Regierungserklärung*), of setting aside the "bureaucratic-centralized system of state leadership" and developing a new relationship of government accountability and initiatives from society. The unitary system must be replaced, he said, with a differentiated and flexible educational system "that does not exclude alternative models." Minister of Education Meyer stressed that the education system must be totally restructured both in form and in content, and should include support for independent schools.[104]

That month, the Initiative Freie Pädagogik held several large meetings at Leipzig University, and gathered 5,000 signatures to a declaration that

> in the interest of children, parents have the right to a free choice of schools. The state must ensure a diversity of schools under State, municipal and free sponsorship. We demand equal opportunity for schools—legally and financially. . . . Schools should declare their educational vision [*ihr Konzept*] publicly, so that parents can make a well-founded choice. A newly-established, public and independent [that is, public but not governmental] school inspection service should monitor equal opportunities, minimum standards and equivalency (not similarity) [*Gleichwertigkeit (nicht Gleichartigkeit)*] of the diverse courses of instruction, schools, and diplomas.

297

The opportunity to operate independent schools became available under a statutory amendment adopted by the East German Volkskammer in July 1990, bringing their status in line with the requirements of article 7 of the West German Constitution. This law, which remains in effect under the reunification treaty unless explicitly changed by the *Länder*, provides for the approval of independent schools if their educational goals, organization, and staff qualifications are equivalent to those of state schools.

Children of school age are required to attend school on the basis of attendance zone, unless they attend an independent school or receive special permission; thus public school choice is limited. All parents are guaranteed the possibility of sending their children to a "substitute" independent school, however, through a public subsidy of between 70 and 90 percent of the costs of corresponding state schools. In exchange, such schools are not allowed to charge excessive supplemental fees and must reserve places for pupils whose parents cannot pay fees at all to prevent an unconstitutional separation of pupils on the basis of social class. The subsidy is not paid to for-profit schools.[105]

"Substitute" independent schools are to be approved and subsidized only if they would offer a distinctive pedagogy or reflect the religious or philosophical views of a group of parents, unless a state school of that religious or philosophical character was already in the community. They could receive waivers from various requirements that apply to state schools, and their pupils could meet their school attendance obligation and receive state-recognized diplomas.[106]

"Supplemental" independent schools (those that do not satisfy the attendance requirement) might also receive approval from local education authorities, and might receive some support from local government, but the presumption was that parents would pay tuition as well. Such schools, in West Germany, have been almost exclusively vocational.

Subsequently, in the preparations for reunification, education came under the control of the newly established *Länder** rather than the central government, as it had been under the Communist regime.

---

*Brandenburg, Mecklenburg-Vorpommern (Mecklenburg-Lower Pommerania), Sachsen (Saxony), Sachsen-Anhalt (Saxony-Anhalt), Thüringen (Thuringia); Berlin continues to be a *Land*, after incorporating the former East Berlin.

Each state was therefore free to develop its own education statutes and regulations. These measures were modeled closely on those already in effect in West Germany, and indeed would become largely required when the West German Constitution took effect in what had been East Germany.

Provisions for independent schools, like other aspects of the new requirements, were subject to constitutional limitations and to the agreements reached over the years among the states of the Federal Republic to ensure the general comparability of their systems.[107] In October 1990, reunification became official and the (formerly West German) Constitution came into force.

The education statutes adopted by the new *Länder* were modeled on those already in effect in different western *Länder*, and thus vary somewhat in how they protect the constitutional right to operate free schools and in the level and timing of public subsidies.[108]

The organizations of independent schools insisted, during the preparation for reunification, that they were pressing for the right to nongovernment schooling not only to further their own interest but also to create an overall educational system in which all schools, state and independent, would be free within a framework of public accountability to determine their own methods and content of instruction and handle their own personnel affairs.[109]

In largely taking over the statutes already in place in West German states, hopes of developing a "third way," distinctively East German, were mostly abandoned in education as they were in many other spheres of social and economic policy. This abandonment was, perhaps, another instance of the "total ideological and material bankruptcy" that "prevented an East German momentum in its own right," so that "only the forces of West German continuity are being felt."[110]

The very spontaneity and easy success of the revolutionary movement in East Germany prevented the development of a coherent program for the future ordering of schools or society. "Democracy Now" was an effective slogan to rally opposition to the Communist regime, but it did not offer a vision of what should be done once democracy had been won.[111]

In contrast with Poland, where habits of grassroots cooperation as an alternative to the state had developed over decades, the opposition movement in East Germany had been largely confined to dissident artists and intellectuals. Some of them, it is now becoming

299

evident, were agents of the *Stasi*. The vacuum of power caused by the collapse of Communist power was filled for a few months by countless ad hoc groups and initiatives. School principals who had been too zealously Communist were spontaneously replaced by others selected by parents and teachers, and elected representatives of teachers, parents, and students began to make decisions about school policy. The required course on citizenship from a Marxist-Leninist perspective was abolished in January 1990, as was the required postgraduate ideological training for teachers.[112]

The education statute developed for Saxony, to take one example, provided a right of parents to an education for their children that is concerned with their dignity and personal development "on the basis of the European traditions of Christianity, Humanism and the ideas of the liberal, democratic and social [not "socialist"] freedom movements." Religious studies were to be a regular subject in the seventh and eighth grade of all state schools, and religious or ethical instruction (by parent and student choice) was to be provided starting in the ninth grade; the latter was to be taught by individuals licensed by the religious denominations. Schools must "respect the philosophical and religious principles upon which parents wish their children to be educated," and avoid political partisanship.[113]

That the educational systems of the West German states provided a well-established model may have inhibited the development of these spontaneous efforts into the vigorous diversity that has been taking shape in Poland, under much more difficult material conditions. Were the textbooks used filled with Marxist-Leninist distortions? The solution was to adopt West German history texts, rather than to go through the painful process of thinking through what should be taught, as in other countries where Communist educational systems must be rebuilt.[114] Generous financial support from the federal government of reunited Germany has solved this and other problems, but perhaps at some cost to fundamental reform.

Recent educational developments in the new *Länder* do not, therefore, go beyond patterns already well-established in West Germany. They are characterized by detailed regulation, with clearly defined rights to establish and operate nonstate schools, but little encouragement for boldness in developing alternative forms of education. Many officials were "imported" from the West with the charge to reorganize education systems with minimum disruption, and are reluctant to encourage initiatives that they perceive as creating confusion. Not having experience with a vigorous independent school sector in the western *Länder*, they are unresponsive to arguments that "model schools—government-sponsored and independent—could be a confidence-building, visible sign of the newly won, free and democratic order. Parents demand this vehemently.... We need this urgently to give impulse to the entire educational system, so that it will tackle renewal in a healthy competition."[115]

On one particularly sensitive issue, although the constitution calls for independent schools to be "equal in value" (*gleichwertig*) to state schools, there may be the same tendency as in the West to insist that they be similar (*gleichartig*) to state schools.[116] This would severely limit the possibility of releasing new and creative energies for education reform.

Advocates of educational freedom challenge the too-easy application of West German models of educational organization as a source of "misunderstandings and a feeling of alienation from the laws, already widely-spread among East German citizens and institutions."

> What should educational legislation in the new *Länder*—after 40 years of a mis-used State school monopoly and unitary school—have as its goal? Most important would be a multiplicity of types of schools and a juxtaposition of State and free sponsors of schooling.... And since a global reform is out of the question, given the continuity of available, irreplaceable teachers, buildings, parents and pupils and given the scarce financial resources, it should be expected that initiatives of individual schools and of independent sponsors [of schools] for a reformed, diverse system of public schooling under state and free sponsorship would be encouraged and assisted.[117]

But unfortunately, from this perspective, it's being handled entirely differently. The proposed education legislation in Brandenburg, for example, specified in great detail the conditions for approval of an independent school; Vogel speculates that this is a dry run for tightened requirements in North Rhine-Westphalia, upon whose statutes those proposed for Brandenburg are otherwise modeled.[118]

Real changes are slower because teachers are accustomed to following centrally prescribed outlines for teaching; "the sudden change means that they now have freedom, but don't know what to do with it." Many parents are apparently skeptical whether teachers are capable of changing what goes on in their schools, even when new forms of schooling are imported from the West.[119]

Despite these misgivings about fundamental reform, the framework has at least been created to develop new alternatives inside and outside the government-operated educational system.

The education statute for Saxony, adopted during the summer of 1991, like those for other new *Länder*, provides procedures to approve nongovernment schools that are fully equivalent to and thus may substitute for state schools, in accordance with the constitution of reunified Germany as well as the political commitments made by the Christian Democrats in power.

In a mark of respect for the role of independent schooling in reforming the educational system, the Saxon *Kultusministerin* (Minister of Religion and Education) spoke at the dedication of a new independent Protestant elementary/secondary school in Leipzig in December 1991. The new school law, she told those who had gathered to celebrate many months of effort to organize the new school, would make possible "a differentiated education for all pupils" to give them the opportunity of a solid formation and also the "free development of personality" guaranteed by the constitution.

> Pupils have very different interests and gifts [and] their parents very different conceptions of what schooling should look like and where its emphasis should be placed. The educational landscape of Saxony will therefore be so arranged that for each different interest there will be a corresponding offering available. Alongside the varied offerings that the state educational system provides, the independent schools are for this reason especially important. With the distinctive characteristics and varied emphases that mark these schools, they contribute significantly to establishing diversity in the supply of schooling. In no sense are these schools to be seen as competition for but rather as a welcome and necessary expansion of the state educational system.[120]

There cannot be many chief state school officers in the United States who are in the habit of making such statements.

Alternative Approaches to Schooling in Eastern *Länder*

On the basis of new legislation (and before reunification was complete), the East German Ministry of Education approved 10 new independent schools in September 1990 and provided a subsidy of 150,000 marks apiece to eight of them and to three existing church schools and to three independent schools for mentally retarded pupils.

By the end of the 1990–91 school year 28 independent schools were operating in what had been East Germany:

Confessional schools	3
New schools approved in September 1990	10
Schools for mentally retarded pupils	11
School for pupils with multiple handicaps	1
Secondary schools	3

All the schools for mentally retarded pupils evolved out of church institutions already providing care to these children. Protestants and Catholics have in fact been very active, even under the restrictions imposed by the Marxist regime, in providing a variety of community services; there are, for example, 383 church-sponsored kindergartens in the former GDR.

One result of the new law of July 1990 has been the official recognition of 20 vocational schools operated by Protestant organizations and 5 operated by Catholic organizations. This will permit these schools to provide state-recognized diplomas in such specialties as the care of the elderly and social work.

Three proposed independent schools (a computer-oriented secondary school, a Waldorf school, and a Protestant secondary school) that requested official recognition were turned down because they failed to meet the criteria. The Waldorf school was started up in Dresden in conscious renewal of the only Waldorf school that operated under the Soviet occupation, from 1945 until it was closed in 1949.[121]

There were thus at the end of the 1990–91 school year 28 approved nonvocational independent schools (compared with some 6,000 state schools in the former GDR), with another 13 requests for approval pending for the 1991–92 school year.[122]

In Leipzig, focal point of the fall 1989 demonstrations demanding freedom, several independent schools have begun operation. In each case, they have received assistance from schools in the West. The Free School of Leipzig, modeled on a school in Hannover, offers what in the United States would be called progressive education, with pupils determining for themselves what they will study and a curriculum organized around projects rather than subjects. A Waldorf school began with grades 1–4 in September 1990, while the Protestant school at whose dedication the education minister spoke began in August 1991 with grades 1 and 4–6, while planning to round out the elementary grades and add the secondary grades. A Protestant school in Nürnberg in Bavaria is in a productive partnership with the group of Christian teachers who established this school, a task which includes persuading reluctant church authorities that their support would not be inconsistent with a concern for the entire educational system.

Not all new school initiatives sought to create independent schools. A predominantly Catholic group of teachers revived the King Albert Gymnasium as a government-sponsored school, and received 350 applications before beginning operations. Another effort, not successful as of late 1991 in obtaining approval from the *Land* officials, gathered 600 parental applications to establish the Leipzig Neighborhood School in a "socially endangered residential area," with a strong emphasis on partnership with the family and the community, and an all-day program.[123]

The establishment of independent schools is of course not the only measure of the growth of freedom within an educational system. There are many indications that teachers and pupils in the states that make up what was East Germany are exploring the implications of a commitment to democracy and to diversity.

In response to a demand to reestablish differentiated and selected secondary education along the lines of the *Gymnasien, Realschulen, and Hauptschulen,* one significant change is that in place of the comprehensive school that was a central article of faith of the postwar changes in East Germany,[124] several of the new *Länder* have settled instead upon a two-tiered rather than a three-tiered model. The *Realschule* and *Hauptschule* are being combined into a single school, to reduce the starkness of selection. Thus it is necessary to concede that "some movement has occurred in educational policy!"[125] It remains to be seen, however, whether the new *Mittelschule* will develop true integration, like the *Gesamtschule* of Hesse and other western *Länder,* or simply operate as two schools under a single roof.[126]

Another approach has been to invent a new *Regelschule* ("standard school"); Anweiler offers this, tongue-in-cheek, as evidence of "linguistic creativity," so as not to use the disfavored term *Hauptschule*.[127]

Thus, while there are some signs of educational change in the *Länder* that were East Germany, it is possible to agree with Vogel that the hopes of late 1989, when everything seemed possible, have been disappointed. It seems a pity that there are not more new initiatives in secondary education to permit exploration of alternatives beyond the rigidity of the existing models. This is where educational freedom and parental choice could make a significant contribution to the reform of German education—in the West as well as the East.

During the difficult period of transition faced by the eastern *Länder*, it may be tempting for policymakers to reach for the familiar tool of education to intervene in the emerging civil society. Before they reinstitute a "command pedagogy," however, they should remember that "a communist command economy is an utterly hopeless way of running an advanced society: not even Germans could make it work. . . . Ideology apart, will their government abandon an ingrained urge to meddle and control?"[128] Let us hope that they place their confidence instead, with respect to education, in the desire of parents and teachers for schooling consistent with a healthy democracy.

> The stability and capacity for development of the political system does not rest . . . on an education that comes down to achieving conformity to the system; the hoped-for fundamental commitment to democratic arrangements does not seek a conflict-free integration and uncritical identification with the state, but rather far more a readiness for acceptance and change through democratic discussion.[129]

Free schools, freely created and chosen by teachers and parents, can be in the forefront of the fundamental educational change needed by post-Communist societies.[130]

References

Valuable help in preparing this chapter was provided by Professors Oskar Anweiler (Bochum), Hans-Georg Hofmann (Berlin), Siegfried Jenkner (Hannover), Günter Lange (Berlin), Heinz Rose (Dresden), and Manfred Weiss (Frankfurt am Main). Portions of this chapter are adapted from the author's 1989 study for the Department of Education, *Choice of Schools in Six Nations*.

1. Frank-Rüdiger Jach, *Schulvielfalt als Verfassungsgebot* (Berlin: Dunker and Humblot, 1991), p. 7.

2. Vladimir Tismaneanu, "Against Socialist Militarism: The Independent Peace Movement in the German Democratic Republic," *In Search of Civil Society*, ed. Vladimir Tismaneanu (New York: Routledge, 1990), p. 136.

3. See the discussion in Charles L. Glenn, *The Myth of the Common School* (Amherst: University of Massachusetts Press, 1988), 100–108.

4. Gerald Grimm, "Expansion, Uniformisierung, Disziplinierung. Zur Sozialgeschichte der Schulerziehung in Österreich im Zeitalter des aufgeklärten Absolutismus" in *Revolution des Wissens? Europa und seine Schulen im Zeitalter der Aufklärung (1750–1825)*, ed. Wolfgang Schmale and Nan L. Dodde (Bochum, Germany: Verlag Dr. Dieter Winkler, 1991), p. 234.

5. Wolfgang Schmale, "Die Schule in Deutschland im 18. and frühen 19. Jh. Konjunkturen, Horizonte, Mentalitäten, Probleme, Ergebnisse" in *Revolution des Wissens?*, pp. 638–39.

6. Ernst Christian Helmreich, *Religious Education in German Schools* (Cambridge, Mass., 1959), p. 134.

7. Helmreich, *Religious Education*, p. 137.

8. Bruno Hamann, *Geschichte des Schulwesens: Werden und Wandel der Schule im ideen- und sozialgeschichtlichen Zusammenhang* (Bad Heilbrunn, Germany: Julius Klinkhardt, 1986), p. 169.

9. Max Planck Institute, *Between Elite and Mass Education: Education in the Federal Republic of Germany*, trans. Raymond Meyer and Adriane Heinrichs-Goodwin (Albany: State University of New York Press, 1983), p. 55.

10. Helmreich, p. 113; Peter Lundgreen, *Socialgeschichte der Deutschen Schule im Überblick*, vol II: 1918–1980 (Göttingen: Vandenhoeck and Ruprecht, 1981), pp. 15–17.

11. Hans-Georg Herrlitz, Wulf Hopf and Hartmut Titze, *Deutsche Schulgeschichte von 1800 bis zum Gegenwart*, 2nd ed. (Königstein/Ts.: Athenaeum, 1986), p. 114.

12. Hamann, p. 179.

13. J. S. Conway, *The Nazi Persecution of the Churches, 1933–45* (New York: Basic Books, 1968), pp. 20, 178; Helmreich, p. 173.

14. Ibid., pp. 366–69.

15. Ibid., p. 369.

16. Ibid., pp. 182–8.

17. Thilo Ramm, "Die Bildungsverfassungen," in *Vergleich von Bildung und Erziehung in der Bundesrepublik Deutschland und in der Deutschen Demokratischen Republik*, ed. Oskar Anweiler (Cologne, Germany: Verlag Wissenschaft und Politik), 1990, p. 35.

18. Wolfgang Mitter, "Politische Bildung und Erziehung," in Ibid., p. 597. *Vergleich von Bildung und Erziehung in der Bundesrepublik Deutschland und in der Deutschen Demokratischen Republik*, Anweiler et al. (Cologne, Germany: Verlag Wissenschaft und Politik, 1990), p. 597.

19. Giesecke (1983) quoted in Mitter, "Politische Bildung," p. 600.

20. Dietmar Waterkamp, "Erziehung in der DDR zwischen Optimismus und Resignation," in *Vergleichende Bildungsforschung: DDR, Osteuropa und interkulturelle Perspektiven: Festschrift für Oskar Anweiler zum 60. Geburtstag*, ed. Bernhard Dilger, Friedrich Kuebart, and Hans-Peter Schäfer (Berlin, Germany: Arno Spitz, 1986), p. 237; Mitter, p. 600.

21. Dietmar Waterkamp, "Erziehung in der Schule," in *Vergleich von Bildung und Erziehung*, pp. 269–71.

22. "Aus dem Gezetz zur Demokratisierung der deutschen Schule, 22. Mai 1946," in *DDR: Dokumente zur Geschichte der Deutschen Demokratischen Republik 1945–1985,* ed. Hermann Weber (Deutscher Taschenbuch Verlag, 1986), p. 71.

23. Siegfried Jenkner, "Schule zwischen Staats- und Selbstverwaltung," *Pädagogik und Schule in Ost und West* 37, no. 1 (1989): 47.

24. Ramm, p. 43.

25. Article 25 (1) and (3), quoted in Ramm, p. 38; Waterkamp, "Erziehung in der Schule," p. 261.

26. Hans-Jörg König, "Schulverfassung in der DDR," *Recht der Jugend und des Bildungswesens* 4 (1990): 414; Oskar Anweiler, "Die 'Wende' in der Bildungspolitik der DDR," *Bildung und Erziehung* 43, no. 1 (March 1990): 97; review by Wolfgang Mitter in Ibid.; Sterling Fishman and Lothar Martin, *Estranged Twins: Education and Society in the Two Germanys* (New York: Praeger, 1987), p. 126.

27. Christine Lost, "Bemerkungen zum Umgang mit Reformpädagogik in der DDR (1945 bis 1989)," *Pädagogische Forschung* 31, nos. 5–6 (1990): 50–51; Waterkamp, p. 263.

28. E. Drefenstedt (1983) quoted in Ekkehard Eichberg, "Gruppenerziehung—Kollektiverziehung—Gemeinschaftserziehung in der Bundesrepublik Deutschland und in der DDR," in *Vergleichende Bildungsforschung: DDR, Osteuropa und interkulturelle Perspektiven,* ed. by Bernhard Dilger, Friedrich Kuebart, and Hans-Peter Schäfer (Berlin: Arno Spitz, 1986), p. 257.

29. James F. Tent, *Mission on the Rhine: Reeducation and Denazification in American-Occupied Germany* (Chicago: University of Chicago Press, 1982), p. 314 and *passim*; "Aus der Entschließung 'Die nächsten Aufgaben der allgemeinbildenden Schule,' 19. Januar 1951," in *DDR: Dokumente zur Geschichte,* p. 179.

30. Rainer Brämer, "Die relative Funktionalität der ideologischen Erziehung im allgemeinbildenden Unterricht der DDR-Oberschule," in *Erziehungs- und Sozialisationsprobleme in her Sowjetunion, der DDR und Polen,* ed. Oskar Anweiler (Hannover, Germany: Hermann Schroedel Verlag, 1978), p. 147; "Aus dem Gesetz über das einheitliche sozialistische Bildungssystem, 25 Februar 1965," *DDR: Dokumente zur Geschichte, Pädagogik* (1978), quoted in Oskar Anweiler, "Ergebnisse und offene Fragen," in *Vergleich von Bildung und Erziehung,* p. 699.

31. Gerhart Eisler, quoted in Peter Grothe, *To Win the Minds of Men: The Story of the Communist Propaganda War in East Germany* (Palo Alto: Pacific Books, 1958), p. 165; "Ergebnisse und offene Frogen."

32. Christa Uhlig, "Erziehung zwischen Engagement und Resignation—Gedanken zur Bildungsgeschichte in der DDR," *Pädagogische Forschung* 31, nos. 5–6 (1990): p. 199.

33. Josef Kraus and Günter Lange, "Schulpolitik im geeinten Deutschland," typescript, no date (received by the author from Lange May 1991).

34. Horst Brandt, "Innovationsbemühungen Leipziger Schulen," in *Schulvielfalt in Hannover (Theorie und Praxis 37)* (Hannover: Fachbereich Erziehungs wissenschaften I der Universität Hannover, 1991), p. 229.

35. Wolfgang Mitter, "Allgemeinbildendes Schulwesen: Grundfragen und Überblick," in *Vergleich von Bildung und Erziehung,* p. 178.

36. Adelheid Busch, "Probleme der Erziehung sozialistischer Persönlichkeiten: Die Diskussion in der DDR seit 1970," *Erziehungs- und Sozialisationsprobleme,* Fishman and Martin, p. 157.

37. Werner Volkmer, "East Germany: Dissenting Views during the Last Decade," in *Opposition in Eastern Europe,* ed. Rudolf L. Tökés (Baltimore: Johns Hopkins University Press, 1979), pp. 117–18.

38. Hans-Peter Schäfer, quoted in Eichberg, p. 254; Waterkamp, p. 241; "Aus einem Protest-Brief DDR-Jugendlicher: Pochen auf die Verwirklichung der Grundrechte, Juli 1985," in *DDR: Dokumente zur Geschichte*, pp. 400–401.

39. Brämer.

40. Oskar Anweiler, "Gesellschaftliche Mitwirkung und Schulverfassung in Bildungssystemen staatssozialistischer Prägung," *Bildung und Erziehung* 26, no. 4 (July–August 1973): 270.

41. Fishman and Martin, p. 40; Kurt Sontheimer and Wilhelm Bleek, *The Government and Politics of East Germany*, trans. Ursula Price (New York: St. Martin's Press, 1975), p. 131.

42. *The German Democratic Republic* (Berlin: Verlag Zeit im Bild, 1984), p. 179; Klaus Bürger, "Es gibt vieles, über das wir miteinander reden müssen," *Bildung und Erziehung* 43, 1 March 1990, pp. 102–104; Grothe, pp. 223–24; Roger Williamson, "East Germany: The Federation of Protestant Churches," *Religion in Communist Lands* 9, nos. 1–2 (Spring 1981): 15n; Sontheimer and Bleek, 124.

43. Fishman and Martin, p. 25.

44. Herrlitz, Hopf, and Titze, p. 142.

45. Frederic Spotts, *The Churches and Politics in Germany* (Middletown, Conn.: Wesleyan University Press, 1973), pp. 11, 212.

46. Ibid., pp. 90, 184–86.

47. Ibid., p. 58n.

48. Ibid., p. 212.

49. Ibid., p. 55.

50. Lundgreen, p. 26.

51. Tent, pp. 170–2; see also Manfred Ertel, Hans Werner Kilz, and Jörg R. Mettke, *Gesamtschule: Modell oder Reformruine?* (Hamburg, Germany: Spiegel-Buch, 1980).

52. Herrlitz, Hopf, and Titze, p. 145f.

53. Tent, p. 206f.

54. Ibid., pp. 112, 127, 139; Spotts, "Erziehung in der Schule," p. 86; Waterkamp, p. 262.

55. Lundgreen, p. 42.

56. Spotts, p. 219.

57. Ibid., p. 228.

58. Ramm, p. 48.

59. Jach, p. 42.

60. Manfred Weiss and Cornelia Mattern, "The Situation and Development of the Private School System in Germany," in *Social Change and Educational Planning in West Germany*, ed. Hasso von Recum and Manfred Weiss (Frankfurt am Main: Deutsches Institut für internationale Pädagogische Forschung, 1991), p. 54.

61. Jach, p. 51.

62. Siegfried Jenkner, "Das Recht auf Bildung," p. 237.

63. Vogel (1979), quoted in Weiss and Mattern, p. 55.

64. Jach, pp. 25–26, 49, 80.

65. Frank Hennecke, *Staat und Unterricht* (Berlin, 1972), quoted in Jach, p. 79.

66. Hermann Giesecke (1985), quoted in Mitter, p. 613.

67. Arbeitsgemeinschaft Freier Schulen, *Freie Schule I. Soziale Funktion der Freien Schulen* (Stuttgart, Germany: 1976), pp. 18–19.

68. Hans Heckel, quoted in Johann Peter Vogel, "Bildungspolitische Perspektiven," in *Freie Schule vol. II. Öffentliche Verantwortung und freie Initiative* (Stuttgart: Arbeitsgemeinschaft Freier Schulen, 1972), p. 38.

69. Weiss and Mattern, p. 55.

70. Ibid., p. 58.

71. John E. Coons, "Educational Choice and the Courts: U.S. and Germany," *The American Journal of Comparative Law* 24, no. 1 (Winter 1986).

72. Bundesverfassungsgericht, *In den Verfahren zur verfassungsrechtlichen Prüfung der . . . Privatschulgesetzes der Freien und Hansestadt Hamburg,*" April 8, 1987, p. 12.

73. Ibid., pp. 30–32.

74. Ibid., p. 35.

75. Jach, pp. 64–65, 81.

76. Max Planck Institute, pp. 45–50.

77. Michael Behr, *Freie Schulen und Internate: Pädagogische Programme und rechtliche Stellung* (Düsseldorf: ECON Taschenbuch Verlag, 1988), pp. 10–11.

78. For a critical but comprehensive account, see Heiner Ullrich, *Waldorfpädagogik und okkulte Weltanschauung* Weinheim and Munich, Federal Republic of Germany: Juventa (1987); for an account from within the Waldorf system, see B. C. J. Lievegoed, "Het kind als geestelijk wezen," in *De levende school* (Zeist, the Netherlands: Uitgeverij Vrij Geestesleven, 1980).

79. Interview with Klaus Schickert, "Die Waldorfschulen—Vorkämpfer eines freien Bildungswesens" [publication unknown], 1990.

80. Vogel "Bildungspolitische Perspektiven," pp. 29–30.

81. Ibid., pp. 34–5.

82. Weiss and Mattern, p. 51.

83. Behr, p. 9.

84. Hans-Georg Hofmann, "Von der Spezial- zur Allgemeinbildung—Zukunftsorientierte gesellschaftspolitische Bildungsarbeit in den fünf neuen Bundesländern," in *Unternehmertun—Wirtschaftlicher Aufschwung und sozialer Fortschrift in einem vereinigten Deutschland*, ed. Hermann Linke, Horst-Udo Niedenhoff, and Wilfried Vetter (Cologne, Germany: Deutscher Instituts-Verlag, 1991), p. 139.

85. Konig, p. 417.

86. Ibid., p. 414.

87. Interview with Sebastien Pflugbeil in *Die Opposition in der DDR*, ed. Gerhard Rein (Berlin: Wichern-Verlag, 1989), pp. 21–22.

88. Hans-Georg Hofmann, *Zu den Programmatischen Erklärungen politisch handlungsfähiger Kräfte zur Bildungsreform in der DDR* (Berlin: Akademie der Paedagogischen Wissenschaften der DDR, 1990), pp. 8–9.

89. Elke Urban, "Neugründungen Leipziger Schulen," in *Schulvielfalt in Hannover*, p. 233.

90. Konrad Gebürek, Heike Kaack, and Günter Lange, " 'Keine Antwort—M. f. s.': Briefe an den Pädagogischen Kongress '89," typescript, no date (sent to the author by Lange in May 1991).

91. Ibid., pp. 11–13.

92. Quoted in Ibid., pp. 14–15.

93. Ibid., pp. 2–3.

94. Quoted in Anweiler, "Die 'Wende,' " p. 100; statements were published in *Neues Deutschland* on November 11–12 and November 18–19, 1989.

95. Hofmann, *Zu den Programmatischen Erklärungen*, pp. 20–21; *Die Opposition in der DDR*, edited by Gerhard Rein (Berlin: Wichern-Verlag, 1989).

96. Hofmann, *Zu den Programmatischen Erklärungen*, p. 31.

97. A French commentator, quoted in J. F. Brown, *Surge to Freedom: The End of Communist Rule in Eastern Europe* (Durham and London: 1991), p. 139.

98. Hofmann, *Zu den Programmatischen Erklärungen*, p. 16.

99. Ibid., p. 40.

100. Ibid., p. 51.

101. Ibid., p. 42.

102. Kraus and Lange, p. 16.

103. H. H. Emons, "Thesen zur Bildungsreform," quoted in Johann Peter Vogel, "Administration statt Konzeption—Bemerkungen zu neuen Schulgesetzen," *Pädagogik und Schulalltag* 46, no. 3 (1991): 301.

104. "Aus der Regierungserklärung von Ministerpräsident Lothar de Maizière vom 19. April 1990," *Bildung und Erziehung* 43, 3 (September 1990): 344; Meyer quoted in Gebürek, Kaack, and Lange, pp. 20–21.

105. "Verfassungsgesetz über Schulen in freier Trägerschaft vom 22. Juli 1990," in "Verfügungen und Mitteilungen des Ministeriums für Bildung und Wissenschaft" (Berlin: September 18, 1990); also explanatory letter from Prof. Günter Lange, April 23, 1991.

106. "Verfassungsgesetz."

107. "Grundsätze und Empfehlungen zur Neugestaltung des Allgemeinbildenden Schulwesens in den Länden Brandenburg, Mecklenburg-Vorpommern, Sachsen, Sachsen-Anhalt und Thüringen sowie in Berlin (Ost)" (September 26, 1990), *Bildung und Erziehung* 44, no. 1 (March 1991): 111.

108. Joachim Böttcher, "Grundsätze für eine verfassungskonforme Privatschulgesetzgebung in den neuen Bundesländern," *Freie Bildung und Erziehung* 66, no. 2 (November 1991): 3–5.

109. Jenkner, "Das Recht auf Bildung," p. 233.

110. Eric Gujer in *Neue Zürcher Zeitung*, October 4, 1991, p. 3.

111. Hofmann (1991), p. 139.

112. Wolfgang Hörner *Bildung und Wissenschaft in der DDR: Ausgangslage und Reform bis Mitte 1990* (Bonn, Germany: Bundesministerium für Bildung und Wissenschaft 1990), pp. 9–10; Gebürek, Kaack, and Lange, 16; Beate Rüther, "Vom marxistisch-leninistischen Grundlagenstudium zum Studium generale in der ehemaligen DDR," in *Systemswandel im Bildungs- und Erziehungswesen in Mittel- und Osteuropa*, ed. Oskar Anweiler (Berlin, Germany: Arno Spitz, 1992), pp. 189–207.

113. "Entwurf eines Landesschulgesetzes des Landes Sachsen," Working Paper, November 13, 1990.

114. Hörner, p. 17.

115. Urban, p. 234.

116. Arbeitsgemeinschaft, p. 21.

117. Vogel, "Administration Statt Konception," p. 301.

118. Ibid.

119. Hans-Georg Hofmann, letter to the author, October 25, 1991; Brandt, p. 230.

120. Stefanie Rehm, "Grußwort sur Eröffnung des Evangelischen Schulzentrums Leipzig," Sächsisches Staatsministerium für Kultus, December 6, 1991.

121. Siegfried Jenkner, "Freie Schule und Staat: Erste Internationale Ost-West-Tagung in der Bundesrepublik," *Pädagogik und Schule in Ost und West* 38, no. 1 (1990): 59.

122. Zeitweilige Arbeitsgruppe 'Alternative Pädagogik,' "Information to algemein-bildenden Schulen, berufsbildenden Schulen und Tageseinrichtungen in freier Trägerschaft," Berlin, October 15, 1990.

123. Urban, p. 234–6.

124. Wolfgang Schmidt, "Die Neustrukturierung der allgemeinbildenden Schulen in den neuen Bundesländen," *Politik und Zeitgeschichte: Beilage zur Wochenzeitung "Das Parlament"* nos. 37–38, September 6, 1991, p. 38.

125. Letters to the author from Oskar Anweiler (February 7, 1992) and Siegfried Jenkner (February 2, 1992); Jenkner, "Deutscher Föderalismus und europäische Integration—unter besonderer Berücksichtigung des Bildungswesens," in *Politische Bildung im vereinten Deutschland* (Opladen, Germany: Leske + Budrich, 1992), pp. 11–12.

126. Brandt, p. 230.

127. Oskar Anweiler, "Wandlungen und Perspektiven des Bildungswesens im östlichen Europa." Paper presented for the opening of the 4th International Glöckel Symposium, Autonomie der Bildung—Anspruch und Wirklichkeit: Bildungsprozesse im Rahmen der europäischen Integration, Vienna, June 3, 1991.

128. Nico Colchester, "The New Germany," *Economist*, June 30, 1990, p. 3.

129. Anweiler, "Ergebnisse und offene Fragen," p. 702.

130. Arbeitsgemeinschaft, p. 34.

10. Conclusion

These final comments on the educational reforms in the post-Communist countries of Eastern Europe are written a full two years after the rest of my study, for reasons which are discussed in the foreword. The tone of the earlier chapters, based upon reports received from each of the countries discussed during the actual process of political change between 1989 and 1991, is essentially optimistic. Tremendous energies had been released by the collapse of totalitarian regimes and dreams that had been nurtured in opposition seemed on the brink of realization.

Today the reforms and initiatives undertaken at the first impetus of freedom have at least the start of a track record, and a more sober assessment is both possible and necessary. A Romanian expert comments that "the passage from communist education to the liberal education systems . . . is proving more difficult than had been supposed. . . . Sometimes the combined weight of bureaucratism and centralism and the sluggishness of top-down reforming impulses result in too much being expected of a new education law."[1] In Bulgaria, "the education system is at present a rather passive reflection of great social change," resulting from decades in which "all strategic decisions and overall management were dictated from above,"

> a natural consequence of the communists' whittling away of
> civic institutions, imparting to the education system a purely
> instrumental servicing role in relation to the political and
> ideological interests of the Nomenklatura and their indus-
> trial system.[2]

Acknowledging the uneven record of reform should not lead to a cynical dismissal of the original impulse. After all, it would be difficult to exaggerate the challenge of "the transformation of a system of government which was operated for more than half a century over a fifth of the earth's surface by a quarter of its population into its exact ideological, political and economic opposite."[3]

313

The difficulty of making fundamental institutional change is compounded by the slow pace of cultural change, the persistence of

> collectivist mentalities and reflexes, egalitarian utopias and populist attitudes, militancy, collective fear and hatred, unconditional submission of the individual to the providential leader or the ruling party. The former captive countries are, it is true, returning to Europe, but they are weighed down by totalitarian experiences and structures whose residual effects will be felt for a long time to come.[4]

New or fundamentally reformed institutions based upon free association and cooperation, and the habits essential to sustain them, are all the more essential in the post-Communist societies because of the rapid pace of social change driven by market forces. As Robert Kuttner has warned, "Capitalism itself depends upon pre-capitalist or extra-capitalist values such as loyalty and community to anchor the stage on which the dynamic market plays." If responsible freedom does not develop vigorously in the civil society and individual consciousness, and if "the dead hand of the past (a useful Marxian phrase) remains, in the form of the state bureaucracy," marketplace freedom may result in systems that "blend the inhuman faces of socialism and early capitalism."[5]

In each of the countries of Eastern Europe, though to a widely varying extent, the all-encompassing bureaucracy of the Communist era remains largely in place, as do the habits and attitudes that sustain its power. It is characteristic of such a system that initiative is strangled at the same time that control is actually quite ineffective.[6] A (West) German educator working in the former East Germany shortly after reunification reported that "the teachers, professors, and administrative staff seemed to be paralyzed by a combination of indignation, indecision, frantic attempts at self-preservation, and, finally, resignation."[7] According to another account, many found it very difficult "to give up their belief in the necessity of central plans and assignments, even though they had seldom had good experiences with them."[8] It was in many respects easier for teachers simply to follow prescribed lesson plans than to make the countless decisions and to take the risks required by a teaching style seeking to develop the ability to question received ideas and to solve problems in fresh ways, skills essential to free markets and democratic political systems.[9]

Bringing about rapid institutional change dependent on school-level initiatives has been particularly difficult in educational systems in which teachers have had little flexibility but have "existed in an ideological and bureaucratic straightjacket."[10] Such habits are difficult to change, even when the political and economic systems are liberalized, and earlier efforts at educational reform in Hungary or the Soviet Union produced meager results because they had been attempted in a top-down manner and had elicited no ferment of energy and creativity at the school level.[11] The habits are even difficult to discuss or to describe accurately, because the social scientists who have studied the post-Communist countries "are more at home in the ramifications of the struggle for power and in matters of economic redeployment . . . than in the . . . world of mentalities and attitudes, institutional and ideological change, renewal of values and social relations."[12]

The problem is compounded, again to a varying extent, by a sharp decline in public expenditure at a time when alternative institutions and sources of revenue have not yet been solidified. In Russia, the condition of the educational system "from bottom to top is a disaster, financial, methodological and in the moral sense. Teachers go on strike, textbooks become expensive, the ceilings of the schools come down."[13] Under totalitarian regimes, "refusing to learn on the part of the students became a means of demonstrating aversion to state-administered education—especially at secondary schools."[14] Despite those discouraging conditions, there are ample signs of life among the ruins, with new schools and interesting initiatives springing up. At the heart of the positive changes is a reorientation of schooling toward serving the interests of students and their parents, rather than those of the state.

> It seems that the renewing Hungarian public education definitely has to enforce the interests of clients in education. One of the ways could be to make allowance for the interests of clients in the internal processes of schools (values, contents, methods). Another similarly important way may be the legal extension of the right to own and run schools.[15]

Efforts on the part of public policy to keep up with social developments have been hampered by the continuing bureaucracy and the focused influence of employees of the existing system, which in Russia has been in place since 1921 and essentially unchanged since the mid 1930s.[16] In the 1992 report of the international advisory committee assisting the Russian Federation, I mentioned the problem of "overlapping and too-prescriptive authority" of different levels of government and suggested that "it would be desirable, indeed, if the law were amended to reduce the potential scope of government intervention to those areas which are strictly necessary and cannot be left to the functioning of the civil society."[17] In his response to the work of our commission, Minister of Education E.V. Tkachenko made explicit reference to my comment, conceding that it was "largely justified" and identified a problem that would have to be addressed.[18]

Despite the exemplary framework of law adopted in 1992, the Russian "government's preference for a gradual process of reform in the educational sector, rather than the shock therapy it has been espousing hitherto," led a Western expert who had been close to the process to ask whether it did not "represent a scaling down of the reform itself." Jan De Groof expresses particular concern about changes made in the draft constitution before its adoption that removed protections for educational freedom. Although "right from the political inception of the Russian Federation, emphasis has been placed on the value of nonstate schools as a source of renewal in the campaign to improve standards," the new constitution does not provide explicit guarantees of the right to establish such schools.[19] The optimism in the preceding chapters about recent developments in Russia, based upon the education law itself and upon the draft constitution, now requires qualification.

Another Western expert confirms that

> the disappearance of these provisions [from the draft Consti-
> tution] means that private schools, created at the initiative
> of private organizations or individuals or acquired by them
> in the process of privatization, no longer enjoy constitutional
> protection, except under the constitutional article on freedom
> of economic activity. Therefore, the freedom of education,
> which is protected under international treaties which Russia
> has joined, is completely neglected in the new Constitution.[20]

It should be noted that the U.S. Constitution also provides no explicit guarantee of freedom of education, and that the 1923 decision of the Supreme Court in *Pierce v. Society of the Sisters of the Holy Names of Jesus and Mary*, 268 U.S. 510, was based essentially on the right to operate a school of the property right under the Fourteenth Amendment, rather than on the right to the free exercise of religion under the First Amendment. For many Western Europeans accustomed to the explicit guarantees of educational freedom in, for example, the German, Dutch, and Belgian constitutions, the American and Russian protections seem insufficient to ensure real freedom of conscience.

If the new Russian Constitution neglects the freedom to provide education, it explicitly guarantees freedom of teaching, in the context of an article that also protects "freedom of literary, artistic, scientific, technical and other types of creativity" (article 44, section 1). In this otherwise entirely appropriate provision lurks the possibility of a problem for those seeking to offer distinctive forms of schooling, since it could be read in conjunction with article 19, prohibiting discrimination on the basis of an "attitude towards religion," to forbid selecting or retaining teachers on the basis of their willingness to support the religious or other distinctive character of the school.[21] This is by no means a far-fetched danger; the issue has been extensively litigated in several Western European nations.[22] The Russian Federation has incorporated into its laws the international covenant protecting educational freedom, which "entails that either the founder of a private school or the pupils and students (the parents thereof) should have the right to direct the method and content of teaching in private schools. Under the [Russian] Law, this right is not guaranteed."[23]

In several of the post-Communist countries—including Lithuania, Bulgaria, and Poland—recent elections have brought to power elements of the former communist establishment, resulting in measures intended to recentralize educational decisionmaking and correspondingly to reduce the autonomy of schools and the support for parents to choose among schools.[24] It seems unlikely, however, that they will succeed in restoring anything like the old system; the social forces that have been unleashed and the new habits and expectations that are being learned continue to have their dynamic effect.

A more generic problem faced by most of the educational systems of formerly communist nations is the low priority given to education by both governments and the growing private sector. In a climate of "disappointed expectations, it is not surprising that the political priority accorded to education has slipped."[25] In Romania, for example, "it is economic and financial questions that have dominated the various government programs since December 1989. Education was regarded as a relatively stable sector . . . hence to reduce the problem of reform to the adoption of a new education law."[26] In the Czech Republic, "no political party has developed its own educational policy. Thus, reforming the educational system is not so much a matter of political debates, and rests, substantially, on educational theorists, researchers, and teacher initiative groups."[27] While depoliticization of decisionmaking about education has its positive side, an inevitable result is difficulty in developing a societywide momentum (and financial support) for fundamental changes.

Expenditure on education as a percentage of gross domestic product has declined, and the situation of teachers has become extremely difficult in most post-Communist countries, with the result that those with other skills marketable in growing economic sectors are leaving teaching or never entering it after their training:

> In 1991 no graduate of English studies from a Polish university took a school teaching job, although the present deficit of English teachers is estimated at over 15,000. . . . The most valuable and innovative teachers leave the education system. This applies, in particular, to those specializations which are in high demand in the market economy. As a result, the teaching potential is decreasing in just those fields for which there is a big demand.

Other teachers have taken on supplemental jobs that often conflict with their teaching. Textbooks and supplies are largely unavailable, and in Poland, for example, 800 elementary schools and 63 secondary schools had to be closed because their physical condition had become so inadequate.[28] State support for education was halved in 1991 as a result of the Polish budget crisis, and similar problems have arisen in other post-Communist countries. Preschool programs, youth activities, libraries, and many other para-educational services have lost their public funding and must seek private sponsors or persuade their users to support them, leading to an extensive growth of all sorts of voluntary associations to meet social and cultural needs. Schools in many cases have had to raise operating funds by engaging in commerce or by charging adults for supplemental educational services, by renting out rooms or equipment to businesses, or by running cafés, canteens or bars.[29]

The distress of the public education systems in these countries has led many parents who can afford the financial burden to place their children in the new nonpublic schools and universities, which can employ teachers from outside the demoralized workforce of the public schools or select the best of those who have taught in them. That is a matter of no small significance in view of the reputation of veteran teachers as time-servers of "low intellectual, professional, cultural and ethical levels," owing to "long years of negative selection" through which "the most valuable persons, and especially those exerting a positive influence on young people, were removed from schools and universities"[30] by the communist authorities.

Nonpublic schooling may be divided into two categories: those schools that are selected by parents because of religious or ideological convictions, or beliefs about desirable approaches to teaching and school life differing from those represented by the public system of schooling, and those that are selected because of a perception that public schooling is inadequate in quality or simply unavailable. The first group is found perhaps in its purest form in those American communities where the public system is reasonably good but some parents choose unsubsidized nonpublic schools—even of inferior resources—because of their religious convictions; the second group is exemplified by some developing nations where only nonpublic schooling may be available above the most basic level. In much of Western Europe, parents are free to choose—on the basis of what can be quite subtle differences—between public and nonpublic schools that are of generally equivalent quality.[31]

In Eastern Europe, especially as described in my chapter on Poland, some of the initial impulses to create nonpublic schools of the first group came from parents and teachers who were closely associated with the anticommunist opposition. Dissidents had long placed an "emphasis on self-organization ... designed to remove from official jurisdiction entire areas of public life which in ideal democratic conditions do not belong under state tutelage."[32] As an important part of this program, they had called for

> the freedom to set up non-state schools (community-managed or private),—the depoliticization of school education, increasing the influence of the parents and the local community on education policy, the acceptance of alternative curricula and teaching methods and systems, the possibility of

319

> introducing new systems of education devised by individu-
> als, and communalism (through local self-government) at
> the level of the district and housing estate.[33]

The schools they created were thus a statement of rejection of the
ideological character of state schools in favor of alternative pedagogies and ways of organizing school life. In the first flush of democratization, most of the postcommunist governments adopted policies
that allowed and even encouraged the establishment of nonpublic
schools "as a specific alternative to state or municipal schools" and
thus as an impetus to their reform.[34] One of the key figures in that
development was Russia's Edvard Dneprov, a leader of the movement for pedagogical renewal before the fall of the communist
regime and minister of education when the 1992 Education Reform
Law was adopted. To Dneprov, the end of the monopoly system of
schooling was more than a practical necessity:

> Educational diversity and a multiple system stipulate the
> state giving up the ownership of the educational system, and
> anticipate both diverse forms of ownership of educational
> establishments and a choice of various channels and forms
> in obtaining education. The realities of life reject the single
> state-controlled and uniform educational system. . . .[35]

It appears, however, that much of the continuing interest in nonpublic schools—of which there appear to be several thousand in
Eastern Europe at latest count—grows out of simple frustration with
the declining quality of the public system and is inevitably taking on
an elitist quality as a result of the high tuitions that many nonpublic
schools charge (even with partial public funding provided in most
cases). Whether such schools are accorded official recognition and
support or not, "parents will opt for private education, offered either
by the black market system of private lessons or by private institutions."[36] To an increasing extent, for-profit schools are created;
"unlike the community [nonpublic] schools, these private schools
are clearly intended for the education of children from better-off
families."[37] Until recently, such schools were able to rent space from
public schools, leading to situations of great inequality:

> "My daughter is in a class of 40. There is a parallel class in
> the same school where there are only 10 children. Of course,
> they pay. They get much better teaching, eat special food, I

think they even have their own playground. The children in
my daughter's class can see them through the glass."[38]

The only solution to the socially undesirable effects of what is
tending to become a two-tier educational system, with different
qualities of schooling based upon wealth rather than merit, would
be to increase the level of public investment in schools, both public
and nonpublic. That would tend to eliminate the connection between
access to particular schools and the wealth of parents. In the Netherlands, for example, elite private schooling has not emerged because
access of all pupils to both independent and government-operated
schools is fully supported on an equal basis by the government, and
they are of a generally comparable quality and prestige. The Eastern
European country that seems most likely to achieve such a balanced
supply of public and nonpublic schooling is the Czech Republic,
where a healthy economy permits a reasonable level of investment
in all schools, and where public funding is provided to nonpublic
schools at a level almost equivalent to that provided to public
schools. In this case, "the autonomy of the school which has legal
identity and the pupil's free choice of school are exerting pressure
for diversifying the supply of educational services, for adapting to
needs and for effective management."[39]

In response to this sorting-out in what had been, at least formally,
egalitarian systems of schooling, new options are being created
within public education systems. In Russia, for example, a new type
of *gymnasium* has been created, admitting students on the basis of
examination, with higher teacher salaries and close cooperation with
universities. In St. Petersburg, 20 out of 631 schools were *gymnasii*
as of 1992, and "the gap in quality . . . is widening fast."[40] In addition,
most Russian public universities now admit tuition-paying students
over and above those who have been accepted into programs under
the quotas set and paid for by government.[41]

A related response to reduction of government support and a
more competitive environment is that schools and cultural institutions must adapt their programs to make them more flexible, up-
to-date, and responsive to the demands of their potential clientele,
including linking them more directly to the demands of employment,
such as proficiency in English, German, and French.[42]

321

If that diversity is to be extended beyond its present relatively narrow scope of schools, staffs, and parents willing to make extraordinary efforts—amounting, in no country of Eastern Europe, to more than 5 percent of the total—it will require changes in the teaching profession and in the legal framework within which schools operate. Dneprov summarized the hindrances to a true "market of educational services" as the ineptness of much of the teaching profession, the failure of "academic pedagogical science" to address alternative means of educating, and legal and tax impediments to privately initiated schooling.

Dneprov warned also of the danger created by a new " 'mafia' in education who were in a hurry to line their pockets, taking advantage of the economic chaos and the legal anarchy" to start profitmaking ventures masquerading as schools,[43] a serious problem in Russia and other countries. Americans should remember our own financial scandals involving "proprietary schools" that offer vocational training to adults in many American cities, but which in some cases exist primarily to exploit government loan programs while producing few qualified graduates. There are many reports of similar ventures in the postcommunist countries, exploiting private rather than public funds and unfortunately contributing to a general cynicism about nonpublic schooling. Despite such negative developments— unknown in Western European countries that provide public support to nonpublic schooling within a framework of accountability— the effect of initiatives by private providers of schooling and training seems likely to be an irreversible diversification of educational systems.

The new diversity of educational systems, then, includes positive developments in situations that otherwise have many discouraging aspects. Like the conversion of the economies of these countries to free-market systems, there are painful dislocations and turmoil associated with the changes, but it is possible to be moderately optimistic about the eventual results. Not only is there both good news and bad news, but the good news is in some respects a result of the bad: it is unlikely that some of the bold, new developments would have taken place absent the near-collapse of the old system.

The same mixed verdict applies to several other aspects of the recent developments in education in Eastern Europe. Structural and organizational changes have been easier to make than changes in the content of education and what actually happens in classrooms.[44] Among the positive developments is a willingness to rethink the goals of schooling, and in many cases to do so in a more clear-eyed fashion than is done by educational leaders in the West. That rethinking has led in several directions, from the humanistic, child-centered approach advocated by some reformers to the insistence by others that "the promotion of individualistic-competitive values, opposing populism and developing an elitist approach, is indispensable for stimulating the spirit of entrepreneurship."[45]

This ferment of ideas and proposals for educational reform does not make for a comfortable environment for policymaking or indeed for teaching; as a Russian official told a Western audience, "The situation in Russia is aggravated by the fact that any image of the desirable future social and governmental structure is totally lacking. Whereas in Soviet Russia there existed a well-known set of dogmas and myths which is ruined now, the philosophers of today's Russia cannot offer anything to replace it."[46] Similarly, a Western authority describes the situation in the post-Communist societies as not yet pluralistic, but rather one of "spiritual anarchy"; the "end of an ideology making an absolutist claim . . . does not necessarily set free democratic ways of thinking" and as a result "there is a struggle of ideas for influence on education."[47] A Polish report puts the same situation in a more positive light: "We do not as yet in Poland have an all-round vision of this new model. We do however know how to aim for the model school that we need."[48]

Whatever their goals, reformers seem to agree that decisions about the content and style of teaching must be made by teachers themselves. After all, even before the fall of the Communist regimes, independent teachers' movements began to emerge and to explore new ways of thinking about education. It is to discussions among such teachers—admittedly a small minority—that reformers of education look for a means of "filling in the spiritual vacuum caused by the collapse of the old ideological system, [and as] one of the main sources of forming a new social ideology capable of changing the mentality of our society."[49]

> The abandonment of the concept that a pupil had to be "shaped" by the state in accordance with a pre-determined scheme makes it possible to implement new strategies which will provide an opportunity for teachers and pupils to exercise more control over the process of education.[50]

For example, a group of Czech educators calling themselves NEMES (Independent Interdisciplinary Group for the Reform of Educational Policy, School System and Education) has worked together to articulate a vision for reform of education, insisting that their goal was not to make "local changes in an otherwise satisfactory system on the level of organizational or structural changes, but such a profound change in the overall conception . . . to result finally in a change in the public attitude." They objected to the suppression, in the existing system of education, of "the function of the transmission of culture" and its equation of the principle of human equality with schooling structured on the basis that "we are all the same. Hence all had to go, in a unified speed, through a unified curriculum, the contents of which were expressing a unified ideology." In place of that deadening system, schooling should be organized on the basis of diversity, choice among public and nonpublic schools, and individualization of educational programs. Such a reform would require the autonomy of schools and the exercise of choice through vouchers or other mechanisms.[51]

Another positive development is an emphasis on setting standards for educational outcomes, rather than supervising in detail how schools operate.

In Bulgaria, for example, "most of the rights ensuring the juridical and financial independence of the educational establishment have been delegated. The State can now influence the functioning of the school only through the system of State standards in education."[53]

Clear and well-publicized outcome standards for each level of schooling, strictly limited to essential academic competencies and leaving most of a school's program to be determined by the parents and teachers directly involved, is the best way to protect "consumers." Common outcome standards can also help to ensure that the schooling received by children in inner-city or rural schools gives them the opportunity to learn what the wider society considers the most important academic skills.

Of course, most parents will also be deeply concerned about how schools help to develop character and compassion, but if this study of the communist manipulation of schooling teaches anything, it is that no free society can afford to entrust to government the definition of these essential aspects of education. The process of setting common standards, even strictly limited in their scope, is unfortunately subject to abuse through overcomplication or overintrusiveness. When designed and implemented appropriately, educational outcome standards can liberate schools from intrusive government supervision and allow teachers to find their own ways to meet the objectives.[54]

Perhaps the most encouraging aspect of the recent developments in education in Eastern Europe is the growing vitality of the civil society, in all its chaotic and uncontrollable variety. As with the other developments mentioned, it is by no means entirely positive and, indeed, is accompanied by the open expression of social tensions that remained latent under communist rule "in the flattened society [where] citizens lacked any political, civic or economic culture." It would be unreasonable to expect that the first expressions of a reviving civil society would be the organization of chapters of the League of Women Voters; it is instead "families, clans, and religious and ethnic communities" that make the first appearances on the stage of democratic decisionmaking and mobilize for grassroots action in their own interests, which may not correspond to those of the wider society. "Unfortunately, the currently compartmentalized societies of the post-totalitarian countries do not offer a basis for the successful participation of citizens" in problem solving and institution building, and it will take some time before the habits of trust and cooperation develop sufficiently to permit effective local coalitions.[55]

This process of social learning by doing is essential both for the political and for the economic development of the countries of Eastern Europe, and many of the difficulties experienced by Russia and other post-Communist countries may be attributed to its inevitable lagging behind the pace of economic and political change. John Gray contends that "the most decisive phenomenon in the collapse of communism is not the adoption of democratic governance, but rather the emergence of civil life."[56]

It is a reflection of the importance of the process of grassroots regeneration that the policy proposals for school-level autonomy in the post-Communist nations have often been more radical than decentralization and school-based management schemes in the West.[57] Civil society cannot be created by government action; it must grow organically through the voluntary association in organizations and institutions of individuals and families for the sake of what is of value to them.

Reforms of the educational systems of the post-Communist countries include elements that are peculiar to their situation, such as the elimination of Communist indoctrination and the removal, in some cases, of staff too closely associated with the old system. In addition to "rectification measures," there are also many "modernization measures" intended to bring schools up to Western standards, dealing with curricular and instructional changes, introduction of new technologies, setting minimum standards, reforming teacher preparation, and adopting new forms of testing.

The more thoughtful reformers have recognized, however, that it is not sufficient to attempt to emulate Western educational systems; the present crisis of the post-Communist societies calls for more fundamental changes, and the structure of schooling may prove to be as important as its content and methods. The hundreds of new school initiatives and schools fundamentally transformed through school-level decisions are highly promising for the growth of the habits of responsible freedom.

> Restoring the civil society entails ... a moral rebuilding: the reconstruction of the sense of solidarity which has been undermined by the system; the reassertion of the dignity of politics, the rehabilitation of the individual against the officially sanctioned cult of the collectivity; and the identification of niches where autonomous actions and initiatives could develop.[58]

As Zbigniew Rau puts it, "The moral character of the individual's decision to leave the structure of the state gives the newly emerged civil society its moral dimension."[59] Teachers and parents who associate together freely to educate a group of children are making a commitment of far deeper moral significance than teachers who take a job in a state system or parents who send their children off to the nearest public school.[60] They have engaged themselves in one of the "little platoons" that, in Edmund Burke's celebrated image, are the first link in responsible citizenship.

Freedom won must always be sustained by virtue, or it ceases to be freedom and falls away into some new tyranny. The freedom that has come almost miraculously to the peoples of Eastern Europe will not continue to be a blessing to them unless they learn how to live as free men and women. That is a lesson not to be learned only through voting in elections but by sustaining the voluntary associations and institutions that make up a healthy civil society. After all, politics truly understood is about more than the balancing of diverse interests; it is also an "ongoing and public deliberation about the good man and the good society,"[61] and it abhors a vacuum of ideas and convictions.

Political life in a free society does *not* depend upon a societywide consensus on which ideas and convictions will prevail; that premise, indeed, was the central unfreedom of the Communist systems. The liberal "public square" of debate welcomes the diversity of views but—rightly understood—it does not elevate rootless opinions over convictions rooted in communities of shared belief and responsibility.[62]

In the Communist systems, according to Rau, there was "a complete lack of personal responsibility for the public good," no "community united around commonly accepted values and shared obligations for implementing them."[63] Free schools, because they are such communities, can teach the adults who work in them and support them as much as they teach the children who attend them about what it means to be a person worthy of trust. To quote Václav Havel at the end of this study, as at the beginning, they are a part of that "parallel polis," that social and political and, ultimately, moral order that

> points beyond itself and only makes sense as an act of deep-ening one's responsibility to and for the whole. . . . Independent initiatives . . . demonstrate that living within the truth is a human and social alternative and they struggle to expand the space available for that life.[64]

References

In some cases I have made minor grammatical corrections in quotations from Eastern European sources.

1. Cézar Bîrzea, *Educational policies of the countries in transition* (Strasbourg, France: Council of Europe Press, 1994), pp. 68–69.

2. Rumen Valchev, *Policy Motives in Education and Training in Bulgaria* (Paris: Organisation for Economic Co-operation and Development, 1992), p. 6, 5.

3. Bîrzea, p. 10.

4. Ibid.

5. Robert Kuttner, "The Dustbin of Economics," *New Republic*, February 25, 1991, p. 27.

6. Jerzy Dietl, *Report on Education and Training in Poland During the Transformation of the Socio-Economic System* (Paris: Organisation for Economic Co-operation and Development, 1992), pp. 18–19.

7. Karlheinz Dühr, "East German Education: A System in Transition," *Phi Delta Kappan*, January 1992, p. 391.

8. Oskar Anweiler, "Politischer Umbruch und Pädagogik im östlichen Europa," *Bildung und Erziehung* 43, no. 3 (1990): 242.

9. Oskar Anweiler, "Wandlungen und Perspektiven des Bildungswesens im östlichen Europa," typescript, June 1991, p. 4–5.

10. Sterling Fishman, "After the Wall: A Case Study of Educational Change in Eastern Germany," *Teachers College Record* (Summer 1993): 2.

11. E.V. Tkachenko, "Educational Reform in the Russian Federation," in *Educational Policy in Russia and Its Constitutional Aspects*, ed. by Jan De Groof (Leuven, Belgium: Acco, 1994), p. 45.

12. Bîrzea, p. 23.

13. K. Malfliet, "Russian Educational Policy as Part of the Political Effort at Reform," in *Comments on the Law on Education of the Russian Federation*, ed. by Jan De Groof (Leuven, Belgium: Acco, 1993), p. 83.

14. Zoltán Báthory, "Some Consequences of the 'Change in Régime' in Hungarian Public Education," in *Recent Trends in Eastern European Education*, ed. by Wolfgang Mitter, Manfred Weiss, and Ulrich Schaefer (Frankfurt am Main: German Institute for International Educational Research, 1992), p. 30.

15. Ibid.

16. Oskar Anweiler, "Bildungsprobleme postkommunistischer Gesellschaften," *Bildung und Erziehung* 45, no. 3 (September 1992): 254.

17. Charles Glenn, "Organizing the Russian Educational System for Freedom and Accountability," in *Comments on the Law on Education*, p. 99.

18. E.V. Tkachenko, "Conclusions," in *Comments on the Law on Education*, p. 196.

19. Jan De Groof, "The 'Renaissance' of Educational Rights in Russia: Conditions for a Common European House," in *Educational Policy in Russia*, pp. 15–22.

20. G.P. van den Berg, "Education and the New Constitution of the Russian Federation," in *Educational Policy in Russia*, p. 82.

21. Ibid., p. 83.

22. Charles Glenn, "Common Standards and Educational Diversity," in *Subsidiarity and Education: Aspects of Comparative Educational Law*, ed. Jan De Groof (Leuven, Belgium: Acco, 1994), pp. 368–72; for a Spanish case, see the ruling of the Tribunal Constitucional, June 27, 1985, reprinted in Francesc Riu i Rovira de Villar, *Todos tienen el derecho a la educación* (Madrid: Consejo General de la Educación Catolica, 1988), pp. 134–37.

23. G.P. van den Berg, "Constitutional Aspects of the Law on Education of the Russian Federation," in *Comments on the Law on Education*, p. 67.

24. Michał J. Kawecki, Letter to the author, October 6, 1994.

25. N.V. Karlov and S.P. Merkuriev, *Education and the Economy in Russia* (Paris: Organisation for Economic Co-operation and Development, 1992), p. 8.

26. Bîrzea, p. 66.

27. Jan Prucha, "Trends in Czechoslovak Education," in *Recent Trends in Eastern European Education*, p. 86.

28. Dietl, pp. 10, 20.

29. Ministry of National Education, *The Development of Education in Poland in 1990–1991* (Warsaw: 1992), pp. 31, 38, 41.

30. Dietl, p. 20.

31. Charles Glenn, *Choice of Schools in Six Nations* (Washington: U.S. Department of Education, 1989).

Conclusion

32. Janusz Bugajski and Maxine Pollack, *East European Fault Lines: Dissent, Opposition, and Social Activism* (Boulder: Westview Press, 1989), p. 93.

33. Ministry of National Education, p. 23.

34. Ministry of Science and Education, *National Report on the Development of Education in the Republic of Bulgaria in 1992–1994* (Sofia: 1994), p. 3.

35. Edvard Dmitrievich Dneprov, "Reform of Education in Russia and Government Policy in the Sphere of Education," *East/West Education* 14, no. 1 (Spring 1993): 21.

36. Ana Maria Sandi and Maria Sandor, *Education and Training for a New Society: The Case of Romania* (Paris: Organisation for Economic Co-operation and Development, 1992), p. 25.

37. Ministry of National Education, p. 27.

38. Pieta Monks, "Brutality of the Market," *Times Educational Supplement*, October 30, 1992.

39. Lubomir Harach, Jan Koucký, et al., *Czech and Slovak Federal Republic* (Paris: Organisation for Economic Co-operation and Development, 1992), p. 26.

40. Karlov and Merkuriev, p. 10.

41. K. Malfliet, "Will the New Constitution Protect Democracy and the Democratization of Education in Russia?" in *Educational Policy in Russia*, p. 78.

42. Ministry of National Education, p. 39.

43. Dneprov, pp. 27, 32.

44. Harach, Koucký, et al., p. 26.

45. Dietl, p. 22.

46. Victor Bolotov, "The Challenge of Educational Reform in Russia," in *Educational Policy in Russia*, p. 61.

47. Anweiler, "Bildungsprobleme," pp. 255–56.

48. Ministry of National Education, p. 23.

49. Dneprov, p. 14, 23.

50. Ministry of National Education, p. 23.

51. NEMES, "Freedom in Education and the Czech School: Project of the Transformation of the Educational System in the Czech Republic," Prague, typescript, July 1991.

52. Glenn, "Organizing the Russian Educational System for Freedom," p. 98.

53. Valchev, p. 8.

54. Charles Glenn, "Outcome-based Education: Can It Be Redeemed?" in *Public Education and Religion: Conversations for an Enlarging Public Square*, ed. by James T. Sears and James Carper (New York: Teachers College Press, forthcoming).

55. Sandi and Sandor, pp. 6, 23.

56. John Gray, "Post-Totalitarianism, Civil Society, and Limits of the Western Model," in *The Reemergence of Civil Society in Eastern Europe and the Soviet Union*, ed. Zbigniew Rau (Boulder: Westview Press, 1991), p. 146.

57. Wolfgang Mitter, "Education in Eastern Europe and the Soviet Union in a Period of Revolutionary Change," in *Recent Trends in Eastern European Education*, p. 128.

58. Vladimir Tismaneanu, "Unofficial Peace Activism in the Soviet Union and East-Central Europe," in *In Search of Civil Society*, ed. Vladimir Tismaneanu (New York and London: Routledge, 1990), p. 5.

59. Zbigniew Rau, "The State of Enslavement: the East European Substitute for the State of Nature," *Political Studies* 39 (1991): 258.

60. Polish sociologists have found that both pupils in nonstate schools and their parents are three times as likely as their counterparts in state schools to report that they have real influence in and responsibility for their schools. Seventy percent of teachers in state elementary schools believe that parents have quite enough influence. Malgorzata Kopcynska, "Kto na kogo wplywa?" (Who is influencing whom?), *Edukacja i Dialog* 37, no. 4 (1992): 10–11, summarized by Malgorzata Radziszewska-Hedderick.

61. George Weigel, "Death of a Heresy," *National Review*, January 20, 1992, p. 46.

62. Richard John Neuhaus, *The Naked Public Square* (Grand Rapids, Mich.: Eerdmans, 1984).

63. Zbigniew Rau, "Human Nature, Social Engineering, and the Reemergence of Civil Society," in *The Reemergence of Civil Society*, p. 42.

64. Václav Havel, *Living in Truth* (London: Faber and Faber, 1987), pp. 102–106.

Index

Accelerated Christian Education, Commonwealth of Independent States, 242–43
Adenauer, Konrad, 282
Alternative schools
  Estonia, 254–55
  nineteenth-century and pre–World War I Germany, 269
  post–World War II East Germany, 275
  West Germany, 290–91
American College, Bulgaria, 84
American University, Bulgaria, 83–84
Andropov, Yuri, 26
Anti-religion campaigns
  Hungary, 205
  Soviet Union, 33–38, 44, 53–56
Antohi, Sorin, 102–3, 106
Anweiler, Oskar, 278
Assimilation
  resistance in Romania to, 99
  in Soviet Union, 40
Atheism
  in Bulgaria, 66–67
  under Communist regime in Poland, 118, 121
  propaganda in Romania, 103

Baer, Richard, 12
Becker, Carl Heinrich, 270
Benda, Václav, 180–81
Billaud-Varenne, 11
Boarding schools
  Czech and Slovak Federal Republic (CSFR), 174
  Soviet Union, 25
Bohemia
  Czechs and Slovaks in (1980), 163
  Nazi rule in, 172
  pre–World War I, 163–64
Bormann, Martin, 272
Botlik, Oldrich, 182, 183, 188–89
Bowen, James, 21
Bräme, Rainer, 277–78
Brezhnev, Leonid, 26

Bukharin, Nikolai, 17, 22, 31
Bulgaria
  pre–World War II educational system, 70
  Communist regime
    education laws and reform (1954, 1979), 67–68
    independent schools, 85
    industrialization policy, 76
    political indoctrination in schools, 66–67
    Soviet model of education, 65–67, 70
    state-run and independent, 69–71
    Turkish educational system, 72–74
  post-Communism
    criticisms of and proposals for state-run system, 80–81
    educational reform proposals, 80–83
    educational system, 313
    independent schools, 83
    proposed school choice initiatives, 80–83
    school policy, 81, 83
  Turkish minority in, 77–79

Calvinist church
  in Hungary, 213–14
  in Romania, 97, 100
Calvinist schools, Hungary, 218–19
Castro, Fidel, 12–13
Catholic church
  in Communist-controlled Hungary, 202
  under Communist regime in CSFR, 167
  in Czech lands, 166
  as force in Polish society, 123–24
  in post-Communist Poland, 145–47
  role under Communist regime in Poland, 115, 120–26
  in Romania, 97–98, 100

Index

Catholic groups, Bulgaria, 70
Catholic schools
  Communist regime in Hungary,
    202–3
  Communist regime in
    Czechoslovakia, 169
  Communist regime in Poland, 117
  Communist regime in Romania, 98
  German public and private (1930s),
    269–70
  nationalization in Slovakia, 172
  post–World War II West Germany, 283
Ceauşescu, Nicolae, 92, 93–96, 101–2
Chernenko, Konstantin, 26
Chervenkov, Vulko, 65
Christian churches, Soviet Union, 27
  See also Eastern Orthodox Church
Christian Democratic Movement
  (KDH), CSFR, 181–82
CIS. See Commonwealth of
  Independent States (CIS)
Civic Educational Association (CEA),
  Poland, 127–32
Civil society
  Catholics predominate in Polish, 139
  defined, 5
  in post-Communist Poland, 153, 155
  reorganization in former Communist
    countries, 7–8
  resistance and return in Poland,
    119–32
  revival of, 7–8
  Romania, 95–97, 104
Common school model, West
  Germany, 282
Commonwealth of Independent States
  (CIS)
  Accelerated Christian Education
    program, 242–43
  constitution, 227–28, 235, 316–17
  creation, 227
  democratic trend for educational
    system, 248
  educational services of private
    businesses, 241
  independent schools, 241–42, 247–48,
    250
  innovative schools, 244–45
  Jewish yeshivas, 241
  laws related to education, 227–40,
    245, 316
  nationalism, 57–58
  public schools in, 241–45

reforms in educational system,
  245–46
trends in educational system, 248
Communist party
  education policy in East Germany,
    276–78
  monopoly on education in Bulgaria, 75
  political surveillance, 24–25
  position on religion in Soviet Union, 29
  religious aspects of, 30
  role in Romania, 91
  role in Soviet Union education
    system, 24–26
  See also Anti-religion campaigns;
    Ideology, Marxist-Leninist
Communist regimes
  control of Orthodox church in
    Bulgaria, 70
  educational program in Bulgaria,
    67–68
  goals in Soviet Union, 19, 30–31
  successes and failures in Romania,
    103–4
  See also Totalitarian regimes
Confessional schools. See Religious
  schools
Constitutions
  Bulgaria, 68
  changes in CSFR, 184
  of Commonwealth of Independent
    States, 227–28, 235, 316–17
  Czech and Slovak Federal Republic
    (1921), 167
  Poland (1952), 133
  Soviet Union (1924), 42
  West Germany, 281, 285–86, 299
Croghan, Michael, 92
CSFR. See Czech and Slovak Federal
  Republic (CSFR)
Curriculum
  anti-religious themes in Soviet
    Union, 35–38
  in Commonwealth of Independent
    States, 248
  renewal of, 7–8
Czech and Slovak Federal Republic
  (CSFR)
  pre-Communism
    ethnic tensions, 163–64
    Nazi rule in Moravia, 172
    pre–World War I Moravia, 163–64
    Slovakia, pre–World War I, 163–64
  Communist regime
    Catholic schools, 169
    Education Acts (1953, 1960), 171,
      174

332

Index

Freedom, religious
  in Communist-controlled Hungary,
    204
  Soviet Union, 28
Freedom of choice. *See* School choice
  concept
Freedom of education, constitution of
  CIS, 316–17

Gellner, Ernest, 7
Geremek, Brownisaw, 125
German Community School (Nazi),
  272, 282
German minority
  in post-Communist Romania, 106
  in Romania, 97, 99–102
Germany
  pre–World War II
    education, 268, 270–71
    public religion-oriented schools
      (1930s), 269
    Nazi, 271–73
  reunified
    education laws, 299–302
    independent schools, 301–2
  See also East Germany (GDR); West
    Germany (FRG)
Gheorghiu-Dej, Gheorghe, 101
Gilberg, Trond, 92, 99, 103
Glenn, Charles, xiv
Glenny, Misha, 178
Gorbachev, Mikhail, 56, 103, 250, 251
Gypsy population
  Czech and Slovak Federal Republic
    (CSFR), 163
  Hungary, 207

Hadjiolov, Asen, 79
Halász, Gábor, 206
Hale, Julian, 103
Havel, Václav, 3, 4, 6, 8, 163, 178–79,
  188, 192–93, 327
Helmreich, Ernst Christian, 271
Hennecke, Frank, 287
Hitler, Adolf, 271–72
Homogeneity, Polish ethnic, 116
Honecker, Margot, 274, 294
Hromadka, Josef, 169
Hungarian minority
  under Communist regime in
    Romania, 97, 99–103
  in post-Communist Romania, 106,
    110
Hungarian revolution (1956), 205

Hungary
  pre–World War II, 199–200
  Communist regime
    educational system reform
      attempts, 210
    organization and function of
      schools, 210–12
    political indoctrination in schools,
      204–7
    selection and tracking in
      educational system, 208
  post-Communism
    educational policy, 199
    educational system reform, 212–23
    voucher system, 215

Ideology, Marxist-Leninist
  Communist party role in formation
    of, 26
  under Communist regime in Poland,
    122–23
  in Czech educational system, 171–77,
    179
  Estonian educational system, 252
  under Hungarian Communist
    regime, 206
  post–World War II East Germany
    (GDR), 276–78
  as religious belief-system, 29
  schools in Soviet Union as
    institutions of, 23–24
  in Soviet Union, 1–4
  taught in Bulgarian schools, 65–68
  taught in Soviet schools, 25–27
  taught in Turkish schools, 75
  teaching in Romanian schools and
    society, 91–97, 105
Ideology, Waldorf schools, 107–9
Independent schools
  Commonwealth of Independent
    States (CIS), 240–42, 247–48, 250
  post-Communist Bulgaria, 83
  post-Communist CSFR, 184–86
  in post-Communist Poland, 127,
    138–55
  post-Communist regime East
    Germany, 298–99, 303–4
  post–World War II West Germany,
    273, 290–91
  reunified Germany, 301–2
Industrialization policy
  Bulgaria, 76
  Soviet Union, 48
Integration program, Romania, 101

Index

Paul, Ilona, 209
Perestroika, 5–6
Petersen, Peter, 290
Pierce v. Society of the Sisters of the Holy Names of Jesus and Mary (1923), 316–17
Pius IX (pope), 280
Podemski, Krzysztof, 125
Poland
  Communist regime
    bureaucratic educational system, 126–30
    education reform, 123–24
    ethnic homogeneity, 116
    movement to reform educational system, 126–32
    prohibition on religious instruction, 121–23
  post-Communism
    education, 127–32
    educational system, 116–17
    educational system reform, 127–32
    independent schools, 127, 138–47
    reforms in educational system, 132–38
    role of CEA in, 127–32
Political education
  East Germany (GDR), 277–78
  Romania, 94–96
Political reform, 6–7
Preobrazhensky, Evgenii, 17, 22, 31
Program for National Renewal (1990), Hungary, 215
Protest actions, Soviet Union, 41
Protestant church
  Bohemia, 166
  Romania, 103, 109
  under Soviet regime, 32
Protestant groups
  Bulgaria, 70
  post–World War II West Germany, 280, 282–83
  Romania, 109
Protestant schools
  under Communist regime in Hungary, 201
  German public (1930s), 269
  post-Communist East Germany, 304
  post–World War II West Germany, 283
  Russia, 241
Public schools
  in CIS, 241–45

common school model in West Germany, 282
German religion-oriented (1930s), 269

Rau, Zbigniew, 2–3, 5, 326
Ravitch, Diane, xi–iii
Religion
  actions in Soviet Union related to, 28–35
  Communism as, 29–30
  under Communist regime in Poland, 117–18
  prohibition in Romania, 94
  as rival of Communism, 10
  teaching in Latvian schools, 255
  toleration in post–World War II East Germany, 279
  See also Anti-religion campaigns; Catholic church; Eastern Orthodox church; Muslim peoples; Protestant church
Religious beliefs
  in Communist-controlled Hungary, 209
  in Soviet Union, 55–56
Religious instruction
  abolition in Polish state schools, 123–24
  of Catholic church in Poland, 123–24
  in CIS schools, 241
  under Communist regime in CSFR, 170, 174–75
  policy in West Germany, 280–81
  in post-Communist Hungarian school system, 217–21
  prohibition in Soviet Union, 31–32
  Romania, 98
  Soviet Union, 18, 29–31
  in state-controlled schools in Hungary, 204–5
  study in post-Communist Bulgarian schools, 85–86
Religious schools
  debate and policy in post–World War II West Germany, 279–84
  Muslim schools in Soviet Union, 53
  in post–World War II West Germany, 283–85
  See also Catholic schools; Protestant schools
Resistance
  of Catholic church in Poland, 124
  to Communist regime in Poland, 116

About the Author

Charles L. Glenn is professor of educational policy at Boston University, where he is chairman of the Department of Administration, Training, and Policy Studies. For 21 years, he was the Massachusetts education official responsible for civil rights and urban education, including an extensive program of improving educational opportunity through school choice. Glenn is author of *The Myth of the Common School* (1988), *Choice of Schools in Six Nations* (1989), and many articles on educational policy and practice. He has worked recently with Russian and Chinese education officials on comprehensive legislation, and is completing a book on how more than a dozen nations educate immigrant minority children.

Cato Institute

Founded in 1977, the Cato Institute is a public policy research foundation dedicated to broadening the parameters of policy debate to allow consideration of more options that are consistent with the traditional American principles of limited government, individual liberty, and peace. To that end, the Institute strives to achieve greater involvement of the intelligent, concerned lay public in questions of policy and the proper role of government.

The Institute is named for *Cato's Letters*, libertarian pamphlets that were widely read in the American Colonies in the early 18th century and played a major role in laying the philosophical foundation for the American Revolution.

Despite the achievement of the nation's Founders, today virtually no aspect of life is free from government encroachment. A pervasive intolerance for individual rights is shown by government's arbitrary intrusions into private economic transactions and its disregard for civil liberties.

To counter that trend, the Cato Institute undertakes an extensive publications program that addresses the complete spectrum of policy issues. Books, monographs, and shorter studies are commissioned to examine the federal budget, Social Security, regulation, military spending, international trade, and myriad other issues. Major policy conferences are held throughout the year, from which papers are published thrice yearly in the *Cato Journal*. The Institute also publishes the quarterly magazine *Regulation*.

In order to maintain its independence, the Cato Institute accepts no government funding. Contributions are received from foundations, corporations, and individuals, and other revenue is generated from the sale of publications. The Institute is a nonprofit, tax-exempt, educational foundation under Section 501(c)3 of the Internal Revenue Code.

CATO INSTITUTE
1000 Massachusetts Ave., N.W.
Washington, D.C. 20001